LITERARY CRITICISM

An Introduction to
Theory and Practice

Second Edition

Charles E. Bressler

Houghton College

Prentice Hall, Upper Saddle River, New Jersey 07458

Library of Congress Cataloging-in-Publication Data

Bressler, Charles E.
    Literary criticism : an introduction to theory and practice /
    Charles E. Bressler. — 2nd ed.
        p.   cm.
    Includes bibliographical references and index.
    ISBN 0–13–897422–5
    1. Criticism.   I. Title.
    PN81.B666   1998
    801'.95—dc21   98-33496
                                                              CIP

For Darlene, my best friend and loving wife, and
For Heidi, my beloved daughter

Editorial Director, Editor-in-Chief, Humanities: Charlyce Jones Owen
Editor-in-Chief, English: Leah Jewell
Acquisitions Editor: Carrie Brandon
Senior Managing Editor: Bonnie Biller
Editorial/Production Supervision: Alison Gnerre
Cover Director: Jayne Conte
Cover Designer: Joe Sengotta
Manufacturing Manager: Nick Sklitsis
Manufacturing Buyer: Mary Ann Gloriande

Acknowledgments appear on page 301, which constitutes a continuation of the copyright page.

This book was set in 10/12 Palatino by DM Cradle Associates
and was printed and bound by Courier Companies, Inc.
The cover was printed by Phoenix Color Corp.

© 1999, 1994 by Prentice-Hall, Inc.
Simon & Schuster/A Viacom Company
Upper Saddle River, New Jersey 07458

Printed in the United States of America

10   9   8   7   6   5   4   3   2

ISBN 0-13-897422-5

Prentice-Hall International (UK) Limited, *London*
Prentice-Hall of Australia Pty. Limited, *Sydney*
Prentice-Hall Canada Inc., *Toronto*
Prentice-Hall Hispanoamericana, S.A., *Mexico*
Prentice-Hall of India Private Limited, *New Delhi*
Prentice-Hall of Japan, Inc., *Tokyo*
Simon & Schuster Asia Pte. Ltd., *Singapore*
Editora Prentice-Hall do Brasil, Ltda., *Rio de Janeiro*

Contents

10 Cultural Poetics   236
or New Historicism

11 Cultural Studies   263

Foreword

Dr. Johnson's character Imlac explains that "To talk in publick, to think in solitude, to read and to hear, to inquire, and to answer inquiries" is the business of a scholar. At some point, as Imlac suggests, our ideas are brought out for review by those in other parts of society. In the process, as we interact with others, we participate in the essential human work of allowing them to help shape the way we think. This interaction admits us to experiences other than our own. It admits us beyond the boundaries of our communities. Developments in literary and cultural theory are intended to help students and teachers explore divergent critical approaches to literary works to expand, not diminish, discussion. Yet many teachers have questioned whether theory has had any positive effect on the quality and depth of classroom practice and discussion.

As we approach the twenty-first century, few would disagree that we have witnessed a proliferation of theory, such as cultural studies, women's studies, interdisciplinary studies, American studies, semiotics, and deconstruction, to name a few. Barbara Christian suggests that this proliferation of theory is more accurately a "race for theory" in which "critics are no longer concerned with literature, but with other critics' texts, for the critic yearning for attention has displaced the writer and has conceived of himself as the center." Many critics are describing these developments in theory as the basis for much needed change in institutional and pedagogical practice. Other critics, hostile to theory and radical curricular change, argue that theoretical changes have resulted in too much division and unnecessary conflict. Terry Eagleton notes, however, that such "hostility to theory usually means an opposition to other people's theories and an oblivion of one's own." Eagleton's point is well taken. There is a particular danger in the totalizing effects of one or two dominant, unchecked opinions in any situation, in the classroom in particular, where theory needs and finds nourishment in discussion and debate, and in meaningful conversation, an old art that needs to be preserved. Gerald Graff has argued that we need to engage students in the conversation about literary study. In *Beyond Culture Wars*, he contends that "It is not the conflicts dividing the university that should worry us but the fact that students are not playing a more active role in them." Graff rightly points out that the literature classroom is an appropriate forum for students to address these conflicts in relation to classroom practice.

Literary Criticism invites students to the ongoing debate about the place of theory and practice in the literature classroom. Charles Bressler has written this book with a developed awareness that, while teachers within and between departments battle for viable approaches to the study of literature and the humanities, students are too often excluded from any number of important critical discussions that most frequently and immediately affect them. Well researched and lucidly written, this book helps students develop and articulate their interpretations from a variety of theoretical approaches by equipping them with the critical tools for reading.

Chapter 1 addresses two of the most prevalent questions in the college literature classroom: What is literature and why do we read it? Obvious questions to many, with obvious answers for some, these two questions in particular reflect the legitimate concern of students that literary study has relevance only in the classroom. Often students feel that developing critical approaches to literary works remains somehow the tired work of academicians, not the work of real citizens. Bressler's discussion addresses this concern, not only providing a working definition of literature, including its epistemological and ontological components, but relating literary study to broader, underlying cultural concerns. Such a discussion provides students a starting point to develop their own definition of literature and criticism, while also providing them an opportunity to discuss their definitions with other students who hold different views.

Chapter 2 traces the historical developments of literary criticism from Plato to the present. This chapter is designed to help students think about how their ideas stand in relation to and participate in the historical debate about such important critical concerns as representation, truth, beauty, nature, form, meaning, gender, class, audience, among others. First, Chapter 2 traces some of the important early influences on what is now modern literary theory so that students can compare the current direction of theory to the bearings of the past. Second, the discussion of historical developments alerts students to the intellectual risks associated with developing a completely contemporary diet of ideas.

Chapters 3 through 11 investigate individually the main critical concerns, or "schools," that have developed in the twentieth-century. This second edition of *Literary Criticism*, in addition to including the now old New Criticism, and including Reader Response Criticism, Structuralism, Deconstruction, Psychoanalytic Criticism, Feminism, Marxism, and New Historicism, has added a chapter on Cultural Studies, Chapter 11. Specifically, Chapter 11 explores the developing trends in Post-colonial, Gender, and African-American studies.

Literary Criticism equips teachers and students to enter into a more meaningful conversation about literary texts. In this new edition, new professional essays follow new student essays at the end of each chapter. In addition, a list of useful web sites and links follow the discussion of each school of criticism beginning with Chapter 3. These Internet listings provide students new and exciting avenues of exploration for each school of criticism. This new design reinforces Bressler's commitment to encouraging students to think of themselves as theorists and critics who play a vital role in literary studies. To enable students to become informed, critical readers, this new edition has also included a Question section at the end of each chapter. This section emphasizes that asking informed questions is most typically the best starting point for conducting literary research and writing effective criticism. Just as importantly, these questions are designed to help students develop their opinion and voice in sometimes vast and impersonal institutional and cultural settings.

It is not the goal of this book to substitute for any important primary readings. Instead, this text intends to engage students in a series of important mutual introductions to primary and secondary works in literary history. It is hoped that students then will decide how reading stands in relation to their own lives inside and outside their own communities. Whatever they decide, they may find that in learning how to be informed readers and thinkers, they are also learning how to be responsible citizens.

Daniel H. Strait
Asbury College

To the Reader

Like the first edition, this new edition of *Literary Criticism* is designed as a supplemental text for introductory courses in both literature and literary criticism. Its purpose is to enable students to approach literature from a variety of practical and theoretical positions and to equip them with a theoretical and a practical understanding of how critics develop and articulate interpretations. Its aim, then, is to take the mystery out of working with and interpreting texts.

Like the first edition, this new text holds to several key premises. First, it assumes that there is no such thing as an innocent reading of a text. Whether our responses to a text are emotional and spontaneous or well-reasoned and highly structured, all such interactions are based upon some underlying factors that cause us to respond in a particular fashion. What elicits these responses and how a reader makes sense out of a text is what really matters. And it is the domain of literary theory to question our initial and final responses, our beliefs, our feelings, and our overall interpretation. To understand why we respond to a text in a certain way, we must first understand literary theory and criticism.

Second, since our responses to a text have theoretical bases, I presume that all readers have a literary theory. Consciously or unconsciously, we as readers have developed a mind-set concerning our expectations when reading any text, be it a novel, a short story, a poem, or any other type of literature. Somehow, as the critic Jonathan Culler maintains, we make sense out of printed material. The methods we use to frame our personal interpretations of any text involve us in the process of literary criticism and theory, and automatically make us practicing literary critics whether we know it or not.

My third assumption rests on the observation that each reader's literary theory and accompanying methodology is either conscious or unconscious, complete or incomplete, informed or ill-informed, eclectic or unified. Since an unconscious, incomplete, ill-informed, and eclectic literary theory more frequently than not leads to illogical, unsound, and haphazard interpretations, I believe that a well-defined, logical, and clearly articulated theory will enable readers to develop their own methods of interpretation, permitting them to order, clarify, and justify their personal appraisals of any text in a consistent and rational manner.

Unfortunately, many readers cannot articulate their own literary theory and have little knowledge of the history and development of the ever-evolving principles of literary criticism. It is the goal of this book to introduce students and other readers to literary theory and criticism, its historical development, and the various theoretical positions or schools of criticism that will enable them as readers to make conscious, informed, and intelligent choices concerning their own methods of interpretation.

Like the first edition, this new edition introduces students to the basic concerns of literary theory and criticism in Chapter 1, but now includes an expanded definition of literature itself. Chapter 2 is also expanded and places literary theory and criticism in historical perspective, starting with Plato and ending with modern-day theorists such as Stephen Greenblatt. Chapters 3 to 11 discuss the eleven major schools of criticism that have developed in the twentieth century: New Criticism, Reader-Response Criticism, Structuralism, Deconstruction, Psychoanalytic Criticism, Feminism, Marxism, Cultural Poetics or New Historicism, and new to the second edition, Post-Colonialism, African-American Criticism, and Gender Studies. To maintain consistency and for ease of study, each of these chapters is identically organized. We begin with a brief **Introduction** followed by the **Historical Development** of each school of criticism. Next is the **Assumptions** section that sets forth the philosophical principles upon which each school of criticism is based. The **Methodology** section follows and serves as a "how to" manual for explaining the techniques used by the various schools of criticism to formulate their interpretations of a text based upon their philosophical assumptions. Readers of the first edition will note that in this new edition each of these sections is greatly expanded and includes a more complete discussion of the varying positions held by literary critics within each school of criticism. Throughout each of the aforementioned sections, all key terms are in boldface type, making them easily found and accessible to the reader.

After the Methodology section, this new edition includes a **Questions for Analysis** section in Chapters 3 through 10. This section provides students with key questions to ask of a text in order to view that text from the perspective of the school of criticism being discussed. Some of these questions also ask students to apply their new-found knowledge to a particular text or texts. After this section come the **Sample Essays**. As in the first edition, undergraduate **student essays** appear in which students apply the principles and methods of interpretation of the school of criticism under discussion to one of six primary texts that can be easily found in literary anthologies. These primary texts include John Keats's "To Autumn," Edgar Allan Poe's "The City in the Sea," Margaret Atwood's "Spelling," Tony Harrison's "Marked with a D.," Susan Glaspell's *Trifles*, and Nathaniel Hawthorne's "Young Goodman Brown." A new addition to this edition is the appearance of outstanding **professional essays** authored by many of the leading scholars of literary theory and criticism. Following the student selections, these professional essays provide a variety of concrete models that readers can emulate to enhance their own theoretical and practical understanding of literary criticism "in action."

After the Sample Essays section, a newly-revised **Further Reading** section follows. Updated and more comprehensive than in the first edition, these selected references complement the more comprehensive and up-to-date **Bibliography** found at the end of the text. After the Further Reading section appears a new section entitled **Internet Sites** that provides many more avenues of exploration for each of the schools of criticism under discussion. Often these World Wide Web addresses include links to many other sites that provide opportunities to venture into the ever-expanding world of literary theory.

Since this new edition is an introductory text, the explanations of the various schools of criticism should not be viewed as exhaustive, but as a first step toward an understanding of some rather difficult concepts, principles, and methodologies. After reading each chapter, it is hoped that readers will continue their own investigations of literary theory and criticism by exploring advanced theoretical texts and the primary works of both theoretical and practical critics.

ACKNOWLEDGMENTS

Like all artistic endeavors, the creation of a text involves the author's relationships with a variety of people. This text is no exception. To the members of my literary criticism classes who heard many parts of this text in lecture form and who continue to inspire me to explore more fully the depths and heights of both critical scholarship and my own personal hermeneutics, I say thank you. Without you, this book would not have been written. I am particularly grateful to Krista Adlhock, Dale Schuurman, Jen Richardson, David Johnson, Kara Roggie, and Juanita Wolfe, the authors of the newly generated student essays that appear in this edition. To Houghton College, for granting me another sabbatical that allowed the time to study, research, and write, I again express my appreciation. Thanks are also due to my colleagues and friends in the Department of English and Communication at Houghton College. Their kind advice and their constant encouragement have been greatly appreciated. In particular, I wish to thank our department secretary, Jane Miner, for her faithful and careful editing and typing of various sections of this manuscript. I also wish to thank Diva Daims, SUNY at Albany and James Heldman, Western Kentucky University. To Carrie Brandon, I am grateful for the superb editing and professional advice. I am particularly grateful to Dr. Daniel Strait for his keen insights, editorial comments, and constant affirmation. Most of all, I wish to express my love and appreciation to my wife, Darlene, and to my daughter, Heidi, for their editorial comments and for freeing me from many of life's daily chores and demands so that I could study, research, and write. Without their support and love this text would not exist. Because of the input of my friends and family, this is a better work. Any mistakes, errors in judgment, or other flaws, however, must be attributed to me alone.

Charles E. Bressler

1

Defining Criticism, Theory, and Literature

EAVESDROPPING ON A LITERATURE CLASSROOM

Having assigned his literature class Flannery O'Connor's short story "A Good Man Is Hard to Find" and knowing O'Connor's canon and her long list of curious protagonists, Professor George Blackwell could not anticipate whether his students would greet him with silence, bewilderment, or frustration when asked to discuss this work. His curiosity would soon be satisfied, for as he stood before the class, he asked a seemingly simple, direct question: "What do you believe O'Connor is trying to tell us in this story? In other words, how do you, as readers, interpret this text?"

Although some students suddenly found the covers of their anthologies fascinating, others shot up their hands. Given a nod from Professor Blackwell, Alice was the first to respond. "I believe O'Connor is trying to tell us the state of the family in rural Georgia during the 1950s. Just look, for example, at how the children, June Star and John Wesley, behave. They don't respect their grandmother. In fact, they mock her."

"But she deserves to be mocked," interrupted Peter. "Her life is one big act. She wants to act like a lady—to wear white cotton gloves and carry a purse—but she really cares only for herself. She is selfish, self-centered, and arrogant."

"That may be," responded Karen, "but I think the real message of O'Connor's story is not about family or one particular character, but about a philosophy of life. O'Connor uses the Misfit to articulate her personal view of life. When the Misfit says Jesus has thrown 'everything off balance,' O'Connor is really asking each of her readers to choose their own way of life or to follow the teachings of Jesus. In effect, O'Connor is saying we all have a choice: to live for ourselves or to live for and through others."

"I don't think we should bring Christianity or any other philosophy or religion into the story," said George. "Through analyzing O'Connor's individual words—words like *tall*, *dark*, and *deep*—and noting how often she repeats them and in what context, we can deduce that O'Connor's text, not

O'Connor herself or her view of life, is melancholy, a bit dark itself. But to equate O'Connor's personal philosophy about life with the meaning of this particular story is somewhat silly."

"But we can't forget that O'Connor is a woman," said Betty. "And an educated one at that! Her story has little to do about an academic or pie-in-the-sky, meaningless philosophical discussion, but a lot to do about being a woman. Being raised in the South, O'Connor would know and would have experienced prejudice because she is a woman. And as we all know, Southern males' opinion of women is that they are to be barefoot, pregnant, and in the kitchen. Seemingly, they are to be as nondescript as Bailey's wife is in this story. Unlike all the other characters, we don't even know this woman's name. How much more nondescript could O'Connor be? O'Connor's message, then, is simple. Women are oppressed and suppressed. If they open their mouths, if they have an opinion, and if they voice that opinion, they will end up like the grandmother, with a bullet in their head."

"I don't think that's her point at all," said Barb. "I do agree that she is writing from personal experience about the South, but her main point is about prejudice itself—prejudice against African Americans. Through the voice of the grandmother we see the Southern lady's opinion of African Americans: They are inferior to whites, uneducated, poor, and basically ignorant. O'Connor's main point is that we are all equal."

"Yes, I agree," said Mike. "But if we look at this story in the context of all the other stories we have read this semester, I see a theme we have discussed countless times before: appearance versus reality. This is O'Connor's main point. The grandmother acts like a lady—someone who cares greatly about others—but inwardly she cares only for herself. She's a hypocrite."

"I disagree. In fact, I disagree with everybody," announced Daniel. "I like the grandmother. She reminds me of my grandmother. O'Connor's grandmother is a bit self-centered, but whose old grandmother isn't? Like my grandma, O'Connor's grandmother likes to be around her grandchildren, to read and to play with them. She's funny, and she has spunk. And she even likes cats."

"But, Dr. Blackwell, can we ever know what Flannery O'Connor really thinks about this story?" asked Jessica. "After all, she's dead, and she didn't write an essay titled "What 'A Good Man Is Hard to Find' Really Means." And since she never tells us its meaning, can't the story have more than one meaning?"

Professor Blackwell instantly realized that Jessica's query—Can a story have multiple meanings?—is a pivotal question not only for English professors and their students but also for anyone who reads any text.

CAN A TEXT HAVE MORE THAN ONE INTERPRETATION?

A quick glance at the discussion of O'Connor's "A Good Man Is Hard to Find" in Professor Blackwell's classroom reveals that not all readers interpret texts in the same way. In fact, all of the eight students who voiced their understandings of the story gave fundamentally different interpretations. Was only one of these eight interpretations correct and the remaining seven simply wrong? If so, how does one arrive at the correct interpretation? Put another way, if there is only one correct interpretation of a text, what are the **hermeneutical principles** readers must use to discover this interpretation?

On the other hand, if a work can have multiple interpretations, are all such interpretations valid? Can and should each interpretation be considered a satisfactory and legitimate analysis of the text under discussion? In other words, can a text mean anything a reader declares it to mean, or are there guiding principles for interpreting a text that must be followed if a reader is to arrive at a valid and legitimate interpretation?

Or need a reader be thinking of any of these particulars when reading a text? Can't one simply enjoy a novel, for example, without considering its interpretation? Need one be able to state the work's theme, discuss its structure, or analyze its tone in order to enjoy the act of reading the novel itself?

These and similar questions are the domain of **literary criticism**: the act of studying, analyzing, interpreting, evaluating, and enjoying a work of art. At first glance the study of literary criticism appears daunting and formidable. Jargon such as **hermeneutics**, **Aristotelian poetics**, **deconstruction**, and a host of other intimidating terms confront the would-be **literary critic**. But the actual process or act of literary criticism is not as ominous as it may first appear.

HOW TO BECOME A LITERARY CRITIC

When the students in Professor Blackwell's class were discussing O'Connor's short story "A Good Man Is Hard to Find," each of them was directly responding to the instructor's initial question: What do you believe O'Connor is trying to tell us in and through this story? Although not all responses were radically different, each student viewed the story from a unique perspective. For example, some students expressed their liking of the grandmother, but others thought she was a selfish, arrogant woman. Still others believed O'Connor was voicing a variety of philosophical, social, and cultural concerns, such as the place of women and African Americans in southern society, or adherence to the teachings of Jesus Christ as the basis for one's view of life, or the structure of the family in rural Georgia in the 1950s. All had an opinion about and therefore an interpretation of O'Connor's story.

When Dr. Blackwell's students stated their personal interpretations of O'Connor's story, they had already become practicing literary critics. All of them had already interacted with the story, thinking about their likes and dislikes of the various characters; their impressions of the setting, plot, and structure; and their overall assessment of the story itself, whether that assessment was a full-fledged interpretation that seeks to explain every facet of the text or simply bewilderment as to the story's overall meaning.

None of the students, however, had had formal training in literary criticism. None knew the somewhat complicated language of literary theory. And none were acquainted with any of the formal schools of literary criticism.

What each student had done was to read the story. The reading process itself produced within the students an array of responses, taking the form of questions, statements, opinions, and feelings evoked by the text. These responses coupled with the text itself are the concerns of formal literary criticism.

Although these students may need to master the terminology, the many philosophical approaches, and the diverse methodologies of formal literary criticism to become trained literary critics, they automatically became literary critics as they read and thought about O'Connor's text. They needed no formal training in literary theory. By mastering the concepts of formal literary criticism, these students, like all readers, can become critical readers who are better able to understand and articulate their own reactions and those of others to any text.

WHAT IS LITERARY CRITICISM?

Matthew Arnold, a nineteenth-century literary critic, describes literary criticism as "A disinterested endeavor to learn and propagate the best that is known and thought in the world." Implicit in this definition is that **literary criticism** is a disciplined activity that attempts to describe, study, analyze, justify, interpret, and evaluate a work of art. By necessity, Arnold would argue, this discipline attempts to formulate aesthetic and methodological principles on which the critic can evaluate a text.

When we consider its function and its relationship to texts, literary criticism is not usually considered a discipline in and of itself, for it must be related to something else—that is, a work of art. Without the work of art, the activity of criticism cannot exist. And it is through this discerning activity that we can knowingly explore the questions that help define our humanity, evaluate our actions, or simply increase our appreciation and enjoyment of both a literary work and our fellow human beings.

When analyzing a text, literary critics ask basic questions concerning the philosophical, psychological, functional, and descriptive nature of the text itself. Since the time of the Greek philosophers Plato and Aristotle, the answers to these questions have been debated. By asking questions of O'Connor's or any other text and by contemplating answers, we too can participate in this debate. Whether we question whether the motives of O'Connor's character the grandmother in wanting to take her cat on the family's vacation or whether the Misfit is the primary reason the grandmother experiences her **epiphany**, we are participating in an ongoing discussion of the value and enjoyment of O'Connor's short story while simultaneously engaging in literary criticism and functioning as practical literary critics.

Traditionally, literary critics involve themselves in either theoretical or practical criticism. **Theoretical criticism** formulates the theories, principles, and tenets of the nature and value of art. By citing general aesthetic and moral principles of art, theoretical criticism provides the necessary framework for practical criticism. **Practical criticism** (also known as **applied criticism**) applies the theories and tenets of theoretical criticism to a particular work. Using the theories and principles of theoretical criticism, the **practical critic** defines the standards of taste and explains, evaluates, or justifies a particular piece of literature. A further distinction is made between the practical critic who posits that there is only one theory or set of principles a critic may use when evaluating a literary work—the **absolutist critic**—and the **relativistic critic**, one who uses various and even contradictory theories in critiquing a piece of literature. The basis for either kind of critic, or any form of criticism, is literary theory. Without theory, practical criticism could not exist.

WHAT IS LITERARY THEORY?

When reading O'Connor's "A Good Man Is Hard to Find," we necessarily interact with the text, asking many specific, text-related questions and oftentimes rather personal ones as well. For example, such questions as these may concern us, the readers:

- What kind of person is the grandmother? Is she like my grandmother or any grandmother I know?
- What is the function or role of June Star? John Wesley? Bailey? The mother?
- Why was the grandmother taking Pitty Sing, the cat, on the family vacation?
- What is the significance of the restaurant scene at The Tower?
- Right before she is shot, what does the grandmother recognize about the Misfit? What is the significance of this recognition?

Such questions immediately involve us in practical criticism. What we tend to forget during the reading of O'Connor's short story or any other text, however, is that we have read other literary works. Our response to any text, then—or the principles of practical criticism we apply to it—is largely a conditioned or socially constructed one; that is, how we arrive at meaning in fiction is in part determined by our past experiences. Consciously or unconsciously, we have developed a mindset or framework concerning our expectations when reading a novel, short story, poem, or any other type of literature. In addition, what we choose to value or uphold as good or bad, moral or immoral, or beautiful or ugly within a given text actually depends on this ever-evolving framework. When we can clearly articulate our mental framework when reading a text and explain how this mindset directly influences our values and aesthetic judgments about the text, we are well on our way to developing a coherent, unified **literary theory**—the assumptions (conscious or unconscious) that undergird one's understanding and interpretation of language, the construction of meaning, art, culture, aesthetics, and ideological positions.

Because anyone who responds to a text is already a practicing literary critic and because practical criticism is rooted in the reader's preconditioned mindset concerning his or her expectations when actually reading a text, every reader espouses some kind of literary theory. Each reader's theory may be conscious or unconscious, whole or partial, informed or ill informed, eclectic or unified. An incomplete, unconscious, and therefore unclear literary theory leads to illogical, unsound, and haphazard interpretations. On the other hand, a well-defined, logical, and clearly articulated theory enables readers to develop a method by which to establish principles that enable them to justify, order, and clarify their own appraisals of a text in a consistent manner.

A well-articulated literary theory assumes that an innocent reading of a text or a sheerly emotional or spontaneous reaction to a work cannot exist, for theory questions the assumptions, beliefs, and feelings of readers, asking why they respond to a text in a certain way. According to a consistent literary theory, a simple emotional or intuitive response to a text does not explain the underlying factors that caused such a reaction. What elicits that response, or how the reader constructs meaning through or with the text, is what matters.

MAKING MEANING FROM TEXT

How we as readers construct meaning through or with a text depends on the mental framework each of us has developed concerning the nature of reality. This framework or **worldview** consists of the assumptions or presuppositions that we all hold (either consciously or unconsciously) concerning the basic makeup of our world. For example, we all struggle to find answers to such questions as these:

- What is the basis of morality or ethics?
- What is the meaning of human history?
- Is there an overarching purpose for humanity's existence?
- What is beauty, truth, or goodness?
- Is there an ultimate reality?

Interestingly, our answers to these and other questions do not remain static, for as we interact with other people, our environment, and our own inner selves, we are continually shaping and developing our personal philosophies, rejecting former ideas and opinions and replacing them with newly discovered ones. But it is our dynamic answers—including our doubts and fears about these answers—that largely determine our response to a literary text.

Upon such a conceptual framework rests literary theory. Whether that framework is well reasoned or simply a matter of habit and past teachings, readers respond to works of art via their worldview. From this philosophical core of beliefs spring their evaluations of the goodness, worthiness, and value of art itself. Using their worldviews either consciously or unconsciously as a yardstick by which to measure and value their experiences, readers respond to individual works of literature, ordering and valuing each separate or collective experience in each text based on the system of beliefs housed in their worldviews.

THE READING PROCESS AND LITERARY THEORY

The relationship between literary theory and a reader's personal worldview is best illustrated in the act of reading itself. When reading, we are constantly interacting with the text. According to Louise M. Rosenblatt's text *The Reader, the Text, the Poem* (1978), during the act or event of reading,

> A reader brings to the text his or her past experience and present personality. Under the magnetism of the ordered symbols of the text, the reader marshals his or her resources and crystallizes out from the stuff of memory, thought, and feeling a new order, a new experience, which he/she sees as the poem. This becomes part of the ongoing stream of the reader's life experience, to be reflected on from any angle important to him or her as a human being.

Accordingly, Rosenblatt declares that the relationship between the reader and the text is not linear, but **transactional**; that is, it is a process or event that takes place at a particular time and place in which the text and the reader condition each other. The reader and the text transact, creating meaning, for meaning does not exist solely within the reader's mind or within the text,

Rosenblatt maintains, but in the transaction between them. To arrive at an interpretation of a text, readers bring their own "temperament and fund of past transactions to the text and live through a process of handling new situations, new attitudes, new personalities, [and] new conflicts in value. They can reject, revise, or assimilate into the resource with which they engage their world." Through this transactional experience, readers consciously and unconsciously amend their worldview.

Because no literary theory can account for all the various factors included in everyone's conceptual framework, and because we, as readers, all have different literary experiences, there can exist no **metatheory**—one overarching literary theory that encompasses all possible interpretations of a text suggested by its readers. And there can be no one correct literary theory, for in and of itself, each literary theory asks valid questions about the text, and no one theory is capable of exhausting all legitimate questions to be asked about any text.

The valid questions asked by the various literary theories often differ widely. Espousing separate critical orientations, each theory focuses primarily on one element of the interpretative process, although in practice different theories may address several areas of concern in interpreting a text. For example, one theory stresses the work itself, believing that the text alone contains all the necessary information to arrive at an interpretation. This theory isolates the text from its historical or sociological setting and concentrates on the literary forms found in the text, such as figures of speech, word choice, and style. Another theory attempts to place a text in its historical, political, sociological, religious, and economic setting. By placing the text in historical perspective, this theory asserts that its adherents can arrive at an interpretation that both the text's author and its original audience would support. Still another theory directs its chief concern toward the text's audience. It asks how the readers' emotions and personal backgrounds affect a text's interpretation. Whether the primary focus of concern is psychological, linguistic, mythical, historical, or from any other critical orientation, each literary theory establishes its own theoretical basis and then proceeds to develop its own methodology whereby readers can apply this theory to an actual text.

Although each reader's theory and methodology for arriving at a text's interpretation differ, sooner or later groups of readers and critics declare allegiance to a similar core of beliefs and band together, thereby founding different **schools of criticism**. For example, critics who believe that social and historical concerns must be highlighted in a text are known as Marxist critics, whereas reader-response critics concentrate on the readers' personal reactions to the text. Because new points of view concerning literary works are continually evolving, new schools of criticism and therefore new literary theories will continue to develop. One of the most recent schools to emerge in the 1980s and 1990s, New Historicism or Cultural Poetics, declares that a text must be analyzed through historical research that assumes that history and fiction are inseparable. The members of this school, known as New Historicists, hope to shift the boundaries between history and literature and thereby produce criticism that accurately reflects what they believe to be the proper relationship between the text and its historical context. Still other newly evolving schools of criticism such as postcolonialism, gender studies, and African-American studies continue to emerge and challenge previous ways of thinking and critiquing texts.

Because the various schools of criticism (and the theories on which they are based) ask different questions about the same work of literature, these theoretical schools provide an array of seemingly endless options from which readers can choose to broaden their understanding not only of the text but also of their society, their culture, and their own humanity. By embracing literary theory, we can thus learn not only about literature but also about tolerance for other people's beliefs. By rejecting or ignoring theory, we are in danger of canonizing ourselves as literary saints who possess divine knowledge and can therefore supply the one and only correct interpretation for a work of literature. To oppose, disregard, or ignore literary theory is also to be against questioning our own concepts of self, society, and culture and how texts help us define and continually redefine these concepts. By embracing literary theory and literary criticism (its practical application), we can participate in that seemingly endless historical conversation and debate concerning the nature of humanity and its concerns as expressed in literature itself.

WHAT IS LITERATURE?

Because literary criticism presupposes that there exists a work of literature to be interpreted, we could assume that formulating a definition of **literature** would be simple. But it is not. For centuries, writers, literary historians, and others have debated about but failed to agree on a definition for this term. Some assume that literature is simply anything that is written, thereby declaring a city telephone book, a cook book, and a road atlas to be literary works along with *David Copperfield* and the *Adventures of Huckleberry Finn*. Derived from the Latin *littera*, meaning "letter," the root meaning of literature refers primarily to the written word and seems to support this broad definition. However, such a definition eliminates the important oral traditions on which much of our literature is based, including Homer's *Iliad* and *Odyssey*, the English epic *Beowulf*, and many Native American legends.

To solve this problem, others choose to define *literature* as an art, thereby leaving open the question of its being written or oral. This further narrows its meaning, equating literature to works of the imagination or creative writing. To emphasize the imaginative qualities of literature, some critics choose to use the German word for literature, *Wortkunst*, instead of its English equivalent, for *Wortkunst* automatically implies that the imaginative and creative aspects of literature are essential components of the word *literature* itself. By this definition, written works such as a telephone or cook book can no longer be considered literature, being replaced or superseded by poetry, drama, fiction, and other imaginative writing.

Although such a narrowing and an equating of the definition of literature to art seemingly simplifies what can and cannot be deemed a literary work, such is not the case. That the J. Crew and Victoria's Secrets clothes catalogues are imaginative (and colorful) writing is unquestioned, but should they be considered works of literature? Or should Madonna's book *Sex* or the lyrics of the rap song "Cop Killer" be called literary works? Is Madonna's text or the rap song an imaginative or creative work? If so, can or should either be considered a work of literature? Defining and narrowing the definition of literature as being a work of art does not immediately provide consensus or a consistent rule concerning whether a work should be called a work of literature.

Whether one accepts the broad or narrow definition, many argue that a text must have certain peculiar qualities before it can be dubbed literature. For example, the artist's creation or secondary world often mirrors the author's primary world, the world in which the creator lives and moves and breathes. Because reality or the primary world is highly structured, so must be the secondary world. To achieve this structure, the artist must create plot, character, tone, symbols, conflict, and a host of other elements or parts of the artistic story, with all of these elements working in a dynamic relationship to produce a literary work. Some would argue that it is the creation of these elements—how they are used and in what context—that determines whether a piece of writing is literature.

Still other critics add the test-of-time criterion to their essential components of literature. If a work such as Dante's *Divine Comedy* withstands the passage of time and is still being read centuries after its creation, it is deemed valuable and worthy to be called literature. This criterion also denotes literature's functional or cultural value: If people value a written work, for whatever reason, they often declare it to be literature whether or not it contains the prescribed elements of a text.

What this work may contain is a peculiar aesthetic quality—that is, some element of beauty—that distinguishes it as literature from other forms of writing. **Aesthetics**, the branch of philosophy that deals with the concept of the beautiful, strives to determine the criteria for beauty in a work of art. Theorists such as Plato and Aristotle declare that the source of beauty is inherent within the art object itself; other critics, such as David Hume, say that beauty is in the eye of the beholder. And some twentieth-century theorists argue that one's perception of beauty in a text rests in the dynamic relationship between the object and the perceiver at a given moment in time. Wherever the criteria for judging beauty of a work of art finally resides, most critics agree that a work of literature does have an appealing aesthetic quality.

While distinguishing literature from other forms of writings, this appealing aesthetic quality directly contributes to literature's chief purpose: the telling of a story. Although it may simultaneously communicate facts, literature's primary aim is to tell a story. The subject of this story is particularly human, describing and detailing a variety of human experiences, not stating facts or bits and pieces of information. For example, literature does not define the word *courage*, but shows us a courageous character acting courageously. By so doing, literature concretizes an array of human values, emotions, actions, and ideas in story form. And it is this concretization that allows us to experience vicariously the stories of a host of characters. Through these characters we observe people in action, making decisions, struggling to maintain their humanity in often inhumane circumstances, and embodying for us a variety of values and human characteristics that we may embrace, discard, enjoy, or detest.

LITERARY THEORY AND THE DEFINITION OF LITERATURE

Is literature simply a story that contains certain aesthetic and literary qualities that all somehow pleasingly culminate in a work of art? If so, can texts be considered **artifacts** that can be analyzed, dissected, and studied to discover their essential nature or meaning? Or does a literary work have **ontological** status; that is, does it exist in and of itself, perhaps in a special **neo-Platonic** realm, or must it have an audience, a reader, before it becomes literature? And can we define the word *text*? Is it simply print on a page? If pictures are included, do they automatically become part of the text? And who determines when print becomes a work of art? The reader? The author? Both?

The answers to these and similar questions have been long debated, and the various responses make up the corpus of literary theory. Providing the academic arena in which those interested in literary theory (literary theorists) can posit philosophical assumptions concerning the nature of the reading process, the **epistemological** nature of learning, the nature of reality itself, and a host of related concerns, literary theory offers a variety of methodologies that enable readers to interpret a text from different and often conflicting points of view. Such theorizing empowers readers to examine their personal worldviews, to articulate their individual assumptions concerning the nature of reality, and to understand how these assumptions directly affect their interpretation not only of a work of art and but also of the definition of literature itself.

Although any definition of literature is debatable, most would agree that an examination of a text's total artistic situation would help us decide what constitutes literature. This total picture of the work involves such elements as the work itself (an examination of the fictionality or secondary world created within the story), the artist, the universe or world the work supposedly represents, and the audience or readers. Although readers and critics will emphasize one, two, or even three of these elements while de-emphasizing the others, such a consideration of a text's artistic situation immediately broadens the definition of literature from the concept that it is simply a written work that contains certain qualities to a definition that must include the dynamic relationship of the actual text and the readers. Perhaps, then, the literary competence of the readers themselves helps determine whether a work should be considered literature. If this is so, then a literary work may be more functional than ontological, its existence and therefore its value being determined by its readers and not the work itself.

Overall, the definition of literature depends on the particular kind of literary theory or school of criticism that the reader or critic espouses. For formalists, for example, the text and text alone contains certain qualities that make a particular piece of writing literature. But for reader-response critics, the interaction and psychological relationships between the text and the reader help determine whether a document should be deemed literary.

THE FUNCTION OF LITERATURE AND LITERARY THEORY

Critics continually debate literature's chief function. Tracing their arguments to Plato, many contend that literature's primary function is moral, its chief value being its usefulness for hidden or undisclosed purposes. But others, like Aristotle, hold that a work of art can be analyzed and broken down into its various parts, with each part contributing to the overall enjoyment of the work itself. For these critics, the value of a text is found within it or inseparably linked to the work itself. In its most simple terms, the debate centers around two concerns: Is literature's chief function to teach (extrinsic) or to entertain (intrinsic)? In other words, can or do we read a text for the sheer fun of it, or must we always be studying and learning from what we read?

Such questions and their various answers lead us directly to literary theory, for literary theory concerns itself not only with ontological questions (whether a text really exists), but also with epistemological issues (how we know or ways of knowing). When we ask, then, if literature's chief function is to entertain or to teach, we are really asking epistemological questions.

Whether we read a text to learn from it or to be entertained, we can say that we know that text once having read it.

We can know a text in two distinct ways. The first method involves the typical literature classroom analysis. When we have studied, analyzed, and critiqued a text and arrived at an interpretation, we can then confidently assert that we know the text. On the other hand, when we stay up all night turning the pages of a mystery novel to discover who the murderer is, we can also say that we know the text, for we have spent time devouring its pages, lost in its secondary world, consumed by its characters, and by novel's end eagerly seeking the resolution of its tensions. Both methods—one whose chief goal is to learn and the other's being entertainment—involve similar yet distinct epistemological ways of knowing.

The French verbs *savoir* and *connaître* can both be translated as "to know" and highlight the difference between these two epistemological ways of knowing a text. *Savoir* means to analyze (from the Greek *analuein*, to undo) and to study. It is used to refer to knowing something that is the object of study and assumes that the object, such as a text, can be examined, analyzed, and critiqued. Knowledge or learning is its ultimate goal.

Connaître, on the other hand, implies that we intimately know or have experienced the text. Interestingly, *connaître* is used for knowing people and refers to our knowing an author's canon. Knowing people and knowing a literary canon imply intimacy, learning the ins and outs of each one of them. And it is such intimacy that one often experiences while reading a mystery novel all night long.

To know how to analyze a text, to discuss its literary elements, and to apply the various methodologies of literary criticism means that we know that text (*savoir*). To have experienced the text, to have cried with or about its characters, to have lost time and sleep immersed in the secondary world of the text, and to have felt our emotions stirred also means that we know that text (*connaître*). From one way of knowing we learn facts or information, and from the other we encounter and participate in an intimate experience.

At times, however, we have actually known the text from both these perspectives, *savoir* and *connaître*. While analyzing and critiquing a text (*savoir*), we have at times (and perhaps more often than not) simultaneously experienced it, becoming emotionally involved with its characters' choices and destinies (*connaître*) and imagining ourselves to be these characters, or at least recognizing some of our own characteristics dramatized by the characters.

Thus, to say that we know a text is no simple statement. Underlying our private and public reactions and our scholarly critiques and analyses is our literary theory, the fountainhead of our most intimate and our most public declarations. The formal study of literary theory therefore enables us to explain our responses to any text and allows us to articulate the function of literature in an academic and a personal way.

BEGINNING THE FORMAL STUDY
OF LITERARY THEORY

This chapter has stressed the importance of literary theory and criticism and its relationship to literature and the interpretative processes. And it has also articulated the underlying premises as to why a study of literary theory is essential:

- Literary theory assumes that there is no such thing as an innocent reading of a text. Whether our responses are emotional and spontaneous or well reasoned and highly structured, all such interactions with and to a text are based on some underlying factors that cause us to respond to the text in a particular fashion. What elicits these responses or how a reader makes sense out of a text is at the heart of literary theory.
- Because our reactions to any text have theoretical bases, all readers must have a literary theory. The methods we use to frame our personal interpretations of any text directly involve us in the process of literary criticism and theory, automatically making us practicing literary critics.
- Because many readers' literary theory is more often than not unconscious, incomplete, ill-informed, and eclectic, their interpretations can easily be illogical, unsound, and haphazard. A well-defined, logical, and clearly articulated literary theory enables readers to consciously develop their own personal methods of interpretation, permitting them to order, clarify, and justify their appraisals of a text in a consistent and logical manner.

It is the goal of this text to enable readers to make such conscious, informed, and intelligent choices concerning their own methods of literary interpretation and to understand their personal and public reactions to a text. To accomplish this goal, this text will introduce readers to literary theory and criticism, its historical development, and the various theoretical positions or schools of criticism that enable readers to become knowledgeable critics of their own and others' interpretations. By becoming acquainted with diverse and often contradictory approaches to a text, readers will broaden their perspectives not only about themselves but also about others and the world in which they live.

FURTHER READING

Atkins, G. Douglas, and Laura Morrow, eds. *Contemporary Literary Theory*. Amherst: University of Massachusetts Press, 1989.
Bonnycastle, Stephen. *In Search of Authority: An Introductory Guide to Literary Theory*. Lewiston, NY: Broadview, 1991.
Cowles, David. *The Critical Experience*. Dubuque: Kendall/Hunt, 1994.

Eagleton, Terry. *Literary Theory: An Introduction.* Minneapolis: University of Minnesota Press, 1983.

Groden, Michael, and Martin Kreiswirth, eds. *The Johns Hopkins Guide to Literary Theory and Criticism.* Baltimore: Johns Hopkins University Press, 1994.

Harmon, William, and C. Hugh Holman. *A Handbook to Literature.* 7th ed. New York: Macmillan, 1996.

Reiss, Timothy J. *The Meaning of Literature.* Ithaca: Cornell University Press, 1992.

Rosenblatt, Louise M. *The Reader, the Text, the Poem.* Carbondale: Southern Illinois University Press, 1978.

Sire, James. *The Joy of Reading: A Guide to Becoming a Better Reader.* Portland, OR: Multnomah Press, 1978.

2

A Historical Survey
of Literary Criticism

Questions about the value, structure, and even definition of literature undoubtedly arose in all cultures as people heard or read works of art. Such practical criticism probably began with the initial hearing or reading of the first literary works. It is the Greeks of the fifth century B.C., however-er, who first articulated and developed the philosophy of art and life that serves as the foundation for most theoretical and practical criticism. These Athenians questioned the very act of reading and writing itself, while pondering the purpose of literature. By so doing, these early critics began a debate concerning the nature and function of literature that continues to the present day. What they inaugurated was the formal study of literary criticism.

From the fifth century B.C. to the present, critics such as Plato, Dante, Wordsworth, and a host of others have developed principles of criticism that have had a major influence on the ongoing discussion of literary theory and criticism. By examining these critics' ideas, we can gain an understanding of and participate in this critical debate while acquiring an appreciation for and a working knowledge of both practical and theoretical criticism.

PLATO (ca. 427–347 B.C.)

Alfred North Whitehead, a modern British philosopher, once quipped that "all of Western philosophy is but a footnote to Plato." Although others have indeed contributed to Western thought, it was Plato's ideas expressed in his *Ion, Crito, The Republic,* and other works, that laid the foundation for many, if not most, of the pivotal issues of philosophy and literature: the concepts of truth, beauty, and goodness; the nature of reality; the structure of society; the nature and relations of being (ontology); questions about how we know what we know (epistemology); and ethics and morality. Since Plato's day, such ideas have been debated, changed, debunked, or simply accepted. None, however, have been ignored.

Before Plato, only fragmentary comments about the nature or value of literature can be found. In the plays and writings of the comic dramatist Aristophanes, a contemporary of Plato, a few tidbits of practical criticism arise, but no clearly articulated literary theory. It is Plato who systematically begins the study of literary theory and criticism.

The core of Platonic thought resides in Plato's doctrine of essences, ideas, or forms. Ultimate reality, he states, is spiritual. This spiritual realm, which Plato calls The One, is composed of "ideal" forms or absolutes that exist whether or not any mind posits their existence or reflects their attributes. It is these ideal forms that give shape to our physical world, for our material world is nothing more than a shadowy replica of the absolute forms found in the spiritual realm. In the material world we can therefore recognize a chair as a chair because the ideal chair exists in this spiritual realm and preceded the existence of the material chair. Without the existence of the ideal chair, the physical chair, which is nothing more than a shadowy replica of the ideal chair, could not exist.

Such an emphasis on philosophical ideals earmarks the beginning of the first articulated literary theory and becomes the foundation for literary criticism. Before Plato and his Academy, Greek culture ordered its world through poetry and the poetic imagination; that is, by reading such works as *The Iliad* and *The Odyssey*, the Greeks saw good characters in action performing good deeds. From such stories, they formulated their theories of goodness and other similar standards, thereby using the presentational mode for discovering truth: observing good characters acting justly, honorably, and courageously and inculcating these characteristics within themselves. With the advent of Plato and his Academy, however, philosophical inquiry and abstract thinking usurped the narrative as a method for discovering truth. Not by accident, then, Plato places above his school door the words, "Let no one enter here who is not a geometer" [a master of geometry; one skilled in formal logic and reasoning]. All his students had to value the art of reason and abstraction, as opposed to the presentational mode, for discovering truth.

Such abstract reasoning and formal logic not only usurps literature's role as an evaluating mode for discerning truth but actually condemns it. If ultimate reality rests in the spiritual realm and the material world is only a shadowy replica of the world of ideals, then according to Plato and his followers, poets (those who compose imaginative literature) are merely imitating an imitation when they write about any object in the material world. Accordingly, Plato declares that a poet's craft is "an inferior who marries an inferior and has inferior offspring," for the poet, declares Plato, is one who is now two steps or degrees removed from ultimate reality. These imitators of mere shadows, contends Plato, cannot be trusted.

While condemning poets for producing art that is nothing more than a copy of a copy, Plato also argues that the poets produce their art irrationally, relying on untrustworthy intuition rather than reason for their inspiration. He writes, "For the poet is a light and winged and holy thing, and there is no invention in him until he has been inspired and is out of his senses, and then the mind is no longer in him." Because such inspiration opposes reason and asserts that truth can be attained intuitively, Plato condemns all poets.

Because poets are untrustworthy and damned, no longer can their works be the basis of the Greeks' morality or ethics. For Plato argues that in the poets' works, lies abound concerning the nature of ultimate reality. In *The Iliad*, for example, the gods lie and cheat and are one of the main causes of suffering among humans. Even the mortals in these works steal, complain, and hate each other. Such writings, contends Plato, set a bad example for Greek citizens and may even lead normally law-abiding people down paths of wickedness and immorality. In *The Republic*, Plato ultimately concludes that such people, the poets, must be banished.

In a later work, Plato recants the total banishment of poets from society, for he seemingly recognizes society's need for poets and their craft to "celebrate the victors" of the state. However, only poets "who are themselves good and also honourable in the state" can be tolerated. Plato thus decrees poetry's function and value in and for his society: to sing the praises of loyal Greeks. Poets must be supporters of the state or risk banishment from their homeland. Being mere imitators of reality, these artisans and their craft must be religiously censured.

By linking politics and literature in an apparently moral and reasoned world view, Plato and his Academy founded a complex theory of literary criticism that initiated the ongoing debate concerning the value, nature, and worth of the artist and literature itself.

ARISTOTLE (384–322 B.C.)

Whereas literary criticism's concern with morality began with Plato, its emphasis on the elements or characteristics of which a work is composed began with Aristotle, Plato's famous pupil. Rejecting some of his teacher's beliefs about the nature of reality, Aristotle opts for a detailed investigation of the material world.

The son of a medical doctor from Thrace, Aristotle reveled in the physical world. After studying at the Academy and mastering the philosophy and the techniques of inquiry taught there, he founded the Lyceum, a school of scientific and philosophical thought and investigation. Applying his scientific methods of investigation to the study of literature, Aristotle answers Plato's accusations against poetry in a series of lectures known as the *Poetics*. Unlike **exoteric treatises** meant for general publication, the *Poetics* is an **esoteric work**, one meant for private circulation to those who attended the

Lyceum. It therefore lacks the unity and coherence of Aristotle's other works, but it remains one of the most important critical influences on literary theory and criticism.

Aristotle's *Poetics* has become the cornerstone of Western literary criticism. By applying his analytic abilities to a definition of tragedy, Aristotle began in the *Poetics* a discussion of the components of a literary work that continues to the present day. Unfortunately, many critics and scholars mistakenly assume that the *Poetics* is a how-to manual, defining and setting the standards for literature (particularly tragedy) for all time. However, Aristotle's purpose was not to formulate a series of absolute rules for evaluating a tragedy, but to state the general principles of tragedy as he viewed them in his time while responding to many of Plato's doctrines and arguments.

Even his title, the *Poetics*, reveals Aristotle's purpose, for in Greek the word *poetikes* means "things that are made or crafted." Like a biologist, Aristotle dissects tragedy to discover its component or crafted parts.

At the beginning of the *Poetics*, Aristotle notes that "epic poetry, tragedy, comedy, dithyrambic poetry, and most forms of flute and lyre playing all happen to be, in general, imitations." All seemingly differ in how and what they imitate, but Aristotle agrees with Plato that all the arts are imitations. In particular, the art of poetry exists because people are imitative creatures who enjoy such imitation. Whereas Plato contends that such pleasure can undermine the structure of society and all its values, Aristotle strongly disagrees. His disagreement is basically a metaphysical argument concerning the nature of imitation itself. Whereas Plato posits that imitation is two steps removed from the truth or realm of the ideal (the poet imitating an object that is itself an imitation of an ideal form), Aristotle contends poetry is more universal, more general than things as they are. For "it is not the function of the poet to relate what has happened, but what may happen—what is possible according to the law of probability or necessity." It is the historian, not the poet, who writes of what has already happened. The poet's task, declares Aristotle, is to write of what could happen. "Poetry, therefore, is a more philosophical and a higher thing than history: for poetry tends to express the universal, history the particular." In arguing that poets present things not as they are but as they should be, Aristotle rebuffs Plato's concept that the poet is merely imitating an imitation, for Aristotle's poet, with his emphasis on the universal, actually attains nearer to the ideal than does Plato's.

But not all imitations by poets are the same, for "writers of greater dignity imitated the noble actions of noble heroes; the less dignified sort of writers imitated the actions of inferior men." For Aristotle, "comedy is an imitation of base men . . . characterized not by every kind of vice but specifically by 'the ridiculous,' some error or ugliness that is painless and has no harmful effects." It is to tragedy written by poets imitating noble actions and heroes that Aristotle turns his attention.

Aristotle's complex definition of *tragedy* has perplexed and frustrated many readers:

> Tragedy is, then, an imitation of a noble and complete action, having the proper magnitude; it employs language that has been artistically enhanced by each of the kinds of linguistic adornment, applied separately in the various parts of the play; it is presented in dramatic, not narrative form, and achieves, through the representation of pitiable and fearful incidents, the catharsis of such pitiable and fearful incidents.

When put in context with other ideas in the *Poetics*, such a complex definition highlights Aristotle's chief contributions to literary criticism:

- Tragedy, or a work of art, is an imitation of nature that reflects a high form of art exhibiting noble characters and noble deeds, the act of imitation itself giving us pleasure.
- Art possesses form; that is, tragedy, unlike life, has a beginning, a middle, and an end, with each of the parts being related to every other part. A tragedy is an organic whole, with all its various parts interrelated.
- In tragedy, concern for form must be given to the characters as well as the structure of the play, for the tragic hero must be "a man who is not eminently good and just, yet whose misfortune is brought about not by vice or depravity, but by some error or frailty. He must be one who is highly renowned and prosperous." In addition, all tragic heroes must have a tragic flaw, or **hamartia**, that leads to their downfall in such a way as not to offend the audience's sense of justice.
- The tragedy must have an emotional effect on its audience and "through pity and fear" effect a **catharsis**; that is, by the play's end, the audience's emotions should be purged, purified, or clarified (what Aristotle really meant by *catharsis* is debatable).
- The universal, not the particular, should be stressed, for unlike history, which deals with what happens, poetry (or tragedy) deals with what could happen and is therefore closer to perfection or truth.
- The poet must give close attention to diction or language itself, be it in verse, prose, or song, but ultimately it is the thoughts expressed through language that are of the utmost concern.

Interestingly, nowhere in the *Poetics* does Aristotle address the didactic value of poetry or literature. Unlike Plato, whose chief concern is the subject matter of poetry and its effects on the reader, Aristotle emphasizes literary form or structure, examining the component parts of a tragedy and how these parts must work together to produce a unified whole.

From the writings of philosopher–artists, Plato and Aristotle, arise the concerns, questions, and debates that have spearheaded the development of most literary schools of criticism. By addressing different aspects of these fifth-century Greeks' ideas and concepts, a variety of literary critics from the Middle Ages to the present have formulated theories of literary criticism that force us to ask different but legitimate questions of a text. But the shadows of Plato and Aristotle loom over much of what these later theorists espouse.

HORACE (65–8 B.C.)

With the passing of the glory that was Greece and its philosopher–artists came the grandeur of Rome and its chief stylist, Quintus Horatius Flaccus, or simply Horace. Friend of Emperor Augustus and many other members of the Roman aristocracy, Horace enjoyed the wealth and influence of these associates. In a letter to the sons of one of his friends and patrons, Maecenas, Horace articulated what became the official canon of literary taste during the Middle Ages, the Renaissance, and much of the Neoclassical period. By reading this letter and his *Ars Poetica*, or *The Art of Poetry*, any Roman aristocrat, any medieval knight, and even Alexander Pope himself could learn the standards of good or proper literature.

Although Horace was probably acquainted with Aristotle's works, his concerns are quite different. Whereas both Plato and Aristotle decree that poets must, and do, imitate nature, Horace declares that poets must imitate other poets, particularly those of the past. Less concerned with metaphysics than his predecessors, Horace establishes the practical do's and don'ts for a writer. To be considered a good writer, he maintains, one should write about traditional subjects in unique ways. In addition, the poet should avoid all extremes in subject matter, word choice, vocabulary, and style. Gaining mastery in these areas could be achieved by reading and following the examples of the classical Greek and Roman authors. For example, because authors of antiquity began their epics in the middle of things, all epics must begin **in medias res**. Above all, writers should avoid appearing ridiculous and must therefore aim their sights low, not attempting to be a new Virgil or Homer.

Literature's ultimate aim, declares Horace, is "dulce et utile" or to be sweet and useful; the best writings, he argues, both teach and delight. To achieve this goal, poets must understand their audience: The learned reader may want to be instructed, whereas others may simply read to be amused. The poet's task is to combine usefulness and delight in the same literary work.

Often oversimplified and misunderstood, Horace opts to give the would-be writer practical guidelines for the author's craft while leaving unattended and unchallenged many of the philosophical concerns of Plato and Aristotle. For Horace, a poet's greatest reward is the adulation of the public.

LONGINUS (FIRST CENTURY A.D.)

Although his date of birth and national origin remain controversial, Longinus garners an important place in literary history for his treatise "On the Sublime." Probably a Greek, Longinus often peppers his Greek and Latin writings with Hebrew quotations, making him the first literary critic to borrow from a different literary tradition and earning him the title of the first comparative critic in literary history.

Unlike Plato, Aristotle, and Horace, who focus respectively on a work's essence, the constituent parts of a work, and literary taste, Longinus concentrates on single elements of a text, and he is the first critic to define a literary classic.

One cannot accurately judge a literary work, he argues, unless one is exceedingly well read. A well-read critic can evaluate and recognize what is great or what Homer calls sublime: "For that is really great which bears a repeated examination, and which it is difficult or rather impossible to withstand, and the memory of which is strong and hard to efface." Homer asserts that all readers are innately capable of recognizing the sublime, for "Nature has appointed us to be no base or ignoble animals . . . for she implants in our souls the unconquerable love of whatever is elevated and more divine than we." When our intellects, our emotions, and our wills harmoniously respond to a given work of art, we know we have been touched by the sublime.

Until the late seventeenth century, few people considered Longinus' "On the Sublime" important or had even read it. By the eighteenth century, its significance was recognized, and it was quoted and debated by most public authors. Emphasizing the author, the work itself, and the reader's response, Longinus' critical method foreshadows New Criticism, reader-response, and other schools of twentieth-century criticism.

DANTE ALIGHIERI (1265–1321)

Born in Florence, Italy, during the Middle Ages, Dante is the only known significant contributor to literary criticism since Longinus and the appearance of his "On the Sublime" approximately 1000 years earlier. Like Longinus, Dante's concern is the proper language for poetry.

Banished from his native Florence for political reasons, Dante wrote many of his works in exile, including his masterpiece *The Divine Comedy*. As an introduction to the third and last section of this *Commedia*, the *Paradiso*, Dante wrote a letter to Can Grande della Scala explaining his literary theory. Known today as *Letter to Can Grande della Scala*, this work decrees that the language spoken by the people (the vulgar tongue or the vernacular) is an appropriate and beautiful language for writing.

Until the publication of Dante's works, Latin was the universal language, and all important works—such as histories, Church documents, and even government decrees—were written in this official Church tongue. Only frivolous or popular works appeared in the "vulgar" language of the common people. But in his *Letter*, Dante asserts and establishes that the vernacular is an excellent vehicle for works of literature.

In the *Letter* Dante also notes that he uses multiple levels of interpretation or symbolic meaning in *The Divine Comedy*. Since the time of St. Augustine and throughout the Middle Ages, the church fathers had followed a tradition of allegoric reading of scripture that interpreted many of the Old Testament laws and stories as symbolic or allegories of Christ's actions. Such a semiotic interpretation—reading of signs—had been applied only to scripture. Until Dante's *Commedia* no secular work had used these principles of symbolic interpretation.

Praising the lyric poem and ignoring a discussion of genres, Dante established himself as the leading, if not the only, significant critic of the Middle Ages. Because he declared the common tongue an acceptable vehicle of expression for literature, literary works found an ever-increasing audience.

SIR PHILIP SIDNEY (1554–86)

The paucity of literary criticism and theory during the Middle Ages is more than made up for by the abundance of critical activity during the Renaissance. One critic of this period far excels all others: Sir Philip Sidney.

The representative scholar, writer, and gentleman of Renaissance England, Sidney is usually considered the first great English critic–poet. His *An Apology for Poetry* (sometimes called *Defence of Poesy*) is the definitive formulation of Renaissance literary theory and the first influential piece of literary criticism in English history. With Sidney begins the English tradition and history of literary criticism.

As evidenced in *An Apology for Poetry*, Sidney is eclectic, borrowing and often amending the theories of Plato, Aristotle, Horace, and a few of his contemporary Italian critics. He begins his criticism by quoting from Aristotle; he writes, "Poesy therefore is an art of imitation, for so Aristotle termeth it in his word *mimesis*, that is to say, a representing, counterfeiting, or figuring forth"; but eight words later he adds a Horatian note, declaring poesy's chief end to be "to teach and delight." Like Aristotle, Sidney values poetry over history, law, and philosophy, but he takes Aristotle's idea one step further by declaring that poetry, above all the other arts and sciences, embodies truth.

Unlike his classical forefathers, Sidney best personifies the Renaissance period when he dictates his literary precepts. After ranking the different literary genres and declaring all to be instructive, he declares poetry to excel all. He mocks other genres (tragicomedy, for example) and adds more dictates to Aristotelian tragedy by insisting on unity of action, time, and place.

Throughout *An Apology for Poetry*, Sidney stalwartly defends poetry against those who view it as a mindless or immoral activity. At the essay's end, a passionate and somewhat platonically inspired poet places a curse on all those who do not love poetry. Echoes of such emotionality reverberate throughout the centuries in English literature, especially in British Romantic writings.

JOHN DRYDEN (1631–1700)

Poet laureate, dramatist, and critic John Dryden, more than any other English writer, embodies the spirit and ideals of Neoclassicism, the literary age that follows Sidney and the Renaissance. Dr. Samuel Johnson attributes to Dryden "the improvement, perhaps the completion of our meter, the refinement of our language, and much of the correctness of our sentiments." The most prolific writer of the Restoration, Dryden excelled in almost all genres. His lasting contribution to literary criticism, *An Essay of Dramatic Poesy*, highlights his genius in most of these genres.

The structure of Dryden's *An Essay of Dramatic Poesy* reflects his brilliance: During a naval battle between the English and the Dutch, four men are floating down a barge on the Thames River, each supporting a different aesthetic theory among those prominently espoused in Renaissance and Neoclassical literary criticism. The Platonic and Aristotelian debate concerning art's being an imitation of nature begins the discussion. Nature, argues one debater, must be imitated directly, whereas another declares that writers should imitate the classical authors such as Homer, for such ancient writers were the best imitators of nature. Through the voice of Neander, Dryden presents the benefits of both positions.

A lengthy discussion ensues over the Aristotelian concept of the three unities of time, place, and action within a drama. Should the plot of a drama take place during one 24-hour cycle (time)? And in one location (place)? Should it be only a single plot with no subplots (action)? The position that a drama must keep the three unities unquestionably wins the debate.

Other concerns center on

- The language or diction of a play, with the concluding emphasis being placed on "proper" speech
- Issues of decorum; that is, whether violent acts should appear on the stage, with the final speaker declaring it would be quite "improper"
- The differences between the English and French theaters, with the English drama winning out for its diversity, its use of the stage, and its Shakespearian tradition

- The value of rhymed as opposed to blank verse in the drama, with rhymed verse being the victor—although Dryden later recanted this position and wrote many of his tragedies in blank verse

Being a reflection of his age, Dryden sides with politesse (courteous formality), clarity, order, decorum, elegance, cleverness, and wit as controlling characteristics of literary works.

ALEXANDER POPE (1688–1744)

Born into a Roman Catholic family in a Protestant-controlled England, born a healthy infant but quickly deformed and twisted in body by spinal tuberculosis, and born at the beginning of the Neoclassical Age and becoming its literary voice by age 20, Alexander Pope embodies in his writings eighteenth-century thought and literary criticism. His early poems such as *The Rape of the Lock,* "Eloisa to Abelard," and "Pastorals" establish him as a major British poet, but with the publication of his *Essay on Criticism,* he becomes for all practical purposes the "literary pope" of England.

Unlike previous literary critics and theorists, Pope in this essay directly addresses the critic rather than the poet while simultaneously codifying Neoclassical literary theory and criticism. Toward the end of the essay, however, he does speak to both critics and poets.

According to Pope, the golden age of criticism is the classical age, the age of Homer, Aristotle, Horace, and Longinus. They are the writers who discovered the rules and laws of a harmonious and ordered nature. It is the critic and poet's task first to know and then to copy these authors and not nature, for "To copy nature is to copy them [the classical authors]."

Pope asserts that the chief requirement of a good poet is natural genius coupled with a knowledge of the classics and an understanding of the rules of poetry (literature). Such knowledge must be tempered with politeness and grace, for "Without good breeding truth is disapproved/ That only makes superior sense beloved."

Natural genius and good breeding being established, the critic/poet must then give heed to certain rules, says Pope. To be a good critic or poet, one must follow the established traditions as defined by the ancients. Not surprisingly, Pope spells out what these rules are and how they should be applied to eighteenth-century verse. Great concern for poetic diction, the establishment of the heroic couplet as a standard for verse, and the personification of abstract ideas, for example, became fixed standards, whereas emotional outbreaks and free verse were *extraordinaire* and considered unrefined.

Governed by rules, restraint, and good taste, poetry, as defined by Pope, seeks to reaffirm truths or absolutes already discovered by the classical writers. The critic's task is clear: to validate and maintain classical values in the ever-shifting winds of cultural change. In effect, the critic becomes the custodian and defender of good taste and cultural values.

By affirming the imitation of the classical writers and through them of nature itself, and by establishing the acceptable or standard criteria of poetic language, Pope grounds his criticism in both the **mimetic** (imitation) and **rhetoric** (patterns of structure) literary theories. By the end of the 1700s, however, a major shift in literary theory occurs.

WILLIAM WORDSWORTH (1770–1850)

By the close of the eighteenth century, the world had witnessed several major political rebellions—among them the American and French revolutions—along with exceptional social upheavals and prominent changes in philosophical thought. During this age of rebellion, a paradigmatic shift occurred in how people viewed their world. Whereas the eighteenth-century valued order and reason, the emerging nineteenth-century worldview emphasized intuition as a proper guide to truth. The eighteenth-century mind likened the world to a great machine with all its parts operating harmoniously, but to the nineteenth-century perception the world was a living organism that was always growing and eternally becoming. Whereas the city housed the centers of art and literature and set the standards of good taste for the rationalistic mind of the eighteenth century, the emerging nineteenth-century citizen saw a rural setting as a place where people could discover their inner selves. Devaluing the empirical and rationalistic methodologies of the previous century, the nineteenth-century thinker believed that truth could be attained by tapping into the core of our humanity or our transcendental natures.

Such radical changes found their spokesperson in William Wordsworth. Born in Cockermouth, Cumberlandshire, and raised in the Lake District of England, Wordsworth completed his formal education at St. John's College, Cambridge, in 1791. After completing his grand tour of the Continent, he published *Descriptive Sketches* and then met one of his literary admirers and soon-to-be friends and coauthors, Samuel T. Coleridge. In 1798 Wordsworth and Coleridge published *Lyrical Ballads*, a collection of poems that heralded the beginning of British romanticism. In the ensuing 15-year period, Wordsworth wrote most of his best poetry, including *Poems in Two Volumes, The Excursion, Miscellaneous Poems*, and *The Prelude*. But it is *Lyrical Ballads* that ushers in the Romantic age in English literature.

In an explanatory Preface written as an introduction to the second edition of *Lyrical Ballads*, Wordsworth espouses a new vision of poetry and the beginnings of a radical change in literary theory. His purpose, he notes, is "to choose incidents and situations from common life, and . . . describe them in language really used by [people] in situations . . . the manner in which we associate ideas in a state of excitement." Like Aristotle, Sidney, and Pope, Wordsworth concerns himself with the elements and subject matter of literature, but changes the emphasis: Common men and women people his poetry, not kings, queens, and aristocrats, for in "humble and rustic life" the poet finds that "the essential passions of the heart find a better soil in which they can attain their maturity, are less under restraint, and speak a plainer and more emphatic language."

Not only does Wordsworth suggest a radical change in subject matter, but he also dramatically shifts focus concerning poetry's "proper language." Unlike Pope and his predecessors, Wordsworth chooses "language really used by [people]"—everyday speech, not the inflated poetic diction of heroic couplets, complicated rhyme schemes, and convoluted figures of speech placed in the mouths of the typical eighteenth-century character. Wordsworth's rustics, such as Michael and Luke in his poetic narrative "Michael," speak in the simple, everyday diction of their trade.

In addition to reshaping the focus of poetry's subject and language, Wordsworth redefines poetry itself: "For all good poetry is the spontaneous overflow of powerful feelings." Unlike Sidney, Dante, and Pope, who decree that poetry should be restrained, controlled, and reasoned, Wordsworth now highlights poetry's emotional quality. Imagination, not reason or disciplined thought, becomes its core.

After altering poetry's subject matter, language, and definition, Wordsworth redefines the role of the poet. The poet is no longer the preserver of civilized values or proper taste, but "he is a man speaking to men: a man . . . endowed with more lively sensibility, more enthusiasm and tenderness, who has a greater knowledge of human nature and a more comprehensive soul than are supposed to be common among mankind." And this poet "has acquired a greater readiness and power in expressing what he thinks and feels, and especially those thoughts and feelings which, by his own choice, or from the structure of his own mind, arise in him without immediate external excitement." Such a poet need no longer follow a prescribed set of rules, for this artist may freely express his or her own individualism, valuing and writing about feelings that are peculiarly the artist's.

Because Wordsworth defines poetry as "the spontaneous overflow of powerful feelings . . . [taking] its origin from emotion recollected in tranquility," his new kind of poet crafts a poem by internalizing a scene, circumstance, or happening and "recollects" that occasion with its accompanying emotions at a later time when the artist can shape that remembrance into words. Poetry, then, is unlike biology or one of the other sciences, for it deals not with something that can be dissected or broken down into its constituent parts, but primarily with the imagination and feelings. Intuition, not reason, reigns.

But what of the reader? What part does the audience play in such a process? Toward the end of the *Preface*, Wordsworth writes, "I have one request to make of my reader, which is, that in judging these poems he would decide by his own feelings genuinely, and not by reflection upon what will probably be the judgement of others." Wordsworth apparently hopes that his readers' responses and opinions of his poems will not depend on critics who freely dispense their evaluations. Wordsworth wants his readers to rely on their own feelings and their own imaginations as they grapple with the same emotions the poet felt when he first saw and then later "recollected in tranquility" the subject or circumstances of the poem itself. Through poetry, declares Wordsworth, the poet and the reader share such emotions.

This subjective experience of sharing emotions leads Wordsworth away from the preceding centuries' mimetic and rhetorical theories of criticism and toward a new development in literary theory: the **expressive school**, which emphasizes the individuality of the artist and the reader's privilege to share in this individuality. By expressing such individuality and valuing the emotions and the imagination as legitimate concerns in poetry, Wordsworth lays the foundation for English romanticism and broadens the scope of literary criticism and theory for both the nineteenth and twentieth centuries.

HIPPOLYTE ADOLPHE TAINE (1828–93)

Wordsworth's romanticism, with its stress on intuition as a guide to learning ultimate truth and its belief that emotions and the imagination form the core of poetry's content, dominated literature and literary criticism throughout the first three decades of the nineteenth century, and its influence still continues today. With the rise of the Victorian era in the 1830s, reason, science, and a sense of historical determinism began to supplant romantic thought. The growing sense of historical and scientific determinism finally found its authoritative voice and culminating influence, in literary criticism and many other disciplines, in Charles Darwin and his text *The Origin of Species*, published in 1859. Humankind was now demystified, for we finally knew our origins and understood our physiological development; science, it seemed, had provided us with the key to our past and an understanding of the present, and would help us determine our future if we relied on the scientific method in all our human endeavors.

Science's methodology, its philosophical assumptions, and its practical applications found an admiring adherent and a strong voice in French historian and literary critic Hippolyte Taine. Born in Vouziers, France, Hippolyte Taine was a brilliant but unorthodox student at the École Normale Supérieure in Paris. After finishing his formal education, he taught in various schools throughout France, continuing his investigations in both aesthetics and history. During the 1850s he published various philosophical and aesthetic treatises, but his chief contribution to literary criticism and history is *The History of English Literature*, published in 1863. In this work, Taine crystallizes what is now known as the historical approach to literary analysis.

In the introduction to *The History of English Literature*, Taine uses a scientific simile to explain his approach to literary criticism:

> What is your first remark on turning over the great, stiff leaves of a folio, the yellow sheets of a manuscript,—a poem, a code of laws, a declaration of faith? This, you say was not created alone. It is but a mould, like fossil shell, an imprint, like one of those shapes embossed in stone by an animal which lived and perished. Under the shell there was an animal, and behind the document there was a man. Why do you study the shell, except to represent to yourself the animal? So do you study the document only in order to know the man.

For Taine, then, a text is like a fossil shell that naturally contains the likeness of its inhabiter, who in this case is the author. To study only the text (discovering its date of composition or the accuracy of its historical references or allusions, for example) without considering the author and his or her inner psyche would therefore result in an incomplete analysis. An investigation of both the text and the author, Taine believed, would result in an accurate understanding of the literary work.

To understand any literary text, Taine asserts that we must examine the environmental causes that joined together in its creation. He divides such influences into three main categories: race, milieu, and moment. By race, Taine posits that authors of the same race, or those born and raised in the same country, share peculiar intellectual beliefs, emotions, and ways of understanding. By examining each author's inherited and learned personal characteristics, Taine believes we will then be able to understand more fully the author's text. In addition, we must also examine the author's milieu or surroundings. English citizens, he believed, respond differently to life than do French or Irish citizens. Accordingly, by examining the culture of the author, Taine asserts that we would understand more fully the intellectual and cultural concerns that inevitably surface in an author's text. And lastly, Taine maintains that we must investigate an author's epoch or moment—that is, the time period in which the text was written. Such information reveals the dominant ideas or worldview held by people at that particular time and therefore helps us identify and understand the characters' actions, motivations, and concerns more fully than if we did not have such information.

Ultimately, for Taine the text becomes a literary object that can be dissected to discover its meaning. By examining the actual text itself, the circumstances of place and race, and the historical times in which the text was written, we will realize, Taine asserts, that no text is written in a vacuum, but is instead the result of its history.

MATTHEW ARNOLD (1822–88)

In the "Preface to *Lyrical Ballads*," Wordsworth asserts that "poetry is the breath and finer spirit of all knowledge; it is the impassioned expression which is the countenance of all science." Such a lofty statement concerning the nature and role of poetry finds an advocate in Matthew Arnold, the self-appointed voice for English Victorianism, the literary epoch immediately following Wordsworth's romanticism.

Born during the Romantic era, Matthew Arnold was the son of an English educator. Following in his family's tradition, Arnold attended Oxford, and upon graduation accepted a teaching position at Oriel College. He spent most of his professional life (nearly 35 years) as an inspector of schools. By age 35 he had already written the majority of his poetry, including "Dover Beach," "The Scholar-Gipsy," and "Sohrab and Rustum," some of his most famous works.

During Arnold's early career, reactions against Wordsworth's romanticism and its adherents began to occur. Writers, philosophers, and scientists began to give more credence to empirical and rationalistic methods for discovering the nature of their world than to the Wordsworthian concepts of emotion, individualism, and intuition as pathways to truth. With the publication of Charles Darwin's *The Origin of Species* in 1859 and the writings of Herbert Spencer and philosopher David Friedrich Strauss, science seemingly usurped the place of Wordsworth's religion of nature and the beliefs of most other traditional religions, while philosophy became too esoteric and therefore less relevant as a vehicle for understanding reality for the average Victorian. Into this void stepped Arnold, proclaiming that poetry can provide the necessary truths, values, and guidelines for society.

Fundamental to Arnold's literary theory and criticism is his reapplication of classical criteria to literature. Quotes and borrowed ideas from Plato, Aristotle, Longinus, and other classical writers pepper his criticism. From Aristotle's *Poetics*, for example, Arnold adapts his idea that the best poetry is of a "higher truth and seriousness" than history, or any other human subject or activity, for that matter. Like Plato, Arnold believes that literature reflects the society in which it is written and thereby heralds its values and concerns. Like Longinus, he attempts to define a classic and decrees that such a work belongs to the "highest" or "best class." And in attempting to support many of his other ideas, he also cites the later "classical" writers such as Dante, Shakespeare, and Milton.

For Arnold, poetry—not religion, science, or philosophy—is humankind's crowning activity. He notes, "More and more [human]kind will discover that we have to turn to poetry to interpret life for us, to console us, to sustain us. Without poetry, our science will appear incomplete; and most of what now passes with us for religion and philosophy will be replaced by poetry." And in the best of this poetry, he declares, we find "in the eminent degree, truth and seriousness." Equating "seriousness" with moral excellence, Arnold asserts that the best poetry can and does provide standards of excellence, a yardstick by which both Arnold and his society should judge themselves.

In his pivotal essays "The Study of Poetry" and "The Function of Criticism at the Present Time," Arnold crystallizes his critical position. Like Plato's critic, Arnold reaffirms but slightly amends the social role of criticism: creating "a current of true and fresh ideas." To accomplish this goal, the critic must avoid becoming embroiled in politics or any other activity that would lead to a form of bias, for the critic must view society disinterestedly, keeping aloof from the world's mundane affairs. In turn, such aloofness will benefit all of society, for the critic will be able to pave the way for high culture—a prerequisite for the poet and the writing of the best poetry.

But how may the best poetry be achieved or discovered? By establishing objective criteria whereby we can judge whether any poem contains or achieves, in Aristotelian terms, "higher truth or seriousness." The critic's task is "to have always in one's mind lines and expressions of the great masters, and to apply them as a touchstone to other poetry." By comparing the newly written lines to classical poems that contain elements of the "sublime," the critic will instantly know whether a new poem is good or bad.

In practice, such apparent objectivity in criticism becomes quite subjective. Whose judgments, for example, shall we follow? Shall lines written by Homer and Dante be considered excellent? How about Sidney's or even Aristophanes'? Need the critic rank all past poets in an attempt to discover who is great and who is not in order to create a basis for such comparisons and value judgments? And whose moral values shall become the yardstick whereby we judge poetry? Arnold's only?

Such "objective" touchstone theory redefines the task of the literary critic and introduces a subjective approach in literary criticism. No longer the interpreter of a literary work, the critic now functions as an authority on values, culture, and tastes. This new literary watchdog must guard and defend high culture and its literature while simultaneously defining what high culture and literature really are.

Decreeing the critic to be the preserver of society's values and poetry to be its most important activity, Arnold became the recognized spokesperson for Victorian England and its literature. By taking Wordsworth's concept of the poet one step further, Arnold separated both the critic and the poet from society in order to create a type of poetry and criticism that could supposedly rescue society from its baser elements and preserve its most noble characteristics.

HENRY JAMES (1843–1916)

While Arnold was decreeing how poetry would rescue humanity from its baser elements and would help lead us all to truth, literary works were also being written in other genres, particularly the novel. Throughout both the Romantic and Victorian eras, for example, people in England and America were reading such works as *Wuthering Heights, Vanity Fair, The House of the Seven Gables,* and *Great Expectations.* However, few were providing for either the writers or the readers of this genre a body of theory or criticism as was being formulated for poetry. As Henry James notes in his critical essay "The Art of Fiction" in 1884, the English novel "had no air of having a theory, a conviction, a consciousness of itself behind it—of being the expression of an artistic faith, the result of choice and comparison." It was left to James himself to provide us with such a theory.

Born in New York City in 1843, Henry James enjoyed the privileges of education, travel, and money. Throughout his early life, he and his family (including his brother William, the father of American pragmatic philosophy) traveled to the capitals of Europe, visiting the sites and meeting the leading writers and scholars of the day. Having all things European injected into his early life and thoughts, James believed he wanted to be a lawyer and enrolled in Harvard Law School. He quickly discovered that writing, not law, captivated him and abandoned law school for a career in writing. By 1875, the early call of Europe on his life had to be answered, and James, a bachelor for life, settled permanently in Europe and began in earnest his writing career.

Noted for his short stories—"The Real Thing," "The Beast in the Jungle," and "The Jolly Corner," to name a few—and his novels—*The American, The Portrait of a Lady, The Bostonians,* and *The Turn of the Screw,* among others—James's favorite theme is the conflict he perceives between Europe and America. The seasoned aristocracy with its refined manners and taste is often infiltrated in his stories by the naive American, who seemingly lacks refined culture and discernment. In addition to being a practicing writer, James is also concerned with developing a theory of writing, particularly for the novel. And in his critical essay "The Art of Fiction" he provides us with the first well-articulated theory of the novel in English literature.

In "The Art of Fiction," James states that "a novel is in its broadest definition a personal, a direct impression of life: that, to begin with, constitutes its value, which is greater or less according to the intensity of the impression"; furthermore, "the only obligation to which in advance we may hold a novel, without incurring the accusation of being arbitrary, is that it be interesting. The ways in which it is at liberty to accomplish this result [are] innumerable." From the start, James's theory rejects the romantic notion of either Wordsworth or Coleridge that the reader suspend disbelief while reading a text. For James, a text must first be realistic, a representation of life as it is and one that is recognizable to its readers. Bad novels, declares James, are either romantic or scientific; good novels show us life in action and, above all else, are interesting.

Bad novels, James continues, are written by bad authors, whereas good novels are written by good authors. Unlike weak authors, good writers are good thinkers who can select, evaluate, and imaginatively use the "stuff of life" (the facts or pictures of reality) in their work. These writers also recognize that a work of art is organic. The work itself is not simply the amassing of realistic data from real-life experiences, but has a life of its own that grows according to its own principles or themes. The writer must acknowledge this fact and distance himself or herself from directly telling the story. Shunning the omniscient narrator as the technical narrative point of view for relating the story, James asserts that a more indirect point of view is essential so that the author shows characters, actions, and emotions to the reader rather than telling us about them. By showing rather than telling us about his characters and their actions, James believes that he creates a greater illusion of reality than if he presents his story through one point of view or one character. Ultimately, however, the reader must decide the worth of the text, and "nothing of course, will ever take the place of the good old fashion 'liking of' a work of art or not liking it: the most improved criticism will not abolish that primitive, that ultimate test."

Thanks to Henry James, the genre of the novel became a respectable topic for literary critics. With his emphasis on realism and "the stuff of life," James formulated a theory of fiction that is still discussed and debated today.

MODERN LITERARY CRITICISM

Matthew Arnold's death in 1888 (and to a lesser degree Henry James's death in 1916) marks a transitional period in literary criticism. Like Dryden, Pope, and Wordsworth before him, Arnold was the recognized authority and leading literary critic of his day, and it is his theories and criticism that embody the major ideas of his era. With the passing of Arnold ends the predominance of any one person or set of ideas representing a broad time period or literary movement. After Arnold, literary theory and criticism became splintered and more diversified, with no one voice speaking ex cathedra or no one theory tenaciously held by all. At the end of the nineteenth century, most critics emphasized either a biographical or historical approach to the text. Using Taine's historical interests in a text and Henry James's newly articulated theory of the novel, many critics investigated a text as if it were the embodiment of its author or a historical artifact. No single, universally recognized voice dominates literary theory in the years that follow Arnold or James. Instead, many distinctive literary voices give rise to a host of differing and exciting ways to examine a text.

What follows in the twentieth century is a variety of schools of criticism, with each school asking legitimate, relevant, but different questions concerning a text. Most of these schools abandon the **holistic approach** to literary study, which investigates, analyzes, and interprets all elements of the artistic situation, in favor of concentrating on one or more specific aspects. For example, modernism (and in particular the New Criticism, the first critical movement of the twentieth century), wishes to break from the past and seemingly disavow the cultural influences on a work of literature. The text, these critics declare, will interpret the text. On the other hand, New Historicism, one of the newest schools of thought to appear, argues that most critics' historical consciousness must be reawakened, for in reality the fictional text and its historical and cultural milieu are amazingly similar. For these critics, a reader can never fully discern the truth about a historical or a literary text, for truth itself is perceived differently from one era to another. The text-only criticism of the early twentieth and mid-century therefore appears biased and incomplete to these New Historicists.

In the remaining chapters of this book we will examine eleven of the most prominent schools of twentieth-century interpretation. For each of these diverse schools we will note the tenets of their philosophy that underlie their literary theory. Most, if not all, have borrowed ideas, principles, and concerns from the literary critics and theories already discussed. We will examine closely what they borrow from these past schools of criticism, what they amend, and what concepts they add. We will also note each school's historical development, examining how new schools of criticism often appear as a reaction to previously existing ones.

After explaining each school's historical development, its working assumptions, and its methodology, we will then examine both a student-written and a professional essay that interprets a text from the point of view of that particular school of criticism under discussion. A close examination of such essays will allow us to see how the theories of the various schools of criticism can be applied directly to a text while simultaneously highlighting the various emphases of each critical school.

By becoming acquainted with the various schools of criticism, we can begin to examine our own theory of interpretation and to articulate our own principles of criticism. We will then come to realize that there is no such thing as an innocent reading of a text, for all readings presuppose either a conscious or unconscious, articulated and well-informed, or piecemeal and uninformed reading of a literary work. An informed and intelligent reading is the better option.

FURTHER READING

Adams, Hazard, ed. *Critical Theory Since Plato*. New York: Harcourt, 1971.

Atkins, G. Douglas, and Laura Morrow, eds. *Contemporary Literary Theory*. Amherst: University of Massachusetts Press, 1989.

Con Davis, Robert, and Laurie Finke, eds. *Literary Criticism and Theory: The Greeks to the Present*. New York: Longman, 1989.

Crane, R. S., et al. *Critics and Criticism: Ancient and Modern*. Chicago: University of Chicago Press, 1952.

Jefferson, Ann, and David Robey. *Modern Literary Theory: A Comparative Introduction*. 2nd ed. London: Batsford, 1986.

Rice, Philip, and Patricia Waugh, eds. *Modern Literary Theory; A Reader*. 2nd ed. London: Arnold, 1992.

Schorer, Mark, et al. *Criticism: The Foundations of Modern Literary Judgment*. New York: Harcourt, 1958.

Selden, Raman, ed. *The Theory of Criticism: From Plato to the Present*. New York: Longman, 1988.

Selden, Raman, and Peter Widdowson. *A Reader's Guide to Contemporary Literary Theory*. 3rd ed. Lexington: The University Press of Kentucky, 1993.

Watson, George. *The Literary Critics*. London: Woburn Press, 1973.

Wimsatt, William K., and Cleanth Brooks. *Literary Criticism: A Short History*. New York: Alfred A. Knopf, 1964.

New Criticism

INTRODUCTION

Sacramental Vision
Sometimes in my dream
he is still alive.
We stand at the fence
talking about the garden.
"Plant kohlrabi," he says,
and I remember the way
he'd slice white wafers
from the bulb, offering
them to me balanced
on his knife blade.

I would eat again
that sharp sacrament
and join myself
to that good world
he walks, but I wake

in time

and know my flesh is one
with frailty. The garden
I must tend is dark
with weeping, grown up
in widow's weeds.

John Leax, *The Task of Adam*, 1985

If John Leax's poem "Sacramental Vision" were to be taught in most high school or introductory level college English courses, the instructor would probably begin the discussion with a set of questions that contain most, if not all, of the following: What is the meaning of the title? What is the title's relationship to the rest of the poem? Who is the *he* in line two? What is *kohlra-bi*? What is a *sacrament*? Are there other words in the text that need to be defined? What words connote sharpness? How are these words related to the garden discussed in the poem? Is Leax discussing any particular garden, or all gardens in general? Can this word be an allusion to some other garden in the canon of Western literature? Is Leax establishing any other relationships between words or concepts in the text? What of the poem's physical structure? Does the arrangement of the words, phrases, or sentences help establish relationships among them? What is the poem's tone? How do you know this is the tone? What tensions does Leax create in the poem? What ambiguities? Based on the answers to these questions, what does the poem mean? In other words, what is the poem's form or its overall meaning and interpretation?

Upon close examination of these discussion questions, a distinct pattern or methodology quickly becomes evident. This interpretive model begins with a close analysis of the poem's individual words, including both denotative and connotative meanings, and then moves to a discussion of possible allusions within the text. Following this discussion, the critic searches for any patterns developed through individual words, phrases, sentences, figures of speech, and allusions. The critic's sharp eye also notes any symbols, either **public** or **private**, used by the poet. Other elements for analysis include point of view, tone, and any other poetic device that will help the reader understand the dramatic situation. After ascertaining how all the above information interrelates and coalesces in the poem, the critic can then declare what the poem means. The poem's overall meaning or form, then, depends solely on the text in front of the reader. No library research, no studying of the author's life and times, and no other extraneous information is needed, for the poem itself contains all the necessary information to discover its meaning.

This method of analysis became the dominant school of thought during the first two thirds of the twentieth century in most high school and college literature classes, English departments, and English and American scholarship. Known as **New Criticism**, this approach to literary analysis provides the reader with a formula for arriving at the correct interpretation of a text using only the text itself. Such a formulaic approach gives both the beginning student of literature and academicians a seemingly objective approach for discovering a text's meaning. Using New Criticism's clearly articulated methodology, any intelligent reader, say the New Critics, can uncover a text's hitherto hidden meaning.

New Criticism's theoretical ideas, terminology, and critical methods are, more often than not, disparaged by present-day critics, who themselves are introducing new ideas concerning literary theory. Despite its current unpopularity, New Criticism stands as one of the most important English-speaking contributions to literary critical analysis. Its easily repeatable principles, teachability, and seemingly undying popularity in the English classroom and in some scholarly English journals have enabled New Criticism to enrich theoretical and practical criticism while helping generations of readers to become **close readers** of texts.

The name *New Criticism* came into popular use to describe this approach to understanding literature with the 1941 publication of John Crowe Ransom's *The New Criticism*, which contained Ransom's personal analysis of several of his contemporary theorists and critics. Ransom himself was a Southern poet, a critic, and one of the leading advocates of this evolving movement. While teaching at Vanderbilt University in the 1920s, Ransom, along with several other professors and students, formed the Fugitives, a group that believed and practiced similar interpretative approaches to a text. Other sympathetic groups, such as the Southern Agrarians at Nashville, soon formed. In *The New Criticism* Ransom articulates the principles of these various groups and calls for an **ontological critic**, one who will recognize that a **poem** (used as a synonym in New Criticism for any literary work) is a concrete entity like Leonardo da Vinci's *Mona Lisa* or the score of Handel's *Messiah* or even any chemical element such as iron or gold. Like these concrete objects, a poem can be analyzed to discover its true or correct meaning independent of its author's intention, or the emotional state, or the values and beliefs of either its author or reader. Because this belief rests at the center of this movement's critical ideas, it is not surprising, then, that the title of Ransom's book quickly became the official calling card for this approach to literary analysis.

Called modernism, formalism, aesthetic criticism, textual criticism, or ontological criticism throughout its long and successful history, New Criticism does not represent a coherent body of critical theory and methodology espoused by all its followers. At best, New Criticism and its adherents (called **New Critics**) are an eclectic group, each challenging, borrowing, and changing terminology, theory, and practices from one another while asserting a common core of basic ideas. Their ultimate unity stems from their opposition to the prevailing methods of literary analysis found in academia in the first part of the twentieth century.

HISTORICAL DEVELOPMENT

At the beginning of the twentieth century (often dubbed the start of the modernist period, or **modernism**), historical and biographical research dominated literary scholarship. Criticism's function, many believed, was to discover the historical context of the text and to ascertain how the authors' lives influenced their writings. Such **extrinsic analysis** (examining elements outside the text to uncover the text's meaning) became the norm in the English departments of many American universities and colleges. Other forms of criticism and interpretation were often intermingled with this emphasis on history and biography. For example, some critics believed we should appreciate the text for its beauty. For these **impressionistic critics**, how we feel and what we personally see in a work of art are what really matters. Others were more philosophical, arguing a naturalistic view of life that emphasizes the importance of scientific thought in literary analysis. For advocates of **naturalism**, human beings are simply animals who are caught in a world that operates on definable scientific principles and who respond somewhat instinctively to their environment and internal drives. Still other critics, the **New Humanists**, valued the moral qualities of art. Declaring that human experience is basically ethical, these critics demanded that literary analysis be based on the moral values exhibited in a text. Finally, remnants of nineteenth-century **romanticism** asserted themselves. For the romantic scholar, literary study concerns itself with the artists' feelings and attitudes exhibited in their work. Known as the **expressive school**, this romantic view values the individual artist's experiences as evidenced in the text.

Along with impressionism, the New Humanism, and naturalism, this romantic view of life and art was rejected by the New Critics. In declaring the objective existence of the poem, the New Critics assert that only the poem itself can be objectively evaluated, not the feelings, attitudes, values, and beliefs of the author or the reader. Because they concern themselves primarily with an examination of the work itself and not its historical context or biographical elements, the New Critics belong to a broad classification of literary criticism called **formalism**. Being formalists, the New Critics espouse what many call "the text and text alone" approach to literary analysis.

Such an approach to textual criticism automatically leads to many divergent views concerning the elements that constitute what the New Critics call the poem. Because many of the practitioners of this formalistic criticism disagree with each other concerning the various elements that make up the poem and hold differing approaches to textual analysis, it is difficult to cite a definitive list of critics who consider themselves New Critics. However, we can group together critics who hold some of the same New Critical assumptions concerning poetic analysis. Among this group are John Crowe Ransom, René Wellek, W. K. Wimsatt, R. P. Blackmur, I. A. Richards, Robert Penn Warren, and Cleanth Brooks. Thanks to the publication of the 1938 college text *Understanding Poetry* by Brooks and Warren, New Criticism emerged in American universities as the leading form of textual analysis throughout the late 1930s until the early 1960s.

Although New Criticism emerged as a powerful force in the 1940s, its roots stem back to the early 1900s. Two British critics and authors, T. S. Eliot and I. A. Richards, helped lay the foundation for this form of formalistic analysis. From Eliot, New Criticism borrows its insistence that criticism be directed toward the poem, not the poet. The poet, declares Eliot, does not infuse the poem with his or her personality and emotions, but uses language in such a way as to incorporate within the poem the impersonal feelings and emotions common to all humankind. Poetry is not, then, the freeing of the poet's emotions, but an escape from them. Because the poem is an impersonal formulation of common feelings and emotions, the successful poem unites the poet's impressions and ideas with those common to all humanity, producing a text that is not a mere reflection of the poet's personal feelings.

The New Critics also borrow Eliot's belief that the reader of poetry must be instructed concerning literary technique. A good reader perceives the poem structurally, maintains Eliot, resulting in good criticism. Such a reader must necessarily be trained in reading good poetry (especially the poetry of the Elizabethans, John Donne, and other metaphysical poets) and be well acquainted with established poetic traditions. A poor reader, on the other hand, simply expresses his or her personal reactions and emotions concerning a text. Such a reader is untrained in literary technique and craft. Following Eliot's lead, the New Critics declare that there are both good and bad readers, and good and bad criticism. A poor reader and poor criticism, for example, may argue that a poem can mean anything its reader or its author wishes it to mean. On the other hand, a good critic and good criticism would assert that only through a detailed structural analysis of a poem can the correct interpretation arise.

Eliot also lends New Criticism some of its technical vocabulary. Thanks to Eliot, for example, the term **objective correlative** has become a staple in poetic jargon. According to Eliot, the only way of expressing emotion through art is by finding an objective correlative: a set of objects, a situation, a chain of events, or reactions that can effectively awaken in the reader the emotional response the author desires without being a direct statement of that emotion. When the external facts are thus presented in the poem, they somehow come together and immediately evoke an emotion. The New Critics readily adopted and advanced such an impersonal theory concerning the arousing of emotions in poetry.

From Eliot's British contemporary, I. A. Richards, a psychologist and literary critic, New Criticism borrows a term that has become synonymous with its methods of analysis: *practical criticism*. In an experiment at Cambridge University, Richards distributed to his students copies of poems without such information as the authors, dates, and oddities of spelling and punctuation, and asked them to record their responses. From these data he identified the difficulties that poetry presents to its readers: matters of interpretation, poetic techniques, and specific meanings. From this analysis Richards devised an intricate system for arriving at a poem's meaning, including a minute scrutiny of the text. It is this close scrutiny or close reading of a text that has become synonymous with New Criticism.

From Eliot, Richards, and other critics, then, New Criticism borrows, amends, and adds its own ideas and concerns. Although few of its advocates would agree on many tenets, definitions, and techniques, there exists a core of assumptions that allow us to identify adherents of this critical approach to texts.

ASSUMPTIONS

New Criticism begins by assuming that the study of imaginative literature is valuable; to study poetry or any literary work is to engage oneself in an **aesthetic experience** (the effects produced on an individual when contemplating a work of art) that can lead to truth. However, the truth discoverable through an aesthetic experience is distinguishable from the truth that science provides us. Science speaks propositionally, telling us whether a statement is demonstrably either true or false. Pure water, says science, freezes at 32 degrees fahrenheit, not 30 or 31. Poetic truth, on the other hand, involves the use of the imagination and intuition, a form of truth that according to the New Critics is discernible only in poetry. In the aesthetic experience alone we are cut off from mundane or practical concerns, from mere rhetorical, doctrinal, or propositional statements. Through an examination of the poem itself we can ascertain truths that cannot be perceived through the language and logic of science. Both science and poetry, then, provide different but valid sources of knowledge.

Like many other critical theories, New Criticism's theory begins by defining its object of concern, in this case a poem. (New Critics use the word *poem* synonymously with *work of art*; however, their methodology works most efficiently with poetry rather than any other genre.) New Critics assert that a poem has **ontological** status; that is, it possesses its own being and exists like any other object. In effect, a poem becomes an artifact, an objective, self-contained, autonomous entity with its own structure. As W. K. Wimsatt declares, a poem becomes a verbal icon.

Having declared a poem an object in its own right, the New Critics then develop their **objective theory of art**. For them, the meaning of a poem must not be equated with its author's feelings or stated or implied intentions. To believe that a poem's meaning is nothing more than an expression of the private experiences or intentions of its author is to commit a fundamental error of interpretation the New Critics call the **Intentional Fallacy**. Because they believe that the poem is an object, they claim that every poem must also be a public text that can be understood by applying the standards of public discourse, not simply the private experience, concerns, and vocabulary of its author.

That the poem is somehow related to its author cannot be denied. In his essay "Tradition and the Individual Talent," T. S. Eliot states the New Critical position concerning this relationship between the author and his or her work. The basis of Eliot's argument is an analogy. We all know, he says, that certain chemical reactions occur in the presence of a **catalyst**, an element that causes but is not affected by the reaction. For example, if we place hydrogen peroxide, a common household disinfectant, in a clear bottle and expose it to the sun's rays, we will no longer have hydrogen peroxide. Acting as a catalyst, the sun's rays cause a chemical reaction to occur, breaking down the hydrogen peroxide into its various parts while the sun's rays remain unaffected.

Similarly, the poet's mind serves as a catalyst for the reaction that yields the poem. During the creative process, the poet's mind, serving as the catalyst, brings together the experiences of the author's personality (not the author's personality traits or attributes), into an external object and a new creation: the poem. It is not the personality traits of the author that coalesce to form the poem, but the experiences of the author's personality. In apparently distinguishing between the personality and the mind of the poet, Eliot asserts that the created entity, the poem, is about the experiences of the author that are similar to all of our experiences. By structuring these experiences, the poem allows us to examine them objectively.

Dismissing the poet's stated or supposed intentions as a means of discovering the text's meaning, the New Critics give little credence to the biographical or contextual history of a poem. If the Intentional Fallacy be correct, then unearthing biographical data will not help us ascertain a poem's meaning. Likewise, trying to place a poem in its social or political context will tell us much social or political history about the time when the poem was authored; although such information may indeed help in understanding the poem, its real meaning cannot reside in this extrinsic or outside-the-text information.

Of particular importance to the New Critics, however, are individual words' etymology. Because the words of a poem sometimes change meaning from one time period to another, the critic often needs to conduct historical research, discovering what individual words meant at the time the poem was written. The *Oxford English Dictionary* (a dictionary that cites a word's various historical meanings chronologically) becomes one of the critic's best friends.

Placing little emphasis on the author, the social context, or a text's historical situation as a source for discovering a poem's meaning, the New Critics also assert that a reader's emotional response to the text is neither important nor equivalent to its interpretation. Such an error in judgment, called the **Affective Fallacy**, confuses what a poem is (its meaning) with what it does. If we derive our standard of criticism, say the New Critics, from the psychological effects of the poem, we are then left with impressionism or worse yet, relativism, believing that a poem has innumerable valid interpretations.

Where, then, can we find the poem's meaning? According to the New Critics, it does not reside in the author, the historical or social context of the poem, or even in the reader. Because the poem itself is an artifact or an objective entity, its meaning must reside within its own structure. Like all other objects, a poem and its structure can be analyzed scientifically. Accordingly, careful scrutiny reveals that a poem's structure operates according to a complex series of laws. By closely analyzing this structure, the New Critics believe that they have devised a methodology and a standard of excellence that we can apply to all poems to discover their correct meaning. It is the critic's job, they conclude, to ascertain the structure of the poem, to see how it operates to achieve its unity, and to discover how meaning evolves directly from the poem itself.

According to New Criticism, the poet is an organizer of the content of human experience. Structuring the poem around these often confusing and sometimes contradictory experiences of life, the poet crafts the poem in such a way that the text stirs its readers' emotions and causes its readers to reflect on the poem's contents. As an artisan, the poet is most concerned with effectively developing the poem's structure, for the artist realizes that the meaning of a text emerges from its structure. The poet's chief concern, maintain the New Critics, is how meaning is achieved through the various and sometimes conflicting elements operating in the poem itself.

The chief characteristic of the poem and therefore its structure is coherence or interrelatedness. Borrowing their ideas from the writings of Samuel T. Coleridge, the New Critics posit the **organic unity** of a poem—that is, the concept that all parts of a poem are interrelated and interconnected, with each part reflecting and helping to support the poem's central idea. Such organic unity allows for the harmonization of conflicting ideas, feelings, and attitudes, and results in the poem's oneness. Superior poetry, declare the New Critics, achieves such oneness through **paradox**, **irony**, and **ambiguity**. Because such tensions are necessarily a part of everyone's life, it is only fitting and appropriate, say the New Critics, that superior poetry present these human experiences while at the same time showing how these tensions are resolved within the poem to achieve its organic unity.

Because the poem's chief characteristic is its oneness, New Critics believe that a poem's form and content are inseparable. For the New Critics, however, **form** is more than the external structure of a poem, for a poem's form encompasses but rises above the usual definition of poetic structure (that is, whether the poem be a Shakespearian or Petrarchan sonnet, or a lyric, or any other poetic structure having meter, rhyme, or some other poetic pattern). In New Criticism, form is the overall effect the poem creates. Because all the various parts of the poem combine to create this effect, each poem's form is unique. When all the elements of a poem work together to form a single, unified effect—the poem's form—New Critics declare that the poet has written a successful poem, one that has organic unity.

Because all good and successful poems have organic unity, it would be inconceivable to try to separate a poem's form and its content, maintain the New Critics. How can we separate what a poem says from how it says it?

Because all the elements of a poem, both structural and aesthetic, work together to achieve a poem's effect or form, it is impossible to discuss the overall meaning of a poem by isolating or separating form and content.

To the New Critic, it is therefore inconceivable to believe that a poem's interpretation is equal to a mere paraphrased version of the text. Labeling such an erroneous belief the **Heresy of Paraphrase**, New Critics maintain that a poem is not simply a statement that is either true or false, but a bundle of harmonized tensions and resolved stresses, more like a ballet or musical composition than a statement of prose. No simple paraphrase can equal the meaning of the poem, for the poem itself resists through its inner tensions any prose statement that attempts to capsulate its meaning. Paraphrases may help readers in their initial understanding of the poem, but such prose statements must be considered working hypotheses that may or may not lead to a true understanding of the poem's meaning. In no way should paraphrased statements about a poem be considered equivalent to the poem's structure or form, insist the New Critics.

METHODOLOGY

Believing in the thematic and structural unity of a poem, New Critics search for meaning within the text's structure by finding the tensions and conflicts that must eventually be resolved into a harmonious whole and inevitably lead to the creation of the poem's chief effect. Such a search first leads New Critics to the poem's diction or word choice. Unlike scientific discourse with its precision of terminology, poetic diction often has multiple meanings and can immediately set up a series of tensions within the text. For example, many words have both a **denotation**, or dictionary meaning, and **connotation(s)**, or implied meanings. A word's denotation may be in direct conflict with its connotative meaning determined by the context of the poem. In addition, it may be difficult to differentiate between the various denotations of a word. For example, if someone writes that "a *fat* head enjoys the *fat* of the land," the reader must note the various denotative and connotative differences of the word *fat*. At the start of poetic analysis, then, conflicts or tensions exist by the very nature of poetic diction. This tension New Critics call **ambiguity**. At the end of a close reading of the text, however, all such ambiguities must be resolved.

Even on a surface level of understanding or upon a first reading, a poem, from a New Critic's perspective, is a reconciliation of conflicts, of opposing meanings and tensions. Its form and content are indivisible, so it is the critic's job to analyze the poetic diction to ascertain such tensions. Although various New Critics give a variety of names to the poetic elements that make up a poem's structure, all agree that the poem's meaning is derived from the oscillating tensions and conflicts that are brought to the surface through the poetic diction. For example, Cleanth Brooks claims that the chief elements in a poem are **paradox** and **irony**, two closely related terms that imply that a word or phrase is qualified or even undercut by its context. Other critics use the word **tension** to describe the opposition or conflicts operating within the text. For these critics, tension implies the conflicts between a word's denotation and its connotation, between a literal detail and a figurative one, and between an abstract and a concrete detail.

Because conflict, ambiguity, or tension controls the poem's structure, the meaning of the poem can be discovered only by analyzing contextually the poetic elements and diction. Because context governs meaning, meanings of individual words or phrases are therefore context related and unique to the poem in which they occur. It is the job of the critic, then, to unravel the various apparent conflicts and tensions within each poem and to show that ultimately the poem has organic unity, thereby showing that all parts of the poem are interrelated and support the poem's chief paradox. This paradox, what the New Critics often call form or overall effect, can usually be expressed in one sentence that contains the main tension and the resolution of that tension. It is this key idea to which all other elements of the poem must relate.

Although most New Critics would agree that the process of discovering the poem's form is not necessarily linear (for advanced readers often see ambiguities and ironies upon a first reading of a text), New Criticism provides the reader with a distinct methodology to help uncover this chief tension. Such guided steps allow both novices and advanced literary scholars together to enter the discussion of a text's ultimate meaning, each contributing to the poem's interpretation. From a New Critical perspective, one begins this journey of discovering a text's correct interpretation by reading the poem several times and by carefully noting the work's title (if it has one) and its relationship to the text. Then, by following the prescribed steps listed here, a reader can ascertain a text's meaning. The more practice one has at following this methodology and the more opportunities one has to be guided by an advanced reader and critic, the more adept one will undoubtedly become at textual analysis.

1. Examine the text's diction. Consider the denotation, connotations, and etymological roots of all words in the text.
2. Examine all allusions found within the text by tracing their roots to the primary text or source, if possible.
3. Analyze all images, symbols and figures of speech within the text. Note the relationships, if any, among the elements, both within the same category (between images, for example) and among the various elements (between an image and a symbol, for example).
4. Examine and analyze the various structural patterns that may appear within the text, including the technical aspects of **prosody**. Note how the poet manipulates metrical devices, grammatical constructions, tonal patterns, and syn-

tactic patterns of words, phrases, or sentences. Determine how these various patterns interrelate with each other and with all elements discussed in steps 1 to 3.

5. Consider such elements as tone, theme, point of view, and any other element— dialogue, foreshadowing, narration, parody, setting, and so forth—that directly relates to the text's dramatic situation.
6. Look for interrelationships of all elements, noting where tensions, ambiguities, or paradoxes arise.
7. After carefully examining all elements, state the poem's chief overarching tension and explain how the poem achieves its dominant effect by resolving all such tensions.

Because all poems are unique, the process of uncovering the poem's chief tension is also unique. By using the prescribed methodology of New Criticism, New Critics believe that readers can justify their interpretations of a text by information gleaned from the text alone while enjoying the aesthetic process that allows them to articulate the text's meaning.

According to such New Critical principles, a **good critic** examines a poem's structure by scrutinizing its poetic elements, rooting out and showing its inner tensions, and demonstrating how the poem supports its overall meaning by reconciling these tensions into a unified whole. By implication, **bad critics** are those who insist on imposing extrinsic evidence such as historical or biographical information on a text to discover its meaning. These critics fail to realize that the text itself elicits its own meaning. They flounder in their analysis, declare the New Critics, because such critics believe more often than not that a text can have multiple meanings.

Asserting that a poem has ontological status, the New Critics believe that a text has one and only one correct interpretation and that the poem itself provides all the necessary information for revealing its meaning. By scrutinizing the text and thus giving it a **close reading**, and by providing readers with a set of norms that will assist them in discovering the correct interpretation of the text, New Criticism provides a teachable, workable framework for literary analysis.

QUESTIONS FOR ANALYSIS

To apply the assumptions and methodology of New Criticism to a given text, one can begin by asking the following questions:

- If the text has a title, what is the relationship of the title to the rest of the poem? Before answering this question, New Critical theory and practice assume that the critic has read the text several times.

- What words, if any, need to be defined?
- What words' etymological roots need to be explored?
- What relationships or patterns do you see among any words in the text?
- What are the various connotative meanings words in the text may have? Do these various shades of meaning help establish relationships or patterns in the text?
- What allusions, if any, are in the text? Trace these allusions to their appropriate sources and explore how the origins of the allusion help elucidate meaning in this particular text.
- What symbols, images, and figures of speech are used? What is the relationship between any symbols or images? Between an image and another image? Between a figure of speech and an image? A symbol?
- What elements of prosody can you note and discuss? Look for rhyme, meter, and stanza patterns.
- What is the tone of the work?
- From what point of view is the content of the text being told?
- What tensions, ambiguities, or paradoxes arise within the text?
- What do you believe the chief paradox or irony is in the text?
- How do all the elements of the text support and develop the text's chief paradox?

SAMPLE ESSAYS

In the sample student essay that follows, note how the student uses the tenets of New Criticism to arrive at an interpretation of John Keats's ode "To Autumn." Be able to explain how the student uncovers ambiguities and tensions within the poem and how the student uses these elements to develop the overarching paradox. Note especially how all the elements of the text that the student cites support his stated chief paradox.

In the sample professional essay that follows, note how Cleanth Brooks's writing style highlights the principles and practices of New Critical theory. For example, observe how many times Brooks quotes directly from Keats's text, noting the various kinds of quotings (single words, phrases, and entire lines). Also recognize the literary vocabulary (elements) Brooks uses and assumes his audience understands: metaphors, irony, paradox, point of view, apostrophe, central paradox, motifs, organic context, and other dramatic terms. And finally, note the style of New Critical writing. Such essays are usually written in the first person and are authoritative. Note particularly such phrases and clauses as "In my opinion," "He misses the point," and "I can see no other interpretation of the lines." After your reading of Brooks's essay, be able to explain what Brooks believes the central paradox is in Keats's poem and how all the various elements of the text support this paradox.

FURTHER READING

Brooks, Cleanth. "My Credo: Formalist Critics." *Kenyon Review* 13 (1951): 72–81.

———. *The Well Wrought Urn: Studies in the Structure of Poetry.* New York: Harcourt, 1975.

Brooks, Cleanth, and Robert Penn Warren, eds. *Understanding Poetry.* New York: Holt, 1938.

Empson, William. *Seven Types of Ambiguity.* 3rd ed. London: Hogarth, 1984.

Ransom, John Crowe. *The New Criticism.* New York: New Directions, 1941.

Richards, I. A. *Practical Criticism.* 1929. Repr. London: Routledge & Kegan Paul, 1964.

———. *Principles of Criticism.* London: Routledge & Kegan Paul, 1964.

Wellek, Rene, and Austin Warren. *Theory of Literature.* Revised. New York: Harcourt, 1977.

Wimsatt, W. K., and Monroe C. Beardsley. *The Verbal Icon.* Lexington: University of Kentucky Press, 1954.

Winters, Yvor. *In Defense of Reason.* Denver: Swallow Press, 1947.

WEB SITES FOR EXPLORATION

www.ipl.org/ref/litcrit/
> The IPL Online Literary Criticism Collection contains 1205 critical and biographical websites about authors and their works. One of the best on the web!

http:/www.130.179.92.25/Arnason_DE/New_Criticism.html
> Provides a working definition of New Criticism

www.scils.english.upenn.edu/~afilreis/50s/ohmann.html
> An excerpt from *English in America: A Radical View of the Profession* by Richard Ohmann

www.sun3.lib.uci.edu/~scctr/Wellek/wellek/1976.html
> Provides a useful New Critical bibliography

www.english.upenn.edu/~afilres/50s/understanding-poetry.html
> Provides the prefatory "Letter to the Teacher" and a selection from Cleanth Brooks and Robert Penn Warren's pivotal New Critical text *Understanding Poetry: An Anthology for College Students*

www.odin.english.udel.edu/teague/brooks.html
> Provides an outline of Cleanth Brooks's essay "Irony as a Principle of Structure"

www.sun3.lib.uci.edu/indiv/scctr/Wellek/wellek/index.html
> Provides a detailed bibliography of the works of René Wellek and links to other New Critical sites

 Student Essay

---

Keats's "To Autumn": Verses of Praise for a Malicious Season?

Written in September of 1891, Keats's ode "To Autumn" describes the work and effect of Autumn on specific aspects of nature. At first glance, the combined verses of Keats sing the praises of a season bestowed with the ability "to bless" (line 3). What seems an ode praising a good-intentioned season, however, in actuality is a paradoxical commentary on the sometimes harsh reality of the beneficial cycle of life. In this cycle, Autumn has the seemingly malevolent job of preparing nature for a wintry death.

Stanza one introduces the reader to a personified character, Autumn, whose personality perfectly fits her job. Stanza two then portrays the guilt faced by Autumn while performing an ostensibly destructive task. By mingling positive images with images of death, stanza three provides hope for life in spring after Autumn and winter have passed. In the end, Autumn's role in the cycle of life is to be a bleak but necessary part of the intricate and beautiful cycles of the seasons.

"To Autumn" is an ode, "a single, unified strain of exalted lyrical verse, directed to a single purpose, and dealing with one theme. The term connotes certain qualities of both manner and form. The ode is elaborate, dignified, and imaginative" (Harmon, *A Handbook to Literature*, 7th ed., p. 358). In addition, the word *autumn* has its origin in the Middle English word *autumpne*, meaning any period of maturity, or the beginning of a decline. When these two definitions are synthesized, "To Autumn" becomes an elaborate, dignified, and imaginative strain of unified verse about either a period of maturity or the beginning of a decline. The combination of these words—autumn and ode—embodies the major paradox around which the poem derives its meaning and effect. In the poem, Autumn is the vehicle that brings about a period of decline while the ode's tone of praise suggests that somehow Autumn's function is beneficial.

In stanza one Autumn's first attribute mentioned is her "mists" (line 1). Autumn uses these mists in an attempt to hide her actions that may and will threaten other parts of nature. She apparently recognizes that nature must remain unsuspecting of her approach and her final actions so that she [Autumn] can accomplish her work without frightening nature, and in particular, summer. The second of Autumn's characteristics mentioned in this stanza is her mellowness (line 1, "mellow"), suggesting Autumn's ability to pleasantly intoxicate her environs. Since *mellow* also implies a relaxed or genial mood, Autumn is thus lulling nature, etherizing her, before Autumn prepares to do the rest of her work.

"To load and bless" in line three perfectly exemplifies the overarching paradox of the entire ode. "Load" is followed directly in the text by "bless," both of these being effects of Autumn on nature. In this combination of infinitives, the order and word choice suggest that nature is blessed to have been loaded. The word *loaded*, however, has the somewhat negative connotation of being overfilled, being weighted or tampered with, thus implying a trick or trap. Such fecundity and such blessing therefore serve as a mask to lull nature into accepting its prescribed destiny.

Though the remainder of stanza one contains images that seem to praise Autumn, upon close examination such images connote more harm than good. For example, Autumn, under the guise of benevolence, "bends" (line 5) the mossed cottaged-trees with unbearable weight, "swells" (line 7) the gourds as if bruised by a violent strike, and "plumps" (line 7) the hazel shells as though fattening them for slaughter. The verbs *bends*, *swells*, and *plumps* clearly connote destruction—the breaking of a tree branch, the bursting of a gourd, the swelling of a shell. The season whose job it is "to load and bless" (line 3) has indeed deceived all of nature into accepting its approaching death!

Even the "bees" (line 9) are lured by "later flowers" (line 9) from their wintry slumber in "clammy cells" (line 11) where they had been safe for the season from cold. Autumn produces these "later flowers" as a trap for the bees that come out, thinking that "warm days will never cease" (line 10). Now that the bees have been seduced from their sleep by Autumn's masterful deception and masquerade, they will be killed in the days that follow by winter's cold. Once again a seemingly gracious gesture on the part of Autumn has proved deadly.

To carry out such treachery, Autumn must possess a certain amount of apparent apathy toward her work (or at least disguised indifference) and its overall effect. Stanza two encapsulates this attitude. Line 14 pictures the character of Autumn "sitting careless on a granary floor" while "thy [Autumn's] hair [is] soft-lifted by the winnowing wind" (line 15). Such an image of peace amidst approaching death directly relates to the ode's major paradox. While Autumn, disguised by both mists and benevolence, carefully plots the death of summer and even herself, she is able to find peace in the seasons' demise, knowing that death is just one part of the cycle of life. Knowledge of this fact enables her to relax while she works.

Three other images in the second stanza serve to develop further the concept of Autumn's finding peace while preparing all nature for death. Autumn now appears "on a half-reap'd furrow sound asleep./ Drows'd with the fume of poppies" (lines 16–17). In this image Keats pictures an attempt by nature and Autumn to escape their coming doom. Emitting perfume, the poppies lull Autumn to sleep in an attempt to delay their own unavoidable destruction and ironically Autumn's too. But their destruction is unavoidable, however, for even as Autumn sleeps, its work continues as seen in Keats's next image when he writes, "while thy hook/ Spares the next swath and all its twined flower" (lines 17–18). The harvest will be gathered, the storehouse will be filled, and the cycle of the seasons will not be delayed or avoided despite any person's efforts or even those of nature herself.

Keats now presents his third image of Autumn's finding peace with her assigned task in lines 19–20, for Autumn is successful in keeping her "laden head" (line 20) "steady across a brook" (line 20). Although Autumn is guilty of bringing about death and although her head is "laden" and apparently heavy with this guilt, she finds peace within herself, believing something is redeemable about her work. She thus marches on, "steady" about her work, knowing that contrary to her seemingly destructive actions, her work is not in vain.

Lines 21 and 22 contain another image of Autumn's coming to grips with the guilt of her actions. Now her personage has a "patient look" (line 21) while the "last oozings" (line 22) are squeezed from the apples and other fruits "ripe to the core" (line 6). Describing Autumn as "patient," Keats creates the impression that she is at peace with the destruction of the fruit. The image of the "cyder-press" (lines 21–22) also contains the first hint of true benefit from her work. The cider that is squeezed from the fruit is a pleasantry to other participants in nature's continuing drama. Hence, instead of being another image solely of death and destruction, this time Keats presents a positive element. Until now, Keats has presented Autumn as deceitful and seemingly uncaring and unfeeling, but now her apparent destructive labors actually begin to prove productive.

The first line of stanza three marks the major turning point of the poem. Line 24 asks, "Where are the songs of spring? Ay, where are they?" Through these questions, Keats develops a tone of lament, suggesting that the songs of spring are to be desired over the destruction of Autumn, implying the beauty and the joy of spring and the songlessness and loss of Autumn. Line 24, however, modifies this lament, for here Keats emphatically declares that Autumn too has her songs: "Think not of them, thou has thy music too." The tone of lament developed throughout stanzas one and two now changes to one of rejoicing as Autumn is reassured of her own beauty and music. Until this point in the ode, the words, the images, the figures of speech, and their overall patterns and interrelationships all seemingly criticize Autumn for her preparations of death. At this turning point in the text, her task does not change, but Keats finally presents Autumn's work as part of nature's continuous cycle of change and renewal.

In lines 25 through 33, Keats introduces several images of Autumn that are consistent with her work of destruction and her previously developed personality as presented in stanzas one and two. Ironically, these images of death are now connected to and triumphantly modified by images of life, birth, and rebirth. The first of these images appears in line 25, where Keats observes that "barred clouds bloom the soft-dying day." Paradoxically, the "barred clouds," an image of an imposing and sometimes deadly storm, "*bloom* the soft-dying day." Now, an image of death created by the clouds blooms or gives birth, not to any day, but to a "soft-dying" one. Yes, notes Keats, the day must die as must the season, but the day's death is "soft" and gentle, connoting a good and positive aspect of death itself. Similarly, the "stubble-plains" in line 26 are now given a "rosy-hue"; that is, the harvested and therefore somewhat barren plains are no longer only an image of death. These once fruitful but now empty fields are rosy, exhibiting their own beauty, somewhat like the "soft-dying day" of the previous line.

Paralleling the "soft-dying day" and the now "rosy-hue[d]" plains is Keats's description in the next three lines of the ode of "a wailful choir . . . of small gnats [mourning]/ Among the river sallows, [and] borne aloft/ Or sinking as the light wind lives or dies." In picturing the "gnat" choir mourning their and all nature's impending doom, Keats adds words that connote hope and life and joy, for this choir floats in "the light wind" that "lives or dies," a wind that carries the gnats from the river willows into the sky. Paradoxically mixed with the images of death, then, are words and images that connote hope, that all is not lost, that something is and will be gained from apparent loss, that even in dying there is cause for rejoicing.

And all of nature's creatures seem to join in the chorus of Autumn, really an ode to joy, for in the last stanza "gnats" sing, "lambs bleat," "hedge-crickets sing," "the redbreast whistles," and "swallows twitter." Such a cooperation among the members of nature is expected, for Keats has prepared us for this cooperation in the opening line of the ode. As the ode begins, we note that at the start of the fall season, Autumn is "conspiring" with its "close bosom friend," the sun, to produce "Seasons of mists and mellow fruitfulness." Now, at the end of Autumn, all of nature's creatures are rejoicing. Seemingly, all of nature is celebrating the end of the season, the end of Autumn. Such music contains both notes of mourning and joy. Like the season itself, many creatures will die, the grass will wither, and no fruit will grow on the trees. But with Autumn's passing comes winter, and when winter too passes, spring will come again. As Autumn prepares all for death, winter allows nature its much needed rest. But from death, from resting, issues life again.

So sing ye animals of Autumn, sing in the midst of impending death, for Autumn is just one season of four that creates the life of nature. Just as Autumn and the sun conspire to produce luscious fruit, just as the animal choir of late Autumn joins to produce Autumn's final ode to joy, so all nature—all its four seasons—are necessary cycles in nature's ever-repeating process of life in death and death in life. Although Autumn be the harbinger of death, because she comes, all will live again.

DALE SCHUURMAN

❧ Professional Essay ❧

Keats's Sylvan Historian: History Without Footnotes

There is much in the poetry of Keats which suggests that he would have approved of Archibald MacLeish's dictum, "A poem should not mean/ But be." There is even some warrant for thinking that the Grecian urn (real or imagined) which inspired the famous ode was, for Keats, just such a poem, "palpable and mute," a poem in stone. Hence it is the more remarkable that the "Ode" itself differs from Keats's other odes by culminating in a statement—a statement even of some sententiousness in which the urn itself is made to say that beauty is truth, and—more sententious still—that this bit of wisdom sums up the whole of mortal knowledge.

This is "to mean" with a vengeance—to violate the doctrine of the objective correlative, not only by stating truths, but by defining the limits of truth. Small wonder that some critics have felt that the unravished bride of quietness protests too much.

T. S. Eliot, for example, says that "this line ["Beauty is truth," etc.] strikes me as a serious blemish on a beautiful poem; and the reason must be either that I fail to understand it, or that it is a statement which is untrue." But even for persons who feel that they do understand it, the line may still constitute a blemish. Middleton Murry, who, after a discussion of Keats's other poems and his letters, feels that he knows what Keats meant by "beauty" and what he meant by "truth," and that Keats used them in senses which allowed them to be properly bracketed together, still, is forced to conclude: "My own opinion concerning the value of these two lines *in the context of the poem itself* is not very different from Mr. T. S. Eliot's." The troubling assertion is apparently an intrusion upon the poem—does not grow out of it—is not dramatically accommodated to it.

This is essentially Garrod's objection, and the fact that Garrod does object indicates that a distaste for the ending of the "Ode" is by no means limited to critics of notoriously "modern" sympathies.

But the question of real importance is not whether Eliot, Murry, and Garrod are right in thinking that "Beauty is truth, truth beauty" injures the poem. The question of real importance concerns beauty and truth in a much more general way: what is the relation of the beauty (the goodness, the perfection) of a poem to the truth or falsity of what it seems to assert? It is a question which has particularly vexed our own generation—to give it I. A. Richards' phrasing, it is the problem of belief.

The "Ode," by its bold equation of beauty and truth, raises this question in its sharpest form—the more so when it becomes apparent that the poem itself is obviously intended to be a parable on the nature of poetry, and of art in general. The "Ode" has apparently been an enigmatic parable, to be sure: one can emphasize *beauty* is truth and throw Keats into the pure-art camp, the usual procedure. But it is only fair to point out that one could stress *truth* is beauty, and argue with the Marxist critics of the thirties for a propaganda art. The very ambiguity of the statement, "Beauty is truth, truth beauty" ought to warn us against insisting very much on the statement in isolation, and to drive us back to a consideration of the context in which the statement is set.

It will not be sufficient, however, if it merely drives us back to a study of Keats's reading, his conversation, his letters. We shall not find our answer there even if scholarship does prefer on principle an investigation of Browning's ironic question, "What porridge had John Keats?" For even if we knew just what porridge he had, physical and mental, we should still not be able to settle the problem of the "Ode." The reason should be clear: our specific question is not what did Keats the man perhaps want to assert here about the relation of beauty and truth; it is rather: was Keats the poet able to exemplify that relation in this particular poem? Middleton Murry is right: the relation of the final statement in the poem to the total context is all-important.

Indeed, Eliot, in the very passage in which he attacks the "Ode" has indicated the general line which we are to take in its defense. In that passage, Eliot goes on to contrast the closing lines of the "Ode" with a line from *King Lear*, "Ripeness is all." Keats's lines strike him as false; Shakespeare's, on the other hand, as not clearly false, and as possibly quite true. Shakespeare's generalization, in other words, avoids raising the question of truth. But is it really a question of truth and falsity? One is tempted to account for the difference of effect which Eliot feels in this way: "Ripeness is all" is a statement put in the mouth of a dramatic character and a statement which is governed and qualified by the whole context of the play. It does not directly challenge an examination into its truth because its relevance is pointed up and modified by the dramatic context.

Now, suppose that one could show that Keats's lines, *in quite the same way*, constitute a speech, a consciously riddling paradox, put in the mouth of a particular character, and modified by the total context of the poem. If we could demonstrate that the speech was "in character," was dramatically appropriate, was properly prepared for—then would not the lines have all the justification of "Ripeness is all"? In such case, should we not have waived the question of the scientific or philosophic truth of the lines in favor of the application of a principle curiously like that of dramatic propriety? I suggest that some such principle is the only one legitimately to be invoked in any case. Be this as it may, the "Ode on a Grecian Urn" provides us with as neat an instance as one could wish in order to test the implications of such a maneuver.

It has seemed best to be perfectly frank about procedure: the poem is to be read in order to see whether the last lines of the poem are not, after all, dramatically prepared for. Yet there are some claims to be made upon the reader too, claims which he, for his part, will have to be prepared to honor. He must not be allowed to dismiss the early characterizations of the urn as merely so much vaguely beautiful description. He must not be too much surprised if "mere decoration" turns out to be meaningful symbolism—or if ironies develop where he has been taught to expect only sensuous pictures. Most of all, if the teasing riddle spoken finally by the urn is not to strike him as a bewildering break in tone, he must not be too much disturbed to have the element of paradox latent in the poem emphasized, even in those parts of the poem which have none of the energetic crackle of wit with which he usually associates paradox. This is surely not too much to ask of the reader— namely, to assume that Keats meant what he said and that he chose his words with care. After all, the poem begins on a note of paradox, though a mild one: for we ordinarily do not expect an urn to speak at all; and yet,

Keats does more than this: he begins his poem by emphasizing the apparent contradiction.

The silence of the urn is stressed—it is a "bride of quietness"; it is a "foster-child of silence," but the urn is a "historian" too. Historians tell the truth, or are at least expected to tell the truth. What is a "Sylvan historian"? A historian who is like the forest rustic, a woodlander? Or, a historian who writes histories of the forest? Presumably, the urn is sylvan in both senses. True, the latter meaning is uppermost: the urn can "express/ A flowery tale more sweetly than our rhyme," and what the urn goes on to express is a "leaf-fring'd legend" of "Tempe or the dales of Arcady." But the urn, like the "leaf-fring'd legend" which it tells, is covered with emblems of the fields and forests: "Overwrought,/ With forest branches and the trodden weed." When we consider the way in which the urn utters its history, the fact that it must be sylvan in both senses is seen as inevitable. Perhaps too the fact that it is a rural historian, a rustic, a peasant historian, qualifies in our minds the dignity and the "truth" of the histories which it recites. Its histories, Keats has already conceded, may be characterized as "tales"—not formal history at all.

The sylvan historian certainly supplies no names and dates—"What men or gods are these?" the poet asks. What it does give is action—of men *or* gods, of godlike men or of superhuman (though not daemonic) gods—action, which is not the less intense for all that the urn is cool marble. The words "mad" and "ecstasy" occur, but it is the quiet, rigid urn which gives the dynamic picture. And the paradox goes further: the scene is one of violent love-making, a Bacchanalian scene, but the urn itself is like a "still unravish'd bride," or like a child, a child "of silence and slow time." It is not merely like a child, but like a "foster-child." The exactness of the term can be defended. "Silence and slow time," it is suggested, are not the true parents, but foster-parents. They are too old, one feels, to have borne the child themselves. Moreover, they dote upon the "child" as grandparents do. The urn is fresh and unblemished; it is still young, for all its antiquity, and time which destroys so much has "fostered" it.

With Stanza II we move into the world presented by the urn, into an examination, not of the urn as a whole—as an entity with its own form—but of the details which overlay it. But as we enter that world, the paradox of silent speech is carried on, this time in terms of the objects portrayed on the vase.

The first lines of the stanza state a rather bold paradox—even the dulling effect of many readings has hardly blunted it. At least we can easily revive its sharpness. Attended to with care, it is a statement which is preposterous, and yet true—true on the same level on which the original metaphor of the speaking urn is true. The unheard music is sweeter than any audible music. The poet has rather cunningly enforced his conceit by using the phrase, "ye soft pipes." Actually, we might accept the poet's metaphor without being forced to accept the adjective "soft." The pipes might, although "unheard," be shrill, just as the action which is frozen in the figures on the urn can be violent and ecstatic as in Stanza I and slow and dignified as in Stanza IV (the procession to the sacrifice). Yet, by characterizing the pipes as "soft," the poet has provided a sort of realistic basis for his metaphor: the pipes, it is suggested, are playing very softly; if we listen carefully, we can hear them; their music is just below the threshold of normal sound.

This general paradox runs through the stanza: action goes on though the actors are motionless; the song will not cease; the lover cannot leave his song; the maiden, always to be kissed, never actually kissed, will remain changelessly beautiful. The maiden is, indeed, like the urn itself, a "still unravish'd bride of quietness"—not even ravished by a kiss; and it is implied, perhaps, that her changeless beauty, like that of the urn, springs from this fact.

The poet is obviously stressing the fresh, unwearied charm of the scene itself which can defy time and is deathless. But, at the same time, the poet is being perfectly fair to the terms of his metaphor. The beauty portrayed is deathless because it is lifeless. And it would be possible to shift the tone easily and ever so slightly by insisting more heavily on some of the phrasings so as to give them a darker implication. Thus, in the case of "thou canst not leave/ Thy song," one could interpret: the musician cannot leave the song even if he would: he is fettered to it, a prisoner. In the same way, one could enlarge on the hint that the lover is not wholly satisfied and content: "never canst thou kiss,/ . . . *yet do not grieve.*" These items are mentioned here, not because one wishes to maintain that the poet is bitterly ironical, but because it is important for us to see that even here the paradox is being used fairly, particularly in view of the shift in tone which comes in the next stanza.

This third stanza represents, as various critics have pointed out, a recapitulation of earlier motifs. The boughs which cannot shed their leaves, the unwearied melodist, and the ever-ardent lover reappear. Indeed, I am not sure that this stanza can altogether be defended against the charge that it represents a falling-off from the delicate but firm precision of the earlier stanzas. There is a tendency to linger over the scene sentimentally: the repetition of the word "happy" is perhaps symptomatic of what is occurring. Here, if anywhere, in my opinion, is to be found the blemish on the ode—not in the last two lines. Yet, if we are to attempt a defense of the third stanza, we shall come nearest success by emphasizing the paradoxical implications of the repeated items; for whatever development there is in the stanza inheres in the increased stress on the paradoxical element. For example, the boughs cannot "bid the Spring adieu," a phrase which repeats "nor ever can those trees be bare," but the new line strengthens the implications of speaking: the falling leaves are a gesture, a word of farewell to the joy of spring. The melodist of Stanza II played sweeter music because unheard, but here, in the third stanza, it is implied that he does not tire of his song for the same reason that the lover does not tire of his love—neither song nor love is consummated. The songs are "for ever new" because they cannot be completed.

The paradox is carried further in the case of the lover whose love is "For ever warm and still to be enjoy'd." We are really dealing with an ambiguity here, for we can take "still to be enjoy'd" as an adjectival phrase on the same level as "warm"—that is, "still virginal and warm." But the tenor of the whole poem suggests that the warmth of the love depends upon the fact that it has not been enjoyed—that is, "warm and still to be enjoy'd" may mean also "warm *because* still to be enjoy'd."

But though the poet has developed and extended his metaphors furthest here in this third stanza, the ironic counterpoise is developed furthest too. The love which a line earlier was "warm" and "panting" becomes suddenly in the next line, "All breathing human passion far above." But if it is *above* all breathing passion, it is, after all, outside the realm of breathing passion, and therefore, not human passion at all.

If one argues that we are to take "All breathing human passion" as qualified by "That leaves a heart high-sorrowful and cloy'd"—that is, if one argues that Keats is saying that the love depicted on the urn is above only that human passion which leaves one cloyed and not above human passion in general, he misses the point. For Keats in the "Ode" is stressing the ironic fact that all human passion *does* leave one cloyed; hence the superiority of art.

The purpose in emphasizing the ironic undercurrent in the foregoing lines is not at all to disparage Keats—to point up implications of his poem of which he was himself unaware. Far from it: the poet knows precisely what he is doing. The point is to be made simply in order to make sure that we are completely aware of what he *is* doing. Garrod, sensing this ironic undercurrent, seems to interpret it as an element over which Keats was not able to exercise full control. He says: "Truth to his main theme [the fixity given by art to forms which in life are impermanent] has taken Keats farther than he meant to go. The pure and ideal are of this 'cold Pastoral,' this 'silent form,' *has* a cold silentness which in some degree saddens him. In the last lines of the fourth stanza, especially the last three lines . . . every reader is conscious, I should suppose, of an undertone of sadness, of disappointments." The undertone is there, but Keats has not been taken "farther than he meant to go." Keats's attitude, even in the early stanzas, is more complex than Garrod would allow; it is more complex and more ironic, and a recognition of this is important if we are to be able to relate the last stanza to the rest of the "Ode." Keats is perfectly aware that the frozen moment of loveliness is more dynamic than is the fluid world of reality *only* because it is frozen. The love depicted on the urn remains warm and young because it is not human flesh at all but cold, ancient marble.

With Stanza IV, we are still within the world depicted by the urn, but the scene presented in this stanza forms a contrast to the earlier scenes. It emphasized, not individual aspiration and desire, but communal life. It constitutes another chapter in the history that the "Sylvan historian" has to tell. And again, names and dates have been omitted. We are not told to what god's altar the procession moves, nor the occasion of the sacrifice.

Moreover, the little town from which the celebrants come is unknown; and the poet rather goes out of his way to leave us the widest possible option in locating it. It may be a mountain town, or a river town, or a tiny seaport. Yet, of course, there is a sense in which the nature of the town—the essential character of the town—is actually suggested by the figured urn. But it is not given explicitly. The poet is willing to leave much to our imaginations; and yet the stanza in its organization of imagery and rhythm does describe the town clearly enough; it is small, it is quiet, its people are knit together as an organic whole, and on a "pious morn" such as this, its whole population has turned out to take part in the ritual.

The stanza has been justly admired. Its magic of effect defies reduction to any formula. Yet, without pretending to "account" for the effect in any mechanical fashion, one can point to some of the elements active in securing the effect: there is the suggestiveness of the word "green" in "green altar"— something natural, spontaneous, living; there is the suggestion that the little town is caught in a curve of the seashore, or nestled in a fold of the mountains—at any rate, is something secluded and something naturally related to its terrain; there is the effect of the phrase "peaceful citadel," a phrase which involves a clash between the ideas of war and peace and resolves it in the sense of stability and independence without imperialistic ambition—the sense of stable repose.

But to return to the larger pattern of the poem: Keats does something in this fourth stanza which is highly interesting in itself and thoroughly relevant to the sense in which the urn is a historian. One of the most moving passages in the poem is that in which the poet speculates on the strange emptiness of the little town which, of course, has not been pictured on the urn at all.

The little town which has been merely implied by the procession portrayed on the urn is endowed with a poignance beyond anything else in the poem. Its streets "for evermore/ Will silent be," its desolation forever shrouded in a mystery. No one in the figured procession will ever be able to go back to the town to break the silence there, not even on to tell the stranger there why the town remains desolate.

If one attends closely to what Keats is doing here, he may easily come to feel that the poet is indulging himself in an ingenious fancy, an indulgence, however, which is gratuitous and finally silly; that is, the poet has created in his own imagination the town implied by the procession of worshipers, has given it a special character of desolation and loneliness, and then has gone on to treat it as if it were a real town to which a stranger might actually come and be puzzled by its emptiness. (I can see no other interpretation of the lines, "and not a soul to tell/ Why thou art desolate can e'er return.") But, actually, of course, no one will ever discover the town except by the very same process by which Keats has discovered it: namely, through the figured urn, and then, of course, he will not need to ask why it is empty. One can well imagine what a typical eighteenth-century critic would have made of this flaw in logic.

It will not be difficult, however, to show that Keats's extension of the fancy is not irrelevant to the poem as a whole. The "reality" of the little town has a very close relation to the urn's character as a historian. If the earlier stanzas have been concerned with such paradoxes as the ability of static carving to convey dynamic action, of the soundless pipes to play music sweeter than that of the heard melody, of the figured lover to have a love more warm and panting than that of breathing flesh and blood, so in the same way the town implied by the urn comes to have a richer and more important history than that of actual cities. Indeed, the imagined town is to the figured procession as the unheard melody is to the carved pipes of the unwearied melodist. And the poet, by pretending to take the town as real—so real that he can imagine the effect of its silent streets upon the stranger who chances to come into it—has suggested in the most powerful way possible its essential reality for him—and for us. It is a case of the doctor's taking his own medicine: the poet is prepared to stand by the illusion of his own making.

With Stanza V we move back out of the enchanted world portrayed by the urn to consider the urn itself once more as a whole, as an object. The shift in point of view is marked with the first line of the stanza by the apostrophe, "O Attic shape . . ." It is the urn itself as a formed thing, as an autonomous world, to which the poet addresses these last words. And the rich, almost breathing world which the poet has conjured up for us contracts and hardens into the decorated motifs on the urn itself: "with brede/ Of marble men and maidens overwrought." The beings who have a life above life—"All breathing human passion far above"—are marble, after all.

This last is a matter which, of course, the poet has never denied. The recognition that the men and maidens are frozen, fixed, and arrested, has, as we have already seen, run through the second, third, and fourth stanzas as an ironic undercurrent. The central paradox of the poem, thus, comes to conclusion in the phrase, "Cold Pastoral." The word "pastoral" suggests warmth, spontaneity, the natural and the informal as well as the idyllic, the simple, and the informally charming. What the urn tells is a "flowery tale," a "leaf-fring'd legend," but the "sylvan historian" works in terms of marble. The urn itself is cold, and the life beyond life which it expresses is life which has been formed, arranged. The urn itself is a "silent form," and it speaks, not by means of statement, but by "teasing us out of thought." It is as enigmatic as eternity is, for like eternity, its history is beyond time, outside time, and for this very reason bewilders our time-ridden minds: it teases us.

The marble men and maidens of the urn will not age as flesh-and-blood men and women will: "When old age shall this generation waste." (The word "generation," by the way, is very rich. It means on one level "that which is generated"—that which springs from human loins—Adam's breed; and yet, so intimately is death wedded to men, the word "generation" itself has become, as here, a measure of time.) The marble men and women lie outside time. The urn which they adorn will remain. The "Sylvan historian" will recite its history to other generations.

What will it say to them? Presumably, what it says to the poet now: that "formed experience," imaginative insight, embodies the basic and fundamental perception of man and nature. The urn is beautiful, and yet its beauty is based—what else is the poem concerned with?—on an imaginative perception of essentials. Such a vision is beautiful but it is also true. The sylvan historian presents us with beautiful histories, but they are true histories, and it is a good historian.

Moreover, the "truth" which the sylvan historian gives is the only kind of truth which we are likely to get on this earth, and, furthermore, it is the only kind that we *have* to have. The names, dates, and special circumstances, the wealth of data—these the sylvan historian quietly ignores. But we shall never get all the facts anyway—there is no end to the accumulation of facts. Moreover, mere accumulations of facts—a point our own generation is only beginning to realize—are meaningless. The sylvan historian does better than that: it takes a few details and so orders them that we have not only beauty but insight into essential truth. Its "history," in short, is a history without footnotes. It has the validity of myth—not myth as a pretty but irrelevant make-belief, an idle fancy, but myth as a valid perception into reality.

So much for the "meaning" of the last lines of the "Ode." It is an interpretation which differs little from past interpretations. It is put forward here with no pretension to novelty. What is important is the fact that it can be derived from the context of the "Ode" itself.

And now, what of the objection that the final lines break the tone of the poem with a display of misplaced sententiousness? One can summarize the answer already implied thus: throughout the poem the poet has stressed the paradox of the speaking urn. First, the urn itself can tell a story, can give a history. Then, the various figures depicted upon the urn play music or speak or sing. If we have been alive to these items, we shall not, perhaps, be too much surprised to have the urn speak once more, not in the sense in which it tells a story—a metaphor which is rather easy to accept—but, to have it speak on a higher level, to have it make a commentary on its own nature. If the urn has been properly dramatized, if we have followed the development of the metaphors, if we have been alive to the paradoxes which work throughout the poem, perhaps then, we shall be prepared for the enigmatic, final paradox which the "silent form" utters. But in that case, we shall not feel that the generalization, unqualified and to be taken literally, is meant to march out of its context to compete with scientific and philosophical generalizations which dominate our world.

"Beauty is truth, truth beauty" has precisely the same status, and the same justification as Shakespeare's "Ripeness is all." It is a speech "in character" and supported by a dramatic context.

To conclude thus may seem to weight the principle of dramatic propriety with more than it can bear. This would not be fair to the complexity of the problem of truth in art nor fair to Keats's little parable. Granted; and yet the principle of dramatic propriety may take us further than would first appear. Respect for it may at least insure our dealing with the problem of truth at the level on which it is really relevant to literature. If we can see that the assertions made in a poem are to be taken as part of an organic context, if we can resist the temptation to deal with them in isolation, then we may be willing to go on to deal with the world-view, or "philosophy," or "truth" of the *poem as a whole* in terms of its dramatic wholeness: that is, we shall not neglect the maturity of attitude, the dramatic tension, the emotional *and* intellectual coherence in favor of some statement of theme abstracted from it by paraphrase. Perhaps, best of all, we might learn to distrust our ability to represent any poem adequately by paraphrase. Such a distrust is healthy. Keats's sylvan historian, who is not above "teasing" us, exhibits such a distrust, and perhaps the point of what the sylvan historian "says" is to confirm us in our distrust.

Essay by Cleanth Brooks. "Keats's Sylvan Historian: History Without Footnotes." *The Well Wrought Urn*, 2nd ed. New York: Harcourt, 1975, pp. 151–66.

4

Reader-Response
Criticism

Once I said to myself it would be a thousand times better for Jim to be a slave
at home where his family was, as long as he'd *got* to be a slave, and so I'd better write a letter to Tom Sawyer and tell him to tell Miss Watson where he was.
But I soon give up that notion, for two things: she'd be mad and disgusted at
his rascality and ungratefulness for leaving her, and so she'd sell him straight
down the river again; and if she didn't, everybody naturally despises an
ungrateful nigger, and they'd make Jim feel it all the time, and so he'd feel
ornery and disgraced. And then think of *me*! It would get all around that Huck
Finn helped a nigger to get his freedom; and if I was to ever see anybody from
that town again I'd be ready to get down and lick his boots for shame. That's
just the way: a person does a low-down thing, and then he don't want to take
no consequences of it. Thinks as long as he can hide it, it ain't no disgrace.
That was my fix exactly. The more I studied about this the more my conscience
went to grinding me, and the more wicked and low-down and ornery I got to
feeling. And at last, when it hit me all of a sudden that here was the plain hand
of Providence slapping me in the face and letting me know my wickedness
was being watched all the time up there in heaven, whilst I was stealing a poor
old woman's nigger that hadn't ever done me no harm, and now was showing
me there's One that's always on the lookout, and ain't agoing to allow no such
miserable doings to go only just so fur and no further, I most dropped in my
tracks I was so scared. Well, I tried the best I could to kinder soften it up somehow for myself by saying I was brung up wicked, and so I warn't so much to
blame; but something inside of me kept saying,"There was the Sunday school,
you could a gone to it; and if you'd a done it they'd a learn't you there that
people that acts as I'd been acting about that nigger goes to everlasting fire."
  It made me shiver.

MARK TWAIN, Adventures of Huckleberry Finn, Chapter 31, 1885

INTRODUCTION

In a college-level, introductory literature course, several class members are
voicing their interpretations of Chapter 31 of Twain's *Adventures of
Huckleberry Finn,* part of which is quoted at the beginning of this chapter.

Student A declares that Huck Finn's struggle is obvious; he is simply debating whether he should listen to his feelings and keep Jim's whereabouts a secret, or listen to his conscience, which dictates that he must report the slave's location to Miss Watson, Jim's lawful owner. This chapter, asserts Student A, illustrates the novel's unifying theme: Huck's struggle to obey his innately good feelings versus his obeying the abstract commandments of an institutionalized system, his society. What unites all the chapters in the text and is now highlighted and climaxed in this chapter, maintains Student A, is Huck's realization that his inner feelings are correct and his society-dominated conscience is wrong. He accordingly opts for declaring Jim's humanity and thus tears up the letter he has written to Miss Watson.

Student B objects, declaring that Student A's interpretation is not relevant for the 1990s. Student A is correct, claims Student B, when she notes that Huck chooses to obey his conscience and disavow his allegiance to society's dictates. This is indeed Twain's chief purpose in his novel. But the novel's significance rests in how it can be applied today. Prejudice, she contends, still exists in our college town. We, like Huck, must see the humanness in all our citizens.

Student C observes that Students A and B have both made valid criticisms. What they have overlooked, however, is the change that now takes place in Huck himself. No longer will we see a Huck who will play dirty tricks on Jim or even consider hurting him in any way, maintains Student C. We now have a Huck who has positioned himself against his society and will not retreat. In the rest of the novel, declares Student C, we will observe this more mature and directed Huck as he responds to Jim's personal needs.

With a quiver in his voice, Student D remarks that Huck reminds him of his friend George. One day when he and George were walking down the hall of their high school on their way to eleventh-grade biology class, they passed a group of students who began cursing and throwing milk cartons at them. "Go home, Jap," "USA all the way," and other derogatory comments came their way. Then George retorted, "Cut it out, guys. Pete has feelings too. Should we call some of you tow-heads, carrot tops, or other names because of how you look and because of your ancestors?" Like George, says Student D, Huck hates prejudice no matter where he finds it. Being on the side of the oppressed, he chooses to guard his friend's dignity and self-worth. He therefore destroys the letter to Miss Watson and will eventually help Jim obtain his freedom.

Each of the four students sees something slightly different in Twain's passage. Consciously or unconsciously, each of their interpretations rests on different theoretical assumptions and their corresponding interpretative methodologies. Of the four interpretations, Student A's is the most theoretically distinct approach to the passage. Seeing an overall textual unity, Student A presupposes that the text is autonomous; it must interpret itself with little or no help from historical, societal, or any other extrinsic factors, with all its parts relating back to its central theme. Using the tenets of New

Criticism, Student A posits the organic unity of the text. For this student, learning and applying literary terminology and searching for the correct interpretation are of utmost importance.

Unlike Student A, who applies a given set of criteria to the text in an attempt to discover its meaning, Students B, C, and D become participants in the interpretive process, actively bringing their own experiences to bear upon the text's meaning. Student B's interpretation, for example, highlights the theoretical difference between a text's meaning (the author's intentions) and its significance or relevance to present-day readers. Student C's approach begins filling in the gaps in the text, hypothesizing how Huck Finn will act in the pages yet unread based on Huck's decision not to write to Jim's owner. Whether Student C is correct or not, and whether she will have to change some of her ideas concerning Jim, remains open. And Student D's theoretical framework objectifies the text and its meaning based on the reader's personal experiences with prejudice.

Although Students B, C, and D differ in their various approaches, none views the text as an objective entity that contains its own meaning (as does Student A). For these students, the text does not and cannot interpret itself. To determine a text's meaning, these students believe they must become active readers and participants in the interpretive process. Their various theoretical assumptions and methodologies used to discover a text's meaning exemplify **reader-response criticism**.

HISTORICAL DEVELOPMENT

Although reader-response criticism rose to prominence in literary analysis in the early 1970s and still influences much contemporary criticism, its historical roots can be traced to the 1920s and 1930s. Such precise dating, however, is artificial, for readers have obviously been responding to what they have read and experienced since the dawn of literature itself. Even the classical writers Plato and Aristotle were aware of and concerned about the reader's (or viewer's) reactions. Plato, for example, asserts that watching a play could so inflame the passions of the audience that the viewers would forget that they were rational beings and allow passion, not reason, to rule their actions. Similarly, in the *Poetics* Aristotle voices concern about the effects a play will have on the audience's emotions. Will it arouse the spectators' pity or fear? Will these emotions purge the viewer? Will they cleanse a spectator of all emotions by the play's end? Such interest in audience response to the artistic creation dominates much literary criticism.

Underlying both Plato's and Aristotle's concerns about audience response, and the concern of many critics who follow in their paths, is the assumption that the audience (or the reader) is passive. As if watching a play or reading a book were a spectator sport, readers sit passively, absorbing the contents of the artistic creation and allowing it to dominate their thoughts and actions. From this point of view, the reader brings little to the play or text. The text provides all that is needed to interpret itself.

From Plato's time until the beginning of the romantic movement in British literature at the beginning of the 1800s, such a passive view of the reader predominated. Although many critics recognized that a text did indeed have an effect on its readers, criticism concerned itself primarily with the text. With the advent of romanticism, emphasis shifted from the text to the author. The author now became the genius who could assimilate truths that were unacknowledged or unseen by the general populace. And as the nineteenth century progressed, concern for the author continued, with literary criticism stressing the importance of the author's life, times, and social context as chief aids in textual analysis.

But by the 1920s, emphasis in textual analysis once again shifted to the text. With the advent of the New Criticism, the text became autonomous—an objective entity that could be analyzed and dissected. If studied thoroughly, the New Critics believed, the text would reveal its own meaning. Extrinsic factors such as historical or social context mattered little. Now considered a verbal icon, the text itself, declared the New Critics, contains what we need to discover its meaning. We need only master the technical vocabulary and the correct techniques to unlock its meaning.

While positing the autonomy of the text, the New Critics did acknowledge the effects a text could have on its readers. Studying the effects of a literary work, they decreed, was not the same as studying the text itself, however. This emphasis on the objective nature of the text once again created a passive reader who did not bring personal experiences or private emotions to bear on textual analysis.

I. A. Richards

In the midst of New Criticism's rise to dominance in textual analysis, which would last for more than 30 years, one of its two founding fathers, I. A. Richards (T. S. Eliot being the other), became interested in the reading process itself. Using a decidedly reader-response approach to textual analysis, Richards distributed to his classes at Cambridge University copies of short poems of widely diverse aesthetic and literary value without citing their authors and titles and with various editorial changes that updated spelling and punctuation. He then asked his students to record their free responses and evaluations of each of these short texts. What surprised Richards was the wide variety of seemingly incompatible and contradictory responses.

After collecting and analyzing these responses, Richards published his findings, along with his own interpretations of the short texts, in *Principles of Literary Criticism* (1925). Underlying Richard's text is his assumption that science, not poetry or any other literary genre, leads to truth—that is, science's view of the world is the correct one. Poems, on the other hand, can produce only "pseudostatements" concerning the nature of reality. But such pseudostatements, declares Richards, are essential to the overall psychological health of each individual. In fact, according to Richards, human beings are basically bundles of desires called **appetencies**. In order to achieve psychic health, one must balance these desires by creating a personably acceptable vision of the world. Richards observes that religion was once able to provide this vision, but has lost its effectiveness to do so. Borrowing from the thoughts of nineteenth-century poet Matthew Arnold, Richards decrees that poetry, above all other art forms, can best harmonize and satisfy humankind's appetencies and thereby create a fulfilling and intellectually acceptable worldview.

After creating such an affective system of analysis, which gives credence to a reader's emotional response to a text, Richards abandons this reader-response approach in his own analysis of his students' responses. Like the New Critics who were to follow him in the next several decades, he declares that the poem itself contains all the necessary information to arrive at the "right" or "more adequate" interpretation. Through textual analysis—that is, by closely examining the poem's diction, imagery, and overall unity—Richards believes a reader can arrive at a better or more correct interpretation of a poem than relying on sheerly personal responses to a text.

Despite his departing from his initial reader-response methodology, Richards recognized the contextual nature of reading poems, for he acknowledged that a reader brings to the text a vast array of ideas amassed through life's experiences, including previous literary experiences, and applies such information to the text. By so doing, the reader is no longer the passive receiver of knowledge but an active participant in the creation of a text's meaning.

Louise M. Rosenblatt

In the 1930s, Louise M. Rosenblatt further developed Richards's earlier assumptions concerning the contextual nature of the reading process. In her text *Literature as Exploration* (1937), Rosenblatt asserts that both the reader and the text must work together to produce meaning. Unlike the New Critics, she shifts the emphasis of textual analysis away from the text alone and views the reader and the text as partners in the interpretive process.

In the late 1930s, however, Rosenblatt's ideas seemed revolutionary, too abstract, and simply off the beaten, critical path. Although New Criticism dominated literary practice for the next 30 years or so, Rosenblatt continued to develop her ideas, culminating her critical work with the publication of *The Reader, the Text, the Poem* (1978). In this work, she clarifies her earlier ideas and presents what has become one of the main critical positions held by many theorists and practical critics today.

According to Rosenblatt, the reading process involves a reader and a text. Both the reader and the text interact or share a **transactional experience**: The text acts as a stimulus for eliciting various past experiences, thoughts, and ideas from the reader, those found in both our everyday existence and in past reading experiences. Simultaneously, the text shapes the reader's experiences, selecting, limiting, and ordering the ideas that best conform to the text. Through this transactional experience, the reader and the text produce a new creation, a poem. For Rosenblatt and many other reader-response critics, a **poem** is now defined as the result of an event that takes place during the reading process, or what Rosenblatt calls the aesthetic transaction. No longer synonymous with the word *text*, a poem is created each time a reader interacts with a text, be that interaction a first reading or any of countless rereadings of the same text.

For Rosenblatt, readers can and do read in one of two ways: efferently or aesthetically. When we read for information—for example, when we read the directions for heating a can of soup—we are engaging in **efferent reading**. During this process we are interested only in newly gained information, not the actual words themselves. When we engage in **aesthetic reading**, we experience the text. We note its every word, its sounds, its patterns, and so on. In essence, we live through the transactional experience of creating the poem.

When reading aesthetically, we involve ourselves in an elaborate encounter of give-and-take with the text. Although the text may allow for many interpretations by eliciting and highlighting different past experiences of the reader, it simultaneously limits the valid meanings the poem can acquire. For Rosenblatt, a poem's meaning is not therefore a smorgasbord of endless interpretations, but a transactional experience in which several different yet probable meanings emerge and thereby create a variety of "poems."

What differentiates Rosenblatt's and all reader-response critics from other critical approaches (especially New Criticism) is their diverting the emphasis away from the text as the sole determiner of meaning to the significance of the reader as an essential participant in the reading process and the creation of meaning. Such a shift negates the formalists' assumption that the text is autonomous and can therefore be scientifically analyzed to discover its meaning. No longer, then, is the reader passive, merely applying a long list of learned, poetic devices to a text in the hope of discovering its intricate patterns of paradox and irony, which, in turn, will lead to a supposed correct interpretation. For reader-response critics, the reader now becomes an active participant along with the text in creating meaning. It is from the **literacy experience** (an event that occurs when a reader and print interact), they believe, that meaning evolves.

ASSUMPTIONS

Like most approaches to literary analysis, reader-response criticism does not provide us with a unified body of theory or a single methodological approach for textual analysis. What those who call themselves reader-response critics, reader-critics, or audience-oriented critics share is a concern for the reader. Believing that a literary work's interpretation is created when a reader and a text interact or transact, these critics assert that the proper study of textual analysis must consider both the reader and the text, not simply a text in isolation. For these critics, the reader + the text = meaning. Only in context with a reader actively involved in the reading process with the text, they decree, can meaning emerge.

Meaning, reader-response critics declare, is context dependent and intricately associated with the reading process. Like literary theory as a whole, several theoretical models and their practical applications exist to explain the reading process, or how we make sense of printed material. Using these various models, we can group these multiple approaches to the literacy experience into three broad categories. Each category emphasizes a somewhat different philosophy, a body of assumptions, and a methodology to explain what these various critics believe happens when a reader interacts with printed material.

Although each model espouses a different approach to textual analysis, all hold to some of the same presuppositions and concerns and ask similar questions. For example, all focus directly on the reading process. What happens, they ask, when a person picks up printed material and reads it? Put another way, their chief interest is what occurs when a text and a reader interact. During this interaction, reader-response critics investigate and theorize whether the reader, the text, or some combination finally determines the text's interpretation. Is it the reader who manipulates the text, they ponder, or does the text manipulate the reader to produce meaning? Does some word, phrase, or image trigger in the reader's mind a specific interpretation, or does the reader approach the text with a conscious or unconscious collection of learned reading strategies that systematically impose an interpretation on the text?

Such questions lead reader-response critics to a further narrowing and developing of terminology. For example, they ask, What is a text? Is it simply the words or symbols on a page? How, they ask, can we differentiate between what is actually in the text and what is in the mind of the reader? And who is this reader, anyway? Are there various kinds of readers? Is it possible that different texts presuppose different kinds of readers?

And what about a reader's response to a text? Are the responses equivalent to the text's meaning? Can one reader's response be more correct than some other reader's, or are all responses equally valid? Although readers respond to the same text in a variety of ways, they ask, why do many readers individually arrive at the same conclusions or interpretations of the same text?

Reader-response critics also ask questions about another person: the author. What part, if any, does the author play in a work's interpretation? Can the author's attitudes toward the reader actually influence a work's meaning? And if a reader knows the author's clearly stated intentions for a text, does this information have any part in creating the text's meaning, or should an author's intentions for a work simply be ignored?

The concerns of reader-response critics can best be summarized in one question: What happens during the reading process? The answer to this question is perplexing, for it involves investigating such factors as

- The reader, including his or her worldview, background, purpose for reading, knowledge of the world, knowledge of words, and other such factors
- The text, with all its various linguistic elements
- Meaning, or how the text and the reader interact so that the reader can make sense of the printed material

How reader-response critics define and explain each of these elements determines their approach to textual analysis. Furthermore, such answers also help determine what constitutes a valid interpretation of a text for each critic.

Although many reader-response critics allow for a wide range of legitimate responses to a text, most agree that reader-response criticism does not mean that any and all interpretations are valid or of equal importance. The boundaries and restrictions placed on possible interpretations of a text vary, depending upon how the critic defines the various elements of the reading process. It is these definitions and assumptions that allow us to group reader-response critics into several broad subgroups.

METHODOLOGY

Although reader-response critics use a wide variety of critical approaches—from those espousing their own particular and modified form of New Criticism to postmodern practitioners such as deconstructionists—most adherents of reader-response theory and practice fall into three distinct groups. Although members of each group may differ slightly, each particular group espouses its own distinct theoretical and methodological concerns. Student B's interpretation at the beginning of this chapter represents the focus of the first group.

Like all reader-response critics, this group believes that the reader must be an active participant in the creation of meaning, but for these critics the text has more control over the interpretative process than does the reader. A few of these critics lean toward New Critical theory, asserting that some interpretations are more valid than others. Others differentiate between a text's meaning and its significance. For them, the text's meaning can be synonymous with its author's intention, while its significance can change from one context or historical period to another. But the majority of critics in this first group belong to the school known as structuralism.

Structuralism

Basing their ideas on the writings of Ferdinand de Saussure, the father of modern linguistics, structuralists often approach textual analysis as if it were a science. Their proponents—Roland Barthes, Gerard Genette, Roman Jakobson, Claude Lévi-Strauss, Gerald Prince, and Jonathan Culler in his early works—look for specific codes within the text that allow meaning to occur. These codes or signs embedded in the text are part of a larger system that allows meaning to occur in all facets of society, including literature. For example, when we are driving a car and we see a red light hanging above an intersection, we have learned that we must stop our car. And if we hear a fire engine or an ambulance siren, we have also learned that we must pull over to the side of the road. Both the red light and the sirens are signs or codes in our society that provide us with ways of interpreting and ordering our world.

According to structuralist critics, a reader brings to the text a predetermined system of ascertaining meaning (a complex system of signs or codes like the sirens and the red light) and applies this sign system directly to the text. The text becomes important because it contains signs or signals to the reader that have established and acceptable interpretations. Many structuralists are therefore more concerned about the overall system of meaning a given society has developed than with textual analysis itself, and concentrate on what a reader needs to know about interpreting any sign (such as a road sign or a word) in the context of acceptable societal standards. Because of this emphasis, structuralists seem to push both the text and the reader to the background and highlight a linguistic theory of communication and interpretation. Because structuralism has become a springboard for many other modern theories of literary criticism, its significance to literary theory and practical criticism will be explored at length in Chapter 5. Meanwhile, the ideas of one leading structuralist, Gerard Prince, will illustrate the methodology of structuralism.

Gerard Prince   In the 1970s, Gerard Prince helped develop a specfic kind of structuralism known as **narratology**, the process of analyzing a story using all the elements involved in its telling, such as narrator, voice, style, verb tense, personal pronouns, audience, and so forth. Prince noted that critics often ask questions concerning the story's technical narrative point of view (omniscient, limited, first person, etc.) but rarely do they ask about the person to whom the narrator is speaking, the **narratee**. Usually the narratee is not the actual person reading the text, for Prince argues that the narrative itself—that is, the story—produces the narratee. By first observing and then analyzing various signs in the text—such as pronoun reference; direct address ("Dear reader"); gender, race, and social class references; and writing style—Prince believes it is possible not only to identify the narratee but also to classify stories based on the different kinds of narratees created by the texts themselves. Such narratees may include the **real reader** (person actually reading the book), the **virtual reader** (the reader to whom the author believes he or she is writing), and the **ideal reader** (the one who explicitly and implicitly understands all the nuances, terminology, and structure of a text).

Although such an approach relies heavily on textual analysis, Prince's concerns about the reader place him in the reader-response school of criticism. Other structuralists, such as Jonathan Culler, who distance themselves from Prince and such close reliance on the text to generate meaning will be discussed in Chapter 5.

Phenomenology

Student C represents the second major group of reader-response critics. For the most part, these critics follow Rosenblatt's assumption that the reader is involved in a transactional experience when interpreting a text. Both the text and the reader, they declare, play roughly equal parts in the interpretive process. For them, reading is an event that culminates in the creation of the poem.

Many adherents in this group—George Poulet, Wolfgang Iser, Hans Robert Jauss, Roman Ingarden, and Gaston Bachelard—are often associated with phenomenology. **Phenomenology** is a modern philosophical tendency that emphasizes the perceiver. Objects can have meaning, phenomenologists maintain, only if an active consciousness (a perceiver) absorbs or notes their existence. In other words, objects exist if and only if we register them on our consciousness. Rosenblatt's definition of a poem directly applies this theory to literary study. The true poem can exist only in the reader's consciousness, not on the printed page. When reader and text interact, the poem and therefore meaning are created; they exist only in the consciousness of the reader. Reading and textual analysis now become an aesthetic experience whereby both the reader and the text combine in the consciousness of the reader to create the poem. As in Student C's interpretation at the beginning of the chapter, the reader's imagination must work, filling in the gaps in the text and conjecturing about characters' actions, personality traits, and motives. The ideas and practices of two reader-response critics, Hans Robert Jauss and Wolfgang Iser, illustrate phenomenology's methodology.

Hans Robert Jauss   Writing toward the end of the 1960s, German critic Hans Robert Jauss emphasized that a text's social history must be considered in interpreting the text. Unlike New Critical scholars, Jauss declares that critics must examine how any given text was accepted or received by its contemporary readers. Espousing a particular kind of reader-response criticism known as **reception theory**, Jauss asserts that readers from any given historical period devise for themselves the criteria whereby they will judge a text. Using the term **horizons of expectation** to include all of a historical period's critical vocabulary and assessment of a text, Jauss points out that how any text is evaluated from one historical period to another (from the Enlightenment to the Romantic period, for example), necessarily changes. For example, Alexander Pope's poetry was heralded as the most nearly perfect poetry of its day, for heroic couplets and poetry that followed prescribed forms were judged as superior. During the Romantic period, however, with its emphasis on content, not form, the critical reception of Pope's poetry was not as great.

Accordingly, Jauss argues that because each historical period establishes its own horizons of expectation, the overall value and meaning of any text can never become fixed or universal, for readers from any historical period establish for themselves what they value in a text. A text, then, does not have one and only one correct interpretation, for its supposed meaning changes from one historical period to another. A final assessment about any literary work thus becomes impossible.

For Jauss, the reader's reception or understanding and evaluation of a text matter greatly. Although the text itself remains important in the interpretive process, the reader, declares Jauss, plays an essential role.

Wolfgang Iser   German phenomenologist Wolfgang Iser borrows and amends Jauss's ideas. Iser believes that any object—a stone, a house, or a poem—does not achieve meaning until an active consciousness recognizes or registers this object. It is thus impossible to separate what is known (the object) from the mind that knows it (human consciousness). Using these phenomenological ideas as the basis for his reader-response theory and practice, Iser declares that the critic's job is not to dissect or explain the text, for once a text is read, the object and the reader (the perceiver) are essentially one. Instead, the critic's role is to examine and explain the text's effect on the reader.

Iser, however, differentiates between two kinds of readers: the "**implied reader**" who "embodies all those predispositions necessary for a literary work to exercise its effect—predispositions laid down, not by an empirical outside reality, but by the text itself. Consequently, the implied reader . . . has his or her roots firmly planted in the structure of the text" (Iser, 1978), as opposed to the **actual reader**, the person who physically picks up the text and reads it. It is this reader who comes to the text shaped by cultural and personal norms and prejudices. By positing the implied reader, Iser affirms the necessity of examining the text in the interpretive process while declaring the validity of an individual reader's response to the text by acknowledging the actual reader.

Like Jauss, Iser disavows the New Critical stance that a text has one and only one correct meaning and asserts that a text has many possible interpretations. For Iser, texts in and of themselves do not possess meaning. When a text is **concretized** by the reader (the phenomenological concept whereby the text registers on the reader's consciousness), the reader automatically views the text from his or her personal worldview. However, because texts do not tell the reader everything that needs to be known about a character, a situation, a relationship, and other such textual elements, readers must automatically fill in these gaps, using their knowledge base grounded in their worldview. In addition, each reader creates his or her horizons of expectation—that is, a reader's expectations about what will or may happen next. (Note that Iser's use of this term is more individual-oriented than that of Jauss, who coined it). These horizons of expectation change frequently, for at the center of all stories is conflict or dramatic tension, often resulting in sudden loss, pain, unexpected joy or fear, and at times great fulfillment. Such changes cause a reader to modify his or her horizons of expectation to fit a text's particular situation.

For example, when in Chapter 31 of the *Adventures of Huckleberry Finn* Huck declares that he will not write a letter to Miss Watson telling her Jim's location, Huck openly chooses to side with Jim against the precepts of Huck's society. A reader may then assume that Huck will treat Jim differently, for now Jim, the slave, has a chance to become a free man. According to Iser, the reader has now established horizons of expectation. When the reader, however, observes in just a few short chapters later that Tom Sawyer has talked Huck into chaining Jim to a table, the reader may need to reformulate his or her previous horizons of expectation, for Huck is not treating Jim as a free man but once again as a slave.

In making sense of the text, filling in the text's gaps, and continually adopting new horizons of expectation, the reader uses his or her own value system, personal and public experiences, and philosophical beliefs. When, according to Iser, each reader makes "concrete" the text, each concretization is therefore personal, allowing the new creation—the text's meaning and effect on the reader—to be unique.

For Iser the reader is an active, essential player in the text's interpretation, writing part of the text as the story is read and concretized and becoming its coauthor.

Subjective Criticism

Student D represents the third group of reader-response critics, who place the greatest emphasis on the reader in the interpretive process. For these psychological or subjective critics, the reader's thoughts, beliefs, and experiences play a greater part than the actual text in shaping a work's meaning. Led by Norman Holland and David Bleich, these critics assert that we shape and find our self-identities in the reading process.

Norman Holland   Using Freudian psychoanalysis as the foundation for his theory and practices formulated in the early 1970s, Norman Holland believes that at birth we receive from our mothers a primary identity. Through our life's experiences we personalize this identity, transforming it into our own individualized **identity theme**, which becomes the lens through which we see the world. Textual interpretation then becomes a matter of working out our own fears, desires, and needs to help maintain our psychological health.

Like Rosenblatt, Holland asserts that the reading process is a transaction between the text and the reader. The text is indeed important, for it contains its own themes, its own unity, and its own structure. A reader, however, transforms a text into a private world, a place where one works out (through the ego) his or her fantasies, which are mediated by the text so that they will be socially acceptable.

For Holland, all interpretations are therefore subjective. Unlike New Criticism, his reader-response approach asserts that there is no such thing as a correct intepretation. From his perspective, there are as many valid interpretations as there are readers, for the act of interpretation is a subjective experience.

David Bleich   The founder of subjective criticism David Bleich (1978) agrees with Holland's psychological understanding of the interpretive process, but Bleich devalues the role the text plays, denying its objective existence. Meaning, Bleich argues, does not reside in the text but is *developed* when the reader works in cooperation with other readers to achieve the text's **collective meaning** (what Bleich calls the interpretation). Only when each reader is able to articulate his or her individual responses within a group about the text, then and only then can the group, working together, negotiate meaning. Such "communally motivated negotiations" ultimately determine the text's meaning.

For Bleich, the starting point for interpretation is the reader's responses to a text, not the text itself. According to Bleich, however, these responses do not constitute the text's meaning, for meaning cannot be found within a text or within responses to the text. Rather, a text's meaning must be *developed* from and out of the reader's responses, working in conjunction with other readers' responses and with past literary and life experiences. In other words, Bleich differentiates between the reader's response to a text (which for Bleich can never be equated to a reader's interpretation) and the reader's interpretation or meaning, which must be developed communally in a classroom or similar setting.

The key to developing a text's meaning is the working out of one's responses to a text so that these responses can be challenged and amended and then accepted by one's social group. Subjective critics such as Bleich assert that when reading a text a reader may respond to something in the text in a bizarre and personal way. These private responses will, through discussion, be pruned away by members of the reader's social group. Finally, the group will decide what is the acceptable interpretation of the text. Like Student D's interpretation cited at the beginning of this chapter, the reader responds personally to some specific element in the text and then seeks to objectify this personal response and declares it to be an interpretation of the text. Only through negotiations with other readers (and other texts), however, can one develop the text's meaning.

A Two-Step Methodology

Although reader-response critics all believe the reader plays a part in discovering a text's meaning, just how small or large a part is debatable. Espousing various theoretical assumptions, these critics must necessarily have different methodologies with regard to textual analysis. According to contemporary critic Steven Mailloux, however, they all share a two-step procedure, which they then adapt to their own theories. All show that a work gives a reader a task or something to do, and the reader's response or answer to that task.

For example, Student D cited at the beginning of this chapter obviously saw something in the text that triggered his memories of his friend George. His task is to discover what in the text triggered his memory and why. He moves, then, from the text to his own thoughts, memories, and past experiences. These personal experiences temporarily overshadow the text, but he realizes that his personal reactions must in some way become acceptable to his peers. He therefore compares George to Huck and himself to Jim and thereby objectifies his personal feelings while having his interpretation deemed socially respectable in his **interpretive community**—a term coined by reader-response critic Stanley Fish to designate a group of readers who share the same interpretive strategies.

Because the term *reader-response criticism* allows for so much divergence in theory and methods, many twentieth-century schools of criticism such as deconstruction, feminism, Marxism, and New Historicism declare their membership in this broad classification. Each of these approaches to textual analysis provides its own ideological basis to reader-response theory and develops its unique methods of practical criticism. Such an eclectic membership ensures the continued growth and ongoing development of reader-response criticism.

QUESTIONS FOR ANALYSIS

Because reader-response critics use a variety of methodologies, no particular list of questions can encompass all their concerns. By asking the following questions of a text, however, one can participate in both the theory and practice of reader-response criticism:

- Who is the actual reader?
- Who is the implied reader?
- Who is the ideal reader?
- Who is the narratee?
- What are some gaps you see in the text?
- Can you list several horizons of expectations and show how they change from a particular text's beginning to its conclusion?

- Using Jauss's definition of horizons of expectations, can you develop first on your own and then with your classmates an interpretation of a particular text?
- Can you identify your identity theme as you develop your personal interpretation of the text?
- Using Bleich's subjective criticism, can you state the difference between your response to a text and your interpretation?
- In a classroom setting, develop your class's interpretive strategies for arriving at the meaning of a text.

SAMPLE ESSAYS

After reading the sample student essay that follows, be able to identify the narratee and the implied and the ideal reader. In addition, be able to identify which one of the various subgroups of reader-response criticism the student uses to write this essay. Is the text, the reader plus the text, or the reader of most importance for this critic in her methodology and philosophy? In addition, can you point out the various personal strategies or moves the author makes to arrive at her interpretation? Also note the style of the essay. From what technical narrative point of view does the author write the essay? Why? Finally, what is the tone of the essay? How does the author establish this tone, and do you believe it is effective?

In the sample professional essay that follows, be able to explain how Norman Holland uses his own theoretical model of reader-response criticism in writing this essay. In other words, explain how Holland uses his own identity theme in his interpretation. According to Holland, how many *Hamlets* and Hamlets are there? In addition, be able to identify the New Critical vocabulary Holland uses throughout the essay. Does Holland redefine these terms or does he use them as a New Critic would? Why do you believe such terms appear in this essay? Finally, be able to discuss the particulars of Holland's style. Does his writing style differ from a New Critic's style? If so, explain. If not, explain.

FURTHER READING

Bleich, David. *Subjective Criticism*. Baltimore: Johns Hopkins University Press, 1978.

Fish, Stanley. *Is There a Text in This Class?* Cambridge, MA: Harvard University Press, 1980.

Holland, Norman N. *5 Readers Reading*. New Haven, CT: Yale University Press, 1975.

————. *Holland's Guide to Psychoanalytic Psychology and Literature-and-Psychology*. Oxford: Oxford University Press, 1990.

Iser, Wolfgang. *The Implied Reader: Patterns of Communication in Prose Fiction from Bunyan to Beckett*. Baltimore: Johns Hopkins University Press, 1974.

————. *The Act of Reading: A Theory of Aesthetic Response*. Baltimore: Johns Hopkins University Press, 1978.

Jauss, Hans Robert. *Aesthetic Experience and Literary Hermeneutics*. Minneapolis: University of Minnesota Press, 1982.

Mailloux, Steven. "Learning to Read: Interpretation and Reader-Response Criticism." *Studies in the Literary Imagination* 12 (1979): 93–108.

McGregor, Graham, and R. S. White, eds. *Reception and Response: Hearer Creativity and the Analysis of Spoken and Written Texts*. London: Routledge, 1990.

Miller, J. Hillis. *Theory Now and Then*. Hemel Hempstead: Harvester Wheatsheaf, 1991.

Rosenblatt, Louise M. *Literature as Exploration*. New York: Appleton-Century-Crofts, 1937.

————. "Towards a Transactional Theory of Reading." *Journal of Reading Behavior* 1 (1969): 31–47.

————. *The Reader, the Text, the Poem*. Carbondale: Southern Illinois University Press, 1978.

Suleiman, Susan, and Inge Crosman, eds. *The Reader in the Text: Essay on Audience and Interpretation*. Princeton, NJ: Princeton University Press, 1980.

Tompkins, Jane, ed. *Reader-Response Criticism: From Formalism to Post-Structuralism*. Baltimore: Johns Hopkins University Press, 1980.

WEB SITES FOR EXPLORATION

http://www.brocku.ca/english/courses/4F70/rr.html
> Provides a good overview of various reader-response positions

www.english.uiuc.edu/hawisher/405/jansen/paradigm.htm
> Provides a paradigm of reader-response criticism

www.scils.rutgers.edu/special/kay/readerresponse.html
> Provides a working definition and a detailed bibliography for reader-response criticism

www.divinity.lib.vanderbilt.edu/div/2504/reader.htm
> Provides a detailed bibliography for reader-response criticism

www.stthomasu.ca/hunt/litread.htm
> Provides an excellent reader-response bibliography

www.ualberta.ca/~dmiall/formalsm.htm
> Provides the text of David S. Miall and Don Kuiken's reader-response essay "Forms of Reading: Recovering the Self-as-Reader"

~ Student Essay ~

The Masks That Separate: A Paradox of Knowing in Glaspell's Trifles

My first reaction to Susan Glaspell's *Trifles* was a vague, unsettled feeling about the characters' relationships with each other. I also must confess wondering if Glaspell, like Edgar Allan Poe, had written merely for effect, since

I initially saw little more than sensationalism in her story. As I reflected on the play, however, I began to realize how central the concept of companionship was to its psychological impact. *Trifles* is not a mere trifle of a play, as I suspected at first, but is a serious warning for the reader to be generous with his or her compassion, for the consequences of selfishness are dire. Overall, *Trifles* taught me much about the human condition and the innate need within each of us to relate with other human beings.

One of the greatest paradoxes in human nature is the longing to know what is unknowable in each other. We hunger for closeness with others, yet the contents of another soul is ultimately a mystery to us. The characters in *Trifles* aptly portray this contradiction by hiding from each other behind masks of unconcern and separating themselves into social groups. The most marked divisions occur between the men and the women. These two groups are quick to stereotype each other ("women are used to worrying about trifles"; "men . . . snooping and criticizing"), but rarely do they honestly and openly communicate in the presence of the opposite sex. Even within the supposedly intimate relationship between husband and wife, estrangement seems to be the norm. Mrs. Peters, for example, hides evidence from her mate, and when the county attorney degrades her by commenting that she is "married to the law," Mr. Peters merely chuckles. Both refuse to treat each other with consideration and honesty.

On the other hand, Mrs. Peters is glad for the company of Mrs. Hale, for without her, the Wright house would seem lonesome. The open camaraderie between these two women contrasts sharply with their other relationships and accentuates the subtle combination of the known and the unknown in the play. Unquestionably, *Trifles* contains some of what Leonardo da Vinci named the "flux" of life—the underlying truth that connects living beings, yet separates us into individual mysteries at the same time. Da Vinci's *Mona Lisa* is a masterpiece precisely because her smile contains this essential unknowability of every person. My positive reaction to *Trifles* is due in part to the psychological impact of this paradox, which Glaspell develops through the relationships of her characters.

The extreme consequences of being completely unknown by another are frighteningly evident in Minnie's transformation. Once a lively town girl who wore pretty clothes and sang in the choir, Minnie has no "close friends" and feels shabby. Her thirty years with John Wright have drained the color from her life. The similarities between Minnie's alteration of character and that of Mattie in the novel *Ethan Frome* by Edith Wharton are strikingly similar. Starkfield is as cheerless a place as Mrs. Wright's kitchen, and the atmosphere is controlled in both cases by a hard, domineering character who entirely disregards the humanity of others and is motivated by self-interest alone. In both texts, silence becomes a weapon, and a bleak and frigid character chokes the spirit out of the optimistic lover of life. Minnie, like a caged bird, is spiritually imprisoned by John's coldness (he's "like a raw wind that gets to the bone"); similarly Mattie's exuberance and color have wasted away under Zeena's heartless and selfish pessimism. The fatal loss of beauty and verve that both women have experienced ominously demonstrates the crippling effect of an absence of communion. Apparently, the intimacy of friendship that we each long to experience is also necessary for vitality in life. If a person is without open and direct communication for a long enough period of time, frigid bitterness becomes characteristic of his or her existence, and bitterness leads to death.

At first, the human desire for sociability may seem like an insignificant need, but like Minnie's trifles in this play, it is the little things in life which are the most important. Mrs. Hale realizes how significant her presence could have been in Minnie's cheerless life, and feels guilty for not visiting her. She says, "I stayed away because it weren't cheerful—and that's why I ought to have come." Mrs. Hale glimpses the truth that the women must assume some of Minnie's guilt because they contributed to her deadening spirit by avoiding her. A small act of selflessness, such as the occasional visit Mrs. Hale wishes she had paid, could indeed have prevented the deformation of Minnie's soul. Mrs. Peters, however, quickly rationalizes away Mrs. Hale's sudden insight by soothing, "somehow we just don't see how it is with other folks until—until something comes up." Blame for sins of omission is difficult to concede.

In the end, Mrs. Hale's knowledge of her own responsibility to Minnie burst from her: "Oh I wish I'd come over here once in a while! That was a crime! That was a crime! Who's going to punish that?" If our failure to recognize and affirm the personhood of our fellow human beings is a criminal offense, how then should we live? If bitterness leads to death, and self-absorption leads to bitterness, then perhaps selfishness is the root of all evil, as C. S. Lewis would seem to claim when he writes, "The 'Great Sin' of pride in ourselves certainly has far-reaching effect." It also follows that the opposite of selfishness would be the root of all righteousness, and that the key to virtue in our world is self-sacrifice.

After she realizes the crime of her failure to help Minnie, Mrs. Hale laments: "We live close together and we live far apart. We all go through the same things—it's all just a different kind of the same thing." The one thing in life more necessary than to be understood is to understand other people. Humility toward our fellow human beings and empathy for their condition, which is simply another reflection of our own, is the truest method of righteousness. As the contemporary song writer Rich Mullins pens in his song "Brother's Keeper," "There's no point in pointing fingers unless you're pointing to the truth." *Trifles* startlingly depicts the dire consequences of a lack of such fellowship. The human need for honesty and selflessness is more than a trifle; without companionship, we wither physically, socially, spiritually, and psychologically. Susan Glaspell's play reminded me once again that empathy, not apathy, should be my attitude toward the human beings with whom I am privileged to spend each moment.

JEN RICHARDSON

❧ Professional Essay ❧

"Hamlet"—My Greatest Creation

You must think, that by my title, I have gone beyond even chutzpah to downright blasphemy. Chutzpah, that would be like the sign I used to pass on the old Yiddish theatre in New York when I was a boy. In big letters, *Hamlet*. In smaller letters, By William Shakespeare. And in the biggest letters of all, Translated and Improved by Moishe Schwartz. But I'm claiming I don't just improve *Hamlet*, I create it. And I fully expect Shakespeare to hurl down, from whatever Elysium he now inhabits, a sonnet shattering me into fourteen pieces where I stand.

Before he does that, I would like to explain what I mean. We used to say purely and simply that Shakespeare created the tragedy *Hamlet*. That is, he wrote down certain words which contained certain ideas, characters, themes, and even unconscious fantasies and defense mechanisms. That is what we mean when we say a text has a certain "content"—the text is a container. This is *Hamlet* as cocktail shaker into which Shakespeare has poured a lovely, cool, exhilarating, and slightly befuddling content.

But if Shakespeare put a certain content into the play, what content did he put in? If he created *Hamlet*, which *Hamlet* did he create? In the three and three-quarters centuries since the play was first produced, we have seen at least three very different versions of the hero and therefore of the play. So far as we can tell, the seventeenth and eighteenth centuries, closest to Shakespeare himself, thought of Hamlet as a young man of great expectation, promise, and vivacity, a Renaissance prince. The nineteenth century enjoyed Goethe's Hamlet, a willowy, delicate, poetic man incapable of committing the revenge his father demands. And, of course, in our own century we have had Hamlet with an oedipus complex. It isn't just that each century has had its own Hamlet the Prince and *Hamlet* the play. If you look at the volumes upon volumes of commentary on this tragedy, you will realize that, finally, each person has his own *Hamlet*. I find, also, that the *Hamlet* I am talking about today is different from the *Hamlet* I wrote about in, say, 1964 or 1966 or 1961. The play changes even for the same person over his lifetime. If *Hamlet* is a container, it is a magician's cocktail shaker from which one can pour at will martinis, daiquiris, Coca-Cola, and vanilla milk shakes. The idea of *Hamlet* as having a fixed content just won't do.

What then did Shakespeare create? When we use the word "create" in the sense of being creative, we mean at least two related, but different things. We mean that the creator creates some physical thing: he makes a movie, embodying it in so many yards of film; he composes a quartet which can be recorded on a paper or disc; he writes a play which can be acted or written down. At the same time we imply that he is able to involve other people in what he has created. When other people are given a chance to see his movie, or hear his quartet, or watch his play, they don't turn their backs—they participate in the aesthetic experience made possible by the artist's creation. Think for a moment about the phrase "failure of creativity." We can mean by it that someone simply stops producing. We can mean equally well that he continues to produce, but that it just doesn't click anymore—people don't take it. Somehow he's lost the knack. That knack is what Freud called the writer's "innermost secret." As he said, "The essential *ars poetica* lies in the technique of overcoming the feeling of repulsion in all of us which is undoubtedly connected with the barriers that rise between each single ego and the others."

At the Center (The Center for the Psychological Study of the Arts, State University of New York at Buffalo) where I work, we believe we have been able to get at that technique. We have built on Freud's writings on creativity, particularly jokes, on some of the concepts developed by the English object relations theorists, and on the identity theory of Heinz Lichtenstein. We have arrived at four quite detailed principles about the way people make experiences out of the raw material presented to them by, for example, a writer like Shakespeare. The general principle is, in the most exact terms, identity replicates itself. Or one could use the older psychoanalytic term, character: *character* creates itself. We use the term *identity*, however, because we define it quite exactly—as the invariant one can abstract from all the ego choices that make up the life of an individual.

Perception is one of those ego choices. Each of us, as we experience not only plays and movies and novels but all of reality, uses the materials that reality gives us within our own personal style of experiencing. Thus each of us creates our own *Hamlet* from the words that Shakespeare gives us. We used to ask, "What in the text accounts for its success with readers?" Or, more precisely, "what in the text accounts for its reader's successful responses?" But we now know that that puts the question the wrong way round. What we really need to ask is, "What in the reader's responses accounts for the success of the text?" In other words, *Hamlet* is not just the words-on-the-page, but, rather, a combination of things in the play with our own ways of assimilating reality. To understand *Hamlet*, we need to begin by understanding our own reactions to the play.

Hamlet is a huge play, Shakespeare's longest. An uncut performance takes from five to six hours. To tell you my reactions to all of it would take weeks, but I can tell you about my five favorite lines from the thirty-nine hundred or so that make up the tragedy as a whole. They are:

O, what a rogue and peasant slave am I! (2.2.550)

What's Hecuba to him, or he to Hecuba,
That he should weep for her? (2.2.559–60)

How all occasions do inform against me
And spur my dull revenge! (4.4.32–33)

What do these lines permit me to do which is so satisfying?

To answer that question, I have to talk not just about the lines, but about me. Let me tell you a few things about myself, things, by the way, that I said in print before I ever became involved with trying to explain my pleasure at these five lines from *Hamlet*. I have "a passionate desire to know about the insides of things with an equally strong feeling that one is, finally, safer on the outside." The core of my identity involves "preserving a sense of self and securing self-esteem by gaining power over relations between things, in particular, mastering them by knowing or seeing them from outside rather than being actually in the relationships." You can see how being a critic of films and drama has fitted my identity particularly in the modern mode of formal, linguistic analysis. "I *like* examining the verbal surface of a text, looking particularly for an 'organic unity' in the way the parts all come together."

Now, when I turn back to those five favorite lines, I am puzzled to notice that each of them lacks, rather than has, the tight kind of organic unity I prize. Each of them has a little something unnecessary in it, a kind of padding, if you will. "O, what a rogue and peasant slave am I!" Why not, "O, what a rogue am I!" or, "O, what a peasant slave am I"? It could just as well be, "What's Hecuba to him that he should weep for her?" Or, "What's he to Hecuba that he should weep for her?" But Shakespeare does it both ways. When I read, "How all occasions do inform against me and spur my dull revenge!" the second phrase seems superfluous. It dangles at the end of the sentence which could just as well be simply, "How all occasions do inform against me." Or, "How all occasions spur my dull revenge!" But Shakespeare gives us both.

Interestingly, it is just this quality in Shakespeare's writing which his friend, Ben Jonson, singled out as his principal fault.

> I remember . . . the players have often mentioned it as an honor to Shakespeare, that in his writing, whatsoever he penned, he never blotted out a line. My answer hath been, "Would he had blotted a thousand!" Which they thought a malevolent speech. I had not told posterity this, but for their ignorance, who choose that circumstance to commend their friend by, where in he most faulted. . . . He flowed with that facility, that sometime it was necessary he should be stopped. . . . Many times he fell into those things, could not escape laughter.

It's amusing that Jonson of all people should complain of this quality in Shakespeare's writing, for Jonson is perhaps the finest example in our literature of an obsessional writer, a man excessively careful about what he would let flow out onto the paper. Another identity creating his own Shakespeare.

Shakespeare was just the opposite of Jonson. Often, he seems to have in excess that quality the Renaissance called *copia* (copy), a fullness of expression. But he does not simply pad his lines. Rather, the extra words permit subtleties and complexities. Consider the single line, "O, what a rogue and peasant slave am I!" "Rogue" could be a noun, but it could also be an adjective modifying "slave," as "peasant" seems to be. A rogue slave. A peasant slave. By the same token "peasant" could also be either an adjective modifying "slave" or a noun, thereby making "slave" the final noun in a series of three, the final and most terrible of the three. "O, what a rogue and peasant—slave! —am I." Because of the extra phrase, I find myself preconsciously following out alternative possibilities and structures within the line.

Thus, for example, first I imagine the player looking toward Hecuba. I see the queen through his eyes but then on the phrase, "or he to Hecuba," I find myself looking the other way from Hecuba to the player. And then the two possibilities are resolved in the final clause, "that he should weep for her."

The third line introduces two complicated and somewhat inconsistent images. At first it seems as though occasions inform against Hamlet like spies reporting to some superior—his father perhaps. Then the second clause suggests his revenge is like a dull horse that has to be spurred to get into action. One of the images has to do with words or information; the other treats a word, "revenge," as though it were something concrete.

I find that my favorite lines make it possible for me to create and explore several grammatical and semantic possibilities within a single thought. They are, in effect, the opposite of denial. They suggest and even ask me to follow out all kinds of complexities and alternate possibilities. So, even if Shakespeare's individual lines do not let me find the tight, organic unity I seek, they do let me master the insides, as it were, of the sentence by understanding verbal and imagistic complexities. I can stand outside the sentence, so to speak, and explore relations within it.

Further, these alternatives take a recurring form or shape. Consider the line "O, what a rogue and peasant slave am I!" It begins with the long vowel O and ends with the long vowel I. The complexities are all in between, as the words "and peasant" bounce off grammatical structure against rhythmical pattern. The same thing happens in the second passage. The sentence begins with the regular foot, "What's Hec-" and then goes into the complexities both in grammar and in sound associated with Hecuba, coming out in the absolutely regular third clause, "That he should weep for her." Just like "And spur my dull revenge!" That sentence, too, begins with the open and regular, "How all" and then becomes involved in the complexities of rhythm and meaning in "occasions" and "inform against."

In short, these sentences begin with a simplicity, move into something full of alternatives and complexities, and come around to a simplicity again. This is, of course, the pattern of the tragedy as a whole. On seeing the ghost, Hamlet resolves purely and simply to set the times right. As you know, we then go into three long and involved acts in which he does anything but. He does not return to his task of revenge until the final scene of the play when he accepts his destiny. "If it be now, 'tis not to come; if it be not to come, it will be now; if it be not now, yet it will come. The readiness is all."

There's a divinity that shapes our end,
Rough-hew them how we will.

Could I not say then that I find in each of these lines the combination of risk-ing and security I enjoy in the tragedy as a whole? They make it possible for me to explore alternatives, but, finally, from their regularity and completion and endstops, I can make a mastery of those alternatives. There is, if not a divinity that shapes their ends, at least a sense for me of regularity and order.

My five favorite lines suggest still another source of my pleasure. All three of these sentences take an external event and make it reflect upon the speaker or, in the Hecuba line, the player whom Hamlet later in this soliloquy will in turn refer to himself. Each one of these sentences creates a situation in which events in the external world acquire their meaning by providing an occasion for an essentially separate and observing Hamlet to reflect upon himself. This is just what Shakespearean plays do for critics like me. But Hamlet does not simply ingest experience. He makes it refer to himself and then from it he cre-ates words, the magnificent speeches that we all admire. Here, too, these three sentences exemplify a pattern that runs all through the play. The very first time we see Hamlet, he appears at Claudius's court in his suit of inky black and watches the goings on, scarcely speaking to Claudius at all, replying to his mother only to point to "that within which passes show." Then, when the rest have left the stage, he lets it all out in the magnificent soliloquy, "O, that this too too sullied flesh would melt." Throughout the play he does the same: after the ghost speaks to him, after Rosencrantz and Guildenstern try to get infor-mation out of him, after he watches the players, after he watches the play within the play, after he sees Fortinbras's army. An event outside him becomes focused on him, and then he turns it into words. Sometimes he gives these words in soliloquy, sometimes he speaks fully to Horatio or his mother. But in all cases the pattern is the same: the whole of external reality, love, statecraft, life and death, heaven and hell, all seemed focused upon Hamlet, and from them all fashions not revenge, but words.

The greatest of *Hamlet* is not the plot alone, nor the character, but the way the thousands, or tens of thousands, of details make it possible for me to explore possibilities and yet master them, to escape reality and yet, in a way, master it, too, by turning it into words.

Notice, too, that all three of these favorite sentences are attacks on a person, two on Hamlet himself, one on his surrogate, the actor. They denigrate—I am a rogue and peasant slave. Or they dehumanize—my revenge is a horse; occa-sions are spies, Hecuba is something to him—what? Yet this killing anger of Hamlet's is turned inward from its real object—his parents. It feels to me as though Hamlet can tolerate his anger toward them better than their anger toward him. They angry at me? No, it is I who am angry at them. Have they left something undone? No, it is I who have left something undone. In effect, by what he does say, Hamlet tells me what he cannot say. My parents are angry at me. My parents are indifferent to me. They value me as a word or a thing.

Thus, Hamlet uses words to build up substitutes for a world of person-al relations, particularly the relations among parents and children, and still more particularly between fathers and sons. It is as though, if there were that personal relation, if there were no words, parents would be violent toward their children or would neglect them. Is this a glimpse at the source of Shakespeare's creativity—a young boy able to substitute words for what he could not tolerate in his relation toward his parents, their violence toward him or their indifference? Perhaps. Perhaps a violence and indifference he imagined as he heard them at night in that doorless bedroom.

At any rate, if words substitute for parental violence or indifference toward a child, then at those points in the play where words are suppressed, violence and parental self-preoccupation should come through. The Ghost's refusing to speak to Horatio and Marcellus, is an example of such an occasion. They "offer it the show of violence." The ghost refuses to tell Hamlet about its purgatory: "I could a tale unfold whose lightest word/ Would harrow up thy soul, freeze thy young blood,/ Make thy two eyes like stars start from their spheres." (Act I, Scene V). And somehow the very silence is worse than what could be told. When Hamlet swears his comrades to silence, the ghost menaces them from beneath the stage. When Polonius forbids Ophelia to "give words or talk with the Lord Hamlet," he is using her for his own advancement. Hamlet's breaking off his "To be or not to be" soliloquy ("Soft you now,/ The fair Ophelia") leads to his brutal rejection of her. Claudius's prayers lead only to an indifferent heaven. When Hamlet swears his mother to silence, she asks, "What shall I do?" and he replies in these words:

Not this, by no means, that I bid you do:
Let the bloat King tempt you again to bed,
Pinch wanton on your cheek, call you his mouse,
And let him, for a pair of reechy kisses,
Or paddling in your neck with his damned fingers,
Make you to ravel all this matter out . . .
(33.181–86)

Is this the violence and indifference that Hamlet and Shakespeare and I share a fear of—the parents loving each other and not me? Certainly it is the first thing Hamlet complains on in his first soliloquy:

That it should come to this:
But two months dead, nay, not so much, not two.
So excellent a king, that was to this
Hyperion to a satyr . . .

—that is, a sun god beaming down perhaps on his "son," as against a creature of lust and lechery.

Hyperion to a satyr, so loving to my mother
That he might not beteem the winds of heaven
Visit her face too roughly. (1.2.137–42)

Why, she would hang on him

> As if increase of appetite had grown
> By what it fed on; and yet within a month—
> Let me not think on't; frailty, thy name is woman—
> A little month, or ere those shoes were old
> With which she followed my poor father's body . . .

—and those shoes I find suggestive—she married.

> Oh, most wicked, speed to post
> With such dexterity to incestuous sheets!

Not in the wind and sunlight now, but in bed. And then Hamlet ends,

> But break my heart, for I must hold my tongue.
>
> (1.2.143–59)

It is as though, when one cannot speak, one is left only the alternatives of an inner sickness, an "imposthume" "That inward breaks and shows no cause without/ Why the man dies," or else the explosion into action which ends the play.

Words in this tragedy are, for me certainly and perhaps also for Hamlet and Shakespeare, a kind of potential space in which I can create alternatives and possibilities instead of being faced with violent action or parental indifference. We have sampled but five, yet there are nearly four thousand lines, each one of which, to some degree, allows me to use words to work out alternatives and so control my very deep fears. I fear that parents or parent-figures will be angry at me—I would rather be angry at them. I fear that they will ignore me—I would rather ignore them. Although I enjoy risking these possibilities, I want, finally, to have them controlled as easily as one can control words. All it takes is a line of verse or a phrase as regular in scansion as "That he should weep for her" or "And spur my dull revenge."

Hamlet has been described as a "great neurotic," a term whose meaning I'm not sure of. I am sure, however, that Hamlet allows me a great counter-transference. And that is the secret of the greatness of this tragedy and, finally, of all great works of art: they permit us to become creators ourselves.

Essay by Norman Holland. "*Hamlet*—My Greatest Creation." *Journal of the American Academy of Psychoanalysis* 3 (1975): 419–27.

5

Structuralism

INTRODUCTION

Having narrowed her list of job candidates to two, the personnel director of a large computer company instructed her secretary to invite each applicant for a job interview. Both candidates seemed equally qualified for the position. Applicant A had graduated from an Ivy League university, earning a B.S. in accounting and business, while applicant B, also a graduate of an Ivy League institution, earned a B.S. in business administration. Each had received outstanding references from his professors and business mentors. And each scored in the 95th percentile on the Graduate Record Examination. The personnel director's choice, no doubt, would be difficult.

On the day of the interview, applicant A arrived wearing a gray suit, a white cotton shirt, a subdued but somewhat bright yellow tie, a pair of highly polished black Oxfords, and an appropriate smile and short haircut. Applicant B arrived a few minutes after applicant A's interview had begun. Wearing a green, fatigue shirt, a pair of stonewashed jeans, and a pair of black suede Birkenstocks, candidate B brushed back his long hair and wondered why the first applicant's interview was lasting more than an hour. After another 15 minutes had passed, applicant A finally exited through the main doors, and the secretary ushered applicant B into the director's office. Eighteen minutes later applicant B passed by the secretary's desk and left the building, his interview apparently over.

Shortly thereafter, the personnel director buzzed for her secretary to come to her office. Upon his entering, the director responded, "Please send applicant A the contract. He will represent our business well. Also, mail applicant B an 'I'm sorry, but . . .' letter. Evidently he doesn't understand our image, our values, and our standards. Jeans, no tie, and long hair, in this office and for this company! Never!"

Applicant A's ability to grasp what his future employer valued earned him his job. Through the language of fashion (**language** being used in a broad sense to convey a system of codes or signs that convey meaning), applicant A demonstrated to the personnel director his understanding of the company's image and its concern for dress and physical appearance. Applicant B, however, silently signaled his lack of understanding of the company's values and public image through his tieless and seemingly inappropriate attire. Whereas applicant B failed to master those fashion codes that represented his understanding of the company's standards, applicant A demonstrated his command of the language of fashion and his potential to learn similar intricate systems or languages used in such areas as economics, education, the sciences, and social life in general. Through his mastery of these codes and his ability (either consciously or unconsciously) to analyze and use them correctly in a given situation, applicant A demonstrated his knowledge of structuralism.

Flourishing in the 1960s, **structuralism** is an approach to literary analysis grounded in **structural linguistics**, the science of language. By using the techniques, methodologies, and vocabulary of linguistics, structuralism offers a scientific view of how we achieve meaning not only in literary works but also in all forms of communication and social behavior.

To understand structuralism, we must trace its historical roots to the linguistic writings and theories of Ferdinand de Saussure, a Swiss professor and linguist of the late nineteenth and and early twentieth century. His scientific investigations of language and language theory provide the basis for structuralism's unique approach to literary analysis.

HISTORICAL DEVELOPMENT

Pre-Saussurean Linguistics

Throughout the nineteenth and early twentieth centuries, **philology**, not linguistics, was the science of language. Its practitioners, **philologists**, described, compared, and analyzed the languages of the world to discover similarities and relationships. Their approach to language study was **diachronic**; that is, they traced language change throughout long expanses of time, discovering how a particular phenomenon such as a word or sound in one language had changed **etymologically** or **phonologically** throughout several centuries, and whether a similar change could be noted in other languages. Using cause-and-effect relationships as the basis for their research, the philologists' main emphasis was the historical development of languages.

Such an emphasis reflected the nineteenth-century philologists' theoretical assumptions of the nature of language. Language, they believed, mirrored the structure of the world it imitated and therefore had no structure of its own. Known as the **mimetic** theory of language, this hypothesis asserts that words (either spoken or written) are symbols for things in the world, each word having its own **referent**—the object, concept, or idea that represents or symbolizes that word. According to this theory, the symbol (a word) equals a thing: Symbol (word) = Thing.

Saussure's Linguistic Revolution

In the first decade of the 1900s, a Swiss philologist and teacher, Ferdinand de Saussure (1857–1913), began questioning these long-held ideas and, by so doing, triggered a reformation in language study. Through his research and innovative theories, Saussure changed the direction and subject matter of linguistic studies. His *Course in General Linguistics*, a compilation of his 1906–1911 lecture notes published posthumously by his students, is one of the seminal works of modern linguistics and forms the basis for structuralist literary theory and practical criticism. Through the efforts of this father of modern linguistics, nineteenth-century philology evolved into the more multifaceted science of twentieth-century linguistics.

Saussure began his linguistic revolution by affirming the validity and necessity of the diachronic approach to language study used by such nineteenth-century philologists as the Grimm brothers and Karl Verner. Using this diachronic approach, these linguists discovered the principles governing consonantal pronunciation changes that occurred in Indo-European languages (the language group to which English belongs) over many centuries. Without abandoning a diachronic examination of language, Saussure introduced the **synchronic** approach, which focuses attention on studying a language at one particular time—a single moment—and emphasizes how the whole state of a particular language functions, rather than tracing the historical development of a single element, as would a diachronic analysis. By highlighting the activity of a whole language system and how it operates rather than its evolution, Saussure drew attention to the nature and composition of language and its constituent parts. For example, along with examining the phonological antecedents of the English sound *b*, as in the word *boy* (a diachronic analysis), Saussure opened a new avenue of investigation, asking how the *b* sound is related to other sounds in use at the same time by speakers of Modern English (a synchronic analysis). This new concern necessitated a rethinking of language theory and a re-evaluation of the aims of language research, and finally resulted in Saussure's articulating the basic principles of modern linguistics.

Unlike many of his contemporary linguists, Saussure rejected the mimetic theory of language structure. In its place, he asserted that language is determined primarily by its own internally structured and highly systematized rules. These rules govern all aspects of a language, including the sounds its speakers identify as meaningful, various combinations of these sounds into words, and how these words may be arranged to produce meaningful communication within a given language.

Structure of Language

According to Saussure, all languages are governed by their own internal rules, which do not mirror or imitate the structure of the world. The basic building block of language is the **phoneme**—the smallest meaningful (significant) sound in a language. The number of phonemes differs from language to language, with the least number of total phonemes for any one language being in the mid-teens, and the most in the mid-sixties. American English, for example, consists of approximately 43–45 phonemes, depending on the dialect being spoken. Although native speakers of American English are capable of producing phonemes found in other languages, it is these 45 distinct sounds that serve as the building blocks for their language. For example, the first sound heard in the word *pin* is the /p/ phoneme, the second /I/, and the last /n/. A phoneme can be identified in writing by enclosing the **grapheme**—the written symbol that represents the phoneme's sound— in virgules, or diagonal lines.

Although each phoneme makes a distinct sound that is meaningful and recognizable to speakers of a particular language, in actuality a phoneme is composed of a family of nearly identical speech sounds called **allophones**. For instance, in the word *pit*, the first phoneme is /p/, and in the word *spin*, the second phoneme is also /p/. Although the /p/ appears in both words, its pronunciation is slightly different. To validate this statement, simply hold the palm of your hand about two inches from your mouth and pronounce the word *pit* followed immediately by the word *spin*. You will quickly note the difference. These slightly different pronunciations of the same phoneme are simply two different allophones of the phoneme /p/.

How phonemes and allophones arrange themselves to produce meaningful speech in any language is not arbitrary, but is governed by a prescribed set of rules developed through time by the speakers of a language. For example, in Modern American English (1755–present), no English word can end with the two phonemes /m/ and /b/. In Middle English (1100–1500), these phonemes could combine to form the two terminal sounds of a word, resulting, for example, in the word *lamb*, where the /m/ and /b/ were both pronounced. Over time, the rules of spoken English have so changed that when *lamb* appears in Modern English, /b/ has no phonemic value. The study of these rules governing the meaningful units of sound in a linguistic system is called **phonology**, whereas the study of the production of these sounds is **phonetics**.

In addition to phonemes, another major building block of language is the **morpheme**—the smallest part of a word that has lexical or grammatical significance (**lexical** referring to the base or root meaning of a word and **grammatical** serving to express relationships between words or groups of words, such as the **inflections** {-ed}, {-s}, and {-ing}). Like the phoneme, the number of lexical and grammatical morphemes varies from language to language. In American English, lexical morphemes far outnumber grammatical morphemes (10 or so). For instance, in the word *reaper*, {reap} is a lexical morpheme, meaning "to ripple flax" and {-er} is a grammatical morpheme, meaning "one who." (Note that in print morphemes are placed in braces.) All words must have a lexical morpheme (hence their great number), whereas not every word need have a grammatical morpheme. How the various lexical and grammatical morphemes combine to form words is highly rule governed and is known in modern linguistics as the study of **morphology.**

Another major building block in the structure of language is the actual arrangement of words in a sentence or **syntax**. Just as the placement of phonemes and morphemes in individual words is a rule-governed activity, so is the arrangement of words in a sentence. For example, although native speakers of English would understand the sentence "John threw the ball into the air," such speakers would have difficulty ascertaining the meaning of "Threw the air into the ball John." Why? Native speakers of a language have mastered which strings of morphemes are permitted by syntactic rules and which are not. Those that do not conform to these rules do not form English sentences and are called **ungrammatical**. Those that do conform to the established syntactic structures are called **sentences** or **grammatical sentences**. In most English sentences, for example, the subject ("John") precedes the verb ("threw"), followed by the complement ("the ball into the air"). Although this structure can at times be modified, such changes must follow tightly prescribed rules of syntax if a speaker of English is to be understood.

Having established the basic building blocks of a sentence—phonemes, morphemes, and syntax—language provides us with one additional body of rules to govern the various interpretations or shades of meaning such combinations of words can evoke: **semantics**. Unlike morphemes, whose meanings can be found in the dictionary or word stock of a language—its **lexicon**—the **semantic features** or properties of words are not so easily defined. Consider, for example the following sentences:

"Charles is a nut."
"I found a letter on Willard Avenue."
"Get a grip, Heidi."

In order to understand each of these sentences, a speaker or reader needs to understand the semantic features that govern an English sentence, for each of the above sentences has several possible interpretations. In the first sentence, the speaker must grasp the concept of metaphor, in the second, lexical ambiguity, and in the third, idiomatic structures. Unless these semantic features are consciously or unconsciously understood by the reader or listener, problems of interpretation may arise. Like the other building blocks of language, an understanding of semantics is necessary for clear communication in any language.

Langue and Parole

By age five or six, native speakers of English or any other language have consciously and unconsciously mastered their language's complex system of rules or its **grammar**—their language's phonology, morphology, syntax, and semantics—which enables them to participate in language communication. They have not, however, mastered such advanced elements as all the semantic features of their language, nor have they mastered its **prescriptive grammar**, the rules of English grammar often invented by eighteenth- and nineteenth-century purists who believed that there were certain constructions that all educated people should know, such as using the nominative form of a pronoun after an intransitive linking verb, as in the sentence, "It is *I.*" But what these five- or six-year-old native speakers of a language have learned Saussure calls **langue**, the structure of the language that is mastered and shared by all its speakers.

Whereas langue emphasizes the social aspect of language and an understanding of the overall language system, an individual's actual speech utterances and writing Saussure calls **parole**. A speaker can generate countless examples of individual utterances, but these are all governed by the language's system, its langue. It is the task of the linguist, Saussure believes, to infer a language's langue from the analysis of many instances of parole. In other words, for Saussure, the proper study of linguistics is the system (langue), not the individual utterances of its speakers (parole).

Saussure's Redefinition of a **Word**

Having established that languages are systems that operate according to verifiable rules and that they must be investigated both diachronically and synchronically, Saussure then re-examined philology's definition of a *word*. Rejecting the long-held belief that a word is a symbol that equals a thing (its referent), Saussure proposed that words are **signs** made up of two parts: the **signifier** (a written or spoken mark) and a **signified** (a concept): sign = signifier / signified.

For example, when we hear the sound *ball*, the sound is the signifier and the concept of a ball that comes to our minds is the signified. Like the two sides of a sheet of paper, the linguistic sign is the union of these two elements. As oxygen combines with hydrogen to form water, Saussure says, so the signifier joins with the signified to form a sign that has properties unlike those of its parts. Accordingly, for Saussure a word does not represent a referent in the objective world, but a sign. Unlike previous generations of philologists who believed that we perceive things (word = thing) and then translate them into units or meaning, Saussure revolutionizes linguistics by asserting that we perceive signs.

Furthermore, the linguistic sign, declares Saussure, is arbitrary: the relationship between the signifier (*ball*) and the signified (the concept of *ball*) is a matter of convention. The speakers of a language have simply agreed that the written or spoken sounds or marks represented by *ball* equal the concept *ball*. With few exceptions, proclaims Saussure, there is no natural link between the signifier and the signified, nor is there any natural relationship between the linguistic sign and what it represents.

If, as Saussure maintains, there is no natural link between the linguistic sign and the reality it represents, how do we know the difference between one sign and another? In other words, how does language create meaning? We know what a sign means, says Saussure, because it differs from all other signs. By comparing and contrasting one sign with other signs, we learn to distinguish each individual sign. Individual signs, then, can have meaning (or signify) only within their own langue.

For Saussure, meaning is therefore relational and a matter of difference. Within the system of sound markers that make up our language, we know *ball*, for instance, because we differentiate it from *hall*, *tail*, and *pipe*. Likewise, we know the concept *bug* because it differs from the concepts *truck*, *grass*, and *kite*. As Saussure declares, "In language there are only differences."

Because signs are arbitrary, conventional, and differential, Saussure concludes that the proper study of language is not an examination of isolated entities but the system of relationships among them. He asserts, for example, that individual words cannot have meaning by themselves. Because language is a system of rules governing sounds, words, and other components, individual words obtain their meaning only within that system. To know language and how it functions, he declares, we must study the system (langue), not individual utterances (parole) that operate according to the rules of langue.

For Saussure, language is the primary sign system whereby we structure our world. Language's structure, he believes, is like that of any other sign system of social behavior, such as fashion, table manners, and sports. Like language, all such expressions of social behavior generate meaning through a system of signs. Saussure proposed a new science called **semiology** that would study how we create meaning through these signs in all our social behavioral systems. Because language was the chief and most characteristic of all these systems, Saussure declared, it was to be the main branch of semiology. The investigation of all other sign systems would be patterned after that of language, for like language's signs, the meaning of all signs was arbitrary, conventional, and differential.

Although semiology never became an important new science as Saussure envisioned, a similar science was being proposed in America almost simultaneously by philosopher and teacher Charles Sanders Peirce. Called **semiotics**, this science borrowed linguistic methods used by Saussure and applied them to all meaningful cultural phenomena. Meaning in society, this science of signs declares, can be studied systematically, in terms of both how this meaning occurs and the structures that allow it to operate. Distinguishing among the various kinds of signs, semiotics as a field of study continues to develop today. Because it uses structuralist methods borrowed from Saussure, the terms *semiotics* and *structuralism* are often used interchangeably, although the former denotes a particular field of study whereas the latter is more an approach and method of analysis.

Assumptions

Borrowing linguistic vocabulary, theory, and methods from Saussure and to a smaller degree from Peirce, structuralists—their studies being variously called structuralism, semiotics, stylistics, and narratology, to name a few—believe that codes, signs, and rules govern all human social and cultural practices, including communication. Whether that communication is the language of fashion, sports, education, friendships, or literature, each is a systematized combination of codes (signs) governed by rules. Structuralists want to discover these codes which they believe give meaning to all our social and cultural customs and behavior. The proper study of meaning and therefore reality, they assert, is an investigation of the system behind these practices, not the individual practices themselves. To discover how all the parts fit together and function is their aim.

Structuralists find meaning, then, in the relationship among the various components of a system. When applied to literature, this principle becomes revolutionary. The proper study of literature, for the structuralists, involves an inquiry into the conditions surrounding the act of interpretation itself (how literature conveys meaning), not an in-depth investigation of an individual work. Because an individual work can express only the values and beliefs of the system of which it is a part, structuralists emphasize the system (langue) whereby texts relate to each other, not an examination of an isolated text (parole). They believe that a study of the system of rules that govern literary interpretation becomes the critic's primary task.

Such a belief presupposes that the structure of literature is similar to the structure of language. Like language, so say the structuralists, literature is a self-enclosed system of rules that is composed of language. And also like language, literature needs no outside referent but its own rule-governed but socially constrained system. Before structuralism, literary theorists discussed the literary conventions—that is, the various genres or types of literature such as the novel, the short story, or poetry. Each genre, it was believed, had its own conventions or acknowledged and acceptable way of reflecting and interpreting life. For example, in poetry a poet could write in nonsentences, using symbols and other forms of figurative language to state a theme or to make a point. For these prestructuralist theorists, the proper study of literature was an examination of these conventions and of how individual texts used these conventions to make meaning or how readers used these conventions to interpret the text. Structuralists, however, seek out the system of codes that they believe convey a text's meaning. For them, how a text convenes meaning rather than what meaning is conveyed is at the center of their interpretative methodology; for example, how a symbol or a metaphor imparts meaning is now of special interest. For instance, in Nathaniel Hawthorne's "Young Goodman Brown," most readers assume that the darkness of the forest equates with evil and images of light represent safety. Of particular interest to the structuralist is how (not that) darkness comes to represent evil. A structuralist would ask why darkness more often than not represents evil in any text and what sign system or code is operating that allows readers to interpret darkness as evil intertextually or in all or most texts they read. For the structuralist, how a symbol or any other literary device functions becomes of chief importance, not how literary devices imitate reality or express feelings.

In addition to emphasizing the system of literature and not individual texts, structuralism claims to demystify literature. By explaining literature as a system of signs encased in a cultural frame that allows that system to operate, no longer, says structuralism, can a literary work be considered a mystical or magical relationship between the author and the reader, the place where author and reader share emotions, ideas, and truth. A scientific and an objective analysis of how readers interpret texts, not a transcendental or intuitive response to any one text, leads to meaning. Similarly, an author's intentions can no longer be equated to the text's overall meaning, for meaning is determined by the system that governs the writer, not an individual author's own quirks. And no longer can the text be autonomous, an object whose meaning is contained solely within itself. All texts, declare structuralists, are part of the shared system of meaning that is intertextual, not text specific; that is, all texts refer readers to other texts. Meaning can therefore be expressed only through this shared system of relations, not in an author's stated intentions or the reader's private or public experiences.

Declaring both isolated text and author to be of little importance, structuralism attempts to strip literature of its magical powers or so-called hidden meanings that can be discovered only by a small, elite group of highly trained specialists. Meaning can be found by analyzing the system of rules that make up literature itself.

METHODOLOGIES

Like all other approaches to textual analysis, structuralism follows neither one methodological strategy nor one set of ideological assumptions. Although most structuralists use many of Saussure's ideas in formulating their theoretical assumptions and foundations for their literary theories, how these assumptions are applied to textual analysis varies greatly. A brief examination of five structuralists or subgroups will help highlight structuralism's varied approaches to textual analysis.

Claude Lévi-Strauss

One of the first scholar/researchers to implement Saussure's principles of linguistics to narrative discourse in the 1950s and 1960s was anthropologist Claude Lévi-Strauss. Attracted to the rich symbols in myths, Lévi-Strauss spent years studying many of the world's myths. Myth, he assumed, possessed a structure like language. Each individual myth was therefore an example of parole. What he wanted to discover was myth's langue, or its overall structure that allows individual examples (parole) to function and have meaning.

After reading countless myths, Lévi-Strauss identified recurrent themes running through all of them. Such themes transcended culture and time, speaking directly to the minds and hearts of all people. These basic structures, which he called **mythemes,** were similar to the primary building blocks of language, the phonemes. Like phonemes, these mythemes find meaning in and through their relationships within the mythic structure. And as with phonemes, such relationships often involve oppositions. For example, the /b/ and /p/ phonemes are similar in that they are pronounced by using the lips to suddenly stop a stream of air. They differ or "oppose" one another in only one aspect: whether the air passing through the wind pipe does or does not vibrate the vocal cords (vibrating vocal cords produce /b/, nonvibrating cords produce /p/ during actual speech). Similarly, a mytheme finds its meaning through opposition. Hating or loving one's parents, falling in love with someone who does or who does not love you, and cherishing or abandoning one's children all exemplify the dual or opposing nature of mythemes. The rules that govern how these mythemes may be combined constitute myth's structure or grammar. The meaning of any individual myth, then, depends on the interaction and order of the mythemes within the story. Out of this structural pattern comes the myth's meaning.

When applied to a specific literary work, the intertextuality of myth becomes evident. For example, in Shakespeare's *King Lear*, King Lear overestimates the value and support of children when he trusts Regan and Goneril, his two oldest daughters, to take care of him in his old age. He also underestimates the value and support of children when he banishes his youngest and most-loved daughter, Cordelia. Like the binary opposition that occurs between the /b/ and /p/ phonemes, the binary opposition of underestimating versus overestimating love automatically occurs when reading the text, for such mythemes have occurred in countless other texts and immediately ignite emotions within the reader.

As we unconsciously master our language's langue, we also master myth's structure. Our ability to grasp this structure, says Lévi-Strauss, is innate. Like language, myths are simply another way we classify and organize our world.

Roland Barthes

Researching and writing in response to Lévi-Strauss was his contemporary, eminent French structuralist Roland Barthes. His contribution to structuralist theory is best summed up in the title of his most famous text, *S/Z*. In Balzac's *Sarrasine*, Barthes noted that the first s is pronounced as the s in snake, and the second as the z in zoo. Both phonemes, /s/ and /z/, are a minimal pair—that is, both are produced by the same articulatory organs and in the same place in the mouth, the difference being that /s/ is **unvoiced** (no vibration of vocal cords) and /z/ is **voiced** (vibration of vocal cords when air is blowing through the breath channel). Like all minimal pairs—/p/and /b/, /t/ and /d/, and /k/ and /g/, for example—this pair operates in what Barthes calls binary opposition. Even within a phoneme, binary opposition exists, for a phoneme is, as Saussure reminded us, a class of nearly identical sounds called allophones that differ **phonetically**—that is, by slightly changing the pronunciation but not altering the recognizable phoneme. Borrowing and further developing Saussure's work, Barthes then declares that all language is its own self-enclosed system based on binary operations.

Barthes then applies his assumption that meaning develops through difference to all social contexts, including fashions, familial relations, dining, and literature, to name a few. When applied to literature, an individual text is simply a message—a parole—that must be interpreted by using the appropriate codes or signs or binary operations that form the basis of the entire system, the langue. Only through recognizing the codes or binary operations within the text, says Barthes, can we explain the message encoded within the text. For example, in Nathaniel Hawthorne's "Young Goodman Brown" most readers intuitively know that Young Goodman Brown will come face to face with evil when he enters the forest. Why? Because one code or binary operation that we all know is that light implies good and dark evil. Thus, Brown enters the "dark" forest and leaves the "light" of his home, only to find the false "light" of evil emanating from the artificial light—the fires that light the baptismal service of those being inducted into Satan's legions. By finding other binary oppositions within the text and showing how these oppositions interrelate, the structuralist can then decode the text, thereby explaining its meaning.

Such a process dismisses the importance of the author, any historical or literary period, or particular textual elements or genres. Rather than discovering any element of truth within a text, this methodology shows the process of decoding a text in relationship to the codes provided by the structure of language itself.

Vladimir Propp

Expanding Lévi-Strauss's linguistic model of myths, a group of structuralists called **narratologists** began another kind of structuralism: **structuralist narratology,** the science of narrative. Like Saussure and Lévi-Strauss, these structuralists illustrate how a story's meaning develops from its overall structure, its langue, rather than each individual story's isolated theme. Using this idea as his starting point, Russian linguist Vladimir Propp investigated Russian fairy tales to decode their langue. According to his analysis, which appears in his work *The Morphology of the Folktale* (1968), all folk or fairy tales are based on 31 fixed elements, or what Propp calls "functions," which occur in a given sequence. Each function identifies predictable patterns or functions that central characters, such as the hero, the villain, or the helper, will enact to further the plot of the story. Any story may use any number of these elements, such as "accepting the call to adventure," "recognizing the hero," and "punishing the villain," but each element occurs in its logical and proper sequence.

Applying Propp's narratological principles to specific literary works is both fun and easy. For example, in Twain's *Adventures of Huckleberry Finn*, Huck, the protagonist or hero, is given a task to do: free Jim. His evil enemy or villain, society, tries to stop him. But throughout the novel various helpers appear to propel the plot forward, until the hero's task is complete, and he frees Jim and flees from his enemy.

Tzvetan Tordorov and Gerard Genette

Another narratologist, Bulgarian Tzvetan Todorov, declares that all stories are composed of grammatical units. For Todorov, the syntax of narrative or how the various grammatical elements of a story combine is essential. By applying a rather intricate grammatical model to narrative—dividing the text into semantic, syntactic, and verbal aspects—Todorov believes he can discover the narrative's langue and establish a grammar of narrative. He begins by asserting that the grammatical clause and, in turn, the subject and verb, is the basic interpretative unit of each sentence and can be linguistically analyzed and further dissected into a variety of grammatical categories to show how all narratives are structured. An individual text (parole) interests Todorov as a means to describe the overall properties of literature in general (langue).

Other narratologists such as Gerard Genette and Roland Barthes have also developed methods of analyzing a story's structure to uncover its meaning, each building on the former work of another narratologist and adding an additional element or two of his own. Genette, for example, believes that **tropes** or figures of speech require a reader's special attention. Barthes, on the other hand, points us back to Tordorov and provides us with more linguistic terminology to dissect a story.

Although these narratologists provide us with various approaches to texts, all furnish us with a **metalanguage**—words used to describe language—so that we can understand how a text means, not what it means.

Jonathan Culler

By the mid-1970s, Jonathan Culler became the voice of structuralism in America and took structuralism in yet another direction. In *Structuralist Poetics* (1975), Culler declared that abstract linguistic models used by narratologists tended to focus on parole, spending too much time analyzing individual stories, poems, and novels. What was needed, he believed, was a return to an investigation of langue, Saussure's main premise.

According to Culler, readers, when given a chance, will somehow make sense out of the most bizarre text. Somehow, readers possess **literary competence**. Through experiences with texts, Culler asserts, they have internalized a set of rules that govern their acts of interpretation. Instead of analyzing individual interpretations of a work, Culler insists, we must spend our time analyzing the act of interpretation itself. We must shift the focus from the text to the reader. How, asks Culler, does interpretation take place in the first place? What system underlies the very act of reading that allows any other system to operate?

Unlike other structuralists, Culler presents a theory of reading. What, he asks, is the internalized system of literary competence readers use to interpret a work? In other words, how do they read? What system guides them through the process of interpreting the work, of making sense of the spoken or printed word?

In *Structuralist Poetics* Culler asserts that three elements undergird any reading, for instance, of a poem:

- A poem should be unified.
- It should be thematically significant.
- This significance can take the form of reflection in poetry.

Accordingly, Culler then seeks to establish the system, the langue, that undergirds the reading process. By focusing on the act of interpretation itself to discover literature's langue, Culler believes he is returning structuralism to its Saussurean roots.

A Model of Interpretation

Many structuralist theories abound, but a core of structuralists believe that the primary signifying system is best found as a series of binary oppositions that the reader organizes, values, and then uses to interpret the text. Each binary operation can be pictured as a fraction, the top half (the numerator) being what is more valued than its related bottom half (the denominator). Accordingly, in the binary operation *light/dark*, the reader has learned to value light over dark, and in the binary operation *good/evil* the reader has similarly valued good over evil. How the reader maps out and organizes the various binary operations and their relationships found within the text but already existing in the mind of the reader determines for that particular reader the text's interpretation.

No matter what its methodology, structuralism emphasizes form and structure, not actual content of a text. Although individual texts must be analyzed, structuralists are more interested in the rule-governed system that underlies texts than in the texts themselves. How a text's underlying structural codes combine to produce the text's meaning rather than a reader's personal interpretation is structuralism's chief interest.

QUESTIONS FOR ANALYSIS

- What are the various binary oppositions or operations that operate in Nathaniel Hawthorne's "Young Goodman Brown" or any other story of your choosing. After you map out these oppositions, show *how* the text means, not what it means.
- What mythemes are evident in Robert Browning's "My Last Duchess"? How do these mythemes show the intertextuality of this particular text with other literary texts you have read?
- How do the various semantic features contained in a text of your choosing directly relate to the codes, signs, or binary oppositions you find in the text?
- Using a text of your choosing, can you apply at least three different methods of structuralism to arrive at how the text achieves its meaning? In the final analysis, is there a difference in how the text achieves its meaning among the three methodologies?
- Can you choose another sign system—sports, music, classroom etiquette—and explain the codes that generate meaning?

SAMPLE ESSAYS

In the student essay that follows, note how the interpretation of Susan Glaspell's play *Trifles* revolves around three major binary oppositions or tensions. The author specifically mentions these oppositions, but she also uses an intricate web of secondary or minor oppositions that become the structural bases of her interpretation. What are the secondary or minor oppositions used in relation to the major binary oppositions? How are both the major and secondary oppositions linked? Can you map out a listing of these binary oppositions on which the interpretation is based?

In the professional essay that follows, observe how Robert Scholes highlights the cultural codes that are internalized by the reader to show how the text means, not what it means. Also, note carefully Scholes's distinction between story and discourse, on one hand, and between text and events on the other. When such distinctions are applied to Hemingway's "A Very Short Story," Scholes believes they will enable the reader to decode the obvious and the hidden social codes that give the text its meaning.

FURTHER READING

Barthes, Roland. *Critical Essays.* Trans. R. Howard. Evanston, IL: Northwestern University Press, 1972.

Culler, Jonathan. *Structuralist Poetics: Structuralism, Linguistics and the Study of Literature.* New York: Cornell University Press, 1975.

Hawkes, Terence. *Structuralism and Semiotics.* London: Methuen, 1977.

Jakobson, Roman, "Linguistics and Poetics" in *Style in Language,* T. Sebeok, ed. Cambridge, MA: MIT Press, 1960, pp. 350–77.

Jameson, Fredric. *The Prison House of Language: A Critical Account of Structuralism and Russian Formalism*. Princeton, NJ: Princeton University Press, 1972.

Lévi-Strauss, Claude. *Structural Anthropology*. Trans. C. Jacobson and B. G. Schoepf. London: Allen Lane, 1968.

Propp, Vladimir. *The Morphology of the Folktale*. Trans. L. Scott. Austin: University of Texas Press, 1968.

Saussure, Ferdinand de. *Course in General Linguistics*. New York: McGraw, 1966.

Scholes, Robert. *Structuralism in Literature: An Introduction*. New Haven, CT: Yale University Press, 1974.

———. *Semiotics and Interpretation*. New Haven, CT: Yale University Press, 1982.

Todorov, Tzvetan. *The Fantastic: A Structural Approach to a Literary Genre*. Trans. R. Howard. Ithaca, NY: Cornell University Press, 1977.

WEB SITES FOR EXPLORATION

http://www.130.179.92.25/Arnason_DE/Backmaterials.html
    Provides necessary background materials for formalism and structuralism
www.colorado.edu/English/ENGL2012Klages/saussure.html
    Provides excerpts from Ferdinard de Saussure's *Course in General Linguistics*
www.brocku.ca/english/courses/4F70/struct.html
    Provides some excellent elements of structuralism and shows its application to literary theory
www.ihi.ku.dk/littvid/publikat/aal/aa/25.html
    An essay that answers the question "What is phenomenology?"
www.130.179.92.25/Arnason_DE/Saussure.html
    Provides a working definition for some of Saussure's basic terms, such as *langue, parole, diachronic, synchronic*
www.130.179.92.25/Arnason_DE/Classes_of_Signs_x.html
    Provides an understanding and application of Saussure's concept of signs to the structure of a poem

∼ Student Essay ∼

A Structuralist Look at Glaspell's Trifles

Susan Glaspell's *Trifles* centers around the investigation of John Wright's murder and takes place entirely within the walls of his farmhouse kitchen. Only five characters command the stage. Three are men, consisting of George Henderson, the country attorney; Henry Peters, the sheriff; and Lewis Hale, a neighboring farmer. The men have come to Wright's house to look for evidence incriminating to Minnie Wright, held in jail for the murder of her husband. Along with them come two of their wives, Mrs. Peters and Mrs. Hale, to collect everyday items needed by Minnie during her imprisonment. Ironically, the women, through noticing the "trifles" of Mrs.

Wright's life common to their own, stumble onto the material searched for by their husbands. A dead canary with a twisted neck found in a pretty box awaiting burial tells them that John Wright killed the only thing of joy in his wife's life. His cruel action spurs Mrs. Wright to kill him, and the knotting on a quilt shows them the method she employed.

Scoffing at the women's interest in minor details such as the quilt, the men overlook the canary and the knotting, and Mrs. Hale and Mrs. Peters keep their discoveries to themselves. They protect Minnie because they empathize with her, sharing the bond of oppression placed over them by their husbands. Though they are horrified at Mrs. Wright's gross act, they respect the woman who put an end to her oppressor, something they do not have the courage to do themselves.

Such an analysis of the play reveals three complex binary oppositions upon which the above interpretation is built, with each binary opposition being connected to and interwoven with the others. The most obvious of the three centers on the relationship between women and men—in this case, how Mrs. Peters and Mrs. Hale interact with each other as opposed to how they do so with their husbands. Part of the way they relate rests heavily on the second binary opposition, the concept of freedom versus oppression that provides a motive both for Mr. Wright's murder and for the protection the two ladies lend his wife at the expense of the destruction of evidence. The evidence falls into the women's hands because male and female opinion differ in what each gender deems as noteworthy, thus revealing the third binary opposition. The men, for example, consider their wives' interest in fruit preserves and quilts as merely "trifles." Yet it is by paying attention to these small things that Mrs. Hale and Mrs. Peters stumble across the material sought by the men.

The opening stage directions establish the first tension between male and female by the men's entering first instead of demonstrating respect by following the "ladies first" rule of that era. The nonchalant manner of the men seems to reflect that they take their wives for granted, and Mr. Hale attests to this fact when he speaks of the late Mr. Wright: "I didn't know as what his wife wanted made much difference to John." The implication is that the husband has command in what goes on in his household.

Shortly thereafter, the Sheriff, Mr. Peters, verbally acknowledges a difference between genders, though he does not articulate the thought completely. "Well, can you beat the women!" he exclaims, referring to one woman but using the plural form, "Held for murder and worryin' about her preserves." Obviously, Mr. Peters thinks that if a man were incarcerated for such a crime, he would not worry about mundane matters but would concern himself with the logistics of his imprisonment. In association with Mrs. Wright's worrying over her preserves, women in general, according to Mr. Hale, "are used to worrying over trifles." Such a statement degrades female concerns and is an insult to Mrs. Hale and Mrs. Peters, whether or not Mr. Hale meant it as one.

Also introduced as a characteristic of women is loyalty to their gender, as observed somewhat condescendingly by the county attorney when Mrs.

Hale defends Mrs. Wright's seeming lack of housekeeping. Stage directions reinforce this idea; the two women stand physically close together until the men exit to go upstairs. After they have gone, Mrs. Hale says that she'd "hate to have men coming into my kitchen, snooping and criticizing." Mrs. Peters, though understanding, merely labels the invasion of privacy as "their duty," but both women imply that their husbands are insensitive to Mrs. Wright's plight. They sympathize with her because they know the physical labor it takes to keep up a farm house and because she did not have time to clean up before she was trundled off to jail.

Other tensions between genders are revealed through the characters' interaction. Every time the men enter the stage, for example, they dominate the conversation, moving boldly and decisively from one place to another. Conversely, the women speak sparingly in the presence of their husbands, timid in their movements and speech until left alone when they can relax once more.

Many of these characteristics arise from the second major binary opposition of freedom over oppression. The best support of this tension develops from the description of Minnie Foster 30 years ago as opposed to the present-day Mrs. Wright. Seeing the drabness of Mrs. Wright's clothes, Mrs. Hale says, "She used to wear pretty clothes and be lively, when she was Minnie Foster, one of the town girls who sang in the choir," and later, "She was kind of like a bird herself—real sweet and pretty. . . . How-she-did-change." This description depicts Miss Foster as a cheerful, pretty woman who loved to sing and be among people. Both women know, however, that 30 years has greatly changed her. Her clothes are "shabby," her home "weren't cheerful," and she no longer sings. Mrs. Hale and Mrs. Peters attribute the change to John Wright. "Wright was close," Mrs. Hale says and continues later, "But he was a hard man, Mrs. Peters. . . . Like a raw wind that gets to the bone." She has no doubt that Wright killed the joy and life out of Minnie Foster, just as she believes he strangled the canary.

Interrelated to the tension of oppression is the women's empathy with Minnie. Mrs. Hale demonstrates this tension early in the play by defending Minnie from the attorney's criticism of her housekeeping. She understands the work involved in maintaining a farm as well as the injustice of having men search through her house when she is not there. Mrs. Peters, though "married to the law," similarly empathizes with Minnie. The dead canary reminds her of her violent reaction to a boy who axed a kitten she owned in her youth, and she remembers the stillness and isolation of her homestead in Dakota after she lost her first child.

The empathy both women feel gives them a common bond with Minnie Wright, causing them first to notice the household details with which she would have been concerned, and second, to hide the "trifles" that would condemn her. Their attention to detail encompasses simple things such as the fruit preserves and the tidiness of the house, but the more significant finds are the dead canary and the quilt, both discovered by accident, both overlooked by the men who fail to recognize the importance of examining her personal belongings. Had the men taken more of an interest in the "trifles," they would have discovered the method of strangulation. Mrs. Wright seemingly "knot-ted" her husband, following the technique used in quilting. Mrs. Hale and Mrs. Peters recognize the knotting method, but the men overlook it, even ridi-culing it: "They wonder if she was going to quilt it or knot it!" At this point in the play the stage directions order the men to laugh and the women to look abashed. The men's superior attitude causes them to miss the evidence which would link Mrs. Wright to the crime, even though it is right in front of them.

Seemingly, the dead bird provides the motive for the murder. Mrs. Hale and Mrs. Peters must believe that Mr. Wright broke the canary's neck or else they would never lie about a cat that does not exist nor would they hide the burial box in the pocket of Mrs. Hale's overcoat. Trifles, then, discovered acci-dentally by the women, explain motive and method, even though the men have searched the entire house and barnyard, going about what even Mrs. Peters calls "important things."

That Mrs. Hale and Mrs. Peters do not turn in their evidence shows that they understand the oppression John Wright placed on his wife and why she chose to liberate herself the way she did. Her freedom is something they will protect, perhaps because they empathize with her or perhaps because they wish for the kind of freedom she now has, even while sitting in the jail cell. The oppression the men place on their women, from their insensitive com-ments about keeping house to the ridicule expressed for interest in simple things, explains why the women do not relinquish the bird and the knotted quilt. Mrs. Hale and Mrs. Peters have the satisfaction of knowing they have solved a crime their husbands could not while still protecting a friend. Their secret is their bid for freedom, something the men cannot dominate or quash.

JULIE CLAYPOOL

❧ Professional Essay ❧

Decoding Papa: "A Very Short Story" as Work and Text[1]

The semiotic study of a literary text is not wholly unlike traditional inter-pretation or rhetorical analysis, nor is it meant to replace these other modes of response to literary works. But the semiotic critic situates the text some-

---

[1]Because of the author's restrictions against reprinting "A Very Short Story" as a whole in any work other than a volume made up exclusively of his own work, the full text of the story has not been included here. The reader should consult the text of "A Very Short Story" in Hemingway's *In Our Time* or *The Short Stories of Ernest Hemingway*, New York: Charles Scribner's Sons, before reading this chapter. My apologies for the inconvenience.

what differently, privileges different dimensions of the text, and uses a critical methodology adapted to the semiotic enterprise. Most interpretive methods privilege the "meaning" of the text. Hermeneutic critics seek authorial or intentional meaning; the New Critics seek the ambiguities of "textual" meaning; the "reader response" critics allow readers to make meaning. With respect to meaning the semiotic critic is situated differently. Such a critic looks for the generic or discursive structures that enable and constrain meaning.

Under semiotic inspection neither the author nor the reader is free to make meaning. Regardless of their lives as individuals, as author and reader they are traversed by codes that enable their communicative adventures at the cost of setting limits to the messages they can exchange. A literary text, then, is not simply a set of words, but (as Roland Barthes demonstrated in *S/Z*, though not necessarily in just that way) a network of codes that enables the marks on the page to be read as a text of particular sort.

In decoding narrative texts, the semiotic method is based on two simple but powerful analytical tools: the distinction between story and discourse, on the one hand, and that between text and events on the other. The distinction between story and discourse is grounded in a linguistic observation by Emile Benveniste to the effect that some languages (notably French and Greek) have a special tense of the verb used for the narration of past events. This tense, the aorist or *passe simple*, emphasizes the relationship between the utterance and the situation the utterance refers to, between the narration and the events narrated. This is *par excellence* the mode of written transcriptions of events: *histoire* or "story." Benveniste contrasts this with the mode of *discours* or "discourse," in which the present contact between speaker and listener is emphasized. Discourse is rhetorical, and related to oral persuasion. Story is referential and related to written documentation. Discourse is now; story is then. Story speaks of he and she; discourse is a matter of you and me, I and thou.

In any fictional text, then, we can discern certain features that are of the story: reports on actions, mentions of times and places, and the like. We can also find elements that are of the discourse: evaluations, reflections, language that suggests an authorial or at least narratorial presence who is addressing a reader or narratee with a persuasive aim in mind. When we are told that someone "smiled cruelly," we can detect more of story in the verb and more of discourse in the adverb. Some fictional texts, those of D. H. Lawrence, for example, are highly discursive. To read a Lawrence story is to enter into a personal relationship with someone who resembles the writer of Lawrence's private correspondence. Hemingway, on the other hand, often seems to have made a strong effort to eliminate discourse altogether—an effort that is apparent in "A Very Short Story."

The distinction between story and discourse is closely related to another with which it is sometimes confused, and that is the distinction between the *recit* and *diegesis* of a narrative. In this case we are meant to distinguish between the whole text of a narration as a text, on the one hand, and the events narrated as events on the other. We can take over the Greek term, *diegesis*, for the system of characters and events, and simply anglicize the other term as recital; or just refer to the "text" when we mean the words and the "diegesis" for what they encourage us to create as a fiction.

The text itself may be analyzed into components of story and discourse, but it may also be considered in relation to the diegesis. One of the primary qualities of those texts we understand as fiction is that they generate a diegetic order that has an astonishing independence from its text. To put it simply, once a story is told it can be recreated in a recognizable way by a totally new set of words—in another language, for instance—or in another medium altogether. The implications of this for analysis are profound. Let us explore some of them.

A fictional diegesis draws its nourishment not simply from the words of its texts but from its immediate culture and its literary tradition. The magical words "once upon a time" in English set in motion a machine of considerable momentum which can hardly be turned off without the equally magical "they lived happily ever after" or some near equivalent. The diegetic processes of "realistic" narrative are no less insistent. "A Very Short Story," by its location in Hemingway's larger text (*In Our Time*), and a few key words—*Padua, carried, searchlights, duty, operating, front, armistice*—allows us to supply the crucial notions of military hospital, nurse, soldier, and World War I that the diegesis requires.

This process is so crucial that we should perhaps stop and explore its implications. The words on the page are not the story. The text is not the diegesis. The story is constructed by the reader from the words on the page by an inferential process—a skill that can be developed. The reader's role is in a sense creative—without it, no story exists—but it is also constrained by rules of inference that set limits to the legitimacy of the reader's constructions. Any interpretive dispute may be properly brought back to the "words on the page," of course, but these words never speak their own meaning. The essence of writing, as opposed to speech, is that the reader speaks the written words, the words that the writer has abandoned. A keen sense of this situation motivates the various sorts of "envoi" that writers supplied for their books in the early days of printing. They felt that their books were mute and would be spoken by others.

In reading a narrative, then, we translate a text into a diegisis according to codes we have internalized. This is simply the narrative version of the normal reading process. As E. D. Hirsch has recently reminded us (in the *Philosophy of Composition* [Chicago, 1977], pp. 122–23), for almost a century research in reading (Binet and Henri in 1894, Fillenbaum in 1966, Sachs in 1967, Johnson-Laird in 1970, Levelt and Kampen in 1975, and Brewer in 1975—specific citations can be found in Hirsch) has shown us that memory stores not the words of texts but their concepts, not the signifiers but the sig-nifieds. When we read a narrative text, then, we process it as a diegesis. If we retell the story, it will be in our own words. To the extent that the distinction between poetry and fiction is a useful one, it is based on the notion of poet-ry as monumental, fixed in the words of the text and therefore untranslat-able; while fiction has proved highly translatable because its essence is not in its language but in its diegetic structure. As fiction approaches the condi-tion of poetry, its precise words become more important; as poetry moves toward narrative, its specific language decreases in importance.

In reading fiction, then, we actually translate from the text to a diege-sis, substituting narrative units (characters, scenes, events, and so on) for verbal units (nouns, adjectives, phrases, clauses, etc.). And we perform other changes as well. We organize the material we receive so as to make it memorable, which means that we systematize it as much as possible. In the diegetic system we construct, time flows at a uniform rate; events occur in chronological order; people and places have the qualities expected of them—unless the text specifies otherwise. A writer may relocate the Eiffel Tower to Chicago but unless we are told this we will assume that a scene below that tower takes place in Paris—a Paris equipped with all the other items accorded it in our cultural paradigm.

Places and other entities with recognizable proper names (Napoleon, Waterloo, Broadway) enter the diegesis coded by culture. The events reported in a narrative text, however, will be stored in accordance with a syntactic code based on a chronological structure. The text may present the events that com-pose a story in any order, plunging *in medias res* or following through from beginning to end, but the diegesis always seeks to arrange them in chronolog-ical sequence. The text may expand a minute into pages or cram years into a single sentence, for its own ends, but the minutes and years remain minutes and years of diegetic time all the same. In short, the text may discuss what it chooses, but once a diegesis is set in motion no text can every completely con-trol it. "How many children had Lady Macbeth?" is not simply the query of a naive interpreter but the expression of a normal diegetic impulse. Where authors and texts delight in equivocation, the reader needs certainty and clo-sure to complete the diegetic processing of textual materials. From this conflict of interests comes a tension that many modern writers exploit.

The semiotician takes the reader's diegetic impulse and establishes it as a principle of structuration. The logic of diegetic structure provides a norm, a benchmark for the study of textual strategies, enabling us to explore the dialogue between the text and diegesis, looking for points of stress, where the text changes its ways in order to control the diegetic material for its own ends. The keys to both affect and intention may be found at these points. Does the text return obsessively to one episode of the diegetic history? Does it disturb diegetic order to tell about something important to its own discur-sive ends? Does it omit something that diegetic inertia deems important?

Does it change its viewpoint on diegetic events? Does it conceal things? Does it force evaluations through the rhetoric of its discourse? The calm inertia of diegetic process, moved by the weight of culture and tradition and the needs of memory itself, offers a stable background for the mapping of textual strategies. And our most esthetically ambitious texts will be those that find it most necessary to put their own stamp on diegetic process.

Hemingway's "A Very Short Story" presents itself as exceptionally reticent. The familiar Hemingway style, which Gerard Genette has called "behaviorist," seems to efface itself, to offer us a pure diegesis. Boy meets girl—a "cute meet," as they used to say in Hollywood—they fall in love, become lovers, plan to marry, but the vicissitudes of war separate them, and finally forces that are too strong for them bring about their defeat. This is the story, is it not; a quasi-naturalistic slice of life that begins almost like a fairy tale ("Once upon a time in another country. . ."—and ends with the negation of the fairy-tale formula ("and they lived unhappily ever after")—a negation that proclaims the text's realistic or naturalistic status? But there is already a tension here, between the open form of the slice of life and the neat closure of the fairy tale, which emerges most clearly if we compare the progress of diegetic time with the movement of the text. We can do this in a crude way by mapping the hours, days, and weeks of diegetic time against the paragraphs of the text. The slowest paragraphs are the first: one night; and the third: one trip to the Duomo. The fastest are the fourth: his time at the front; the sixth: Luz's time in Pordenone; and the seventh or last: which carries Luz to the point of infinity with the word "never." The narrative thus increases its speed throughout, and achieves its effect of culmination by the use of the infinite terms in the last paragraph. The text might easily have contented itself with recounting the fact that the major did not marry Luz in the spring, but it feels obliged to add "or any other time," just as it is obliged to use the word "never" in the next sentence. Something punitive is going on here, as the discourse seems to be revenging itself upon the character. Why?

Before trying to answer that question we would do well to consider some other features of the text/diegesis relationship. From the first paragraph on, it is noticeable that one of the two main characters in the diegesis has a name in the text while the other is always referred to by a pronoun. Why should this be? The answer emerges when we correlate this detail with other features of the text/diegesis relationship. The text, as we have observed, is reticent, as if it, too, does not want to "blab about anything during the silly, talky time." But it is more reticent about some things than others. In the first paragraph, the male character is introduced in the first sentence. Luz appears in the fifth. When she sits on the bed we are told, "she was cool and fresh in the hot night." Why this information about her temperature? She is the nurse, after all, and he the patient. In fact it is not information about how she feels at all, but about how she appears to him. The text is completely reticent about how he feels himself, though the implication is that he finds her coolness attractive. How he seems to her or how she feels about him are not considered relevant. This is a selective reticence. Our vision is subjectively with him (as the personal pronoun implies), while Luz is seen more objectively (as the proper name implies). The final implication of paragraph 1 is that they make love right then and there. But the reticent text makes the reader responsible for closing that little gap in the diegesis.

This matter of the point of view taken by the text can be established more clearly with the use of a sort of litmus test developed by Roland Barthes. If we rewrite the text substituting the first-person pronoun for the third, we can tell whether or not we are dealing with what Barthes calls a "personal system," a covert, first-person narration (see "Introduction to the Structural Analysis of Narrative," in *Image-Music-Text*, p. 112). In the case of "A Very Short Story," where we have two third-person characters of apparently equal consequence, we must rewrite the story twice to find out what we need to know. Actually, the issue is settled conclusively after the first two paragraphs, which are all I will present here:

The first two paragraphs of "A Very Short Story" rewritten—"he" transposed to "I":

> One hot evening in Padua they carried me up onto the roof and I could look out over the top of the town. There were chimney swifts in the sky. After a while it got dark and the searchlights came out. The others went down and took the bottles with them. Luz and I could hear them below on the balcony. Luz sat on the bed. She was cool and fresh in the hot night.
>
> Luz stayed on night duty for three months. They were glad to let her. When they operated on me she prepared me for the operating table; and we had a joke about friend or enema. I went under the anaesthetic holding tight on to myself so I would not blab about anything during the silly, talky time. After I got on crutches I used to take the temperatures so Luz would not have to get up from the bed. There were only a few patients, and they all knew about it. They all liked Luz. As I walked back along the halls I thought of Luz in my bed.

The same paragraph—"Luz" transposed to "I":

> One hot evening in Padua they carried him up onto the roof and he could look out over the top of the town. There were chimney swifts in the sky. After a while it got dark and the searchlights came out. The others went down and took the bottles with them. He and I could hear them below on the balcony. I sat on the bed. I was cool and fresh in the hot night.
>
> I stayed on night duty for three months. They were glad to let me. When they operated on him I prepared him for the operating table; and we had a joke about friend or enema. He went under the anaesthetic holding tight on to himself so he would not blab about anything during the silly, talky time. After he got on crutches he used to take the temperatures so I would not have to get up from the bed. There were only a few patients, and

they all knew about it. They all liked me. As he walked back along the halls he thought of me in his bed.

"He" transposes to "I" perfectly, but "Luz" does not. In the second rewriting the first person itself enters the discourse with a shocking abruptness, since the earlier sentences seem to have been from the male patient's point of view. The stress becomes greater in the last sentence of the first paragraph, which has been constructed to indicate how she appeared to him, not how she seemed to herself. But the last two sentences of the second paragraph in the second rewriting are even more ludicrous, with the first-person narrator informing us of how well liked she was, and finally describing his thoughts about her. In this rewriting there is simply too great a tension between the angle of vision and the person of the voice. The discourse loses its coherence. But the first rewriting is completely coherent because in it voice and vision coincide. It is really his narrative all the way. The third-person narration of the original text is a disguise, a mask of pseudo-objectivity worn by the text for its own rhetorical purposes.

The discourse of this text, as I have suggested, is marked by its reticence, but this reticence of the text is contrasted with a certain amount of talkativeness in the diegesis. He, of course, doesn't want to "blab," but *they* want "every one to know about" their relationship. Implication: *she* is the one who wants the news spread. There is absolutely no direct discourse in the text, but there are two paragraphs devoted to letters and one to recounting a quarrel. Here, too, we find reticence juxtaposed to talkativeness. Luz writes many letters to him while he is at the front. But the text does not say whether he wrote any to her. Hers are clearly repetitive and hyperbolic. The style of the discourse becomes unusually paratactic—even for Hemingway—whenever her letters are presented. "They were all about the hospital, *and how* much she loved him *and how* it was impossible to get along without him *and how* terrible it was missing him at night" (my italics). The repetitive "how's," the hyperbolic "impossible" and "terrible," and all the "and's" suggest an unfortunate prose style even without direct quotation. Above all, they indicate an ominous lack of reticence.

The quarrel is not represented in the text but the "agreement" that causes it is summarized for us, at least in part. It takes the form of a series of conditions that *he* must fulfill in order to be rewarded with Luz's hand in marriage. Curiously, the conditions are represented not only as things it is "understood" that he will and will not do but also as things he wants and does not want to do. He does not "want to see his friends or any one in the States. Only to get a job and be married." It is not difficult to imagine a man being willing to avoid his friends, to work, and to stay sober in order to please a woman, but it is hard to imagine any human being who does not "*want* to see his friends or *anyone*." Not *want* to? Not *anyone*? The text seems to be reporting on the diegesis in a most curious way here. This is not simply reticence but irony. There is a strong implication that he is being coerced, pushed too far, even having his masculinity abused. If there are any conditions laid upon Luz, we do not hear of them.

Finally, the final letter arrives. In reporting it the text clearly allows Luz's prose to shine through once again, complete with repetition of the horrible phrase about the "boy and girl" quality of their relationship and the splendidly hyperbolic cacophony of "expected, absolutely unexpectedly." Her behavior belies her words. Her true awfulness, amply suggested earlier by the reticent text, blazes forth here as her hideous discourse perfectly complements her treacherous behavior.

But how did *he* behave while she was discovering the glories of Latin love? *Nihil dixit*. The text maintains what we can now clearly see as a specifically manly reticence. Did he drink? Did he see his friends? Or anyone? Did he want to? We know not. We do know, however, of his vehicular indiscretion in Lincoln Park and its result. The text is too generous and manly to say so, of course, but we know that this, too, is Luz's fault. She wounded him in the heart and "a short time after" this salesgirl got him in an even more vital place. The discourse leaves them both unhappy, but it clearly makes Luz the agent of the unhappiness.

And what does it make him? Why, the patient, of course. He is always being carried about, given enemas, operated on, sent to the front, sent home, not wanting anything, reading letters. He is wounded at the beginning and wounded at the end. The all-American victim: polite, reticent, and just waiting for an accident to happen to him. Who is to blame if his accidents keep taking the form of women? Who indeed? Whose discourse is this, whose story, whose diegesis, whose world? It is Papa's, of course, who taught a whole generation of male readers to prepare for a world where men may be your friends but women are surely the enema.

The story quite literally leaves its protagonist wounded in his sex by contact with a woman. From the bed in Padua to the back seat in Lincoln Park our Hero is carried from wound to wound. We never hear the accents of his voice or the intonations of his prose. We do not have to. The text speaks for him. Its voice is his. And its reticence is his as well. In this connection we should look once again at a passage in the second paragraph: "they had a joke about friend or enema. He went under the anaesthetic holding tight on to himself so he would not." Up to this point in the second sentence we are not aware that there has been a change of topic from that which closed the earlier sentence. The language of oral retentiveness coincides neatly with that of anal retentiveness. Logorrhea and diarrhea are equally embarrassing. Enemas are enemies and to "blab about anything during the silly, talky time" (to finish the sentence) would be as bad as to discharge matter freely from the opposite end of the alimentary canal. As Hemingway put it on another occasion: "If you talk about it, you lose it."

The point of this discussion is that the text reveals the principle behind its reticent prose style through an impartial and equal distress at the idea of excessive discharge of either verbal or fecal matter. It is an anal retentive style, then, in a surprisingly literal way. And through this style the text presents us with a lesson about women. Luz first gives our retentive hero a literal enema and then she metaphorically emasculates him by making him renounce alcohol, friends, and all the pleasures of life. The salesgirl from the loop merely administers the literal coup de grace to his already figuratively damaged sexuality.

Having come this far with a semiotic analysis, we can begin to distinguish it more precisely from New Critical exegesis. In doing so, we must begin by admitting that the two approaches share a certain number of interpretive gestures. We must also recognize that no two semiotic analyses or New Critical exegeses are likely to be identical. The major differences in the two critical approaches can be traced to their different conceptions of the object of study: for New Criticism, the work; for semiotics, the text. As a work, "A Very Short Story" must be seen as complete, unified, shaped into an aesthetic object, a verbal icon. The pedagogical implications of this are important.

The student interpreting "A Very Short Story" as a "work" is put into an interesting position. Like many of Hemingway's early stories, this one presents a male character favorably and a female unfavorably. In fact, it strongly implies favorable things about masculinity and unfavorable things about femininity. It does this, as our semiotic analysis has shown, by mapping certain traits onto a value structure. The good, loyal, reticent male character is supported by the discourse, through its covert first-person perspective and the complicity of its style with those values. The bad, treacherous, talkative female is cast out. Even the carefully established point of view is violated in the last paragraph so that the narrator can track Luz through eternity and assure us that she never married her major "in the spring, or any other time." But for the most part Hemingway's control over his text is so great that the anger at the root of the story is transformed into what we may take as cool, lapidary prose of the pure, impersonal artist.

And there definitely is an anger behind this story, to which we shall soon turn our attention. For the moment we must follow a bit further the situation of the student faced with this story in the form of a "work" to be interpreted. The concept of "the student" is one of those transcendental abstractions that we accept for convenience's sake and often come to regret. We can begin to break it down by reminding ourselves that students come in at least two genders. Actual students read this story in different ways. Most male students sympathize with the protagonist and are very critical of Luz—as, indeed, the discourse asks them to be. Many female students try to read the story as sympathetic to Luz, blaming events on the "weakness" of the young man or the state of the world. This is a possible interpretation, but it is not well supported by the text. Thus the female student must either "misread" the work (that is, she must offer the more weakly supported of two inter- pretations) or accept one more blow to her self-esteem as a woman. Faced with this story in a competitive classroom, women are put at a disadvantage. They are, in fact, in a double mind.

By the New Critical standards the narrator is impersonal and reliable. The words on the page are all we have, and they tell us of a garrulous, faith- less woman who was unworthy of the love of a loyal young man. But semi- otic analysis has already suggested alternatives to this view. Seen as a text that presents a diegesis, this story is far from complete. There are gaps in the diegesis, reticences in the text, and a highly manipulative use of covert first- person narrative. There are signs of anger and vengefulness in the text, too, that suggest not an omniscient impersonal author but a partial, flawed human being—like the rest of us—behind the words on the page.

Essay by Robert Scholes. "Decoding Papa: 'A Very Short Story' As Work and Text." *Semiotics and Interpretation*. New Haven, CT: Yale University Press, pp. 110–26.

6

Deconstruction

STRUCTURALISM AND POSTSTRUCTURALISM: TWO VIEWS OF THE WORLD

Throughout the 1950s and 1960s, a variety of different forms of structuralism dominated European and American literary theory: the French structuralism of Roland Barthes, the Russian structuralist narratology of Vladimir Propp, and Jonathan Culler's American brand of structuralist poetics, to name a few. The application of structuralist principles varies from one theoretician to another, but all believe that language is the primary means of **signification** (how we achieve meaning) and that language comprises its own rule-governed system to achieve such meaning. Although language is the primary sign system, it is not the only one. Fashions, sports, dining, and other activities all have their own "language" or codes whereby the participants know what is expected of them in a particular situation. When dining at a restaurant, for example, connoisseurs of fine dining know that it is inappropriate to drink from a finger bowl. Similarly, football fans know that it is appropriate to shout, scream, and holler to support their team.

From a structuralist perspective, such expectations highlight that all social and cultural practices are governed by rules or codes. Wanting to discover these rules, structuralists declare that the proper study of reality and meaning is the system behind such individual practices, not the individual practices themselves. Like football or fine dining, the act of reading is also a cultural and a social practice that contains its own codes. Meaning in a text resides in these codes, which the reader has mastered before he or she even picks up an actual text. For the structuralist, the proper study of literature is an inquiry into the conditions surrounding the act of interpretation itself, not an investigation of the individual text.

Holding to the principles of Ferdinand de Saussure, the founding father of structuralism, structuralists seek to discover the overall system (langue) that accounts for an individual interpretation (parole) of a text. Meaning and the reasons for meaning can be both ascertained and discovered.

With the advent of **deconstruction** theory and practice in the late 1960s, however, the structuralist assumption that a text's meaning can be discovered through an examination of its structural codes was challenged and replaced by the maxim of undecidability: A text has many meanings and therefore no definitive interpretation. Rather than providing answers about the meaning of texts or a methodology for discovering how a text means, deconstruction asks a new set of questions, endeavoring to show that what a text claims it says and what it actually says are discernibly different. By casting doubt on most previously held theories, deconstruction declares that a text has an almost infinite number of possible interpretations. And the interpretations themselves, declare some deconstructionists, are just as creative and important as the text being interpreted.

With the advent of deconstruction and its challenge to structuralism and other preexisting theories, a paradigmatic shift occurs in literary theory. Before deconstruction, literary critics—New Critics, some reader-response theorists, structuralists, and others—found meaning within the literary text or the codes of the various sign systems within the world of the text and the reader. The most innovative of these theorists, the structuralists, provided new and exciting ways to discover meaning, but nonetheless, these theorists maintained that meaning could be found. Underlying all of these predeconstructionist views of the world is a set of assumptions called **modernism** (or the modern worldview) that provided the philosophical, ethical, and scientific bases for humankind for about 300 years. With the coming of deconstruction, these long-held beliefs were challenged, creating **poststructuralism**, a new basis for understanding and guiding humanity (its name denotes that it historically comes after, or *post*, structuralism). Often historians, anthropologists, literary theorists, and other scholars use the term **postmodernism** synonymously with *deconstruction* and *poststructuralism*, although the term *postmodernism* was coined in the 1930s and has broader historical implications outside the realm of literary theory than do the terms *poststructuralism* and *deconstruction*. To place in context the somewhat turbulent reception of the first of several poststructural schools of criticism—deconstruction theory and practice—a working understanding of modernism and postmodernism is necessary.

MODERNISM

For many historians and literary theorists, the Enlightenment or the Age of Reason (eighteenth century) is synonymous with modernism. That its roots predate this time period is unquestioned, with some even dating to 1492 (Columbus's journeys to the Americas) and its overall spirit lasting until the middle of the twentieth century. At the center of this view of the world lie two prominent beliefs: that reason is humankind's best guide to life and that science, above all other human endeavors, could lead humanity to a new promised land. Philosophically, modernism rests on the foundations laid by René Descartes (1596–1650), a French philosopher, scientist, and mathematician. Ultimately, declares Descartes, the only thing one cannot doubt is one's own existence. Certainty and knowledge begin with the self. "I think, therefore I am" thus becomes the only solid foundation on which knowledge and a theory of knowledge can be built. For Descartes, the rational essence freed from superstition, from human passions, and from one's often irrational imagination will allow humankind to discover truth about the physical world.

As Descartes's teachings elevated to new heights humankind's ability to reason and an individual's rational essence, the scientific writings and discoveries of Francis Bacon and Sir Isaac Newton allowed science to be likewise coronated. Thanks to Francis Bacon (1561–1626), the scientific method has become part of everyone's elementary and high school education. It is through experimentation, in the doing of experiments, in making inductive generalizations, and in verifying the results that one can discover truths about the physical world. And thanks to Sir Isaac Newton (1642–1727), the physical world is no longer a mystery but a mechanism that operates according to a system of laws that can be understood by any thinking, rational human being who is willing to apply the principles of the scientific method to the physical universe.

Armed with an unparalleled confidence in humankind's capacity to reason—the ability to inquire and to grasp necessary conditions essential for seeking out such undoubtable truths as provided by mathematics—and the assurance that science can lead the way to a complete understanding of the physical world, the modern or Enlightenment scholar was imbued with a spirit of progress. Anything the enlightened mind set as its goal, so these scholars believed, was attainable. Through reason and science, all poverty, all ignorance, and all injustice would finally be banished.

Of all Enlightenment people, Benjamin Franklin (1706–90) may best exemplify the characteristics of modernity. Gleaned from self-portraits contained in his *Autobiography*, Franklin is the archetypal modern philosopher/scientist. Self-assured, Franklin declares that he literally pulled himself up by his own bootstraps, overcoming poverty and ignorance through education to become America's first internationally known and respected scientist/philosopher/statesman. Believing in the power and strength of the individual mind, he delighted in the natural world and decided early in life to know all possible aspects of his universe. Accordingly, he abandoned superstitions and myths and placed his trust in science to lead him to truths about his world. Through observations, experiments, and conclusions drawn upon the data discovered from using the scientific method, Franklin believed he could obtain and know the necessary truths to guide him through life.

Like Descartes, Franklin does not abandon religion and replace it with science. Holding to the tenets of Deism, he rejects miracles, myths, and much of what he called religious superstitions. What he does not reject is a belief in the existence of God. He asserts, however, that God leaves it to humanity, to each individual, to become masters of his or her own fate. According to Franklin, individuals must find salvation within themselves. By using one's God-given talents of reason and rational abilities coupled with the principles of science, each person, declares Franklin, can experience and enjoy human progress.

For Franklin and other enlightened minds, truth is to be discovered scientifically, not through the unruly and passionate imagination or through one's feelings or intuition. And what is to be known and discovered via the scientific method is reality: the physical world. All people, declares Franklin, must know this world objectively and must learn how to investigate it to discover its truths.

Self-assured, self-conscious, and self-made, Franklin concludes that all people possess an essential nature. It is humanity's moral duty to investigate this nature contained within ourselves and to investigate our environment through rational thinking and the methods of science so that we can learn and share the truths of the universe. By devoting ourselves to science and to the magnificent results that will necessarily follow, Franklin proclaims that human progress is inevitable and will usher in a new golden age.

Franklin and modernity's spirit of progress permeated humankind's beliefs well into the twentieth century. For several centuries modernity's chief tenets—that reality can be known and investigated and that humanity possesses an essential nature characterized by rational thought—became the central ideas on which many philosophers, scientists, educators, and writers constructed their worldviews. In particular, writers and literary theoreticians—New Critics, structuralists, and others—believed that texts had some kind of objective existence and therefore could be studied and analyzed with appropriate conclusions to follow from such analyses. Whether a text's actual value and meaning were intrinsic or extrinsic was debatable; nevertheless, an aesthetic text's meaning could be discovered. With the advent of deconstruction, the first poststructuralist or postmodern school of criticism, the belief in the objective reality not only of texts but also of objective reality itself becomes questionable.

POSTSTRUCTURALISM OR POSTMODERNISM

What is truth? How can truth be discovered? What is reality? Is there an objective reality on which we can all agree? If so, how can we best investigate this reality so that all humanity can understand the world in which we live and prosper from such knowledge? Until the late 1960s (with a few notable exceptions), the worldview espoused by modernity and symbolized by Benjamin Franklin provided acceptable and workable answers to these questions. For Franklin and other modern thinkers, the primary form of discourse is like a map. The map itself is a representation of reality as known, discovered, and detailed by humanity. By looking at a map, a traveler could see a delineated view of the world and therefore an accurate picture of reality itself: the mountains, rivers, plains, cities, deserts, and forests. By placing his or her trust in this representation of reality, the traveler could plot a journey, feeling confident in the accuracy of the map and its depictions. For the modern mind, objective reality as pictured on the map was knowable and discoverable by any intelligent person who wished to do so.

With the advent of deconstruction, Jacques Derrida's poststructural view of the world in the mid-1960s, modernity's understanding of reality is challenged and turned on its head. For Derrida and other postmodernists, no such thing as objective reality exists. For these thinkers, all definitions and depictions of truth are subjective, simply creations of the minds of humanity. Truth itself is relative, depending on the various cultural and social influences in one's life. Because these poststructuralist thinkers assert that many truths exist, not one, they declare that modernity's concept of one objective reality must be disavowed and replaced by many different concepts, each being a valid and reliable interpretation and construction of reality.

Postmodernist thinkers reject modernity's representation of discourse (the map) and replace it with the collage. Unlike the fixed, objective nature of a map, a collage's meaning is always changing. Whereas the viewer of a map relies on and obtains meaning and direction from the map itself, the viewer of a collage actually participates in the production of meaning. And unlike a map, which allows one interpretation of reality, a collage permits many possible meanings, for the viewer can simply juxtapose a variety of combinations of images, thereby constantly changing the meaning of the collage. Each viewer, then, creates his or her own subjective picture of reality.

To say postmodernism popped onto the American literary scene with the coming of Derrida to America in 1966 would be inaccurate. Although historians disagree as to who actually coined the term, scholars generally agree that it first appeared in the 1930s. Previously, however, its seeds had already germinated in the writings of Friedrich Nietzsche (1844–1900). As Nietzsche's Zarathustra, the protagonist of *Thus Spake Zarathustra*, proclaims the death of God, the death knell begins to sound for objective reality and ultimate truth. World Wars I and II, a decline in the influence of Christianity and individualism, and the appearance of a new group of theologians led by Thomas Altizer, who in the 1950s echoed Nietzsche's words that God is dead, all spelled the demise of objective reality and the autonomous scholar who seeks to discover ultimate reality.

Beginning in the 1960s and continuing to the present, the voices of French philosopher Jacques Derrida, French cultural historian Michel Foucault, aesthetician Jean-François Lyotard, and ardent American pragmatist Richard Rorty, professor of humanities at the University of Virginia, all declare univocally the death of objective truth. These leading voices of postmodernism assert that modernity failed because it searched for an external point of reference—God, reason, and science, among others—on which to build its philosophy. For these postmodern thinkers, there is no such point of reference, for there is no ultimate truth or inherently unifying element in the universe and thus no ultimate reality.

According to postmodernism, all that is left is difference. We must acknowledge, they say, that each person shapes his or her own concepts of reality. Reality becomes a human construct that is shaped by each individual's dominant social group. There is no center and no one objective reality, but as many realities as there are people. Each person's interpretation of reality is necessarily different. No one has a claim to absolute truth; therefore, tolerance of each other's points of view is the postmodern maxim.

Because postmodern philosophy is constantly being shaped, reshaped, defined, and articulated by its present followers, no one voice can adequately represent it or serve as its archetypal spokesperson, as Franklin does for modernity. By synthesizing the beliefs of Derrida, Foucault, Lyotard, and Rorty, however, we can hypothesize what this representative postmodern thinker would possibly espouse:

> I believe, like my forebears before me, that we, as a race of people, will see progress, but only if we all cooperate. The age of the lone scholar, working diligently in the laboratory, is over. Cooperation among scholars from all fields is vital. Gone are the days of individualism. Gone are the days of conquest. Now is the time for tolerance, understanding, and collaboration.
>
> Because our knowledge always was and always will be incomplete, we must focus on a new concept: holism. We must realize that we all need each other, including all our various perspectives on the nature of reality. We must also recognize that our rationality, our thinking process, is only one of many avenues that can lead to an understanding of our world. Our emotions, feelings, and intuition can also provide us with valid interpretations and guidelines for living.
>
> And we have finally come to realize that no such thing as objective reality exists; there is no ultimate truth, for truth is perspectival, depending on the community and social group in which we live. Because many truths exist, we must learn to accept each other's ideas concerning truth, and we must learn to live side by side, in a pluralistic society, learning from each other while celebrating our differences.
>
> We must stop trying to discover the undiscoverable—absolute truth— and openly acknowledge that what may be right for one person may not be right for another. Acceptance, not criticism; open-mindedness, not closed-mindedness; tolerance, not bigotry; and love, not hatred must become the guiding principles of our lives. When we stop condemning ourselves and others for 'not having truth,' then we can spend more time interpreting our lives and giving them meaning, as together we work and play.

When such principles are applied to literary interpretation, the postmodernist realizes that no such thing as "the" meaning or the correct meaning of an aesthetic text exists. As in a collage, meaning develops as the reader interacts with the text, for meaning does not reside within the text itself. And because each reader's view of truth is perspectival, the interpretation of a text that emerges when a reader interacts with a text will necessarily be different from every other reader's interpretation. For each text, then, there exists an almost infinite number of interpretations, or at least as many interpretations as there are readers.

HISTORICAL DEVELOPMENT

Beginnings of Deconstruction

Coined by its founding father, Jacques Derrida, deconstruction first emerged on the American literary stage in 1966 when Derrida, a French philosopher and teacher, read his paper "Structure, Sign, and Play" at a Johns Hopkins University symposium. By questioning and disputing in this paper the metaphysical assumptions held to be true by Western philosophy since the time of Plato, Derrida inaugurated what many critics believe to be the most intricate and challenging methods of textual analysis as yet to appear.

Derrida himself, however, would not want deconstruction dubbed a critical theory, a school of criticism, a mode or method of literary criticism, or a philosophy. Nowhere in Derrida's writings does he state the encompassing tenets of his critical approach, nor does he ever present a codified body of deconstructive theory or methodology. Although he gives his views in bits and pieces throughout his canon, he believes that he cannot develop a formalized statement of his rules for reading, interpretation, and writing. Unlike a unified treatise, Derrida claims, his approach to reading (and literary analysis) is more a strategic device than a methodology, more a strategy or approach to literature than a school or theory of criticism. Such theories of criticism, he believes, must identify with a body of knowledge that they claim to be true or to contain truth. It is this assertion (that truth or a core of metaphysical ideals actually exists and can be believed, articulated, and supported) that Derrida and deconstruction wish to dispute and "deconstruct."

Because deconstruction uses previously formulated theories from other schools of criticism, coins many words for its newly established ideas, and challenges beliefs long held by Western culture, many students, teachers, and even critics avoid studying it, fearing its supposed complexity. By organizing deconstruction and its assumptions into three workable areas of study rather than plunging directly into some of its complex terminology, we can begin to grasp this approach to textual analysis. In order to understand deconstruction and its strategic approach to a text, then, we must first gain a working knowledge of the historical and philosophical roots of structuralism, a linguistic approach to textual analysis that gained critical attention and popularity in the 1950s and 1960s. (See Chapter 5 for a detailed analysis of structuralism.) From this school of criticism Derrida borrows the basis of and the starting point for his deconstructive strategy. After examining structuralism, we must investigate the proposed radical changes Derrida makes in Western philosophy and metaphysics. Such changes, Derrida readily admits, turn Western metaphysics on its head. Finally, we must master a set of new terminology coupled with new philosophical assumptions and their corresponding methodological approaches to textual analysis if we wish to understand and use deconstruction's approach to interpreting a text.

Structuralism at a Glance

Derrida begins formulating his strategy of reading by critiquing Ferdinand de Saussure's *Course in General Linguistics*. Saussure, the father of modern linguistics, dramatically shifted the focus of linguistic science in the early twentieth century. It is his ideas concerning language that form the core of structuralism, the critical body of literary theory from which Derrida borrows many of the major philosophical building blocks of deconstruction.

According to Saussure, structural linguistics (and structuralism itself) rests on a few basic principles. First, language is a system of rules, and these rules govern its every aspect, including individual sounds that make up a word (the *t* in *cat*, for example), small units that join together to form a word (*garden* + *er* = *gardener*), grammatical relationships between words (such as the rule that a singular subject must combine with a singular verb, as in *John eats ice cream*), and the relationships among all words in a sentence (such as the relationship between the phrase *under a tree* and all remaining words in the sentence *Mary sits under a tree to eat her lunch*). Consciously and unconsciously every speaker of a language learns these rules and knows when they are broken. Speakers of English know, for example, that the sentence *Simon grew up to be a brilliant doctor* seems correct and thereby follows the rules of the English language, but that the sentence *Simon up grew a brilliant doctor* is somehow incorrect and violates the rules of English. These rules that make up a language and that we learn both consciously and unconsciously Saussure dubs **langue**. Saussure recognizes that individual speakers of a language evidence langue in their individual speech utterances, which he calls **parole**. It is the task of the linguist, Saussure believes, to infer a language's langue from the analysis of many instances of parole.

Emphasizing the systematized nature of language, Saussure then asserts that all languages are composed of basic units or **emes**. Identifying these paradigms (models) or relationships among symbols (the letters of the alphabet, for example) in a given language is the job of a linguist. This task becomes especially difficult when the emes in the linguist's native language and those in an unfamiliar language under investigation differ. Generally, linguists must first recognize and understand the various emes in their native language. For example, one eme in all languages is the individual sounds that make up words. The number of distinct and significant sounds (or **phonemes**) that make up a language ranges from the low teens to 60 and above. English, for instance, has approximately 45 phonemes. But telling the difference among sounds and knowing when any alteration in the pronunciation of a phoneme can change the meaning of a group of phonemes (i.e., a word) or when a simple variation in a phoneme's pronunciation is linguistically insignificant can be difficult. For example, in English the letter *t* represents the sound /t/. But is there one distinct pronunciation for this sound whenever and wherever it appears in an English word? Is the *t* in the word *tip*, for instance, pronounced the same as the *t* in *stop*? Obviously not, for the first *t* is **aspirated**, or pronounced with a greater force of air than the *t* in *stop*. In either word, however, a speaker of English could still identify the /t/ as a phoneme, or a distinct sound. If we then replace the *t* in *tip* with a *d*, we now have *dip*, the difference between the two words being the sounds /t/ and /d/. Upon analysis, we find that these sounds are pronounced in the same location in the mouth but with one difference: /d/ is **voiced**, or pronounced with the vocal cords vibrating, whereas /t/ is **unvoiced**, with the vocal cords remaining basically still. It is this difference between the sounds /t/ and /d/ that allows us to say that /t/ and /d/ are phonemes or distinct sounds in English. Whether the eme (any linguistic category such as a phoneme) is a sound, or a minimal unit of grammar such as the adding of an *-s* in English to form most plurals, or any other distinct category of a language, Saussure's basic premise operates: Within each eme, distinctions depend on differences.

That distinctions or meaning in language depend on differences within each eme radically changes some fundamental concepts long held by linguists preceding Saussure. Before Saussure, linguists believed that the structure of language was **mimetic**, merely mimicking the outside world; language, then, had no structure of its own. It simply copied its structure from the reality exhibited in the world in which it was used. Saussure denies that language is intrinsically mimetic and demonstrates that it is determined primarily by its own internal rules, such as phonology (individual sounds), grammar (the principles and rules of a language), and syntax (how words combine within an utterance to form meaning). Furthermore, these rules are highly systematized and structured. But most importantly, Saussure argues that the **linguistic sign** (Saussure's linguistic replacement for the word *word*) that makes up language itself is both arbitrary and conventional. For example, most languages have different words for the same concept. For instance, the English word *man* is *homme* in French. And in English we know that the meaning of the word *pit* exists not because it possesses some innate acoustic quality but because it differs from *hit, wit*, and *lit*. In other words, the linguistic sign is composed of two parts: the **signifier**, or the spoken or written constituent such as the sound /t/ and the orthographic (written) symbol *t*, and the **signified**, the concept signaled by the signifier. It is this relationship between the signifier (the word *dog*, for example) and the signified (the concept or the reality behind the word *dog*) that Saussure maintains is arbitrary and conventional. The linguistic sign, then, is defined by differences that distinguish it from other signs, not by any innate properties.

Believing that our knowledge of the world is shaped by the language that represents it, Saussure insists on the arbitrary relationship between the signifier and the signified. By so doing, he undermines the long held belief that there is some natural link between the word and the thing it represents. For Saussure, meaning in language resides in a systematized combination of sounds that rely chiefly on the differences among these signs, not any innate properties within the signs themselves. It is this concept that meaning in language is determined by the differences among the language signs that Derrida borrows from Saussure as a key building block in the formulation of deconstruction.

Derrida's Interpretation of Saussure's Sign

Derridean deconstruction begins with and emphatically affirms Saussure's decree that language is a system based on differences. Derrida agrees with Saussure that we can know the meaning of signifiers through and because of their relationships and their differences among themselves. But unlike Saussure, Derrida also applies this reasoning to the signified. Like the signifier, the signified (or concept) can also be known only through its relationships and its differences among other signifieds. Furthermore, declares Derrida, the signified cannot orient or make permanent the meaning of the signifier, for the relationship between the signifier and the signified is both arbitrary and conventional. And, accordingly, signifieds often function as signifiers. For example, in the sentence *I filled the glass with milk*, the spoken or written word *glass* is a signifier; its signified is the concept of a *container* that can be filled. But in the sentence *The container was filled with glass*, the spoken or written word *container*, a signified in the previous sentence, is now a signifier, its signified being the concept of an object that can be filled.

ASSUMPTIONS

Transcendental Signified

Believing that signification (how we arrive at meaning from the linguistic signs in language) is both arbitrary and conventional, Derrida now begins his process of turning Western philosophy on its head. He boldly asserts that the entire history of Western metaphysics from Plato to the present is founded upon a classic, fundamental error: the searching for a **transcendental signified**, an external point of reference on which one may build a concept or philosophy. Once found, this transcendental signified would provide ultimate meaning, being the origin of origins, reflecting itself, and as Derrida says, providing a "reassuring end to the reference from sign to sign." In essence, it would guarantee to those who believe in it that they do exist and have meaning. For example, if we posit that *I* or *self* is a transcendental signified, then the concept of *self* becomes the unifying principle on which I structure my world. Objects, concepts, ideas, or even people take on meaning in my world only if I filter them through my unifying, ultimate signified *self*.

Unlike other signifieds, the transcendental signified would have to be understood without being compared to other signifieds or signifiers. In other words, its meaning would originate directly with itself, not differentially or relationally, as does the meaning of all other signifieds or signifiers. These transcendental signifieds would then provide the center of meaning, allowing those who believed in them to structure their ideas of reality around them. Such a center of meaning could not subject itself to structural analysis, for by so doing it would lose its place as a transcendental signified to another center. For example, if I declare the concept *self* to be my transcendental signified and then learn that my mind or self is composed of the id, the ego, and the superego, I could no longer hold the *self* or *I* to be my transcendental signified. In the process of discovering the three parts of my conscious and unconscious mind, I have both structurally analyzed and decentered *self*, thus negating it as a transcendental signified.

Logocentrism

According to Derrida, Western metaphysics has invented a variety of terms that function as centers: *God, reason, origin, being, essence, truth, humanity, beginning, end,* and *self,* to name a few. Each can operate as a concept that is self-sufficient and self-originating and can serve as a transcendental signified. This Western proclivity for desiring a center Derrida names **logocentrism**: the belief that there is an ultimate reality or center of truth that can serve as the basis for all our thoughts and actions.

That we can never totally free ourselves from our logocentric habit of thinking and our inherited concept of the universe Derrida readily admits. To decenter any transcendental signified is to be caught up automatically in the terminology that allows that centering concept to operate. For example, if the concept *self* functions as my center and I then "discover" my unconscious self, I automatically place in motion a binary operation or two opposing concepts: the *self* and the *unconscious self*. By decentering and questioning the *self*, I cause the *unconscious self* to become the new center. By questioning the old center, I establish a new one.

Such logocentric thinking, declares Derrida, has its origin in Aristotle's principle of noncontradiction: A thing cannot both have a property and not have a property. Thanks to Aristotle, maintains Derrida, Western meta-physics has developed an either–or mentality or logic that inevitably leads to dualistic thinking and to the centering and decentering of transcendental signifieds. Such a logocentric way of thinking, asserts Derrida, is natural for Western readers, but problematic.

Binary Oppositions

Because the establishing of one center of unity automatically means that another is decentered, Derrida concludes that Western metaphysics is based on a system of **binary operations** or conceptual oppositions. For each center, there exists an opposing center (God/humankind, for example). In addition, Western philosophy holds that in each of these binary operations or two opposing centers, one concept is superior and defines itself by its opposite or inferior center. We know *truth*, for instance, because we know *deception*; we know *good* because we know *bad*. The creating of these hierarchal binaries is the basis of Western metaphysics to which Derrida objects.

Phonocentrism

Such a fragile basis for believing what is really real Derrida wishes to dismantle. In the binary oppositions on which Western metaphysics has built itself from the time of Plato, Derrida declares that one element will always be in a superior position, or **privileged**, whereas the other becomes inferior, or **unprivileged**. According to this way of thinking, the first or top elements in the following list of binary oppositions are privileged: man/woman, human/animal, soul/body, good/bad. Most importantly, Derrida decrees that Western thought has long privileged speech over writing. This privileging of speech over writing Derrida calls **phonocentrism**.

In placing speech in the privileged position, phonocentrism treats writing as inferior. We value a speaker's words more than the speaker's writing, says Derrida, for words imply presence. Through the vehicle of spoken words, we supposedly learn directly what a speaker is trying to say. From this point of view, writing becomes a mere copy of speech, an attempt to capture the idea that was once spoken. Whereas speech implies presence, writing signifies absence, thereby placing into action another binary opposition: presence/absence.

Because phonocentrism is based on the assumption that speech conveys the meaning or direct ideas of a speaker better than writing (a mere copy of speech), phonocentrism assumes a logocentric way of thinking, that the self is the center of meaning and can best ascertain ideas directly from other selves through spoken words. Through speaking, the self declares its presence, its significance, and its being (or existence).

Metaphysics of Presence

Accordingly, Derrida coins the phrase **metaphysics of presence** to encompass ideas such as logocentrism, phonocentrism, the operation of binary oppositions, and other notions that Western thought holds concerning language and metaphysics. His objective is to demonstrate the shaky foundations on which such beliefs have been established. By deconstructing the basic premises of metaphysics of presence, Derrida believes he gives us a strategy for reading that opens up a variety of new interpretations heretofore unseen by those who are bound by the restraints of Western thought.

METHODOLOGY

Acknowledging Binary Operations in Western Thought

The first stage in a deconstructive reading is to recognize the existence and operation of binary oppositions in our thinking. One of the most "violent hierarchies" derived from Platonic and Aristotelian thought is speech/writing, with speech being privileged. Consequently, speech is awarded presence, and writing is equated with absence. Being the inferior of the two, writing becomes simply the symbols of speech, a second-hand representation of ideas.

Once the speech/writing hierarchy or any other hierarchy is recognized and acknowledged, Derrida asserts, we can readily reverse its elements. Such a reversal is possible because truth is ever elusive, for we can always decenter the center if any is found. By reversing the hierarchy, Derrida does not wish merely to substitute one hierarchy for another and to involve himself in a negative mode. When the hierarchy is reversed, says Derrida, we can examine the values and beliefs that give rise to both the original hierarchy and the newly created one. Such an examination reveals how the meanings of terms arise from the differences between them.

Arche-writing

In *Of Grammatology*, Derrida spends much time explaining why the speech/writing hierarchy can and must be reversed. In short, he argues for a redefining of the term *writing* that will allow him to assert that writing is actually a precondition for and prior to speech. According to Derrida's metaphysical reasoning, language is a special kind of writing which he calls **archi-écriture** or **arche-writing**.

Using traditional Western metaphysics that is grounded in phonocentricism, Derrida begins his reversal of the speech/writing hierarchy by noting that language and writing share common characteristics. For example, both involve an encoding or inscription. In writing, this coding is obvious, for the written symbols represent various phonemes. And in language or speech, a similar encoding exists. As Saussure has already shown, there exists an arbitrary relationship between the signifier and the signified (between the spoken word *cat* and the concept of cat itself). Thus, there is no innate relationship between the spoken word and the concept, object, or idea it represents. Nevertheless, once a signifier and a signified join to form a sign, some kind of relationship then exists between these components of the sign. For example, some kind of inscription or encoding has taken place between the spoken word *cat* (the signifier) and its concept (the signified).

For Derrida both writing and language are means of signification, and each can be considered a signifying system. Traditional Western metaphysics and Saussurean linguistics equate speech (language) with presence, for speech is accompanied by the presence of a living speaker. The presence of the speaker necessarily links sound and sense and therefore leads to understanding—one usually comprehends the spoken word. Writing, on the other hand, assumes an absence of a speaker. Such absence can produce misunderstanding, for writing is a depersonalized medium that separates the actual utterance of the speaker and his or her audience. This absence can lead to misunderstanding of the signifying system.

But Derrida asserts that we must broaden our understanding of writing. Writing, he declares, cannot be reduced to letters or other symbols inscribed on a page. Rather, it is directly related to what Saussure believed to be the basic element of language: difference. We know one phoneme or one word because each is different from another. And we know that there is no innate relationship between a signifier and its signified. The phoneme /b/, for example, could have easily become the symbol for the phoneme /d/, just as the coined word *bodt* could have become the English word *ball*. It is this free play or element of undecidability in any system of communication that Derrida calls writing. This free play with the various elements of signification in any system of communication totally eludes a speaker's awareness when using language, for the speaker falsely assumes a position as supposed master of his or her speech.

By equating writing with the free play or the element of undecidability at the center of all systems of communication, Derrida declares that writing actually governs language, thereby negating the speech/writing hierarchy of Western metaphysics. Writing now becomes privileged and speech unprivileged, for speech is a kind of writing called arche-writing.

This being so, Derrida then challenges Western philosophy's concept that human consciousness gives birth to language. Without language (or arche-writing), argues Derrida, there can be no consciousness, for consciousness presupposes language. Through arche-writing, we impose human consciousness on the world.

Supplementation

The relationship between any binary hierarchy, however, is always unstable and problematic. It is not Derrida's purpose simply to reverse all binary oppositions that exist in Western thought but rather to show the fragile basis for the establishment of such hierarchies and the possibility of inverting these hierarchies to gain new insights into language and life. Derrida uses the term *supplement* to refer to the unstable relationship between elements in a binary operation. For example, in the speech/writing opposition, writing supplements speech and in actuality takes the place of speech (arche-writing). In all binary oppositions such supplementation exists. In the truth/deception hierarchy, for example, Western thought would assert the supremacy of truth over deception, attributing to deception a mere supplementary role. Such a logocentric way of thinking asserts the purity of truth over deception. Upon examination, deception more often than not contains at least some truth. And who is to say, asks Derrida, when truth has been spoken, achieved, or even conceived? The purity of truth may simply not exist. In all human activity, then, supplementation operates.

Différance

By realizing that supplementation operates in all of Western metaphysics' binary operations and by inverting the privileged and unprivileged elements, Derrida begins to develop his reading strategy of deconstruction. Once he turns Western metaphysics on its head, he asserts his answer to logocentrism and other Western elements by coining a new word and concept: *différance*. The word itself is derived from the French word *différer*, meaning both to defer, postpone, or delay, and to differ, to be different from. Derrida deliberately coins his word to be ambiguous, taking on both meanings simultaneously. And in French the word is a pun, for it exists only in writing; in speech there is no way to tell the difference between the French word *différence* and Derrida's coined word *différance*.

Understanding what Derrida means by *différance* is one of the basic keys to understanding deconstruction. Basically, *différance* is Derrida's what-if question. What if no transcendental signified exists? What if there is no presence in whom we can find ultimate truth? What if all our knowledge does not arise from self-identity? What if there is no essence, being, or inherently unifying element in the universe? What then?

The presence of such a transcendental signified would immediately establish the binary operation presence/absence. Because Western metaphysics holds that presence is supreme or privileged and absence unprivileged, Derrida suggests that we temporarily reverse this hierarchy to become absence/presence. By such a reversal, no longer can we posit a transcendental signified. No longer is there some absolute standard or coherent unity from which all knowledge proceeds and develops. All human knowledge and all self-identity must now spring from difference, not sameness, from absence, not presence.

When such a reversal of Western metaphysics' pivotal binary operation occurs, two dramatic results follow: First, all human knowledge becomes referential; that is, we can know something only because it differs from some other bit of knowledge, not because we can compare this knowledge to any absolute or coherent unity (a transcendental signified). Human knowledge, then, must now be based on *différence*. We know something because it differs from something else to which it is related. Nothing can be studied or learned in isolation, for all knowledge becomes context-related. Second, we must also forgo closure; that is, because no transcendental signified exists, all interpretations concerning life, self-identity, and knowledge are possible, probable, and legitimate.

But what is the significance of différance in reading texts? If we, like Derrida, assert that différance operates in language and therefore also in writing (Derrida sometimes equates différance and arche-writing), what are the implications for textual analysis? The most obvious answer is that texts lack presence. Once we do away with the transcendental signified and reverse the presence/absence binary operation, texts can no longer have presence; that is, in isolation, texts cannot possess meaning. Because all meaning and knowledge are now based on differences, no text can simply mean one thing. Texts become intertextual. Meaning evolves from the interrelatedness of one text to many other texts. Like language itself, texts are caught in a dynamic, context-related interchange. Never can we state a text's definitive meaning, for it has none. No longer can we declare one interpretation to be right and another wrong, for meaning in a text is always illusive, always dynamic, also transitory.

The search, then, for the text's correct meaning or the author's so-called intentions become meaningless. Because meaning is derived from differences in a dynamic, context-related, ongoing process, all texts have multiple meanings or interpretations. If we assert, as does Derrida, that no transcendental signified exists, then there can exist no absolute or pure meaning supposedly conveyed by authorial intent or professorial dictates. Meaning evolves as we, the readers, interact with the text, with both the readers and the text providing social and cultural context.

Deconstructive Suppositions for Textual Analysis

A deconstructor would thus begin textual analysis assuming that a text has multiple interpretations and that it allows itself to be reread and thus reinterpreted countless times. Because no one correct interpretation of any text exists, the joy of textual analysis resides in discovering new interpretations each time a text is read and reread. Ultimately, a text's meaning is undecidable, for each reading or rereading can elicit different interpretations.

When beginning the interpretative process, deconstructors seek to override their own logocentric and inherited ways of viewing a text. Such revolutionary thinkers find the binary oppositions at work in the text itself. These binary oppositions, they believe, represent established and accepted ideologies that usually posit the existence of transcendental signifieds. These binary operations restrict meaning, for they already assume a fixed interpretation of reality. They assume, for instance, the existence of truth and falsehood, reason and insanity, good and bad. Realizing that these hierarchies presuppose a fixed and a biased way of viewing the world, deconstructors seek out the binary oppositions operating in the text and reverse them. By reversing these hierarchies, deconstructors wish to challenge the fixed views assumed by such hierarchies and the values associated with such rigid beliefs.

By identifying the binary operations that exist in the text, deconstructors can then show the preconceived assumptions on which most of us base our interpretations. For example, we all declare some activity, being, or object to be good or bad, valuable or worthless, significant or insignificant. Such values or ideas automatically operate when we write or read any text. By reversing the hierarchies on which we base our interpretations, deconstructors wish to free us from the constraints of our prejudiced beliefs. Such freedom, they hope, will allow us to see a text from exciting new perspectives that we have never before recognized.

These various perspectives cannot be simultaneously perceived by the reader or even the writer of a text. In Nathaniel Hawthorne's "Young Goodman Brown," for example, many readers believe that the 50-year-old character who shepherds Goodman Brown through his night's visit in the forest is Satan and therefore necessarily an evil character. Brown's own interpretation of this character seems to support this view. According to deconstructionist ideas, at least two binary operations are at work here: good/evil and God/Satan. But what if we reverse these hierarchies? Then the scepteral figure may not be Satan and therefore may not be evil! Such a new perspective may dramatically change our interpretation of the text.

According to deconstructors, we cannot simultaneously see both of these perspectives in the story. To discover where the new hierarchy Satan/God or evil/good will lead us in our interpretation, we must suspend our first interpretation. We do not, however, forget it, for it is locked in our minds. We simply shift our allegiance to another perspective or level.

Such oscillating between interpretations, levels, or perspectives allows us to see the impossibility of ever choosing a correct interpretation, for meaning is an ongoing activity that is always in progress, always based on différance. By asking what will happen if we reverse the hierarchies that frame our preconceived ways of thinking, we open ourselves to a never-ending process of interpretation that holds that no hierarchy or binary operation is right and no other is wrong.

Deconstruction: A New Reading Strategy

Deconstructors do not wish, then, to set up a new philosophy, a new literary theory of analysis, or a new school of literary criticism. Instead, they present a new reading strategy that allows us to make choices concerning the various levels of interpretation we see operating in a text. All levels, they maintain, have validity. They also believe that their approach to reading frees them and us from ideological allegiances that restrict our finding meaning in a text.

Because meaning, they believe, emerges through interpretation, even the author does not control a text's interpretation. Although writers may have clearly stated intentions concerning their texts, such statements must be given little credence. Like language itself, texts have no outside referents (or transcendental signifieds). What an author thinks he or she says or means in a text may be quite different from what is actually written. Deconstructors therefore look for places in the text where the author **misspeaks** or loses control of language and says what was supposedly not meant to be said. These "slips of language" often occur in questions, figurative language, and strong declarations. For example, suppose we read the following words: "Important Seniors' Meeting." Although the author thinks that readers will interpret these words to mean that it is important that all seniors be present at this particular meeting, the author may have misspoken, for these words can actually mean that only important seniors should attend this meeting. By examining such slips and the binary operations that govern them, deconstructors are able to demonstrate the undecidability of a text's meaning.

At first glance, a deconstructionist reading strategy may appear to be linear—that is, having a clearly delineated beginning, middle, and end. If this is so, then to apply this strategy to a text, we must do the following:

- Discover the binary operations that govern a text.
- Comment on the values, concepts, and ideas beyond these operations.
- Reverse these present binary operations.
- Dismantle previously held worldviews.
- Accept the possibility of various perspectives or levels of meaning in a text based on the new binary inversions.
- Allow meaning of the text to be undecidable.

Although all these elements operate in a deconstructionist reading, they may not operate in this exact sequence. Because we all tend toward logocentrism when reading, we may not note some logocentric binary operations functioning in the text until we have reversed some obvious binary oppositions and are interpreting the text on several levels. In addition, we must never declare such a reading to be complete or finished, for the process of meaning is ongoing, never allowing us to pledge allegiance to any one view.

Such a reading strategy disturbs most readers and critics, for it is not a neat, completed package whereby if we follow step A through to step Z we arrive at "the" reading of the text. Because texts have no external referents, their meanings depend on the close interaction of the text, the reader, and social and cultural elements, as does every reading or interpretive process. Denying the organic unity of a text, deconstructors declare the free play of language in a text. Because language itself is reflexive, not mimetic, we can never stop finding meaning in a text, whether we have read it once or a hundred times.

Overall, deconstruction desires an ongoing relationship between the interpreter (the critic) and the text. By examining the text alone, deconstructors hope to ask a set of questions that continually challenges the ideological positions of power and authority that dominate literary criticism. And in the process of discovering meaning in a text, they declare that criticism of a text is just as valuable as the creative writing being read, thus inverting the creative writing/criticism hierarchy.

AMERICAN DECONSTRUCTORS

After Derrida's introduction of deconstruction to his American audience in 1966, Derrida found several sympathetic listeners who soon became loyal adherents and defenders of his new reading strategy: Romantic scholar Paul de Man (*Blindness and Insight*, 1971), rhetorical deconstructor Hayden White (*Tropics of Discourse*, 1978), the sometimes terse metaphysical deconstructor Geoffrey Hartman (*Criticism in the Wilderness*, 1980), the strong voice of Barbara Johnson (*The Critical Difference*, 1980), and phenomenological critic turned deconstructor J. Hillis Miller (*Fiction and Repetition: Seven English Novels*, 1982). These critics asserted that deconstruction would find a voice and an established place in American literary theory. Although the voices of other poststructural theories such as New Historicism and Postcolonial theory now clamor to be heard, deconstruction's philosophical assumptions and practical reading strategies form the basis of many postmodern literary practices.

QUESTIONS FOR ANALYSIS

- Interpret a short story or poem of your choice. After you have completed your interpretation, cite the binary operations that function both within your chosen text and within your thinking to allow you to arrive at your perspective.
- Using the same text and interpretation you used for the first question, reverse one of the binary operations and reinterpret the text. When you are finished, reverse two additional binaries and reinterpret the story. What differences exist between the two interpretations?

- Using Robert Browning's "My Last Duchess" or a poem of your choice, demonstrate how the author misspeaks, or where the text involves itself in paradox. Be specific. Be able to point to lines, figurative speech, or imaginative language to support your statements.
- Using Robert Browning's "My Last Duchess," cite at least four dramatically different interpretations, all based on a deconstructive reading.
- Reread the student essay found at the end of Chapter 3, "New Criticism." What elements of the story does the author simply ignore or dismiss? Consider how Derrida's concept of supplementation is operating in this critic's analysis.
- Using the professional essay found at the end of Chapter 4, "Reader-Response Criticism," state the binary operations that control the critic's interpretation of the text. From these binaries, cite the ideological positions of the critic, and note what elements in the story she must ignore to arrive at her conclusions.
- Read the student essay located at the end of this chapter. Because this essay approaches textual analysis from a deconstructive point of view, the author must assume that all essays can be so analyzed. On this assumption, deconstruct the student essay, noting where the author of the essay misspeaks and how the essay dismantles itself.

SAMPLE ESSAYS

In the student essay that follows, note how the author uses the various binary operations she discovers in the text to show how the text misspeaks and dismantles itself. Also note and be able to explain how the binaries used by the author of the parable of the wedding banquet involve the text in paradoxes. Based on the binary oppositions at work in the parable, be able to explain at least four different interpretations. In addition, note how the author tries to divorce herself from logocentric thinking and the metaphysics of presence as she seeks to analyze the parable.

In the professional essay that follows, J. Hillis Miller asserts that Wordsworth's short poem "A Slumber Did My Spirit Seal" appears to be organized around several sets of binary oppositions that seem logical and systematic. Using deconstructive methodology, Miller then demonstrates how these interrelated and supposedly orderly binary oppositions prevent one from declaring that the poem achieves organic unity. Be able to explain how Miller arrives at such a conclusion and what principles of deconstruction he uses in his interpretation.

FURTHER READING

Atkins, G. Douglas. *Reading Deconstruction: Deconstructive Reading.* Lexington: University Press of Kentucky, 1983.

Bloom, Harold. *A Map of Misreading.* New York: Oxford University Press, 1975.

Caputo, John D. "The Good News About Alterity: Derrida and Theology." *Faith and Philosophy* 10.4 (Oct. 1993): 453–70.

Culler, Jonathan. *On Deconstruction: Theory and Criticism after Structuralism.* Ithaca, NY: Cornell University Press, 1982.

de Man, Paul. *Blindness and Insight: Essays in the Rhetoric of Contemporary Criticism.* New York: Oxford University Press, 1971.

———. *The Rhetoric of Romanticism.* New York: Columbia University Press, 1984.

Derrida, Jacques. "Structure, Sign, and Play in the Discourse of the Human Sciences." *Writing and Difference.* Trans. Alan Bass. Chicago: University of Chicago Press, 1978.

Ellis, John M. *Against Deconstruction.* Princeton: Princeton University Press, 1989.

Gasche, Rodolphe. "Deconstruction as Criticism." *Glyph Textual Studies* 6 (1979): 177–215.

Hartman, Geoffrey. *Criticism in the Wilderness.*

Hartman, Geoffrey. *Saving the Text: Literature/Derrida/Philosophy.* Baltimore: Johns Hopkins University Press, 1981.

Jefferson, Ann. "Structuralism and Post Structuralism." *Modern Literary Theory: A Comparative Introduction.* Totowa, NJ: Barnes & Noble, 1982, pp. 84–112.

Johnson, Barbara. *The Critical Difference: Essays in the Contemporary Rhetoric of Reading.* Baltimore: Johns Hopkins University Press, 1980.

Miller, J. Hillis. *Fiction and Repetition: Seven English Novels.* Cambridge, MA: Harvard University Press, 1982.

———. *Tropes, Parables and Performatives: Essays on Twentieth-Century Literature.* Hemel Hempstead, London: Harvester Wheatsheaf, 1990.

Norris, Christopher. *Deconstruction: Theory and Practice.* London: Meuthen, 1982.

Rajnath, ed. *Deconstruction: A Critique.* London: Macmillan, 1989.

Saussure, Ferdinand de. *Course in General Linguistics.* Ed. Charles Baly and Albert Reidlinger. Trans. Wade Baskin. New York: Philosophical Library, 1959.

White, Hayden. *Tropics of Discourse: Essays in Cultural Criticism.* Baltimore: Johns Hopkins University Press, 1978.

WEB SITES FOR EXPLORATION

http://www.brocku.ca/english/course/4F70/deconstruction.html
    Provides some basic assumptions of deconstruction
www.stg.brown.edu/projects/hypertext/landow/SSPCCluster/Derrida.html
    Provides links to a variety of deconstructive articles
www.130.179.92.25/Arnason_DE/Derrida.html
    Provides a working definition of deconstruction and includes definitions of terms essential to deconstruction theory
www.tile.net/tile/listserv/derrida.html
    Provides access to Internet discussion groups concerning Jacques Derrida and deconstruction
www.sun3.lib.uci.edu/~scctr/Wellek/derrida.html
    Provides access to two bibliographies of works by Jacques Derrida
www.colorado.edu/English/ENGL2012Klages/1derrida.html
    Provides a basic understanding of and shows the differences between structuralism and poststructuralism

⋙ Student Essay ⋙

Banquet of Contradiction

According to *A Handbook to Literature*, a parable is "an illustrative story teaching a lesson. A true *parable* parallels, detail for detail, the situation that calls forth the *parable* for illustration. A *parable* is, in this sense, an allegory. In Christian countries the most famous parables are those told by Christ" (Harmon and Holman, 7th ed., p. 372). As Harmon and Holman note, Jesus Christ, the founder of Christianity, often used parables to teach his followers. The Gospel of Matthew records one such instance, for it contains the parable of the wedding banquet. [The text of this parable can be found at the end of this essay.] Many interpretations of this text explain that this parable illustrates God's unwarranted mercy toward humanity. God, the gracious host of the feast, provides garments of righteousness to all who respond to His invitation. He accepts both the good and the bad, calling them "friend," and He rejects those who refuse His invitation.

According to the deconstructive critic Geoffrey Hartman, however, such interpretations as the one cited above rely upon an "older hermeneutics" of Biblical texts that tends to soften what the actual text says and tries to reconcile a rather harsh picture of God as depicted in the text with a gentle, all-merciful father image. A more critical reader can readily discover several passages in this parable in which the text misspeaks and dismantles itself.

One of the most obvious instances where the text dismantles itself is the paradoxical situation created when the king calls the intruder at his banquet "Friend," and then treats him like an enemy. In his disappointment and anger at the behavior of his original guests, the king has ordered his servants to invite anyone they can find to fill his wedding hall. As requested, the servants have arbitrarily brought people in off the streets without questioning their background. The king's treatment of one such individual whom he has invited to his banquet and subsequently named "Friend" is highly unusual. Interestingly, the text of the parable fails to mention that the king provided his guests with the required wedding garments. Although Biblical commentators attest that such a service was probably a custom at the time, the truth of this assumption is undocumented by the text itself. The man's (or "friend's") speechlessness at the king's demand that he have garments that he obviously had no opportunity to obtain is hardly surprising. The sudden command that the "friend" be thrown "outside, into the darkness, where there will be weeping and grinding of teeth" is, then, a most unexpected treatment of one so highly named as a friend.

Similarly, the conceptual contradiction intrinsic in the privileging of both the invited guests and the chosen is also problematic. At the beginning of the story, those who are invited to the wedding banquet are elevated by the simple raising of status involved in their receiving an invitation from the king. When these now-important people refuse the gift of the king's invitation and are either indifferent ("they paid no attention") or violently opposed to the king's plans (they "mistreated [his servants] and killed them"), they quickly lose their privileged status.

Not only do they lose their newly-acquired, prestigious social rank but they also lose their lives, for the king has them destroyed. The use of the word "destroyed" is particularly important. When the king's servants are murdered by these would-be wedding guests, the text announces that the servants are "killed" (verse 6). But when the king, in turn, kills uncooperative wedding guests, the text declares they are "destroyed." The connotation and implications of being "destroyed" are certainly more derogatory, more damning, and more pernicious than being "killed." Suddenly, the king's servants (who were "killed" and "mistreated" by "murderers") have gained a higher social status than the violent, once-invited wedding guests. Interestingly, however, the privileging of the concept of "the invited" remains intact, for the king's next act after having the first set of wedding guests "destroyed" is to bestow the honor of invitation on others.

Another conflict of ideas and dismantling of the text occurs near the end of the story when the king expels an invited guest who does not wear the appropriate "wedding clothes." Nowhere in the text or in the invitation to the wedding does it state that one had to be dressed a certain way to attend the wedding banquet. The text simply says that the king's servants "gathered all the people they could find, both good and bad, and the wedding hall was filled with guests." And nowhere in the text does it decree that one must be "chosen" to stay at the wedding feast or even how one becomes chosen.

But the parable ends with the homily, "For many are invited, but few are chosen." The "chosen" are thus privileged over the "invited" who are privileged over those unfortunates who were never asked to come to the wedding banquet in the first place. Apparently, to be invited to the king's banquet is good, but the invitation has no lasting value unless the guest is also chosen. But what a contradiction! Is it any better, in the long run, to be merely invited but not chosen and to be thrown "into the darkness" then to be unbidden and never see the light? And, how, anyway, does one become "chosen"? The privileging, then, of both the invited people and those who are chosen is problematic and perplexing. The author has apparently misspoken, causing pain not only to the invited but not chosen guests but also to the readers of the parable.

But the text continues to dismantle itself in regard to the vengeance/mercy binary operation. Enraged by the ingratitude, the indifference, and the injustice of the invited guests, the king "destroy[s] those murderers and burn[s] their city." In a sublime act of mercy in the very next paragraph, he then fills his wedding hall with guests off the streets, "both the good and the bad." One ill-clad guest arouses the king's anger, however, and once again vengeance for the man's impertinence is privileged over mercy. Such arbitrary behavior hardly seems fair, and certainly not kingly or loving, for this king wreaks vengeance on those that disappoint him.

The most convoluted of binary oppositions in the story, however, occurs with the selective/inclusive binary. At first, the guests are a select number, specifically invited to the king's banquet. When for various reasons the preferred guests revolt, the king says that they "did not deserve to come." Instead of filling his hall with a select company, the king indiscriminately brings in the nobodies. The resulting assemblage contains "both good and bad," a rather inclusive group. These guests certainly deserve the king's invitation no more than the first bunch, but the king seems to have changed the rules, and luckily for the second group, eligibility is no longer based on worthiness. The idea of the inclusive and the undeserved is therefore now privileged over the selective and the merited. The binary flips once more, however, with the king's treatment of the "friend." Apparently, the gathering is not quite so inclusive after all. The only valid guests are those wearing the correct clothes. In the end, the selective is valued above the inclusive once again, "For many are invited, but few are chosen."

The parable of the wedding banquet becomes more and more obscure and problematic as each binary opposition operating in the text comes under scrutiny. By using deconstructive principles to guide an interpretation of the text, one's analysis generates seemingly endless queries and puzzlement. For example, is the king merciful or vengeful? Is this parable a reassurance of grace or a warning against refusing the invitation? Or is it perhaps both? From a deconstructor's perspective, the joy of such analysis is found in devising multiple interpretations obtained from the text's dismantling of itself, not in pontificating or in trying to discover its so-called correct interpretation.

JENNIFER RICHARDSON

"The Parable of the Wedding Banquet"

The kingdom of heaven is like a king who prepared a wedding banquet for his son. He sent his servants to those who had been invited to the banquet to tell them to come, but they refused to come.

Then he sent some more servants and said, "Tell those who have been invited that I have prepared my dinner: My oxen and fattened cattle have been butchered, and everything is ready. Come to the wedding banquet."

But they paid no attention and went off—one to his field, another to his business. The rest seized his servants, mistreated them and killed them. The king was enraged. He sent his army and destroyed those murderers and burned their city.

Then he said to his servants, "The wedding banquet is ready, but those I invited did not deserve to come. Go to the street corners and invite to the banquet anyone you find." So the servants went out into the streets and gathered all the people they could find, both good and bad, and the wedding hall was filled with guests.

But when the king came in to see the guests, he noticed a man there who was not wearing wedding clothes. "Friend," he asked, "how did you get in there without wedding clothes?" The man was speechless.

Then the king told the attendants, "Tie him hand and foot, and throw him outside, into the darkness, where there will be weeping and gnashing of teeth."

For many are invited, but few are chosen.

GOSPEL OF MATTHEW, CHAPTER 22
NEW INTERNATIONAL VERSION

❧ Professional Essay ❧

from On Edge: The Crossways of Contemporary Criticism

The relation of metaphysics and the deconstruction of metaphysics finds a parable in the strange relation of kinship among apparent opposites in Wordsworth's "A Slumber Did My Spirit Seal." Here is the poem:

> A slumber did my spirit seal;
> I had no human fears:
> She seemed a thing that could not feel
> The touch of earthly years.
>
> No motion has she now, no force;
> She neither hears nor sees;
> Rolled round in earth's diurnal course,
> With rocks, and stones, and trees.

This beautiful, moving, and apparently simple poem was written at Goslar in Germany in the late fall or early winter of 1798–1799, during Wordsworth's miserable sojourn there with his sister Dorothy. It seems at first to be organized around a systematically interrelated set of binary oppositions. These seem to be genuinely exclusive oppositions, with a distinct uncrossable boundary line between them. Such a systematic set of oppositions, as always, invites interpretation of the dialectical sort. In such an interpretation, the oppositions are related in some scheme of hierarchical subordination. This makes possible a synthesis grounded in an explanatory third term constituting the logos of the poem. This logos is the poem's source and end, its ground and meaning, its "word" or "message." This particular text, I am arguing, forbids the successful completion of such a procedure.

The method does not work. Something is always left over, a plus value beyond the boundaries of each such interpretation.

A surprising number of oppositions are present in the poem. These include slumber as against walking; male as against female; sealed up as against open; seeming as against being; ignorance as against knowledge; past as against present; inside as against outside; light as against darkness in the "diurnal" course of the earth; subject or consciousness, "spirit," as against object, the natural world of stones and trees; feeling as "touch" as against feeling as emotion, "fears"; "human fears" as against—what?—perhaps inhuman fears; "thing" in its meaning of "girl," young virgin, as against "thing" in the sense of physical object; years as against days; hearing as against seeing; motion as against force; self-propulsion as against exterior compulsion; mother as against daughter or sister, or perhaps any female family member as against some woman from outside the family, that is, mother, sister, or daughter as against mistress or wife, in short, incestuous desires against legitimate sexual feelings; life as against death.

The invitation to interpret the poem in terms of oppositions is sustained in part by its syntactical and formal structure. Syntactically it is structured around words or phrases in apposition or opposition. The second line, for instance, repeats the first, and then lines three and four say it over again:

> A slumber did my spirit seal;
> I had no human fears:
> She seemed a thing that could not feel
> The touch of earthly years.

To have no human fears is the same thing as to have a sealed spirit. Both of these are defined by the speaker's false assumption that Lucy will not grow old or die. Formally the poem is organized by the opposition between the first stanza and the second. Each stanza sets one line against the next, the first two against the last two, by way of the interlaced pattern of rhymes— abab, cdcd. The bar or barrier or blank on the page between the two stanzas constitutes the major formal structuring principle of the poem. In the shift from past to present tense this bar opposes then to now, ignorance to knowledge, life to death. The speaker has moved across the line from innocence to knowledge through the experience of Lucy's death. The poem expresses both eloquently restrained grief for that death and the calm of mature knowledge. Before, he was innocent. His spirit was sealed from knowledge as though he were asleep, closed in on himself. His innocence took the form of an ignorance of the fact of death. Lucy seemed so much alive, such an invulnerable vital young thing, that she could not possibly be touched by time, reach old age, and die. Her seeming immortality reassured the speaker of his own, and so he did not anticipate with fear his own death. He had no human fears. To be human is to be mortal, and the most specifically human fear, it may be, is the fear of death.

Wordsworth, in fact, as we know from other texts both in poetry and in prose, had as a child, and even as a young man, a strong conviction of his immortality. The feeling that it would be impossible for him to die was associated with a strong sense of participation in a nature both enduringly material, therefore immortal, and at the same time enduringly spiritual, therefore also immortal, though in a different way. In this poem, as in many others by Wordsworth—"The Boy of Winander," the Matthew poems, and "The Ruined Cottage," for example—the speaker confronts the fact of his own death by confronting the death of another. He speaks as a survivor standing by a grave, a corpse, or a headstone, and his poem takes the form of an epitaph.

The second stanza of "A Slumber Did My Spirit Seal" speaks in the perpetual "now" of a universal knowledge of death. The speaker knows his own death through the death of another. Then Lucy seemed an invulnerable young "thing"; now she is truly a thing, closed in on herself like a stone. She is a corpse, without senses or consciousness, unable to feel any touch, unable to move of her own free will, but unwillingly and unwittingly moved by the daily rotation of the earth.

The structure of the poem is temporal. It is also "allegorical" in the technical sense in which that term is used by Walter Benjamin or by Paul de Man. The meaning of the poem arises from the interaction of two emblematic times. These are juxtaposed across an intervening gap. They are related not by similarity but by radical difference. The ironic clash between the two senses of "thing" is a miniature version of the total temporal allegory which constitutes the poem.

The play on the word "thing" exists, it happens, also in German. Two curious passages in Martin Heidegger's work will perhaps help to understand it better in Wordsworth. The first is in a passage in "Der Ursprung des Kunstwerkes" ("The Origin of the Work of Art"), in which Heidegger is giving examples of times when we do or do not call something a "thing":

> A man is not a thing. (*Der Mensch ist kein Ding.*) It is true that we speak of a young girl who is faced with a task too difficult for her as being a young thing, still too young for it, but only because we feel that being human is in a certain way missing here and think that instead we have to do here with the factor that constitutes the thingly character of things. We hesitate even to call the deer in the forest clearing, the beetle in the grass, the blade of grass a thing. We could sooner think of a hammer as a thing, or a shoe, or an ax, or a clock. But even these are not mere things. Only a stone, a clod of earth, a piece of wood are for us such mere things.

Strangely, though perhaps in response to a deep necessity, Heidegger gives almost exactly the same list of mere things as Wordsworth. His young girl, stone, clod of earth, piece of wood, correspond to Wordsworth's Lucy, rocks, stones, trees, and the earth itself. Moreover, Heidegger, certainly not known for his attention to the sexual aspect of things, finds himself of necessity, in his account of the uses of the word "thing," introducing the fact of sexual difference. A young girl is a thing because something is missing in her which men have. "A man is not a thing." This something missing makes her "too young for it," too young for the burdens of life. She is too innocent, too light.

This lightness of the maiden thing, which makes a young girl both beneath adult male knowledge and lightheartedly above it, appears in another odd passage in Heidegger, in this case in *Die Frage nach dem Ding* (*What Is a Thing?*). Heidegger first recalls the story in Plato's *Thaetetus* about the "goodlooking and whimsical maid from Thrace" who laughed at Thales when he fell down a well while occupied in studying the heavens. In his study of all things in the universe, "the things in front of his very nose and feet were unseen by him." "Therefore," says Heidegger in commentary on Plato's story, "the question 'What is a thing?' must always be rated as one which causes housemaids to laugh. And genuine housemaids must have something to laugh about." The question, "What is a thing?", which is the question implicit in "A Slumber Did My Spirit Seal," would be a laughable nonquestion to Lucy. She would not understand it because she *is* a thing. Being a thing makes her both immeasurably below and immeasurably above laughable man with his eternal questions. By dying Lucy moves from the below to the above, leaving the male poet in either case in between, excluded, unable to break the seal.

As the reader works his or her way into the poem, attempting to break its seal, however, it comes to seem odder than the account of it I have so far given. My account has been a little too logical, a little too much like Thales' account of the universe, an analogical oversimplification. For one thing, the speaker has in fact not died. Lucy, it may be, has achieved immortality by joining herself to the perpetual substance of earth, which cannot die, as Wordsworth very forcefully says at the beginning of Book V of *The Prelude*. The speaker by not dying remains excluded from that perpetual vitality. His immortality is the bad one of a permanent empty knowledge of death and a permanent impossibility of dying. The "I" of the first stanza ("I had not human fears") has disappeared entirely in the impersonal assertions of the second stanza. It is as though the speaker has lost his selfhood by waking to knowledge. He has become an anonymous impersonal wakefulness, perpetually aware that Lucy is dead and that he is not yet dead. This is the position of the survivor in all Wordsworth's work.

Moreover, an obscure sexual drama is enacted in this poem. This drama is a major carrier of its allegorical significance. The identification of this drama will take the reader further inside. As we know from *The Prelude* as well as from the Lucy poems, nature for Wordsworth was strongly personified. It was, oddly, personified as both male and female, as both father and mother. The earth was the maternal face and body he celebrates in the famous "Infant Babe" passage in the earliest version of *The Prelude*, written also in Goslar in 1798:

> No outcast he, bewilder'd and depress'd;
> Along his infant veins are interfus'd
> The gravitation and the filial bond
> Of nature, that connect him with the world.

Nature was also, however, in certain other episodes of the earliest *Prelude*, a frightening male spirit threatening to punish the poet for wrongdoing. The poem "Nutting," also written at Goslar and later incorporated into *The Prelude*, brings the two sexes of nature together into the astonishing scene of a rape of female nature which brings the terror of a reprisal from another aspect of nature, a fearsome male guardian capable of revenge.

Wordsworth's mother died when he was eight, his father when he was thirteen. His father's death and Wordsworth's irrational sense of guilt for it are the subject of another episode of the two-book *Prelude*, another of the "spots of time." His mother's death, however, is curiously elided, so that the reader might not even be sure what the poet is talking about:

> For now a trouble came into my mind
> From obscure causes. I was left alone. . . .

The death of Wordsworth's mother hardly seems an "obscure cause" for sorrow, and yet the poet wants to efface that death. He wants to push the source of the sorrow of solitude further back, into deeper obscurity. In the Lucy poems the possession of Lucy alive and seemingly immortal is a replacement for the lost mother. It gives him again that direct filial bond to nature he had lost with the mother's death. It perhaps does not matter greatly whether the reader thinks of Lucy as a daughter or as a mistress or as an embodiment of his feelings for his sister Dorothy. What matters is the way in which her imagined death is a reenactment of the death of the mother as described in *The Prelude*.

The reenactment of the death of the mother takes a peculiar form in "A Slumber Did My Spirit Seal," however. This poem, and the Lucy poems as a group, can be defined as an attempt to have it both ways, an attempt which, necessarily, fails. Within his writing, which is what is meant here by "Wordsworth," the poet's abandonment has always already occurred. It is the condition of life and poetry once Wordsworth has been left alone, once he has become an outcast, bewildered and depressed. His only hope for reestablishing the bond that connected him to the world is to die without dying, to be dead, in his grave, and yet still alive, bound to maternal nature by way of a surrogate mother, a girl who remains herself both alive and dead, still available in life and yet already taken by Nature. Of course this is impossible, but it is out of such impossibilities that great poems are made.

Wordsworth's acting out of this fantasy is described in an extraordinary passage by Dorothy Wordsworth. This is her entry in the "Grasmere Journals" for April 29, 1802, three and a half years after the composition of "A Slumber Did My Spirit Seal":

We then went to John's Grove, sate a while at first. Afterwards William lay, and I lay in the trench under the fence—he with his eyes shut and listening to the waterfalls and the Birds. There was no one waterfall—it was the sound of waters in the air—the voice of the air. William heard me breathing and rustling now and then but we both lay still, and unseen by one another. He thought that it would be as sweet thus to lie so in the grave, to hear the *peaceful* sounds of the earth and just to know that our dear friends were near.

"A Slumber Did My Spirit Seal" dramatizes the impossibility of fulfilling this fantasy, or rather it demonstrates that it can only be fulfilled in fantasy, that is, in a structure of words in which "thing" can mean both "person" and "object," in which one can have both stanzas at once, and can, like Lucy, be both alive and dead, or in which the poet can be both the dead–alive girl and at the same time the perpetually wakeful survivor. To have it as word-play, however, is to have it as the impossibility of having it, to have it as permanent loss and separation, to have it as the unbridgeable gap between one meaning of the word "thing" and the other.

In "A Slumber Did My Spirit Seal" this simultaneous winning and losing, winning by losing, losing by winning, is expressed in a constant slipping of entities across borders into their opposites. As a result the mind cannot carry on that orderly thinking which depends on keeping "things" firmly fixed in their conceptual pigeon-holes. Lucy was a virgin "thing." She seemed untouchable by earthly years, that is, untouchable by nature as time, as the bringer of death, as death. The touch of earthly years is both a form of sexual appropriation which leaves the one who is possessed still virgin if she dies young, and at the same time it is the ultimate dispossession which is death. To be touched by earthly years is a way to be sexually penetrated while still remaining virgin.

The speaker of the poem rather than being the opposite of Lucy, male to her female, adult knowledge to her prepubertal innocence, is the displaced representative of both the penetrated and the penetrator, of both Lucy herself and of her unravishing ravisher, nature or death. The speaker was "sealed," as she was. Now he knows. He is unsealed, as she is. To know, however, as the second stanza indicates, is to speak from the impersonal position of death. It is to speak as death. Death is the penetrator who leaves his victim intact, unpierced, but at the same time wholly open, as an unburied corpse is exposed, open to the sky, like rocks and stones and trees. The speaker's movement to knowledge, as his consciousness becomes dispersed, loses its "I," is "the same thing" as Lucy's death. It finds its parable in that death.

Whatever track the reader follows through the poem he arrives at blank contradictions. These contradictions are not ironic. They are the copresence of difference within the same, as, for example, time in the poem is not different from space but is collapsed into the rolling motion of the earth, or as Lucy in her relation to the speaker blurs the difference of the sexes. Lucy is both the virgin child and the missing mother, that mother earth who gave birth to the speaker and has abandoned him. Male and female, however, come together in the earth, and so Lucy and the speaker are "the same," though the poet is also the perpetually excluded difference from Lucy, an unneeded increment, like an abandoned child. The two women, mother and girl child, have jumped over the male generation in the middle. They have erased its power of mastery, its power of logical understanding, which is the male power *par excellence*. In expressing this, the poem leaves its reader with no possibility of moving through or beyond or standing outside in sovereign control. The reader is caught in an unstillable oscillation unsatisfying to the mind and incapable of being grounded in anything outside the activity of the poem itself.

"A Slumber Did My Spirit Seal" shimmers between affirming male mastery as the consciousness which survives the death of the two generations, mother and daughter or sister, and *knows*, and lamenting the failure of consciousness to join itself to the dead mother, and therefore to the ground of consciousness, by way of its possession of the sister or daughter. On the one hand, he does survive; if he does not have possession or power, he has knowledge. On the other hand, thought or knowledge is not guiltless. The poet has himself somehow caused Lucy's death by thinking about it. Thinking recapitulates in reverse mirror image the action of the earthly years in touching, penetrating, possessing, killing, encompassing, turning the other into oneself and therefore being left only with a corpse, an empty sign.

Lest it be supposed that I am grounding my reading of the poem on the "psychobiographical" details of the poet's reaction to the death of his parents, let me say that it is the other way around. Wordsworth interpreted the death of his mother according to the traditional trope identifying the earth with a maternal presence. By the time we encounter her in his writing she exists as an element in that figure. His life, like his poetry, was the working out of the consequences of this fictitious trope, or rather of the whole figurative system into which it is incorporated. This incorporation exists both in Wordsworth's language and in the Western tradition generally, both before and after him. To put this as economically as possible, "A Slumber Did My Spirit Seal," in the context of the other Lucy poems and of all Wordsworth's work, enacts one version of a constantly repeated occidental drama of the lost sun. Lucy's name of course means light. To possess her would be a means of rejoining the lost source of light, the father sun as logos, as head power and fount of meaning. As light she is the vacant evidence that that capital source seems once to have existed. Light is dispersed everywhere but yet may not be captured or held. It is like those heavens Thales studied. To seek to catch or understand it is to be in danger of falling into a well. The fear of the death of Lucy is the fear that the light will fail, that all links with the sun will be lost, as, in "Strange Fits of Passion," another of the Lucy poems, the setting of the moon, mediated female image of the sun, makes the poet-lover fear Lucy's death:

"Oh mercy!" to myself I cried,
"If Lucy should be dead."

The fulfillment of that fear in her actual death is the loss both of light and of the source of light. It is the loss of the logos, leaving the poet and his words groundless. The loss of Lucy is the loss of the poet's female reflex or narcissistic mirror image. In the absence of the filial bond to nature, this has been the only source of his solid sense of selfhood. In one version of the Narcissus story, Narcissus' self-love is generated by the hopeless search for a beloved twin sister, who has died. For Wordsworth, "The furiously burning father fire" (Wallace Stevens' phrase) has sunk beneath the horizon, apparently never to return. In spite of the diurnal rotation of the earth that earth seems to have absorbed all the light. Even the moon, reflected and mediated source of sunlight at night, and so the emblem of Lucy, has set. The consciousness of the poet has survived all these deaths of the light to subsist as a kind of black light. His awareness is the light-no-light which remains when the sun has sunk and Lucy has died, when both have gone into the earth.

This loss of the radiance of the logos, along with the experience of the consequences of that loss, is the drama of all Wordsworth's poetry, in particular of "A Slumber Did My Spirit Seal." In the absence of any firm grounding the poem necessarily takes on a structure of chiasmus. This is the perpetual reversal of properties in crisscross substitutions I have tried to identify. The senses of the poem continually cross over the borders set up by the words if they are taken to refer to fixed "things," whether material or subjective. The words waver in their meaning. Each word in itself becomes the dwelling place of contradictory senses, as though host and parasite were together in the same house. This wavering exceeds the bounds of the distinction between literal and figurative language, since literal ground and figurative derivative change places too within the word, just as do the other opposites. This wavering within the word is matched by an analogous wavering in the syntax. That in turn is matched by the large-scale relation of going and coming between the two stanzas. Each of these waverings is another example of the disparate in the matching pair which forbids any dialectical synthesis. The tracing out of these differences within the same moves the attention away from the attempt to ground the poem in anything outside itself. It catches the reader within a movement in the text without solid foundation in consciousness, in nature, or in spirit. As groundless, the movement is, precisely, alogical.

This explanation of Wordsworth's little poem has led me seemingly far away from a sober description of the state of contemporary literary study. It is meant, however, to "exemplify" one mode of such interpretation. In a passage in *The Will to Power* Nietzsche says: "To be able to read off a text as a text without interposing an interpretation is the last-developed form of 'inner experience'—perhaps one that is hardly possible." If it is hardly possible, it may not even be desirable, since interpretation, as Nietzsche also elsewhere says, is an active, affirmative process, a taking possession of something for some purpose or use. In the multitudinous forms of this which make up the scene of literary study, perhaps the true fork in the road is between two modes of this taking possession, two modes of teaching literature and writing about it. One mode already knows what it is going to find. Such a mode is controlled by the pre-supposition of some center. The other alternative mode of reading is more open to the inexhaustible strangeness of literary texts. This enigmatic strangeness much literary study busily covers over. The strangeness of literature remains, however. It survives all attempts to hide it. It is one of the major cor-relatives of the human predicament, since our predicament is to remain, always, within language. The strangeness lies in the fact that language, our Western languages at least, both affirm logic and at the same time turn it on edge, as happens in "A Slumber Did My Spirit Seal." If this is the case, the alternative mode of literary study I have tried to exemplify both can and should be incorporated into college and university curricula. This is already happening to some extent, but, as I see it, the development of programs for this, from basic courses in reading and writing up to the most advanced grad-uate seminars, is one task in humanistic studies today.

Essay by J. Hillis Miller. "On Edge: The Crossways of Contemporary Criticism." *Bulletin of the American Academy of Arts and Sciences* 32 (Jan. 1979).

7

Psychoanalytic Criticism

The Imagination may be compared to Adam's dream—he awoke and found it truth.

JOHN KEATS, "Letter to Benjamin Bailey"
November 22, 1817

INTRODUCTION

Our dreams fascinate, perplex, and often disturb us. Filled with bizarre twists of fate, wild exploits, and highly sexual images, our dreams can bring us pleasure or terrorize us. Sometimes they cause us to question our true feelings, to contemplate our unspoken desires, and even to doubt the nature of reality itself. Do dreams, we wonder, contain any degree of truth, and do they serve any useful function?

Chemist Friedrich August Kekule answers in the affirmative. For years, Kekule was investigating the molecular structure of benzene. One night he saw in a dream a string of atoms shaped like a snake swallowing its tail. Upon awakening, he drew this serpentine figure in his notebook and realized it was the graphic structure of the benzene ring he had been struggling to decipher. When reporting his findings at a scientific meeting in 1890, he stated, "Let us learn to dream, gentlemen, and then we may perhaps find the truth."

Giuseppe Tartini, an Italian violinist of the eighteenth century, similarly discovered the value of dreams. One night he dreamed the devil came to his bedside and offered to help him finish a rather difficult sonata in exchange for his soul. Tartini agreed, whereupon the devil picked up Tartini's violin and completed the unfinished work. Upon awakening, Tartini jotted down from memory what he had just heard. Known as *The Devil's Trill Sonata*, this piece is Tartini's best known composition.

Like numerous scientists and composers, many writers have claimed that they too have received some of their best ideas from their dreams. Robert Louis Stevenson, for example, maintained that many of his ideas for *Dr. Jekyll and Mr. Hyde* came directly from his nightmares. Similarly, Dante, Goethe, Blake, Bunyan, and a host of others owed much of their writings, they claimed, to their world of dreams. And others, such as Poe, DeQuincey, and Coleridge borrowed from their drug-induced dreams the content of some of their most famous works.

That our dreams and those of others fascinate us cannot be denied. Whether it is their bizarre and often erotic content or even their seemingly prophetic powers, dreams cause us to question and explore the part of our minds over which we have seemingly little control: the unconscious.

Without question, the foremost investigator of the unconscious and its activities is Vienna neurologist and psychologist Sigmund Freud. Beginning with the publication of *The Interpretation of Dreams* in 1900, Freud lays the foundation for a new model of how our minds operate. Hidden from the workings of the conscious mind, the unconscious, he believes, plays a large part in how we act, think, and feel. According to Freud, the best avenue for discovering the content and the activity of the unconscious is through our dreams. It is through the interaction of both the conscious and unconscious working together, argues Freud, that we shape ourselves and our world.

Developing both a body of theory and a practical methodology for his science of the mind, Freud became the founding father of **psychoanalysis**, a method of treating emotional and psychological disorders. During psychoanalysis, Freud had his patients talk freely in a patient-analyst setting about their early childhood experiences and dreams. When we apply these same methods to our interpretations of works of literature, we engage in **psychoanalytic criticism**.

Unlike some other schools of criticism, psychoanalytic criticism can exist side by side with any other critical method of interpretation. Because this approach attempts to explain the hows and whys of human actions without developing an **aesthetic theory**—a systematic, philosophical body of beliefs concerning how meaning occurs in literature—Marxists, feminists, and New Historicists, for example, can use psychoanalytic methods in their interpretations without violating their own hermeneutics. Psychoanalytic criticism, then, may best be called an approach to literary interpretation rather than a particular school of criticism.

Although Freud is unquestionably the father of this approach to literary analysis, psychoanalytic criticism has continued to develop in theory and practice throughout the twentieth century. Carl Jung, Freud's rebellious student, borrowed some of Freud's ideas while rejecting many others. Jung branched out into new theories and concerns and established **analytical psychology**. Using some of Jung's ideas, Northrop Frye, an English professor and literary theorist, developed symbolic or **archetypal criticism** in the mid-

1950s that changed the direction of twentieth-century literary analysis. In the 1960s, French neo-Freudian psychoanalyst Jacques Lacan revised and expanded Freud's theories in light of new linguistic and literary principles, and thereby revitalized psychoanalytic criticism and ensured its continued influence on literary criticism today. And many present-day feminist critics turn to psychoanalytic criticism, using the ideas of Lacan as the basis of their critical methodology.

HISTORICAL DEVELOPMENT

Sigmund Freud

The theories and practice of Sigmund Freud provide the foundation for psychoanalytic criticism. While working with patients whom he diagnosed as hysterics, Freud theorized that the root of their problems was psychological, not physical. His patients, he believed, had suppressed incestuous desires with which they had unconsciously refused to deal. Suffering from his own neurotic crisis in 1887, Freud underwent self-analysis. Results from this self-analysis coupled with his research and analyses of his patients led Freud to posit that fantasies and wishful thinking, not actual experiences, play a large part in the onset of neuroses.

Models of the Human Psyche: Dynamic Model   Throughout his lifetime Freud developed various models of the human psyche that became the changing bases of his psychoanalytic theory and practice. Early in his career, he posited the **dynamic model,** asserting that our minds are a dichotomy consisting of the **conscious** (the rational) and the **unconscious** (the irrational). The conscious, Freud argued, perceives and records external reality and is the reasoning part of the mind. Unaware of the presence of the unconscious, we operate consciously, believing that our reasoning and analytical skills are solely responsible for our behavior. But Freud is the first to suggest that it is the unconscious, not the conscious, that governs a large part of our actions.

This irrational part of our psyche, the unconscious, receives and stores our hidden desires, ambitions, fears, passions, and irrational thoughts. Freud did not coin this term; this honor goes to C. G. Carus. Carus and many of Freud's other contemporaries viewed the unconscious as a static system that simply collects and maintains our memories. Freud dramatically redefined the unconscious, believing it to be a dynamic system that not only contains our biographical memories but also stores our suppressed and unresolved conflicts. For Freud, the unconscious is the storehouse of disguised truths and desires that want to be revealed in and through the conscious. These disguised truths and desires inevitably make themselves known through our dreams, art, literature, play, and accidental slips of the tongue known as **Freudian slips**.

Economic Model   Freud's second model of the human psyche enlarges on but retains most of his ideas housed in the dynamic model. In both models, the conscious and the unconscious battle for control of a person's actions. And in both models a person's unconscious desires force their way to the conscious state. But in the **economic model**, Freud introduces two new concepts that describe and help govern the human psyche: the pleasure principle and the reality principle. According to Freud, the **pleasure principle** craves only pleasures, and it desires instantaneous satisfaction of instinctual drives, ignoring moral and sexual boundaries established by society. Immediate relief from all pain or suffering is its goal. The pleasure principle is held in check, however, by the **reality principle**, that part of the psyche that recognizes the need for societal standards and regulations on pleasure. Freud believed that both these principles are at war within the human psyche.

Topographic Models   Throughout his career Freud developed yet another model of the human psyche, the **topographic model**. In an earlier version of this model, Freud separated the human psyche into three parts: the conscious, the **preconscious**, and the unconscious. The conscious is the mind's direct link to external reality, for it perceives and reacts with the external environment, allowing the mind to order its outside world. The preconscious is the storehouse of memories that the conscious part of the mind allows to be brought to consciousness without disguising these memories in some form or another. As in his previously devised models, Freud contends that the third part of the psyche, the unconscious, holds the repressed hungers, images, thoughts, and desires of human nature. Because these desires are not housed in the preconscious, they cannot be directly summoned into the conscious state. These repressed impulses must therefore travel in disguised forms to the conscious part of the psyche and surface in their respective disguises in our dreams, our art, and in other unsuspecting ways in our lives.

But the most famous model of the human psyche is Freud's later version of the topographic model, the **tripartite model**. This model divides the psyche into three parts: the id, the ego, and the superego. The irrational, instinctual, unknown, and unconscious part of the psyche Freud calls the **id**. Containing our secret desires, our darkest wishes, and our most intense fears, the id wishes only to fulfill the urges of the pleasure principle. In addition, it houses the **libido**, the source of all our psychosexual desires and all our psychic energy. Unchecked by any controlling will, the id operates on impulse, wanting immediate satisfaction for all its instinctual desires.

The second part of the psyche Freud calls the **ego**, the rational, logical waking part of the mind, although much of its activities remain in the unconscious. Whereas the id operates according to the pleasure principle, the ego operates in harmony with the reality principle. It is the ego's job to regulate the instinctual desires of the id and to allow these desires to be released in some nondestructive way.

The third part of the psyche, the **superego**, acts as an internal censor, causing us to make moral judgments in light of social pressures. In contrast to the id, the superego operates according to the morality principle and serves primarily to protect society and us from the id. Representing all of society's moral restrictions, the superego serves as a filtering agent, suppressing the desires and instincts forbidden by society and thrusting them back into the unconscious. Overall, the superego manifests itself through punishment. If allowed to operate at its own discretion, the superego will create an unconscious sense of guilt and fear.

It is left to the ego to mediate between the instinctual (especially sexual) desires of the id and the demands of social pressure issued by the superego. What the ego deems unacceptable it suppresses and deposits in the unconscious. And what it has most often repressed in all of us is our sexual desires of early childhood.

Freud's Pre-Oedipal Developmental Phases   In addition to his various models of the human psyche, Freud developed several stages of human development that are important to the healthy development of one's psyche. According to Freud, in our early childhood all of us go through three overlapping phases: the oral, anal, and phallic stages. As infants, we experience the **oral phase**: As we suck our mother's breast in order to be fed, our sexuality (or libido) is activated. Our mouths then become an erotogenic zone that will later cause us to enjoy sucking our thumbs and, still later, kissing. In the second or **anal stage**, the anus becomes the object of pleasure when children learn the delights of defecation while simultaneously learning that they are independent persons who are separate from their mothers. During this stage the anus becomes an erotogenic zone, for children become sadistic, expelling and destroying through defecation as a means of expressing both their anger and their excitement upon discovering their independence from their mothers. By withholding feces, children also learn that they can control others. In the final phase, the **phallic stage**, a child's sexual desire or libido is directed toward the genitals when the child learns the pleasure that results from stimulating one's sexual organs.

At this point in a child's development, Freud asserts that the pleasure principle basically controls the child. Being self-centered, sadistic, and assertive, the child cares for nothing but his or her own pleasure. If a child, however, is to grow up as a normal adult, he or she must develop a sense of sexuality, a sense of his maleness or her femaleness. Freud maintains that this awareness can be achieved by a successful handling of either the Oedipus or the Electra complex.

The Oedipus, Castration, and Electra Complexes   The formulation of the **Oedipus complex** is one of Freud's most significant contributions not only to psychoanalytic criticism but also to all literary criticism in general. Freud borrows the name from the play *Oedipus Rex*, written by Greek playwright

Sophocles. In this play, Oedipus, the protagonist, is prophesied to kill his father and marry his mother. His attempts to abort the prophecy fail, and the once-foretold events occur as predicted. According to Freud, the essence of Oedipus' story becomes universal human experience.

Using Sophocles' plot as the basis for his Oedipus complex, Freud asserts that during the late infantile stage (somewhere between ages 3 and 6), all infant males possess an erotic attachment to their mother. Unconsciously, the infant desires to engage in sexual union with his mother. He recognizes, however, a rival for his mother's affection: the father. Already in the phallic stage and therefore sexually aware of his own erogenous organs, the child perceives the father's attention given to the mother as sexual.

If a child's sexual development is to proceed normally, Freud maintains, each must then pass through the **castration complex**. From observing themselves, their mothers, and perhaps their sisters, little boys know they have a penis like their fathers whereas their mothers and sisters do not. What prevents the male child from continuing to have incestuous desires for his mother is fear of castration by his father. The child therefore represses his sexual desire, identifies with his father, and hopes someday to possess a woman as his father now possesses his mother. Unconsciously, the boy has thus successfully made the transition to manhood.

Whereas a boy must successfully negotiate the Oedipus complex in order to become a normal man, a girl must successfully negotiate the **Electra complex** if she is to make the transition from a girl to a normal woman. Like a boy, a young girl is also erotically attracted to her mother, and like the boy, she too recognizes a rival for her mother's affection: the father. Unconsciously, however, the girl realizes that she is already castrated, as is her mother. Because she knows her father possesses that which she desires, a penis, she turns her desires to him and away from her mother. After the seduction of her father fails, she turns back toward the mother and identifies with her. Her transition into womanhood being complete, the girl realizes that one day she, like her mother, will possess a man. Through her relationships with a man, her unfulfilled desire for a penis (**penis envy**) will be mitigated, and her sense of lacking will be somewhat appeased.

The process of becoming a man or a woman, Freud maintained, may be long and difficult, but necessary. For within this process, the child passes from basing his or her life on the pleasure principle, in which all decisions are based on the immediate gratification of pleasure, to the reality principle, in which societal needs and the operation of the superego occur. During this stage, Freud believed that a child's moral development and conscience appear for the first time.

The Significance of Dreams   Even though the passage into manhood or womanhood may be successful, according to Freud the child has stored many painful memories of repressed sexual desires, anger, rage, and guilt in his or her unconscious. Because the conscious and the unconscious are part of the same psyche, the unconscious with its hidden desires and repressed wishes continues to affect the conscious in the form of inferiority feelings, guilt, irrational thoughts and feelings, and dreams and nightmares.

In his magnum opus, *The Interpretation of Dreams* (1900), Freud asserts that the unconscious expresses its suppressed wishes and desires. Even though the conscious mind has repressed these desires and has forced them into the unconscious, such wishes may be too hard for the conscious psyche to handle without producing feelings of self-hatred or rage. The unconscious then redirects and reshapes these concealed wishes into acceptable social activities, presenting them in the form of images or symbols in our dreams or writings. By so doing, the psyche creates a window to the id by allowing these softened and socially acceptable desires to seep into the conscious state.

The psyche may create this window to the id in a variety of ways. Through the process of **displacement**, for example, the unconscious may switch a person's hatred for someone named Mr. Appleby onto a rotting apple in a dream. Or through **condensation**, the psyche may consolidate one's anger to a variety of people and objects into a simple sentence. Whatever the case, through symbols and images, but not directly, the unconscious continually asserts its influence over our motivations and behavior.

When certain repressed feelings or ideas cannot be released adequately through dreams, jokes, or other methods, the ego must act and block any outward response. In so doing, the ego and id become involved in an internal battle that Freud called **neurosis**. From a fear of heights to a pounding headache, neurosis can create many physical and psychological abnormalities. According to Freud, it is the job of the psychoanalyst to identify the unresolved conflicts that give rise to a patient's neurosis. Through psychoanalytic therapy and dream analysis, the psychotherapist attempts to return the patient to a state of well-being or normalcy.

Literature and Psychoanalysis   For Freud, the unresolved conflicts that give rise to any neurosis are the stuff of literature. A work of literature, he believes, is the external expression of the author's unconscious mind. Accordingly, the literary work must be treated like a dream, applying psychoanalytic techniques to the text to uncover the author's hidden motivations and repressed desires.

Carl G. Jung

Freud's most famous pupil is Carl Gustav Jung (1875–1961), a Swiss physician, psychiatrist, philosopher, and psychologist. Selecting Jung as his favorite "son," Freud appointed him his successor. Toward the end of their 7-year teacher–disciple relationship (1912), however, Jung prophetically wrote to Freud, quoting from Nietzsche's *Thus Spake Zarathustra*, "One repays a teacher badly if one remains only a pupil." A year later, the pupil broke away from his master and eventually became one of the leading forces in the psychoanalytic movement.

Jung's dissatisfaction with some elements of Freudian psychoanalysis arose from theoretical differences with Freud concerning the interpretation of dreams and each psychologist's models of the human psyche. According to Freud, all human behavior, including dreams, is fundamentally sexual, being driven by one's sexual energy or libido. Interpreting dreams almost exclusively in sexual terms, Freud linked most dreams to the Oedipus or Electra complexes. Jung disagreed with Freud's basic premise that all human behavior is sexually driven. More than sexual imagery, Jung argued, appears in dreams. In 1912 Jung published his seminal work *Symbols of Transformation*, which ultimately led to his separation from Freud. In this work, Jung asserts that dreams include mythological images as well as sexual ones. Jung's new ideas caused him to be banished from the psychoanalytic community for the next 5 years. During this time, however, he formulated his own model of the human psyche that would eventually become his most important contribution to psychology and literary criticism.

In forming his model of the human psyche, Jung accepts Freud's assumption that the unconscious exists and that it plays a major role in our conscious decisions. But he rejects Freud's analysis of the contents of the unconscious. According to Jung, the human psyche consists of three parts: the personal conscious, the personal unconscious, and the collective unconscious. The **personal conscious,** or waking state, is the image or thought of which we are aware at any given moment. Like a slide show, every moment of our lives provides us with a new slide. As we view one slide, the previous slide vanishes from our personal consciousness, for nothing can remain in the personal conscious. Although these vanished slides are forgotten by the personal consciousness, they are stored and remembered by the **personal unconscious**. Jung asserts that all conscious thoughts begin in the personal unconscious. Because each person's moment-by-moment slide show is different, everyone's personal unconscious is unique.

But in the depths of the psyche and blocked off from human consciousness lies Jung's third part of his model of the human psyche: the **collective unconscious.** This part of the psyche houses the cumulative knowledge, experiences, and images of the entire human race. According to Jung, people from all over the world respond to certain myths or stories in the same way not because everyone knows and appreciates the same story, but because lying deep in our collective unconscious are the racial memories of humanity's past. These memories exist in the form of **archetypes**: patterns or images of repeated human experiences such as birth, death, rebirth, the four seasons, and motherhood, to name a few, that express themselves in our stories, dreams, religions, and fantasies. Archetypes are not ready-made ideas, but predispositions, causing us to respond to stimuli in a certain way.

Furthermore, they are inherited genetically (a psychic, not a biological, inheritance), making up an identical collective unconsciousness for all humankind. For Jung, these archetypes "give form to countless typical experiences of our ancestors [and are] the psychic residue of innumerable experiences of the same type, of joys and sorrows that have been repeated countless times in our ancestral history." Occurring in literature in the form of recurrent plot patterns, images, or character types, these archetypes stir profound emotions in the reader because they awaken images stored in the collective unconscious and thereby produce feelings or emotions over which the reader initially has little control.

Jung was the first to suggest that such archetypes directly affect the way we respond to external elements. For example, when we see or read about an infant in diapers surrounded by a litter of puppies licking the child's face, feelings of contentment, warmth, and love seemingly pop up in most of us. These somewhat uncontrollable emotions, Jung would claim, are the results of the stirring of an archetype.

Many anthropologists would argue that archetypes are inherited cultural responses that are passed down from one generation to another in a particular social group. Eventually, such social phenomena become myths or stories that help give meaning and significance to people's lives. Jung would strongly disagree, asserting that myths are "symbolic expressions of the inner, unconscious drama of the psyche." For Jung, myths are the means by which archetypes evidence themselves not only in our dreams but also in the personal conscious.

Throughout the 1920s and until his death in 1961, Jung continued developing his methods of **analytical psychology**. When we apply his theories and methods to literature, we engage in **archetypal criticism**. Unquestionably, the foremost archetypal critic of the twentieth century is Northrop Frye.

Northrop Frye

With the publication of his work *Anatomy of Criticism* in 1957, Frye became the primary advocate of the principles of archetypal criticism in literary theory. Although he never declares allegiance to Jung's concept of the collective unconscious, Frye borrows Jung's ideas concerning myths and archetypes and develops a systematic approach to archetypal or **mythic criticism.** Divorcing a text from its social history, Frye maintains that there exists an overall structure or mythic development that can explain the structure and significance of all texts.

Frye believes that all of literature makes up one complete and whole story called the **monomyth**. This monomyth can best be diagrammed as a circle containing four separate phases, with each phase corresponding to a season of the year and to peculiar cycles of human experiences. The Romance phase, which is located at the top of the circle, is our summer story.

In this kind of story, all our wishes are fulfilled, and we can achieve total happiness. At the bottom of the circle is winter, or the Anti-romance phase. The opposite of summer, this phase tells the story of bondage, imprisonment, frustration, and fear. Midway between Romance and Anti-romance and to the right of the middle of the circle is spring, or Comedy. This phase relates the story of our rise from Anti-romance and frustration to freedom and happiness. Correspondingly, across the circle is Tragedy, or fall, narrating our fall from the Romance phase and from happiness and freedom to disaster. According to Frye, all stories can be placed somewhere on this diagram.

What Frye provides for us is a schema of all possible kinds of stories. Such a structural framework furnishes the context whereby we can identify stories according to their particular genre, kinds of symbolization, themes, points of view, and other literary elements. In addition, Frye's schematic supplies the background and context for his form of literary criticism and allows us to compare stories on the basis of their relationship among themselves.

With the advent of archetypal criticism and Frye's schematics in the 1950s, few critics used Freudian analysis in their practical criticism. But in the 1960s, French psychoanalyst, neo-Freudian, and poststructuralist critic Jacques Lacan helped revive Freudian criticism and rescued it from its overwhelmingly **phallocentric** or a male-dominated position.

Jacques Lacan

Like Freud, Lacan believes that the unconscious greatly affects our conscious behavior. But unlike Freud, who pictures the unconscious as a chaotic, unstructured, bubbling cauldron of dark passions, hidden desires, and suppressed wishes, Lacan asserts that the unconscious is structured, much like the structure of language. And like language, this highly structured part of the human psyche can be systematically analyzed. What we will learn from such an analysis, claims Lacan, is that all individuals are fragmented: No one is whole. The ideal concept of a wholly unified and psychologically complete individual is just that: an abstraction that is simply not attainable.

Like Freud, Lacan devises a tripartite model of the human psyche. In Freud's model, the interactions of the id, ego, and superego greatly determine our behavior. Underlying Lacan's model, however, is the basic assumption that language shapes and ultimately structures our unconscious and conscious minds and thus shapes our self-identity.

According to Lacan, the human psyche consists of three parts, or what Lacan calls orders: the **Imaginary,** the **Symbolic,** and the **Real**. As in Freud's tripartite model, each of these orders interacts with the others. From our birth until somewhere around 6 months, we function primarily in the Imaginary Order, or the part of the psyche that contains our wishes, fantasies, and, most importantly, images. In this phase of our psychic development we are joyfully united as one with our mother, receiving our food, our care, and all our comfort from her. In this preverbal state, we rely on images as a means of perceiving and interpreting the world. Consequently, our image of ourselves is always in flux, for we are not able to differentiate where one image stops and another begins.

Somewhere between the age of 6 and 18 months, we enter what Lacan calls the mirror stage. In this stage we literally see ourselves in a mirror, or we may metaphorically see ourselves in our mothers' image. Seeing this mirror image permits us to perceive images that have discrete boundaries, thereby allowing us to become aware of ourselves as independent beings who are separate from our mothers. This mirror image of ourselves as a whole and complete being is in itself an ideal, for unlike the actual mirror image, we are not in full control of ourselves. For example, we cannot move our bodies as we want or eat when we so desire.

During this mirror stage, we come to recognize certain objects—what Lacon calls **objet a**—as being separate images from ourselves. These include bodily wastes, our mothers' voices and breasts, and our own speech sounds. When these objects or sounds are not present, we yearn for them. According to Lacan, such objects become for us symbols of lack. This sense of lack will continue to plague us for the rest of our lives.

While we are passing through the Imaginary Order, one great consuming passion dominates our existence: the desire for our mother. Mother, we believe, can fulfill all our wishes just as we can fulfill all of hers. But like our mothers before us, we must learn that we are separate entities who can never be totally unified with our mothers. According to Lacan, such total unity and wholeness is in itself an illusion.

Once we learn that we are individual beings who are separate from our mothers, we are ready to enter Lacan's second developmental phase, the Symbolic Order. Whereas the mother dominates the Imaginary Order, the father dominates the Symbolic Order. In this phase, we learn language. Lacan, however, would argue that language masters us, for he believes that it is language that shapes our identity as separate beings and molds our psyches. Using linguistic principles formulated by Ferdinand de Saussure, Lacan declares that we differentiate between individual sounds and words on the basis of difference. We know the word *might*, for example, because it is different from *sight*, and we know *hill* because it differs from *bill*. Knowing and mastering this concept of difference enables us to enter and pass through the Symbolic Order successfully.

Lacan contends that in the Symbolic Order we learn to differentiate between male and female. This process of learning gender identity is based on difference and loss. Whereas in the Imaginary Order we delighted in the presence of our mother, in the Symbolic Order we learn that our father comes to represent cultural norms and laws. It is he who stands between us and our mother, and it is he who enforces cultural rules by threatening to castrate us if we do not obey. Because the castration complex is obviously different for boys and girls, the process of completing the Symbolic Order successfully is different for each sex.

For Lacan, what sex we are—male or female—is biologically determined. Our gender or our sexuality, however, is culturally created. For example, society decrees that a little boy should play with cars and a little girl with dolls. And it is the father, the power symbol, who enforces society's rules and ensures we follow them. Both sexes, then, come to understand their own sexuality by observing what they are not, a boy noting that he does not do the things a young girl does and vice versa. Each must recognize that he or she will forever be a splintered self, never again being able to experience the wholeness and joy of being one with his or her mother in the Imaginary Order.

For the boy, entry into the Symbolic Order dictates that he identifies and acknowledges the father as the symbol of society's power and as the object that blocks his desire for sexual union with his mother. For the girl, entry into the Symbolic Order demands that she too acknowledge the father or the male as the symbol of power in society and as her personal superior. Like the boy, she wishes to return to the happy state of union with her mother in the Imaginary Order. Unlike the boy, however, she maintains more access than he to this pre-Oedipal stage as she grows up.

Lacan maintains that entering the Symbolic Order is a form of castration for either sex. For Lacan, castration is symbolic, not literal, and represents each person's loss of wholeness and his or her acceptance of society's rules. For the male, it means accepting the father, the power symbol who possesses a **phallus,** or penis. Likewise, the female must not only accept the father figure as dominant but also accept her lack of phallus. Similar to his differentiation between sex and gender, Lacan distinguishes between the penis, the actual biological organ, and the phallus, what becomes for Lacan, in poststructural terms, the transcendental signified—the object that gives meaning to all other objects. In other words, for Lacan the phallus is the ultimate symbol of power. Although neither males or females can ever possess the phallus and therefore can never be complete or whole, males do have a penis, giving them a slight claim to such power.

At the heart of Lacan's theory and his understanding of the human psyche is lack and fragmentation. We have longings for love, for physical pleasure, and for countless objects, but nothing can fulfill our desire to return to the Imaginary Order and be at one with our mother. It is this fragmentation, this divided self, that concerns Lacan when he examines a literary text. For Lacan, literary texts hold the possibility of capturing, at least for a moment, our desire to return to the Imaginary Order and to regain that sense of pure joy we felt when we were whole and united with our mothers.

In examining a text, Lacan also looks for elements of the third and most remote and unreachable part of the human psyche: the Real Order. On one hand, the Real Order consists of the physical world, including the material universe and everything in it. On the other hand, the Real Order also symbolizes all that a person is not. Or as Lacan would say, the Real Order contains countless *objet a*—objects that continually function for us as symbols of primordial lack. Because these objects, and indeed the entire physical universe, can never be parts of us, we therefore can never experience or really know them except through language. And as Lacan contends, it is language that causes our fragmentation in the first place. For Lacan literature's particular ability is to capture **jouissance**, or a brief moment of joy or terror or desire that somehow arises from deep within our unconscious psyche and reminds us of a time of perfect wholeness when we were incapable of differentiating among images from the Real Order. More often than not, these experiences are sexual, although other images and experiences such as birth or death can serve this function. Such moments of joy Lacan often finds in the writings of Poe, Shakespeare, and Joyce.

The Present State of Psychoanalytic Criticism

Thanks primarily to Lacan, psychoanalytic criticism has enjoyed new popularity. In particular, feminist critics such as Sandra Gilbert and Susan Gubar (*Madwoman in the Attic*, 1979) and a host of others continue to adapt both Freud and Lacan's theoretical models to show the psychological conflicts and concerns encountered by female writers in a male-dominated world. Other critics such as Felix Guattari continue to challenge both Freud and Lacan's ideas, devising their own models of the human psyche. Without question, however, Freud and his models of the human psyche remain at the core of psychoanalytic criticism.

Assumptions

The foundation for all forms of psychoanalytic criticism irrefutably belongs to Freud and his theories and techniques developed during his psychiatric practice. Whether any practicing psychoanalytic critic uses the ideas of Jung, Frye, Lacan, or any other psychoanalyst, all must acknowledge Freud as the intellectual founding father of this form of criticism.

Central to psychoanalytic criticism is Freud's assumption that all artists, including authors, are neurotic. Unlike most other neurotics, however, the artist escapes many of the outward manifestations and results of neurosis such as madness or self-destruction by finding a pathway back to saneness and wholeness in the act of creating his or her art.

According to Freud, an author's chief motivation for writing any story is to gratify some secret desire, some forbidden wish that probably developed during the author's infancy and was immediately suppressed and dumped in the unconscious. The outward manifestation of this suppressed wish becomes the literary work itself. Freud declares that the literary work is therefore the author's dream or fantasy. By using Freud's psychoanalytic techniques as they are used in dream therapy, psychoanalytic critics believe we can unlock the hidden meanings contained within the story and housed in symbols. Only then can we arrive at an accurate interpretation of the text.

Because Freud believes that the literary text is really an artist's dream or fantasy, the text can and must be analyzed like a dream. For Freud, this means that we must assume that the dream is a disguised wish. All of our present wishes, Freud believed, originated in some way during infancy. As an infant, we longed to be both sensually and emotionally satisfied. The memory of these satisfied infantile desires provides the fertile ground for our present wishes to occur. All present wishes are therefore re-creations of a past infantile memory—especially elements of the Oedipal phase—brought to the surface of our unconscious and conscious states through sensations, emotions, and other present-day situations.

But the actual wish is often too strong and too forbidden to be acknowledged by the mind's censor, the ego. Accordingly, the ego distorts and hides the wish or **latent content** of the dream, thereby allowing the dreamer to remember a somewhat changed and often radically different dream. It is this changed dream or **manifest content** of the dream that the dreamer tells the dream analyst. In turn, the dream analyst must strip back the various layers of the patient's conversation and carefully analyze the multiple layers of the dream. The analyst's job is much like that of an archaeologist who painstakingly uncovers a valued historical site layer by layer. Like the archaeologist, the analyst must peel back the various layers of a dream until the true wish is uncovered.

Like the dream analyst, the psychoanalytic critic believes that any author's story is a dream that on the surface reveals only the manifest content of the true tale. Hidden and censored throughout the story on various levels lies the latent content of the story, its real meaning or interpretation. Usually this latent content directly relates to some element and memory of the Oedipal phase of our development. By directly applying the techniques used in Freudian dream analysis, the psychoanalytic critic believes the actual, uncensored wish can be brought to the surface, thereby revealing the story's true meaning.

As noted earlier in this chapter, not all psychoanalysts agree with Freud's basic assumptions. For example, Jung believes that mythological as well as sexual images appear in our dreams. Frye borrows this assumption from Jung and develops a schematic for interpreting all dreams and stories. Lacan, another psychoanalytic critic, disavows Freud's assumption that the unconscious is a cauldron of boiling passions and announces that the unconscious is as highly structured as language itself. By analyzing this structure, Lacan declares that no one can achieve wholeness, for we are all and will always remain fragmented individuals who are seeking completeness. However, all of these theorists and their theories relate in some way to Freud's presuppositions.

Methodologies

First introduced to literary studies in the 1920s and 1930s, Freud's psychoanalytic criticism still survives today. Although its methods have been challenged, revised, and supplemented, psychoanalytic criticism provides a stimulating approach to literary analysis that holds that we humans are complex yet somewhat understandable creatures who often fail to note the influence of the unconscious on our motivations and our everyday actions.

For several decades after its introduction, psychoanalytic criticism focused mainly on the author. Known as **psychobiography**, this method of analysis begins by amassing biographical data of an author through biographies, personal letters, lectures, and any other document deemed related in some way to the author. Using these documents and the author's canon, these psychoanalytic critics believed they could theoretically construct the author's personality with all its idiosyncrasies, internal and external conflicts, and most importantly, neuroses. In turn, such a devised theory, they believed, could illuminate an author's individual works, giving rise to the latent content in the author's texts. By gaining an in-depth understanding of the author, these critics assumed they would be better able to interpret an author's canon. Of particular interest to them were the lives and works of Edgar Allan Poe, William Blake, and Leonardo da Vinci.

In the 1950s, psychoanalytic critics turned their attention away from psychobiography to character analysis, studying the various aspects of characters' minds found in an author's canon. Such a view gave rise to a more complex understanding of a literary work. Individual characters within a text now became the focus. Believing that the author had in mind a particular personality for his or her characters, critics also noted that readers develop their own conceptions of each character's personality. A character's motivations and actions, then, became more complex than simply the author's ideas. How the readers interpreted the various characters now became an integral part of the text's interpretation. Whereas the author creates a character, a reader re-creates the same character, bringing to the text and to an individual character all the reader's past experiences and knowledge. The character simultaneously becomes a creation of both the author and of the reader. In order to interpret the story, a psychoanalytic analysis of the author and the reader were thus needed.

Today, many psychoanalytic critics realize that the reader plays a major role in interpreting a work. Understanding ourselves from a Freudian point of view and the context in which we live is therefore essential if we are to interpret a text.

One of the most controversial psychoanalytic techniques used today involves applying Freud's key assumption—that all human behavior is sexually driven—directly to a text. In the hands of novice critics who are often ill- or misinformed about Freud's psychoanalytic techniques, everything in a text becomes a sexual image. For these critics, every concave image, such as a flower, cup, cave, or vase, is a **yonic** or female symbol, and any image whose length exceeds its diameter, such as a tower, sword, knife, or pen, becomes a phallic or male symbol. Consequently, a text containing a boat floating into a cave or a pen being placed within a cup is interpreted as a symbol of sexual intercourse. From this perspective, all images and actions within a text must be traced to the author's id, for everything in a text is ultimately the hidden wishes of the author's libido.

Another psychoanalytic approach is archetypal criticism first developed by Jung and then later by Frye. In this form of analysis, critics examine a text to discover the various archetypes that they claim appear in it. According to Jung, these archetypes have the same meaning for all readers. The color red, for example, signifies danger just as water symbolizes life. By showing where and how these archetypes appear in the text and form recognizable patterns, the archetypal critic believes that he or she can discover the text's meaning. To apply this method accurately, a critic must be greatly conversant with Jung's rather complex theories and terminology.

But the most recent type of psychoanalytic criticism to appear is that developed by Lacan. A Lacanian critic would attempt to uncover how a text symbolically represents elements of the Real, the Imaginary, and the Symbolic Orders. By identifying the symbolic representations of these orders within the text, the critic would then examine how each of these symbols would demonstrate the fragmentary nature of the self. Such a demonstration would show the reader that all individuals are in actuality splintered selves. The overall purpose, then, of a Lacanian analysis is to teach us that a fully integrated and psychologically whole person does not exist and that we must all accept fragmentation.

Whichever psychoanalytic method a critic chooses to use, he or she must master the psychoanalytic theories and practices of Freud and some of his pupils in order to devise an interpretation that is credible and clear. Although mastering the theory and its appropriate applications may be difficult, the result could be a rewarding discovery of the truth that lies within each of us.

QUESTIONS FOR ANALYSIS

- Because psychoanalytic criticism is based on various models of the mind rather than any aesthetic theory, this critical approach to textual analysis can use the methodology of a variety of schools of criticism. Explain how the critical methods of New Criticism, reader-response, and deconstruction can be used in a psychoanalytic reading of a text.
- Using Hawthorne's "Young Goodman Brown," analyze the character of Goodman Brown from the Freudian, Jungian, and Lacanian perspectives.

- Apply Freud's theories to Robert Browning's "My Last Duchess" and articulate a psychoanalytic interpretation of this poem.
- Using a short story or poem of your choice, identify the various images and structural patterns that occur. Then, using your understanding of psychoanalytic criticism, explain the presence of these images and patterns and how each of them relates to an overall psychoanalytic interpretation of the text itself.
- Investigate the life of John Keats and apply the principles of pyschobiography to his poem "Ode on a Grecian Urn." When your psychobiographical analysis is completed, apply the theories of Freud to this same poem, pointing out and explaining any phallic or yonic symbols that appear in the text.

SAMPLE ESSAYS

In the student essay that follows, note carefully how the author, David Johnson, applies Freudian psychoanalytic terminology and methodology to arrive at his interpretation. After briefly reviewing basic elements of Freudian psychology, what primary psychoanalytic approach does he use in his analysis? Is the author concentrating his psychoanalysis more on the poet or on the poem? Can you find any evidence that the author interacts with the text and imposes his own personality traits on his interpretation of the text? In your opinion, is this psychoanalytic essay a valid and legitimate interpretation of the text? Be able to defend your response.

In the professional essay that follows, note how E. Pearlman uses psychoanalytic theory and methodology to arrive at an interpretation of David Copperfield's dreams as they appear in Charles Dickens's *David Copperfield*. In this essay, is Pearlman using a Freudian, Jungian, or Lacanian approach to the text? After deciding which approach the critic is employing, be able to cite the psychoanalytic terminology and methodological principles the critic uses to develop the critical essay. In addition, be able to cite and explain the many New Critical methods used by Pearlman in this psychoanalytic essay.

FURTHER READING

Benvenuto, Bice, and Roger Kennedy. *The Works of Jacques Lacan: An Introduction.* New York: St. Martin's, 1986.

Crews, Frederick C. *Out of My System.* New York: Oxford University Press, 1975.

Felman, Shoshana. *Jacques Lacan and the Adventure of Insight: Psychoanalysis in Contemporary Culture.* Cambridge: Harvard University Press, 1987.

Freud, Sigmund. *Introductory Lectures on Psycho-Analysis.* Trans. Joan Riviere. London: Allen, 1922.

———. *The Interpretation of Dreams.* Trans. A. A. Brill. New York: Random House, 1950.

Frye, Northrop. *Anatomy of Criticism.* Princeton, NJ: Princeton UP, 1957.

Gilbert, Sandra, and Susan Gubar. *Madwoman in the Attic*. New Haven: Yale University Press, 1979.

Hoffman, Frederick J. *Freudianism and the Literary Mind*. 2nd ed. Baton Rouge: Louisiana State UP, 1957.

Holland, Norman N. *The Dynamics of Literary Response*. New York: Oxford University Press, 1968.

————. "The 'Unconscious' of Literature" in *Contemporary Criticism*, Norman Bradbury and David Palmer, eds. Stratford-upon-Avon Series, vol. 12. New York: St. Martin's, 1970.

Jung, Carl G. *Symbols of Transformation*. 2nd ed. Trans. by R. F. C. Hull. Bollingen Series XX. Princeton: Princeton University Press, 1967.

Meisel, Perry, ed. *Freud: Twentieth Century Views*. Englewood Cliffs, NJ: Prentice-Hall, 1981.

Scott, Wilbur. *Five Approaches to Literary Criticism*. London: Collier-Macmillan, 1962.

Wright, Elizabeth. *Psychoanalytic Criticism: Theory in Practice*. New York: Methuen, 1984.

WEB SITES FOR EXPLORATION

http://www.brocku.ca/english/courses/4F70/psychthry.html
> Provides links to the contributions of psychoanalytic thought to the study of literature, to key terms and concepts, and to recent articles concerning Freud

www.colorado.edu/English/ENGL2012Klages/freud.html
> Provides an overview of psychoanalysis and Sigmund Freud

www.twics.com/~melmoth2/freud.html
> Provides a guide to Freud's dream theory (graphics included)

www.stg.brown.edu/projects/h...andow/HTatBrown/Freud_OV.html
> Provides a variety of links that help explain Freud's theories

www.colorado.edu/English/ENG2012Klages/lacan.html
> Provides an overview of the differences between Sigmund Freud and Jacques Lacan

www.enteract.com/~jwalz/Jung
> Provides an understanding of the writings of Carl Gustav Jung

~ Student Essay ~

A Psychoanalytic Approach to Poe's "The City in the Sea"

Unlike many other schools of criticism, psychoanalytic theory with its accompanying practical applications is unique, for it can be used with a variety of other literary theories when analyzing a text. Although this particular approach to textual analysis has been criticized for its lack of attention toward the aesthetic elements of a work, a psychoanalytic approach can reveal intriguing details not only about the text but also about the author and the reader, elements of the interpretative process that other literary techniques often overlook.

Psychoanalytic theory finds its roots in psychoanalysis, a medical technique developed by Sigmund Freud (1856–1938). Freud bases his psychoanalytic theories on his tripartite model of the human mind. This model represents the unconscious part of the human psyche as housing three parts: the id, the ego, and the superego. According to Freud, the id is the reservoir of the primal instincts of sexuality and aggression. Being dominated by the "pleasure principle" that knows only desire, the id is lawless and amoral, striving only to gratify the dark desires it houses. Freud believes that if the id is left unchecked, it can result in a person's self-destruction. To counterbalance this dangerous part of the unconscious, the mind possesses two regulating agencies: the ego and the superego. The superego is the exact opposite of the id, working to protect society and to allow a person to abide by certain moral restrictions. Dominated by the "morality principle," an overactive superego will result in an unconscious and often overwhelming sense of guilt. But it is the ego that regulates between these two psychic forces (the id and the superego), acting as the rational governing agency of the mind. Though it may lack the vitality of the id, the ego more frequently than not succeeds in redirecting the strong and potentially dangerous urges housed in the unconscious mind into non-destructive activities.

When Freud first developed psychoanalysis, he did not intend it to be a school of literary criticism. He did believe, however, that literature contains elements relevant to his psychological theories, taking, for example, the name of his "Oedipus Complex" from Sophocles' Greek tragedy. A major component of psychoanalysis is dream interpretation in which the analyst probes the patient's dreams for hidden symbols. In this probing, the analyst must distinguish among four key elements of a dream: repression, sublimation, displacement, and condensation. Repression represents the powerful urges of the id that have been forced into the unconscious by the ego. These repressed desires resurface in dreams through the other three processes. For example, in sublimation the unconscious mind redirects unacceptable desires into acceptable activities. In actuality, the mind leaks these forbidden desires into the acceptable activity of dreaming, thereby providing a pathway for and a view into the previously inaccessible id. Through displacement, the id disguises a repressed urge so as to sneak this forbidden desire past the mind's censor, often making the most interesting element of the dream the most trivial detail. All of these forces working together constitute what Freud calls a condensed dream—that is, in a person's dream the images in that dream become a highly compressed array of the dreamer's psychic expressions, offering an extensive assortment of meanings. According to Freud, a literary work is similar to a dream in that such a text is deemed an acceptable activity by society and the mind, making a work of fiction a virtual playground for the author's repressed instincts.

In her comprehensive, psychoanalytic study of Edgar Allan Poe, Marie Bonaparte, a follower of Sigmund Freud, analyzes Poe's canon, utilizing psychobiography, one of the first literary applications of psychoanalytic criticism. Rarely used today, psychobiography is the study of an author's life and events, and includes the excavation of the residue of these events in the author's work. Bonaparte extensively studied Poe's life, and through the application of Freud's dream analysis techniques, she linked characters and events from Poe's writing to actual characters and events in his life.

From her study of Poe's life, Bonaparte deduced that Poe's existence was one of loneliness, poverty, and despair. Before Poe turned three, his father had already deserted the family. Shortly thereafter, his mother died of consumption, leaving Poe in the hands of a somewhat uncaring but financially successful foster father, John Allan. Poe spent the next five years in England, for the Allans' profitable business ventures had taken them abroad. Returning a somewhat lonely and introverted child, Poe lacked the self-motivation of a disciplined student, but nonetheless was an outstanding classical scholar. At age seventeen, Poe matriculated at the University of Virginia where his excessive drinking, gambling, and aristocratic airs eventually led to his leaving the university and joining the United States Army.

Poe's lack of discipline once again surfaced, and about two years later—thanks, in part, to the intervention of his foster father—Poe left the army. A short time later, however, he gained entrance to West Point, remaining only eight months. Receiving little or no support from his foster father and loathing the discipline of military life, Poe deliberately violated the academy's rules and was thereby dismissed.

After his second military stint, Poe moved to Baltimore, Maryland, in 1831, where he lived with his aunt. A few years later, he married his thirteen-year-old cousin, Virginia Clemm. Many scholars believe the marriage, however, was never consummated. Throughout the remainder of Poe's brief life, bouts of depression, bursts of creativity, periods of extreme poverty, the death of his wife, and difficulties maintaining stable employment haunted him until his death in 1849.

By applying Freud's psychoanalytic principles to Poe's life and his canon, Bonaparte believes that Poe was still erotically attached to his mother at the time of her death, leaving a void in his libido. Through his marriage to his cousin and his avoiding the sexual consummation of the marriage, Poe preserved his sexuality. According to Bonaparte, Poe's self-imposed abstinence forced the powerful urges of his libido back into his unconscious. Through the process of sublimation, his repressed sexual forces then made themselves apparent in his fiction. His unacceptable activities of his sex drive thus became sublimated to the acceptable activity of writing.

Such sublimation evidences itself in Poe's poem "The City in the Sea" (1845). In this text Poe paints a dark image of an ancient Gothic city that is abandoned and desolate. Throughout the poem Poe describes this solemn city with its once magnificent buildings and monuments as the remnants of a once seething metropolis. A psychoanalytic approach to this text reveals explicit sexual imagery, signifying the emergence of Poe's repressed libido. Three types of such sexual imagery abound in the poem: phallic symbols (any object whose length exceeds its diameter and which represents the penis); yonic symbols (round, hollow objects that symbolize the vagina); and symbols of the actual sex act. The presence of this sexual imagery combined with an understanding and the utilization of Freud's theories of displacement, repression, and sublimation reveal the resurfacing of Poe's forgotten and suppressed sexual desires in this poem.

Interestingly, "The City in the Sea" was not the poem's original title. Before the present title, Poe opted for "The Doomed City" (1831) and the "City of Sin" (1836). Both of these former titles illustrate the concept of displacement. Poe's ego probably deemed these earlier titles unacceptable; his id then developed a title that seems trivial enough, but one that still contains a highly sexual but more repressed image. For the "City" with its buildings and pulsating activities symbolizes the penis, and the "Sea," a frequent yonic symbol, represents the vagina. "The City in the Sea," Poe's final title, then represents the sex act itself.

The poem begins with a brief description of the city, with phallic symbols immediately becoming apparent. As early as line 6 we find evidence of the phallus: "There shrines and palaces and towers/ Time-eaten towers that tremble not!" These shrines, palaces, and towers we quickly recognize as symbolic of the penis, but a penis that "tremble[s] not"! For in lines 8–11, Poe reveals his repressed sexual desires: "Resemble nothing that is ours./ Around, by lifting winds forgot,/ Resignedly beneath the sky/ The melancholy waters lie." Poe now describes the phallic symbols he previously addressed—the shrines, palaces, and towers—as "forgotten" and as those that "resign beneath the sea in melancholy waters." The use of this description illustrates Poe's forced but self-imposed sexual abstinence. The penis, as any kind of pleasure center, Poe has completely neglected.

Phallic symbols continue to abound in the second stanza of the poem. Lines 14–18 reveal these symbols and Poe's repressed sexuality:

> But light from out the lurid sea
> Streams up the turrets silently—
> Gleams up the pinnacles far and free
> Up domes—up spires—up kingly halls
> Up fanes—up Babylon-like walls.

Apparently Poe's ego sees the quickening of the penis as unacceptable, and his repressed feelings of sexuality become sublimated into poetry.

In stanzas three and four the imagery changes to include not only phallic but also yonic symbols. In stanza three, for example, "The melancholy waters lie" (an obvious yonic symbol) and "a proud tower . . . looks gigantically down" (an obvious phallic symbol). But it is in stanza four where such imagery becomes even more apparent. In lines 30–31, Poe writes: "There open fanes and gaping graves/ Yawn level with the luminous waves." These gaping graves represent the vagina. Poe's use of the adjective "gaping" is particularly indicative of sexual activity and possesses many sexual connotations. In addition, the "ripples" and "swellings" that follow in the rest of the stanza represent breast-like images and the curves of a woman's body.

Whereas phallic and yonic symbolism abound in the first three stanzas of the poem, the fourth and last stanza contains a symbolic representation of the actual sex act. The first two lines of the stanza (42–43) imply the activity that is to come: "But lo, a stir is in the air!/ the wave—there is a movement there!" The sexual imagery becomes more explicit in the next four lines:

> As if the towers had thrust aside,
> In slightly sinking, the dull tide—
> As if their tops had feebly given
> A void within the filmy Heaven.

In these lines where the "thrusting towers" give a "void within the filmy heaven," the sex act becomes apparent. The phallic symbol, the towers, couples with the yonic symbol, the void, signifying sexual intercourse. Such imagery represents sexual climax, with the lines that follow containing images of the post-climactic sexual state:

> The eaves have now a redder glow—
> The hours are breathing faith and low—
> And when, amid no earthly moans,
> Down, down that town shall settle hence.

Overall, the poem "The City in the Sea" is incredibly rich with sexual imagery and shows Poe's id at work, striving to convey the deep passions and desires of his unconscious mind. And thanks to Freud's psychoanalytic methods of dream analysis applied to this text, we can uncover such a rich and varied interpretation.

DAVID JOHNSON

➷ Professional Essay ➷

David Copperfield Dreams of Drowning

When Betsy Trotwood comes to London to tell her nephew that she is financially ruined, and that he must henceforth shift for himself, David Copperfield is not unnaturally shocked and distraught. His sleep is nightmarish, as it often is (more than twenty of his dreams are recounted in the novel). He imagines himself

> hopelessly endeavouring to get a license to marry Dora, havng nothing but one of Uriah Heep's gloves to offer in exchange, which the whole commons rejected; and still more or less conscious of my room, I was always tossing about like a distressed ship in a sea of bedclothes.[1]

The rejection by the Commons is a form of public humiliation, not infrequent in dreams; it is also a close echo of a preceding incident. Just prior to Aunt Betsey's arrival, David had encountered Edward Murdstone at the offices of Spenlow and Jorkins. Murdstone had at that moment procured a license to marry a beautiful girl "just of age"—a girl, we are to understand, very like David's mother. The fantasy of seeking and failing to get a marriage license is clearly a re-enactment of this event. Again David competes with Murdstone, and again he fails, just as he had failed in competing with him for the attention of Clara Copperfield. Equally revealing is the object which David offers to the Commons—"one of Uriah Heep's gloves." The implication is that David, now deprived of the status that accompanies financial well-being, unconsciously acknowledges his new kinship with the unpropertied social climber Heep. But is there any significance to the glove itself? Dickens, most economical of novelists, frequently defines characters in terms of objects, as for instance Jane Murdstone is denoted a sadist by her iron beads ("fetters" to David). Heep's hand, and by association his gloves, are a metonym for his character, for his body, for his sexuality. The gloves figure prominently in the scene in which Heep reveals his desire to marry Agnes (an action with a number of ironic parallels to David's wooing of Dora). "He was close beside me, slowly fitting his long skeleton fingers into the still longer fingers of a great Guy Fawkes pair of gloves" (XXV, 436). He was "so humble in respect of those scarecrow gloves, that he was still putting them on, and seemed to have made no advance in that labour, when we got to my place." Heep's incomplete penetration of the glove is a marvelous image of sexual aggression, none of the less nauseous for its futility. But the key terms in the passage are "scarecrow" and "Guy Fawkes," which categorize Heep as repulsive and sub-human and also suggest that he is a scapegoat slated for ritual expulsion. The dream hints at the depth of the relationship between David and Heep, one aspect of which is that Heep is freighted with the baser elements of human nature which are apparently missing from David's character. David and Uriah are, in psychological terms, "splits." But a close reading of the novel, with special attention to the unraveling of fantasies, shows that David Copperfield is split not twofold but triply, and that James Steerforth is as important in David's psychological life as is Heep.

On the night of David's first meeting with Uriah Heep, his sleep is also troubled by dreams. In his odd circular office at Canterbury, the villainous clerk has fearfully suggested that David is ambitious to usurp his place in

---

[1]XXXV, 566. Page references are to the convenient Penguin edition of Treavor Blount (1966).

Wickfield's firm. David denies such an intention. Heep leaves the office by an outside door, and extinguishes the light. As he is about to return to Wickfield's home by a connecting passage, David falls over Heep's stool.

> This was the proximate cause, I suppose, of my dreaming about him, for what appeared to me to be half the night; and dreaming, among other things, that he [Heep] had launched Mr. Peggotty's house on a piratical expedition, with a black flag at the masthead, bearing the inscription "Tidd's Practice," under which diabolical ensign he was carrying me and little Em'ly to the Spanish Main, to be drowned. (XVI, 293)

The controlling form of this dream of drowning is flashback, or regression, to childish fantasies based on the semi-surreptitious reading of picaresque adventure. For an imaginary moment, David is once again one of Smollett's seagoing heroes, or "Captain Somebody of the Royal British Navy" (IV, 106). Sometime in daylight and sometime in dreams, David longs to be a great heroic figure ("Whether I shall turn out to be the hero of my own life . . ."), and the Spanish Main is one of the demesnes of great men. It is, in fact, the part of the world Dickens had sent Walter Gay, the hero of *Dombey and Son* (1848) to seek his fortune. But David's odyssey is landlocked, and he comes no closer to the sea than to study nautical law at Doctors' Commons. Even in the dream, he does not command the ship. David is a passenger; Heep is the captain.

But a closer look at the dream reveals that a third person, shadowy but nevertheless real, is also present. For it is Steerforth, not David, who carries off little Em'ly and drowns. David fantasizes for himself the role that Steerforth enacts or, stated another way, Steerforth represents that part of David which desires to philander and seduce. As a child, David had wished to marry Em'ly; now older and wiser, he recognizes that a gentleman does not marry a fisherman's niece. The fantasy reveals what society and civilization make David deny, even to himself. The dream of drowning, then, contains David and the two men who stand for alternative moral paths, and at least in the world of dreams, symbolize parts of the self. Uriah Heep represents what David fears he is or might become; Steerforth, briefly, stands for what David wishes to be, but can neither achieve nor reject.

In terms of the dream, all three men "drown," and this too has an obvious significance. The traditional association between water and sexuality is not unknown to Dickens, as is clear from the splendid comic excess of the account of David's infatuation with Dora.

> If I may so express it, I was steeped in Dora. I was not merely over head and ears in love with her, but was saturated through and through. Enough love might have been wrung out of me, metaphorically speaking, to drown anybody in; and yet there would have remained enough within me, and all over me, to pervade my entire existence.[2] (XXXIII, 535)

---

[2] The extension of this metaphor leads to delectable but submerged puns, as when David says of his love that its "profundity was quite unfathomable" (XXXIV, 551). Or note Julia Mill's use of the term "the Desert of Sahara" to indicate trouble between the lovers.

Drowning is not only a way of dying—it is the plunge into the sea of passion; its ineluctable corollary is that sex and sexual passion are dangerous and destructive. Therefore Dora dies of the consequences of miscarriage— she dies of the love that is "wrung out of" David. The association between water and passion permeates the novel. Little Em'ly, for instance, is first seen running "along a jagged timber" which protrudes over the water, as if "springing forward to her destruction." David tells us that he is "afraid of her falling over" (III, 86), but in the dream, exercising the prerogative of the unconscious, he falls with her. She elopes across the water, and Steerforth even christens his clipper ("clip her") the *Little Em'ly*. The rechristening of the *Stormy Petrel* is transparently an emblem of her fall. In fact, a number of the highly sexed, and therefore potentially or actually immoral figures in the novel are drawn to the water. Martha Endell, a prostitute, tries to commit suicide in the river. Jack Maldon, the principal threat to the marriage of impotent Dr. Strong and his child-bride Annie, says that "when a plunge is to be made into the water, it's no use lingering on the bank" (XVI, 287), and he plows the sea as far as to India and back. Maldon is a swashbuckler, a parody of Steerforth, and a ne'er-do-well even at seduction. He attempts to violate Annie's virginity, but only succeeds in taking her cherry-colored ribbon.[3] A more effective plunger is Steerforth himself—a great lover of the sea, naturally adept at sailing, a "nautical phenomenon" (XXII, 383). Mr. Peggotty remembers his name as Rudderford, and the confusion is a Dickensian manner of definition. David, who magically cannot drown, and Agnes are specifically identified as land—chaste—characters by the second components of their surnames.[4]

The medium of the dream is water; the primary subject is Uriah Heep, who is a sexual, an economic, and a moral threat to David. In terms of simple male rivalry, Heep opposes David for the hand of Agnes, just as another Uriah was once a rival of David for possession of Bathsheba. Repulsive in himself, Heep is more loathsome when considered as a partner for Agnes. It has been suggested that Heep's physique bears the iconology of the habitual masturbator;[5] whether or not this is true, there is certainly something indecent about him. In this novel, a male character's genital is occasionally represented by his hand. Old Dr. Strong's, for instance, "did nothing for itself" (XVI, 282); nor is it accidental that when the oedipal struggle between David and Murdstone comes to a crisis, Murdstone is bitten on the hand. Heep's hands are long, dangly, and wet, and he manipulates them constantly.

[3]Dolly Varden is also decked in cherry when she is molested by "Hugh of the Maypole" in *Barnaby Rudge*.

[4]The meaning of David's name is unclear. I would derive it from Edward Moor, *Suffolk Words and Phrases* (London, 1827), which Dickens used as a source for Yarmouth dialect. Moor defines "COPPEROZE. The common red field poppy" (86). The conjunction of "copper" and "field" is persuasive, especially since Dickens rejected such names as "Topflower" and "Flowerbury" for his hero. Cf. also Steerforth's "Daisy." Flowers seem to have been on Dickens' mind.

[5]Steven Marcus, *The Other Victorians* (New York, 1966), p. 19.

> It was not fancy of mine about his hands, I observed; for he frequently ground the palms against each other as if to squeeze them dry and warm, besides often wiping them, in a stealthy way, on his pocket-handkerchief. (XVI, 291)

Heep's writhing, rufous, snaky appearance suggest flaccidity rather than self-abuse. His Christian name, no less than his appearance, associates him with micturition. "Heep" might refer to a heap of money, but again the excremental reading is the more likely.[6] Indeed, tradition tells us that the two are the same (cf. Mr. Merdle and the dust-heaps in *Our Mutual Friend*). Heep, though, is not an anal character in Freud's sense, although he does participate to some extent in the type. Taken as a whole he is, to put it as simply as possible, repulsively cloacal. He therefore represents a kind of immature or diseased or perverted sexuality which David finds sometimes attractive—"[he] had a sort of fascination for me" (XVI, 290); "I was attracted to him in very repulsion" (XXV, 443–4)—but more often despicable. When David dreams that Heep launches Him, the latent meaning is that he is initiated into a new world of dangerous and potentially degenerate sexuality. In it also clear that David would be willing to launch himself, but can only deal with his desires when he scapegoats them onto Heep (it is, after all, David's dream). Heep is not scapegoat only, but the Yahoo within David, projected outward.

Heep also causes David distress of a social order, for in essence Uriah is Mealy Potatoes with social pretensions. David lives in fear that he might lose gentlemanly status and fall again into the proletariat. The special nightmare of Murdstone and Grinby is not the loss of education—it is the horror of manual labor and low associations. Had David not run away to Dover, and succeeded in becoming a gentleman through the transforming magic of his Aunt, his path through life would have been the same as Heep's. The dream is very clear on the subject, for in it David is an unwilling participant in Heep's enterprise. David dreams that Heep "had launched Mr. Peggotty's house on a piratical expedition, with a black flag at the masthead, bearing the inscription, 'Tidd's Practice.'" The "piratical expedition" is the means by which Heep attempts to clamber upward—the foray into Wickfield's accounts. "Tidd's Practice" is the law book that Heep pores over, and therefore an appropriate symbol for his ambition.[7] The ship itself is a telescoping of the Wickfield and

---

[6]Cf. also Traddles. Moor defines "Trattles—or trottles. The globular excrementitious droppings of sheep. The following are the similar words I have met with. *Tirdles* or *treadles*, or *treddles*, the dung of a sheep. *Trettles*, the dung of a rabbit or coney." Perhaps Durdles in *Edwin Drood* should be mentioned here.

[7]Heep's intercourse with "Tidd's Practice" is just a bit disgusting.

"'I found Uriah reading a great fat book, with such demonstrative attention, that his lank forefinger followed up every line as he read, and made clammy tracks along the page (or so I fully believed) like a snail.'" (XVI, 290). But a "tid" in Victorian slang is a woman, and Heep's molesting of Tidd suggests an unpleasant sexual practice.

"'Have you been studying much law lately?' I asked to change the subject.

"'Oh, Master Copperfield,' he said, with an air of self-denial, 'my reading is hardly to be called study. I have passed an hour or two in the evening, sometimes, with Mr. Tidd.'" (XVII, 311).

The "air of self-denial" is deliberately unpersuasive, and the idea of passing "an hour or two" with Tidd is curiously suggestive.

Peggotty residences. They are comparable: in the Peggotty home (a boat), a complete family appears to be in residence, yet there is no relationship of real intimacy until the doomed engagement of Ham to Em'ly. At Wickfield's, Agnes is surrogate wife to her father—a chaste and slightly insane relationship later duplicated by that of Mr. Peggotty and Em'ly in Australia. Each family is initially free of sexual passion, but in the course of the novel each is invaded, the one by Steerforth, at David's invitation; the other by Heep, who exclaims to David: "To think that you should be the first to kindle the sparks of ambition in my umble breast!" (XXV, 438). Both invasions are disastrous in their consequences; both lead to "shipwrecks"; both are alluded to in the dream.

Heep is also, as the dream reveals, "diabolical"—an Iago-like figure who enjoys villainy for its own sake, and whose hatred for David is as intense as its motivation is obscure. His devilishness is part of a religious content of the novel that has never been fully explored.[8] Steerforth, for instance, is the "bad angel"—the misleader of youth in attractive shape. Heep is Vice in form as well as fact. Agnes, the good angel (Dickens is consistent in his use of morality nomenclature) is also, as her name suggests, *agnus*. Clearly David does not want Heep to creep and climb and intrude into her fold. But Heep is also parody of Christ. He preaches "umbleness," but his humility is false and hypocritical. The great scene in which David slaps Heep and dislodges a tooth is a burlesque of true Christianity. Heep literally turns the other cheek.

> "Copperfield," he said, "there must be two parties to a quarrel. I won't be one. . . . I forgive you . . . I'm determined to forgive you. But I do wonder that you should lift your hand against a person that you knew to be so umble." (XLII, 686–7)

His humility and fraudulent forgiveness are designed to arrogate power to himself. Heep is also "subtle," a "devil," and generally snaky. In addition, he is designed to be a Jew in everything but fact. His red hair, as Dickens well knew, is a theatrical badge with antecedents in Judas, Shylock, and Fagin. In *Our Mutual Friend*, Dickens conveniently splits Heep into Fledgeby and Mr. Riah. Fledgeby works on much the same principle as Heep—exercise of power over the "better" people by exploiting weakness and acquiring privileged information, while Mr. Riah preserves Heep's "Christian" name. Another of the complex reverberations that make Heep terrifying is his connection with death. He is "cadaverous" and has long "skeleton" hands. He generally wears "decent black," and his mother continues to wear weeds throughout the novel, although even at the time of David's dream, her husband had been dead four years. Heep's father, incidentally, was a sexton and like Gabriel Grub in *Pickwick Papers*, probably also a gravedigger. The association explains why Heep appears in the dream as an angel of death.

---

[8]The theme is touched on by J. Hillis Miller in *Charles Dickens: The World of His Novels* (Cambridge, 1958), p. 157.

Another property of Heep's that is connected with the dream is his stool. The clerk, it will be remembered, lives in a "little round tower that formed one side of the [Wickfield] house"[9] (XV, 275). His room is circular, and he sits, with Tidd, on a high stool. The stool is associated with his ambitions and David, characteristically, trips on it. In fact, the stool is the catalyst that precipitates the dream.

> Being, at last, ready to leave the office for the night, he asked me if it would suit my convenience to have the light put out; and on my answering, 'Yes,' instantly extinguished it. After shaking hands with me—his hand felt like a fish, in the dark—he opened the door into the street a very little, and crept out, and shut it, leaving me to grope my way back into the house: which cost me some trouble and a fall over his stool. This was the proximate cause, I suppose, of my dreaming about him, for what appeared half the night, and dreaming. (XV, 292)

This is Dickens at his best. Every element in the description combines primary meaning with deeper reference. Here is Heep, under the guise of serving David's convenience, inconveniencing him severely. Here is Heep, cribb'd confined, cabin'd, opening doors "a very little." His personality is as locked up as that of Shylock, or Barkis, or Tulkinghorn. Or Heep as snake, creeping about; as an odious sexual creature, waiting until the light is extinguished to shake hands. And there is the symbolic fall over the stool which represents Heep's economic power, and which also seems to carry a sexual reference. It is like the stool in Dr. Strong's school on which Mr. Dick sits. "He always sat in a particular corner, on a particular stool, which was called 'Dick' after him" (XVII, 310). Mr. Dick parodies Heep's pretensions, as his *Memorial* is a parody of David's autobiography and Dickens' *roman a clef*.[10] And though it is Sterne and not Dickens who is generally thought to be novelist of stools and corners, the import of a stool named Dick is clear.

Uriah is for David a nightmare of a special kind. He is ostentatiously immoral, sexually diseased, and socially unacceptable. Steerforth is the

---

[9]The "image cluster' involving towers (Dickens calls Heep's stool a tower), the sea, and dreams is recapitulated when the subject again turns to drowning (Steerforth's).

"I now approach an eventide in my life, so indelible, so awful, so bound by an infinite variety of ties to all that has preceded it, in these pages, that, from the beginning of my narrative, I have seen it growing larger and larger as I advanced, *like a great tower in a plain*, and throwing its fore-cast shadow even on the incidents of my childish days.

"For years after it occurred, I *dreamed* of it often. I have started up so vividly impressed by it, that its fury has yet seemed raging in my quiet room, in the still night. I *dream* of it sometimes, though at lengthened and uncertain intervals, to this hour. *I have an association between it and a stormy wind, or the lightest mention of a seashore, as strong as any of which my mind is conscious.*" (LV, 854, my italics).

[10]Dr. Strong's *Dictionary* and its search for "Greek roots" is another example of parodic authorship. It is linked to Mr. Dick's *Memorial* by the simpleton's delight in it, and by a curious detail. "Adams, our head-boy, who had a turn for mathematics, had made a calculation, I was informed, of the time this Dictionary would take in completing, on the Doctor's plan, and at the Doctor's rate of going. He considered that it might be done in one thousand six hundred and forty-nine years, counting from the Doctor's last, or sixty-second, birthday" (XXXIV, 293). The *Memorial* is obsessed with the execution of Charles I, A.D. 1649.

opposite. Aristocratic in manner if not in fact, he is unconcerned with what preoccupies David: respectability, love, duty, work. He is clearly modeled on Shelley (a try at Oxford, curls, physical beauty, elopement with a member of the underclass, heroic drowning).[11] David, hypnotized, fails to notice his abundantly obvious faults. He does not see that Steerforth's exploitation of him is as offensive as the viciousness of employers, waiters, coachmen, and schoolteachers. "I feel as if you were my property" (XX, 348), says Steerforth, who is nothing if not frank. David becomes his "plaything" (358) and finds the unequal relationship satisfactory. The colonial–colonizer relationship never changes. And, as is characteristic of members of an exploited class, David identifies with his idolized victimizer, especially when Steerforth acts out the wish that is revealed in the dream. "I had never loved Steerforth better than when the ties that bound me to him were broken" (XXXII, 516).

David and Steerforth share adolescent crushes on each other. Later the two share love objects. Dickens flirts with this classic homosexual theme, but does not take it very far. Little Em'ly is loved by both, and so, in a less obvious way, is Rosa Dartle. Steerforth seduces them both; David loves them both, but loves them passively, unsuccessfully, and therefore morally. Miss Dartle is one of Dickens' angry women, not so magnificent as Edith Dombey, not so perverse as Miss Wade. She is ferociously jealous of the women in Steerforth's life, and she is also jealous of David. When David first comes to the Steerforth home, he learns the story of Miss Dartle's remarkable scar— the mark that cuts through her lips.

> "Why, the fact is," he returned, "I did that."
> "By an unfortunate accident!"
> "No. I was a young boy, and she exasperated me, and I threw a hammer at her. A promising young angel I must have been!"
> I was deeply sorry to have touched on such a painful theme, but that was useless now.
> "She has borne the mark ever since, as you see," said Steerforth, "and she'll bear it to her grave, if she ever rests in one—though I can hardly believe she will ever rest anywhere. She was the motherless child of a sort of cousin of my father's. He died one day. My mother, who was then a widow, brought her here to be company to her. She has a couple of thousand pounds of her own, and saves the interest of it every year, to add to the principal. There's the history of Miss Rosa Dartle for you."
> "And I have no doubt she loves you like a brother?" said I.
> "Humph!" retorted Steerforth, looking at the fire. "Some brothers are not loved overmuch; and some love—but help yourself, Copperfield." (XX, 352)

The passage is brimming with suggestions.[12] Miss Dartle's scar is an emblem of the sexual violation which was produced by Steerforth's hammer

---

[11] And the first boat that appears in *David Copperfield* is called the *Skylark*.

[12] Some of which have been elucidated by Mark Spilka, *Dickens and Kafka, a Mutual Interpretation* (Bloomington, Indiana, 1963), to which this passage is indebted.

and which passed through her lips (i.e., *labiae*). Her restlessness allies her to Steerforth and Maldon and suggests that she is among those fated to "drown." The sudden death of Rosa's father, so casual in report, is reminiscent of the death of Mr. Spenlow. David, of course, is attracted to women with weak or absent fathers. In the closing exchange, David, fishing for information, intimates that the relation between Steerforth and Rosa ought to be that of brother and sister. This is rejected, and the implication of the aposiopesis is what we later learn directly from Miss Dartle: that Steerforth has "used" her, and continues to use her at his whim. The parting expression—"Help yourself, Copperfield" is entirely apt. Steerforth is willing and anxious to share.

Miss Dartle is about thirty years old, which is the same age as the elder Miss Larkins, after whom David's heart launches still another of its undisciplined impulses. The first stirrings of lust for Rosa come when he spends the night at Steerforth's home. He is surprised to discover his room dominated by a portrait of his new love, and again he is transfixed by the scar.

> It was a startling likeness, and necessarily had a startling look. The painter hadn't made the scar, but I made it; and there it was, coming and going; now confined to the upper lip as I had seen it at dinner, and now showing the whole extent of the wound inflicted by the hammer, as I had seen it when she was passionate. (XX, 356)

The wound which grows larger with passion is a cliche of Victorian pornography, and the italicized "I made it" enforces the identity with Steerforth, as David, in fantasy, duplicates the act of violation. The sexual import of the passage is implicit not only in metaphor, but in the very rhythm of the sentence, especially in the phrase, "coming and going." David's repressed and stylized imaginings are parallel to the content of the dream of drowning— David would do what Steerforth can do.

But Steerforth is more than the conventional gentleman-seducer. How frequently does David refer to his wasted powers, to his easy learning and bored novelty seeking. He is rather a precursor of Des Esseintes than a successor to Lovelace. And there is a hint of perversity here too—the same that is implicit in the notion of drowning together.

> "You haven't got a sister, have you?" said Steerforth, yawning.
> "No," I answered.
> "That's a pity," said Steerforth. "If you had had one, I should think that she would have been a pretty, timid, little bright-eyed sort of a girl. I should have like to have known her." (VI, 140)

The implication of Steerforth's remarks are as clear as is the effeminate nickname which he gives to David—"Daisy." And perhaps this is the solution to what has been considered a puzzle—what exactly does Steerforth find attractive about Em'ly? Steerforth is more interested in David than he admits, and of all the daisies in the field he chooses a girl most like David—his "sister."

David Copperfield's dream of drowning is then a path into the central structural pattern of the novel, which is the rich and complex relationship between David and two complementary figures. Dickens is an extraordinarily subtle novelist, though the depth of his psychological vision is not as apparent as that of the novelist of manners whose fiction is dense with the involuted analysis of personality and motive. Here, Dickens has created a brilliant tripartite relationship; perhaps its immediacy is accounted for by the same reasons that made this novel a "favorite child." And if an understanding of his method can only be effected on dwelling on details and trifles, then we must fall back on David's own observation, that "trifles make the sum of life" (LIII, 838).

Essay by E. Pearlman, as found in *The Practice of Psychoanalytic Criticism*, Leonard Tennenhouse, ed. Detroit: Wayne State University Press, 1976, pp. 105–17.

Original source: E. Pearlman. "David Copperfield Dreams of Drowning." *American Imago* 28 (1971): 391–403.

8

Feminism

What enrages me is the way women are used as extensions of men, mirrors of men, devices for showing men off, devices for helping men get what they want. They are never there in their own right, or rarely. The world of the Western contains no women.

Sometimes I think *the world* contains no women.

JANE TOMPKINS, "Me and My Shadow"

INTRODUCTION

In 1972, Judith Viorst, a well-known author of children's literature, published her short, poetic, revised version of the fairy tale *Cinderella*. In "... And Then the Prince Knelt Down and Tried to Put the Glass Slipper on Cinderella's Foot," Viorst writes:

> I really didn't notice that he had a funny nose.
> And he certainly looked better all dressed up in fancy clothes.
> He's not nearly as attractive as he seemed the other night.
> So I think I'll just pretend that this glass slipper feels too tight.

Viorst's recasting of Cinderella may make us smile or laugh or simply wonder what has happened to our childhood version of this story that was read to us countless times by our parents, our teachers, and our friends. Viorst's Cinderella is, after all, certainly not the Cinderella we remember. The Cinderella we have been taught would never think or act the way Viorst's re-creation does. Our Cinderella is beautiful, but poor. Treated cruelly by her ugly stepsisters and her arrogant, scheming, selfish step-mother, our Cinderella dutifully cleans the family home while she quietly weeps, lamenting that she will not be able to attend the upcoming ball to be held at the castle. Bearing with great patience her trials, our Cinderella will triumphantly get her wish, for her fairy godmother comes to her rescue. Now clothed in a magnificent gown, the lovely Cinderella is driven to the ball in a coach fit for a queen. At the ball, she meets her handsome prince, who is immediately overwhelmed by her beauty, grace, and charm. But at the stroke of midnight, the Cinderella we remember must return home, losing her glass slipper in her haste to return to her carriage.

Dressed once again in rags, our childhood Cinderella finds herself once again cooking and cleaning for her ugly stepsisters and her wicked stepmother. Bearing her lot in life with unspeakable patience, she is scorned and rebuked time and time again by her older siblings. And then one day the prince and his attendants come to her home, seeking the owner of the glass slipper accidently left on the steps of the castle. After her ugly stepsisters try unsuccessfully to squeeze their big feet into the small slipper, the Cinderella we remember comes face to face with her handsome prince and successfully puts her petite foot into the magical shoe. Immediately the prince recognizes her as the woman of his dreams and proposes marriage. And after their marriage, they live happily ever after.

Viorst's version of this fairy tale characterizes Cinderella a bit differently. In this re-creation, Cinderella now has opinions of her own. In the light of day, she observes that the prince does not seem to be as attractive as he was the other night at the ball. Asserting her own independence, she pretends the glass slipper does not fit. Accordingly, there will be no marriage, for Cinderella herself has decided she does not want to marry the prince.

This new Cinderella refuses to be defined as the nonsignificant other. Unlike the old Cinderella, she will not allow herself to be shaped by her society. She realizes that her culture has all too often presented her with stereotypes that she and many others like her have so blindly accepted. Beautiful women, her society decrees, are often oppressed and belittled. If, however, these beautiful people will only bear with patience their lot in life, they will be rewarded. For like the traditional Cinderella, society says that they must accept that in addition to their beauty, they must also be good natured and meek. After all, ugly women like Cinderella's stepsisters are cruel and heartless. Beautiful women like Cinderella must bear patiently their suffering and accept that they are victims of the circumstances of life. If they accept their lot in life, they will, in time, be rewarded. According to their society's decrees, they will meet some handsome, wealthy prince who will marry them, care for them, and dote over them the rest of their lives.

This re-created Cinderella debunks the false standards and ideas concerning women and their portrayal in both life and literature that have been carefully perpetuated by the traditional Cinderella and her society. Women, says this new Cinderella, should not mindlessly wait around for a handsome prince to come to their rescue. Women must not be like the traditional Cinderella: dependent creatures who blindly accept the commandments of their patriarchal society. Unlike the traditional Cinderella, women must not weep about their lot in life, but take an active part in creating and determining their own lives and their own futures. They must therefore reject many of their culture's stereotypes of women such as "the wicked stepmother" syndrome that asserts that only ugly women are aggressive and self-motivated. They must also reject the notion that marriage is a woman's ultimate goal, one that can assure her of financial security. And they must reject the idea that women (like the traditional Cinderella) are mindless, weepy, passive, helpless creatures who must wait for a man to come and make their lives meaningful. Success in life, these new Cinderellas assert, is not dependent on physical beauty as it is for the traditional Cinderella. And above all, they must realize that they are not limited by their sex; like any man, they can shape their personhood and assert their resourcefulness, their wit, and their personal drive to become what they desire to be. For the re-created Cinderella knows something the old Cinderella never knew: Whereas sex is biologically determined, gender is culturally determined. And like the revised Cinderella, all women must therefore reject the patriarchal standards of society and become persons in their own right. What they must become is a "significant person," not the other.

In essence, this new version of the Cinderella fairy tale crystallizes the central issues of feminism:

- Men, either unconsciously or consciously, have oppressed women, allowing them little or no voice in the political, social, or economic issues of their society.
- By not giving voice and value to women's opinions, responses, and writings, men have therefore suppressed the female, defined what it means to be feminine, and thereby devoiced, devalued, and trivialized what it means to be a woman.
- In effect, men have made women the "nonsignificant other."

Feminism's goal is to change this degrading view of women so that all women will realize that they are not a "nonsignificant Other," but that each woman is a valuable person possessing the same privileges and rights as every man. Women, feminists declare, must define themselves and assert their own voices in the arenas of politics, society, education, and the arts. By personally committing themselves to fostering such change, feminists hope to create a society where the male and female voices are equally valued.

HISTORICAL DEVELOPMENT

According to feminist criticism, the roots of prejudice against women have long been embedded in Western culture. Such gender discrimination may have begun, say some feminists, with the Biblical narrative that places the blame for the fall of humanity on Eve, not Adam. In similar fashion, the ancient Greeks abetted such gender discrimination when Aristotle, one of their leading philosophers and teachers, asserted that "the male is by nature superior, and the female inferior; and the one rules and the other is ruled."

Following Aristotle's lead, religious leaders and philosophers such as Thomas Aquinas and St. Augustine declared that women are really "imperfect men." These imperfect and spiritually weak creatures, they maintained, possess a sensual nature that lures men away from spiritual truths, thereby preventing males from achieving their spiritual potential. And in the centuries to follow, other theologians, philosophers, and scientists continued such gender discrimination. For example, in *The Descent of Man*, Darwin announces that women are of a "characteristic of . . . a past and lower state of civilization." Such beings, he noted, are inferior to men, who are physically, intellectually, and artistically superior.

For century after century, men's voices continued to articulate and determine the social role and cultural and personal significance of women. In the late 1700s, a faint voice crying in the wilderness against such patriarchal opinions arose and began to be heard. Believing that women along with men should have a voice in the public arena, Mary Wollstonecraft authored *A Vindication of the Rights of Women* (1792). Women, she maintained, must stand up for their rights and not allow their male-dominated society to define what it means to be a woman. Women themselves must take the lead and articulate who they are and what role they will play in society. Most importantly, they must reject the patriarchal assumption that women are inferior to men.

It was not until the Progressive era of the early 1900s, however, that the major roots of feminist criticism began to grow. During this time, women gained the right to vote and became prominent activists in the social issues of the day, such as healthcare, education, politics, and literature. But equality with men in these arenas remained outside their grasp.

Virginia Woolf

Then in 1919, British scholar, teacher, and early feminist Virginia Woolf laid the foundation for present-day feminist criticism in her seminal work *A Room of One's Own*. In this text, Woolf declares that men have and continue to treat women as inferiors. It is the male, she asserts, who defines what it means to be female and who controls the political, economic, social, and literary structures. Agreeing with Samuel T. Coleridge, one of the foremost nineteenth-century literary critics, that great minds possess both male and female characteristics, she hypothesizes in her text the existence of Shakespeare's sister, one who is as gifted a writer as Shakespeare. Her gender, however, prevents her from having "a room of her own." Because she is a woman, she cannot obtain an education or find profitable employment. Her innate artistic talents will therefore never flourish, for she cannot afford her own room, Woolf's symbol of solitude and autonomy needed to seclude one's self from the world and its accompanying social constraints in order to find time to think and write. Ultimately, Shakespeare's sister dies alone without any acknowledgment of her personal genius. Even her grave does not bear her name, for she is buried in a unmarked grave simply because she is female.

Such loss of artistic talent and personal worthiness, says Woolf, is the direct result of society's opinion of women: that they are intellectually inferior to men. Women, Woolf argues, must reject this social construct and establish their own identity. Women must challenge the prevailing, false cultural notions concerning their gender identity and develop a female discourse that will accurately portray their relationship "to the world of reality and not to the world of men." If women accept this challenge, Woolf believes that Shakespeare's sister can be resurrected in and through women living today, even those who may be "washing up the dishes and putting the children to bed" right now. But the Great Depression of the 1930s and World War II in the 1940s focused humankind's attention on other matters and delayed the development of such feminist ideals.

Simone de Beavoir

With the 1949 publication of French writer Simone de Beavoir's *The Second Sex*, however, feminist interests once again surfaced. Heralded as the foundational work of twentieth-century feminism, Beavoir's text declares that both French and Western societies are **patriarchal**, controlled by males. Like Woolf before her, Beavoir believed that the male in these societies defines what it means to be human, including, therefore, what it means to be female. Because the female is not male, Beavoir asserted, she becomes "the Other," an object whose existence is defined and interpreted by the male, who is the dominant being in society. Always subordinate to the male, the female finds herself a secondary or nonexistent player in the major social institutions of her culture, such as the church, government, and educational systems. According to Beavoir, a woman must break the bonds of her patriarchal society and define herself if she wishes to become a significant human being in her own right and defy male classification as the Other. She must ask herself, "What is a woman?" Beavoir insists that a woman's answer must not be "mankind," for such a term once again allows men to define women. This generic label must therefore be rejected, for it assumes that "humanity is male and man defines woman not in herself but as relative to him."

Beavoir insists that women see themselves as autonomous beings. Women, she maintains, must reject the societal construct that men are the subject or the absolute and that women are the Other. Embedded in this false assumption is the supposition that males have power and define cultural terms and roles. Accordingly, women must define themselves outside the present social construct and reject being labeled as the Other.

Kate Millett

With the advent of the 1960s and its political activism and social concerns, feminist issues found new voices. One such voice was Kate Millett. With her publication of *Sexual Politics* in 1969, a new wave of feminism began. Millet was one of the first feminists to challenge the ideological social characteristics of both the male and the female. According to Millet, a female is born and a woman is created. In other words, one's sex, be that male or female, is determined at birth. One's gender, however, is a social construct, being created by cultural ideals and norms. Consciously or unconsciously women and men conform to the cultural ideas established for them by society. Little boys, for example, must be aggressive, self-assertive, and domineering, whereas little girls must be passive, meek, and humble. These cultural norms and expectations are transmitted through television, movies, songs, and literature. Conforming to these prescribed sex roles dictated by society is what Millett calls **sexual politics.** Women, Millett maintains, must revolt against the power center of their culture: male dominance. In order to do so, women must establish female social conventions for themselves by establishing female discourse, literary studies, and feminist criticism.

Feminism in the 1960s and 1970s

Moving from the political to the literary arena throughout the 1960s and 1970s, feminist critics began examining the traditional literary canon and discovered an array of male dominance and prejudice that supported Beavoir and Millet's assertion that males considered the female "the Other," an unnatural or deviant being. First, stereotypes of women abounded in the canon: Women were sex maniacs, goddesses of beauty, mindless entities, or old spinsters. Second, whereas Dickens, Wordsworth, Hawthorne, Thoreau, Twain, and a host of other male authors were "canonized," few female writers achieved such status. Third, for the most part, the roles of female, fictionalized characters were limited to secondary positions, usually occupying minor parts within the stories or simply reverting to the male's stereotypical images of women. And fourth, female scholars such as Virginia Woolf and Simone de Beavoir were ignored, their writings seldom if ever referred to by the male crafters of the literary canon.

Feminist critics of this era asserted that males who created and enjoyed a place of prominence within the canon assumed that all readers were males. Women reading such works could unconsciously be duped into reading as a male. In addition, because most university professors were males, female students were usually trained to read literature as if they were males. But the feminists of the 1960s and 1970s now postulated the existence of a female reader who was affronted by the male prejudices abounding in the canon. Questions concerning the male or female qualities of literary form, style, voice, and theme became the rallying points for feminist criticism, and throughout the late 1970s books that defined women's writings in feminine terms abounded.

Having highlighted the importance of gender, feminist critics then discovered a body of literary works authored by females that their male counterparts decreed inferior and therefore unworthy to be part of the canon. In America, for example, Kate Chopin's late nineteenth-century novel *The Awakening* served as the archetypal rediscovered feminist text of this period, whereas in England Doris Lessing's *The Golden Notebook* (1962) and in France Monique Wittig's *Les Guerilleres* (1969) fulfilled these roles. Throughout the universities and in the reading populace, readers turned their attention to historical and current works authored by women. Simultaneously, works that attempted to define the feminine imagination, to categorize and explain female literary history, and to attempt to define the female aesthetic or concept of beauty became the focus of feminist critics.

The ongoing debate concerning definitive answers to these key feminist interests continued throughout the 1980s, as it does today.

Elaine Showalter

The predominant voice of feminist criticism throughout the 1980s is that of Elaine Showalter. In her text *A Literature of Their Own*, Showalter chronicles what she believes to be the three historical phases of evolution in female writing: the feminine phase (1840–1880), the feminist phase (1880–1920), and the female phase (1970–present). During the feminine phase, writers such as Charlotte Brontë, George Eliot, and George Sand accepted the prevailing social constructs of their day concerning the role and therefore the definition of women. Accordingly, these female authors wrote under male pseudonyms, hoping to equal the intellectual and artistic achievements of their male counterparts. During the feminist phase, female authors dramatized the plight of the slighted woman. These authors depicted the harsh and often cruel treatment of female characters at the hands of their more powerful male creations. In the female phase of today, women reject the imitation prominent during the feminine phase and the protest that dominated the feminist phase. According to Showalter, feminist critics now concern themselves with developing a peculiarly female under-standing of the female experience in art, including a feminine analysis of literary forms and techniques. Such a task necessarily includes the uncovering of **misogyny** in male texts, a term Showalter uses to describe the male hatred of women.

Showalter asserts that female authors were consciously and therefore deliberately excluded from the literary canon by the male professors who first established the canon itself. Authors such as Susan Warner, E. D. N. Southworth, and Mary E. Wilkins Freeman—by far the most popular authors of the second half of the nineteenth century in American fiction—were not deemed worthy to be included in the canon. Showalter urges that such exclusion of the female voice must be stopped. She coins the term *gyno-critics* to "construct a female framework for analysis of women's literature to develop new models based on the study of female experience, rather than to adapt to male models and theories." Through gynocritics, Showalter hopes to expose the false cultural assumptions of women as depicted in literature. By exposing these inaccurate pictures of women, she hopes to establish women as both readers and writers in their own right.

Showalter's term **gynocriticism** has now become synonymous with the study of women as writers and provides critics with four models concerning the nature of women's writing that help answer some of the chief concerns of feminist criticism: the biological, linguistic, psychoanalytic, and cultural. Each of Showalter's models is sequential, subsuming and developing the preceding model. The biological emphasizes how the female body marks itself upon a text by providing a host of literary images and a personal, intimate tone. The linguistic model concerns itself with the need for a female discourse. This model investigates the differences between how women and men use language. It asserts that women can and do create a language peculiar to their gender and how this language can be used in their writings. The psychoanalytic model, based on an analysis of the female psyche and how such an analysis affects the writing process, emphasizes the flux and fluidity of female writing as opposed to male rigidity and structure. And the cultural model investigates how the society in which female authors work and function shape women's goals, responses, and points of view.

Geographical Strains of Feminism

Because no one critical theory of writing dominates feminist criticism and few theorists agree on a unifying feminist approach to textual analysis, physical geography plays a great part in determining the major interests of various voices of feminist criticism. Three distinct geographical strains of feminism have thus emerged: American, British, and French. According to Elaine Showalter, American feminism is essentially textual, stressing repression; British feminism is essentially Marxist, stressing oppression; and French feminism is essentially psychoanalytic, stressing repression. All groups attempt to rescue women from being considered the Other.

American feminist critic Annette Kolodny helps set the major concern of American feminism: the restoration of the writings of female authors to the literary canon. Believing that literary history is itself a fiction, Kolodny wishes to restore the history of women so that they themselves can tell "herstory." In order to tell and write herstory, however, women must first find a means to gain their voice in the midst of numerous voices—particularly male—clamoring for attention in society.

Like Kolodny, Sandra M. Gilbert and Susan Gubar, authors of *The Madwoman in the Attic: The Woman Writer and the Nineteenth-Century Literary Imagination* (1979), assert that the male voice has for too long been the dominant one in society. Because males have also had the power of the pen and therefore the press, they have been able to define and create images of women as they so choose in their male texts. According to Gilbert and

Gubar, such male power has caused "anxiety of authorship" in women, causing them to fear the act of literary creation itself and the act of writing. Such creation, they fear, will isolate them from society and may even destroy them. Gilbert and Gubar's solution is that women develop a "woman's sentence" that would encourage literary autonomy. By inventing such a sentence, a woman can thus sentence a man just as for centuries men have been sentencing women to isolation, anxiety, and literary banishment. In effect, by formulating a woman's sentence, women writers can finally free themselves from being defined by men.

Such a sentence could also free women from being reduced to the stereotypical images that all too often appear in literature. According to Gilbert and Gubar these two major images are "the angel in the house" and the "madwoman in the attic." If a woman is depicted as the angel in the house, she supposedly realizes that her physical and material comforts are gifts from her husband. Her goal in life, therefore, is to please her husband, to attend to his every comfort, and to obey him. Through these selfless acts, she finds the utmost contentment by serving her husband and children. If, perchance, a female character should reject this role, the male critics quickly dub her a monster, a freakish anomaly who is obviously sexually fallen.

Gilbert and Gubar assert that both of these images—the angel and the madwoman—are unrealistic images of women in society. One canonizes and places the woman above the world and the other denigrates and places her below the world. And the message, say Gilbert and Gubar, is clear to all women: If you are not an angel, then you are a monster. Such stereotypical male-created images of women in literature must be uncovered, examined, and transcended if women are to achieve literary autonomy.

Whereas American feminism emphasizes repression, British feminism stresses oppression. Essentially Marxist, British feminism refuses to separate art—literature—and life. Denying the existence of any spiritual reality, British feminists view reading, writing, and publishing as facets of material reality. Being part of material reality, literature, like one's job and one's social activities, is part of a great whole, with each part affecting the other. How women are depicted in life, then, directly affects how they are treated in real life. Particularly in the West, women are exploited not only in literature but also in economic and social conditions. From this perspective, the traditional Western family structure helps to subordinate women, causing them to be economically dependent. Such dependency is then reflected in literature. And it is the job of feminist critics, British feminism maintains, to change this unfair social status of women economically and socially and also in texts. For these feminist critics, the goal of criticism is to change society, not simply critique it.

Believing that women are oppressed both in life and art, French feminism, the third geographical division of present-day feminism, typically stresses the repression of women. As a whole, French feminism is closely associated with the theoretical and practical applications of psychoanalysis. At first, the association with psychoanalysis may be a bit puzzling, for the father of psychoanalysis is Sigmund Freud. Believing that the penis is power, Freud viewed women as incomplete males. All women, he thought, were envious of a male's power as symbolized by the penis. Wanting this power, all women possess penis envy, desiring to gain the male phallus and thereby obtain power. The French psychoanalytic critic Jacques Lacan, however, rescues psychoanalysis from some of Freud's misogynistic theories. (For a detailed explanation of Lacan's theories, see "Jacques Lacan," Chapter 7.) According to Lacan, language, not the phallus, ultimately shapes and structures our conscious and unconscious minds and thus shapes our self-identity. And it is language that ultimately denies women the power of language and therefore the power of literature and writing.

Lacan believes that the human psyches consists of three parts, or what he calls orders: the Imaginary, the Symbolic, and the Real. Each of these orders interacts with the others. From birth to 6 months or so, we function primarily in the Imaginary Order, a preverbal state that contains our wishes, fantasies, and physical images. In this state we are basically sexless, for we are not yet capable of differentiating ourselves from our mothers. Once we successfully pass through the Oedipal crisis, we depart from a biological language into a socialized language into the second of the Lacanian orders: the Symbolic Order. Unfortunately, in this Order the male is socialized into the dominant discourse whereas the female is socialized into a subordinated language. Upon entering this Order, the father becomes the dominant image, or the law. In this stage of our psychic development, both the male and the female fear castration at the hands of the father. For the male, castration means obeying and becoming like the father while simultaneously repressing the Imaginary Order that is most closely associated with the female body. The Imaginary Order, with its pre-Oedipal male desires, becomes a direct threat for the male to the third Lacanian Order, the Real Order, or the actual world as perceived by the individual. Similarly, for the female, entrance into the Symbolic Order means submission to law of the father. Such submission means subservience to the male. Being socialized into a subordinated language, the female becomes a second-class citizen. Because language, for Lacan, is a psychological, not biological, construct, women can learn the dominant discourse of both the Symbolic and the Real Orders and become tools of social change.

Other French feminists, such as Julia Kristeva and Hélène Cixous, further develop and apply Lacan's theories to their own form of feminist criticism. Kristeva, for example, posits that the Imaginary Order is characterized by a continuous flow of fluidity or rhythm, which she calls **chora**. Upon entering the Symbolic Order, both males and females are separated from the chora and repress the feelings of fluidity and rhythm. Similar to a Freudian slip, whereby an unconscious thought breaks through the conscious mind, the chora can break through into the Real Order and disturb the male-dominant discourse. On the other hand, Hélène Cixous explores an entirely different mode of discourse that arises from the Imaginary, not the Symbolic, Order. Cixous maintains that there exists a particular kind of female writing that she calls **l'écriture féminine**. Characterized by fluidity, this particularly feminine discourse, when fully explored, transforms the social and cultural structures within literature.

In addition to the three geographical strains of feminism, other significant feminist strains such as black and lesbian feminism transcend geographical boundaries. For example, Alice Walker, a spokesperson for black feminism, refuses to be associated with traditional feminist criticism and with the term *feminist* itself. She prefers to be called a womanist. On the other hand, French lesbian feminist Monique Wittig rejects the label *woman,* asserting that this term does not include lesbians. She prefers to be called a lesbian, believing that this nomenclature will allow women "to name and redefine themselves."

No matter what they emphasize in theory, however, all feminist critics assert that they are on a journey of self-discovery that will lead them to a better understanding of themselves. And once they understand and then define themselves as women, they believe they will be able to change their world.

ASSUMPTIONS

To the onlooker, feminist theory and practice appear to be a diffuse, loosely connected body of criticism that is more divided than unified, housing more internal disagreements than unity among its adherents than are found in perhaps any other approach to literary analysis. Because it claims no ultimate spokesperson but many different voices, there is not one but a variety of feminist theories. Behind all these seemingly contradictory voices and theories, however, is a set of principles that unites this criticism.

Although feminist critics' ideas concerning the directions of their criticism vary, feminists possess a collective identity: They are women (and some men) who are struggling to discover who they are, how they arrived at their present situation, and where they are going. In their search, they value differing opinions, thereby giving significance to the personal rather than a group of people or a codified and authoritative collection of texts. Their search, they assert, is political, for their aim is to change the world in which they live, a world that they maintain must be changed if all individuals, all cultures, all subcultures, and both sexes are to be valued as creative, rational people who can all contribute to their societies and their world. Such a revisionist, revolutionary, and ideological stance seeks to understand the place of women in society and to analyze all aspects that affect women as writers and their writings in what feminists believe is a male-dominated world. In this masculine world, the feminists declare that it is man who defines what it means to be human, not woman. Because a woman is not a man, she has become the other, the not-male. Man is the subject, the one who defines meaning; woman is the object, having her existence defined and determined by the male. The man is therefore the significant figure in the male/female relationship and the woman is subordinate.

Such female insignificance did not first appear in the twentieth century, declare feminists such as Jane Tompkins. Long before the existence of our present-day, male-dominated world, most societies have been governed by males. These patriarchal societies, say the feminists, have simply passed down their erroneous beliefs from generation to generation, culminating with the predominant Western assumption that women are less than, not equal to, men. Arbitrarily using the male as the standard, these societies apparently agree with Aristotle's assertion that "the female is female by virtue of a certain lack of qualities." Or they support St. Thomas Aquinas' conviction that all women are simply imperfect men. And some still believe that Freud is correct when he argues that female sexuality is based on a lack of a penis, the male sexual organ.

According to feminist critics, by defining the female in relation to the male while simultaneously decreeing the superiority of the male, Western and other cultures have decreed that the female, by nature, is inferior. Once Western culture consciously or unconsciously assimilated this belief into its social structures and allowed it to permeate all levels of its society, females became the oppressed people, inferiors who must be suppressed lest humankind fail to reach its potential.

Feminist critics want to show humankind the errors of such a way of thinking. Women, they declare, are people in their own right; they are not incomplete or inferior men. Despite how often literature and society fiction-alize and stereotype women as angels, barmaids, bitches, whores, brainless housewives, or old maids, women must break free from such oppression and define themselves. No longer, assert these critics, can they allow their male-dominated society to define and articulate their roles, values, and opinions.

To free themselves from such oppression, say feminist critics, women must analyze and challenge the established literary canon that has helped shape the images of female inferiority and oppression ingrained in our culture. Women must create an atmosphere that is less oppressive by contesting the long-held patriarchal assumptions concerning their sex. Because no female Aristotle has articulated a philosophy or coined a battle cry for women's equality, all women must muster a variety of resources to clarify, assert, and implement their beliefs. By re-examining the established literary canon, validating what it means to be a woman, and involving themselves in literary theory and its multiple approaches to a text, women can legitimize their responses to texts written by both males and females, their own writings, and their political, economic, and social positions in their culture.

METHODOLOGY

Just as there is no single feminist theory but many theories, so there exists not one but a variety of feminist approaches to a text. Wanting to challenge and change Western culture's assumption that males are superior to females and therefore are better thinkers, more rational, more serious, and more reflective than women, feminist critics may begin their debunking of male superiority by exposing stereotypes of women found throughout the literary canon. Women, they argue, cannot be simply depicted and classified as either angels or demons, saints or whores, or brainless housewives or eccentric spinsters. Such characterizations must be identified and challenged throughout the canon, and such abuse of women by male authors must be acknowledged as ways men have consciously or unconsciously demeaned, devalued, and demoralized women.

Having identified the antifeminist characterization that occurs in many texts, the feminist critic may then turn to either the American, English, or a non-Western literary canon, seeking to discover works written by women. This is usually a difficult task because males have authored the majority of texts. The American literary canon, for example, is decidedly male. With the works of Hawthorne, Melville, Poe, and other male notables filling the pages of the canon, little or no room is allowed for the writings of Susan Warner, E. D. N. Southwick, and Mary E. Wilkins Freeman, three of the most widely read authors in nineteenth-century America. Feminists assert that these female authors must be "rediscovered" by having their works republished and re-evaluated. When complete, this rediscovery will reveal a valuable body of female authors who share common themes, histories, and often writing styles.

Other feminist critics suggest that we reread the canonized works of male authors from a woman's point of view. Such an analysis is possible, they maintain, by developing a uniquely female consciousness based on female experience rather than the traditional male theories of reading, writing, and critiquing. Known as gynocriticism, this female model of literary analysis offers four areas of investigation:

- Images of the female body as presented in a text. Such an anatomical study, for example, would highlight how various parts of the female body such as the uterus and breasts often become significant images in works authored by women.
- Female language. Such a concern centers on the differences between male and female language. Because we live in patriarchal societies, would it be fair to assume, wonder feminists, that our language is also male-dominated? Do women speak or write differently from men? Although there is little consensus

in the answers to these questions, critics interested in this kind of investigation analyze grammatical constructions, recurring themes, and other linguistic elements.

- The female psyche and its relationship to the writing process. Such an analysis applies the psychological works of Freud and Lacan to a text and shows how the physical and psychological development of the female evidences itself in the writing process through penis envy, the Oedipus complex, and other psychological stages.
- Culture. By analyzing cultural forces (such as the importance and value of women's roles in a given society), critics who emphasize this area of study investigate how society shapes a woman's understanding of herself, her society, and her world.

QUESTIONS FOR ANALYSIS

Whatever method of feminist criticism we choose to apply to a text, we can begin textual analysis by asking some general questions.

- Is the author male or female?
- Is the text narrated by a male or female?
- What types of roles do women have in the text?
- Are the female characters the protagonists or secondary, minor characters?
- Do any stereotypical characterizations of women appear?
- What are the attitudes toward women held by the male characters?
- What is the author's attitude toward women in society?
- How does the author's culture influence her or his attitude?
- Is feminine imagery used? If so, what is the significance of such imagery?
- Do the female characters speak differently from the male characters? In your investigation, compare the frequency of speech for the male characters to the frequency of speech for the female characters.

By asking any or all of these questions of a text, we can begin our journey in feminist criticism while helping ourselves to understand better the world in which we live.

SAMPLE ESSAYS

In the student essay that follows, note how the author uses the psychoanalytic theories of Jacques Lacan to highlight feminist issues. Be able to explain Lacan's feminist theories and to show how the author uses these ideas to arrive at her interpretation of Margaret Atwood's poem "Spelling." After reading the essay, ask yourself whether this interpretation has brought to your attention any feminist issues with which you were previously unaware. If so, what are they?

In the professional essay that follows, note how Elizabeth A. Meese uses the assumptions, terminology, and methodology of feminist criticism to arrive at her interpretation of Zora Neale Hurston's *Their Eyes Were Watching God*. Be able to explain her theoretical assumptions and her methodology. In particular, be able to explain Meese's conclusions. As you did in the student essay, ask yourself whether Meese's interpretation has brought to your attention any feminist issues with which you were unaware. If so, be able to state these concerns.

FURTHER READING

Beauvoir, Simone de. *The Second Sex*. 1949. Ed. and trans. H. M. Parshley. New York: Modern Library, 1952.

Cohen, Ralph, ed. "Feminist Directions." *New Literary History: A Journal of Theory and Interpretation* 19 (Autumn 1987): 1–208.

Eagleton, Mary, ed. *Feminist Literary Theory: A Reader*. 2nd ed. Oxford: Blackwell, 1996.

Gilbert, Sandra M., and Susan Gubar. *The Madwoman in the Attic: The Woman Writer and the Nineteenth-Century Literary Imagination*. New Haven, CT: Yale University Press, 1979.

Humm, Maggie, ed. *Feminisms: A Reader*. Hemel Hempstead, London: Harvester Wheatsheaf, 1992.

Kolodny, Annette. "Some Notes on Defining a 'Feminist Literary Criticism.'" *Critical Inquiry* 2 (1975): 75–92.

Meese, Elizabeth. *Crossing the Double-Cross: The Practice of Feminist Criticism*. Chapel Hill: University of North Carolina Press, 1986.

Millett, Kate. *Sexual Politics*. New York: Doubleday, 1970.

Moi, Toril. *Sexual/Textual Politics: Feminist Literary Theory*. London: Methuen, 1985.

Showalter, Elaine. *A Literature of Their Own: British Women Novelists from Brontë to Lessing*. Princeton, NJ: Princeton University Press, 1977.

———, ed. *The New Feminist Criticism: Essays on Women, Literature, Time*. New York: Pantheon, 1985.

Viorst, Judith. ". . . And Then the Prince Knelt Down and Tried to Put the Glass Slipper on Cinderella's Foot."

Warhol, Robin, and Diane Price Herndl, eds. *Feminisms: An Anthology of Literary Theory and Criticism*. Basingstoke: Macmillan, 1992.

Wollstonecraft, Mary. *A Vindication of the Rights of Women*. Harmondsworth, England: Penguin Books, 1975.

Woolf, Virginia. *A Room of One's Own*. London: Hogarth, 1929; London: Grafton, 1987.

WEB SITES FOR EXPLORATION

http://www.stg.brown.edu/projects/h...xt/landow/SSPCluster/FemTheory.html
   Provides a variety of links to feminist theory and criticism
www.igc.apc.org/women/feminist.html
   Provides more links to feminist issues and resources

www.feminist.org/research/chronicles/biblio.html
   Provides a working bibliography for feminist concerns in America
www.umbc7.umbc.edu/~korenman/wmnst/links.html
   Provides links to women's studies and women's issues
www.colorado.edu/English?ENGL2012Klages/cixous.html
   Provides an essay that distinguishes between the feminism of Sandra Gilbert
   and that of Hélène Cixous

~ Student Essay ~

A Feminist Critique of Margaret Atwood's "Spelling"

Written in 1981, Margaret Atwood's poem "Spelling" echoes the cries of all
women who have been, are, and will be repressed by the dominance of male
discourse. The poem provides the reader with strong images of women who
are attempting to break out of what Jacques Lacan calls the Symbolic Order
and return to the Imaginary Order. The women Atwood pictures in this
poem must wrestle from society its symbol of power: the pen. In this process,
they must reject the image of the female as constructed by males using a
male-dominated discourse and re-define themselves according to their
biologically determined sex, not their gender, for gender is a social construct
defined by the dominant male discourse.

   According to Lacan, in our infancy to about six months of age, we all
pass through the Imaginary Order, a stage of psychic development characterized by flux and fluidity. This stage is closely related to a woman's body,
especially the vagina. During this stage we are able to communicate in a
language not governed by laws or gender or power. All too quickly,
however, Lacan asserts that the next stage of psychic development
approaches, the Symbolic Order. Juxtaposed to the fluidity and flux of the
Imaginary Order, the Symbolic order is characterized by structure and
rigidity. During this stage male discourse becomes dominant, suppressing
the kind of discourse learned during the Imaginary Order. In order to break
out of the Symbolic Order and return to the Imaginary Order dominated by
fluidity and motion, the women Atwood pictures in "Spelling" must take
from society the symbol of power, the pen, and write in their own female-
dominated discourse.

   In the first stanza Atwood describes the persona's daughter playing
with "plastic letters" and "learning how to spell." The language she is
spelling is androgynous, one unaffected by social and cultural influences.
She thus spells boldly with colors of "red, blue & hard yellow" (line 3). Hers
is a semiotic language possessing an innocence that has not been confronted
by castration anxiety. She therefore plays contentedly on the floor with no
one telling her how to spell.

The persona then compares her daughter's bold use of semiotic language to those women who "[deny] themselves daughters" by conforming to the Symbolic language by which men maintain power not only in literature but also in society (line 8). In conforming to the Symbolic Order, these women close themselves up in rooms; they conceal their true discourse, the fluid female chora, in order to "mainline words" (line 11). To be heard and accepted by society, such women must mimic the Symbolic language of male-dominated discourse, or they must sacrifice not being heard at all, thereby repressing the language of their Imaginary Order.

In the next stanza the persona alludes to the necessity of developing a new androgynous language in order to solve the dilemma faced by these women. By stating that "a child is not a poem,/ a poem is not a child," the persona asserts that the Imaginary Order is not acceptable to the poem any more than the Symbolic Order is acceptable to a child (lines 12–13). She therefore suggests that there need not be any distinction between female and male discourse, but rather that both should be revolutionized into a new language that embodies both male and female properties. Both male and female should harmonize together in language with equal distribution of power. In effect, there should be no "either/or" (line 14).

But the power of language remains unequal, and the persona returns to reality by replaying the story of a woman "caught in the war" between society and herself (lines 15–17). In this story, the woman is laboring to give birth to her true self—that is, a language unaffected by male discourse—but the enemy, the male, binds her legs to prevent her intended revolution. And simultaneously an ancestress is also kept from spelling her language as leather is placed over her mouth to "strangle" the words that will give her power (line 23). After all, "a word after a word/ after a word is power;" a power that society struggles to repress and destroy (lines 24–25). This male-dominated society cannot allow these "radical" women to give birth to a new language that would make women and men equals, for then men would be forced to relinquish power and to share it with women whom they believe are merely deformed men. Males, therefore, symbolically close the womb, forcing women to use male discourse if they wish to "mainline words."

As language "falls away/ from the hot bones," the rock-hard conventions of patriarchy break open and melt away (lines 25–26). Only under the kind of pressure that will break rock and melt granite is the hollowness of Symbolic language exposed. The word that was strangled to deny power to women, "splits & doubles & speaks/ the truth & the body/ itself becomes a mouth" (lines 33–35). Symbolically, the persona paints a picture of an embryo splitting inside a woman's womb, slowly giving shape to a new language. Simultaneously, the metaphorical womb contends with the metaphorical penis. When the words of the womb become words, each word leading to the production of more words, and the body becomes a mouth, then the female can rise above the rigidity and structure of the Symbolic Order, embrace the Imaginary Order, and communicate in a new language without hesitation or restriction. Through revolutionizing and creating language, the metaphorical womb can then triumph over the metaphorical penis, taking the penis's pen.

In the final stanza, the persona challenges us, the readers, to consider how we learn to spell. Do we learn inside of gendered constructs, or do we learn by our biological nature? Do we allow society to name us as a man or a woman, or do we learn to spell by our first word learned in the Imaginary Order, a language that ultimately fails to distinguish between genders?

The reader, and in particular the female, is left to seek and to regain the innocence of the pre-Oedipal infant who is untouched by the Symbolic Order. The persona exhorts the reader to challenge socialized conventions of language and to relate to one's biological sex rather than to gender. As women spell their language according to their sex, then and only then will they be able to define themselves and their world views rather than accepting the definitions that the male-dominated society has already constructed for them.

KARA ROGGIE

⚜ Professional Essay ⚜

Orality and Textuality in Zora Neale Hurston's Their Eyes Were Watching God

Through her novel *Their Eyes Were Watching God*, Zora Neale Hurston presents a forceful resistance to black women's oppression in a sexist and racist society. She does so by means of her own artistic accomplishment, which she shares with her character Janie Crawford. The work has attracted varied attention since it was first published in 1937. June Jordan called it the greatest novel of Blacklove ever written. Alice Walker has explored its place in Hurston's presentation of herself as a role model for black women artists. A host of critics have discussed the significance of Janie as a black woman who creates herself in her own image. Not all of the commentary, however, has been positive. Ignoring her critique of sexual politics, some writers have criticized Hurston's political views, comparing her unfavorably with Richard Wright and Ralph Ellison and describing her as an opportunist and a reactionary. While we have finally developed a fuller understanding of

Hurston's work, critics still feel obliged to begin their discussions by reconstructing the author's life and works, continually reestablishing their right to undertake the more specialized literary analysis this black feminist writer deserves. Few critics have talked at any length about the literary value and construction of meaning in *Their Eyes Were Watching God*, one of the century's finest works of fiction.

Hurston remains something of an enigma. She incited jealousy, dedication, love, and anger in her friends and associates; later writers have shared these responses in varying degrees. Certainly no one is immune to them because Hurston's position, like Freeman's, refuses a one-dimensional reduction. Her defiant individualism frequently displays itself in the bias, equivocation and obliquity of her critics' commentaries. In her exceptional essay, "On Refusing to Be Humbled by Second Place in a Contest You Did Not Design: A Tradition by Now," which serves as the Dedication to the Feminist Press edition of Hurston's selected writings, Alice Walker summarizes the puzzle surrounding the author and her work:

> Is *Mules and Men* racist? Or does it reflect the flawed but nonetheless beautiful creative insights of an oppressed people's collective mythology? Is "Gilded Six-Bits" so sexist it makes us cringe to think Zora Neale Hurston wrote it? Or does it make a true statement about deep love functioning in the only pattern that at the time of its action seemed correct? Did Zora Neale Hurston never question "America" or the status-quo, as some have accused, or was she questioning it profoundly when she wrote phrases like "the arse-and-all of Democracy"? Is Janie Crawford, the main character in *Their Eyes Were Watching God*, light-skinned and silken-haired because *Hurston* was a colorist, as a black male critic has claimed, or because Hurston was not blind and therefore saw that black men (and black women) have been, and are, colorist to an embarrassing degree?
>
> Is Hurston the messenger who brings the bad news, or is she the bad news herself? Is Hurston a reflection of ourselves? And if so, is that not, perhaps, part of our "problem" with her?[1]

Through the use of countervailing questions, Walker defends the writer against her critics and provides us with badly needed corrective in her remembering of Hurston. Walker concludes her litany of questions by cautioning us to restrict our comments to Hurston's artistry.

Obviously, this is an injunction that is difficult for Walker to heed. She cites a Wellesley College student's comment: *"What does it matter what white folks must have thought about her?"*[2] Aside from Hurston's association with and patronage by liberal whites, and the influence they exerted on the shape of her art and career,[3] we must ask an equally pressing question with respect

[1]Walker, "On Refusing to Be Humbled," 2.

[2]Walker, "Looking for Zora," 302.

[3]See Robert Hemenway's *Zora Neale Hurston*, 104–35, for a discussion of the effects of Mrs. Charlotte Mason's patronage on Hurston's life and works.

to the development of her reputation as an artist: What does it matter what black men thought about Hurston? Sharing her oppression as a black American, black male critics read Hurston the way most men read women. The need to construct a defense against those male critics has preoccupied black women writing on her. Langston Hughes's comment in *The Big Sea* exemplifies the problem. Rivaling Hemenway's remarks on Stein, Hughes writes his sense of jealous competition with Hurston between the lines: "In her youth she was always getting scholarships and things from wealthy white people, some of whom simply paid her just to sit around and represent the Negro race for them, she did it in such a racy fashion . . . . To many of her white friends, no doubt, she was a perfect 'darkie,' in the nice meaning they give the term—that is a naïve, childlike, sweet, humorous, and highly colored Negro."[4] Hurston, along with her character Janie, transgresses the boundaries of gender roles. In "Zora Neale Hurston: A Woman Half in Shadows," Mary Helen Washington criticizes Darwin Turner and Nathan Huggins for confusing the personal with the artistic as a means of dismissing Hurston's contribution to literature.[5] Larry Neal's remarks have escaped much qualification. Discussing Hurston's view of the South, he describes her as "an inveterate romantic" who managed to avoid the oppressive forces that characterized the region for political radicals such as Wright. He supports this assertion with the observation: "Perhaps it was because she was a black woman, and therefore not considered a threat to anyone's system of social values."[6] Black women who have written about Hurston adopt a very different position, reflecting the awareness they share with her of the effects of male power.

Hurston, as a black woman, poses a double threat. In her article, "'This Infinity of Conscious Pain': Zora Neale Hurston and the Black Female Literary Tradition," Lorraine Bethel assesses Hurston's place within literature in terms of a confluence of oppressive forces: "The codification of Blackness and femaleness by whites and males is contained in the terms 'thinking like a woman' and 'acting like a nigger,' both based on the premise that there are typically negative Black and female ways of acting and thinking. Therefore, the most pejorative concept in the white male world view would be thinking and acting like a 'nigger woman.' This is useful for understanding literary criticism of Hurston's works, which often attacks her personally for simply conducting herself as what she was: a Black woman."[7] By insisting on her

---

[4]Hughes, *The Big Sea*, 239.

[5]Washington, "Zora Neale Hurston," 11.

[6]Neal, "Zora Neale Hurston," 161. In the final chapters of *Zora Neale Hurston*, Hemenway provides a useful assessment of Hurston's political views. The critiques presented by black intellectuals are both accurately and narrowly construed; their obvious silences obscure the question of what Hurston does say as well as the black community's singular role in character assassination surrounding the false morals charge against Hurston.

[7]Bethel, "'This Infinity of Conscious Pain,'" 178–79.

right to be a "Black woman," free from prescribed roles, Hurston was perhaps as immediately intimidating to black men as to white. Because she was a black woman without independent resources, her white patrons undoubtedly experienced a more secure relationship based on dominance. Hurston necessarily tolerated the situation, although it did little to earn public praise for her literary accomplishments when she struggled to tell her own story rather than the one whites constructed for her to tell. Within this arena of sexual and racial conflict, Hurston's literary reputation suffered.

Over the years, critics have commented variously on the central theme of *Their Eyes Were Watching God*. Washington argues that the novel's most powerful theme "is Janie's search for identity, an identity which finally begins to take shape as she throws off the false images which have been thrust upon her because she is both black and woman in a society where neither is allowed to exist naturally and freely."[8] Hurston expresses this theme, Washington maintains, through the images of the horizon and the pear tree, the former symbolizing Janie's personal, individual quest, the latter, her search for fulfillment through union with another.[9] Ann Rayson argues similarly that Hurston chooses "becoming" rather than "being" as the principal focus of her fiction, suggesting a parallel with Ellison's protagonist, who says, "the end is the beginning."[10] While Rayson's comment reveals her sensitivity to Hurston's choice of narrative strategy, she does not examine that sense of circularity or the reasons underlying Hurston's choice. This question of creating form through narrative technique, which serves as the basis for Janie's deconstruction of the effects of power, provides the focus for my discussion of *Their Eyes Were Watching God* and offers one way of relating this work to those of other feminist writers.

The puzzle of the novel's structure is inseparable from considerations of its theme. Despite Larry Neal's contention that "Zora Neale Hurston was not an especially philosophical person,"[11] Hurston employs a narrative strategy that is culturally, philosophically, and aesthetically complex. This complexity reveals itself through Hurston's decision to re-tell the story rather than to tell it. Barbara Christian makes an important observation about this choice, which the scope of her book does not permit her to develop: "*Their Eyes Were Watching God* is a story within a story. Janie Stark tells the story of her childhood, her life, and her loves to her best friend, Phoebe [sic], and to the community to which she has just returned. This aspect of the novel is critical to its substance, for Janie Stark is not an individual in a vacuum; she is an intrinsic part of a community, and she brings her life and its richness, joys,

[8]Washington, "Zora Neale Hurston," 15.
[9]Ibid.
[10]Rayson, "The Novels of Zora Neale Hurston," 4.
[11]Neal, "Zora Neale Hurston," 164.

and sorrows back to it. As it has helped to form her, so she also helps to form it."[12] Lillie Howard, however, finds fault with Hurston's method and maintains that "the story is rather awkwardly told by both the heroine, Janie Crawford, and an omniscient narrator, and is revealed, for the most part, in a flashback to Janie's best friend, Phoeby Watson. The narrative is awkward in some places because much of what Janie tells Phoeby, Phoeby must already know, partly because she is Janie's best friend, and partly because Phoeby was a part of Eatonville just as Janie was."[13] It is neither through accident nor uncalculated device that Janie's story is re-told rather than told. Phoeby—the audience for the fiction within the fiction—surely knows much of the story she is being told? The value of the approach as strategy exists in what Hurston accomplishes through its use; here as well rests much of the novel's significance for feminist readers today.

Hurston's artistic method displays a keen awareness of the performative quality of fiction as it emerges from the tradition of oral narrative, as well as a clever consciousness of the storyteller/writer's role in constructing the history of a people through language. Her brilliant use of dialect, specifying pride and ownership, lends credibility to the novel's claim as a work for the black community. It is a testament to the power and beauty of blackness. Hurston is culturally and artistically at ease with the narrative convention of re-telling the tale, just as her character Janie has grown used to an audience: "Phoeby's hungry listening helped Janie to tell her story."[14] On this point, Bethel comments that "In presenting Janie's story as a narrative related by herself to her best Black woman friend, Phoebe, Hurston is able to draw upon the rich oral legacy of Black female storytelling and mythmaking that has its roots in Afro-American culture."[15] But this is not an end in itself. Hurston's aim is textuality—the process of producing a text through the transformation of other texts— and through this textuality, a form of feminist self-definition. By transforming Janie's orality—Hurston's intertexts—into textuality, the writer creates both herself as a writer and her own story, while Janie creates her life through language. Creator and character fuse in Hurston's description of Janie's motivation for relating the story that follows: "that oldest human longing—self revelation" (p. 18). All the events of the novel's one long evening find their center in the act of telling the tale.

To understand the effects of the novel's frame, the embodiment of Hurston's narrative strategy, it is useful to suspend consideration of that device for the moment in order first to examine the story Janie tells. The frame consists only of the first chapter and the final three pages of the novel's twentieth and last chapter. Since the story within the story comprises

[12]Christian, *Black Women Novelists*, 57.

[13]Howard, *Zora Neale Hurston*, 94.

[14]Hurston, *Their Eyes Were Watching God*, 23. Further references are cited in the text.

[15]Bethel, "'This Infinity of Conscious Pain,'" 180.

much of the novel, it always commands the greatest critical attention. Here Hurston offers the tale of Janie Crawford's development from puberty to womanhood as a model of black female development. The story begins in the home of her grandmother, moves to the homes of her two husbands, Logan Killicks and then Joe Starks, and concludes with the death of her third husband and lover Vergible "Tea Cake" Woods. Janie orders the story in such a way that she chronicles her progress from dependence to independence, while Hurston gives us the story of Janie's development from silent "object" to speaking "subject."

At the beginning of the story within the story, Janie receives her sense of definition from others. She is woman as object under the control of a racist, patriarchal culture. Failing to recognize herself as the one black child in a photograph, she begins her story without name or color: "'Dey all useter call me Alphabet 'cause so many people had done named me different names'" (p. 21). Initially she reconciles herself to the received wisdom, the history of black women's place in the prevailing power structure as imparted by Nanny, her grandmother: "'Honey, de white man is de ruler of everything as fur as Ah been able tuh find out. Maybe it's some place way off in de ocean where de black man is in power, but we don't know nothin' but what we see. So de white man throw down de load and tell de nigger man tuh pick it up. He pick it up because he have to, but he don't tote it. He hand it to his womanfolks. De nigger woman is de mule uh de world so fur as Ah can see. Ah been prayin' fuh it tuh be different wid you. Lawd, lawd, lawd'" (p. 29). Nanny projects a stereotypical identity (wife) and a secure future (house and land) for Janie based upon what she knows, which is limited by the historical constraints of what she has seen of the white man's power over blacks and the black man's relationship to the black woman. Thus, she explains to Janie: "'Ah was born back due in slavery so it wasn't for me to fulfill my dreams of whut a woman oughta be and to do. Dat's one of de hold-backs of slavery'" (p. 31).

Nanny arranges Janie's marriage to Logan Killicks and his sixty acres of land, thereby "desecrating" Janie's vision from the pear tree of idyllic union. Bethel explains Nanny's behavior as a protective measure: "She is attempting to adjust Janie to the prevailing sexual and racial milieu, and her protectiveness emerges as violence directed against Janie. Nanny attempts to explain to Janie the historical and social forces that make her innocent actions so serious."[16] Bethel sees in this cross-generational relationship the pattern of black women's victimization by oppressive racial and sexual forces. "In this sense," she concludes, "Janie and her grandmother illustrate the tragic continuity of Black female oppression in white/male America."[17] While it is true that the oppression continues, it is also evident that Hurston makes Janie differ from nanny in some important ways. Part of what the

[16]Ibid., 181.
[17]Ibid., 182.

character learns is to place her grandmother's words in perspective—to understand how Nanny's recounting of experience shaped what Janie was later able to see. In this respect, Hurston stages a break with the oppressor's culture and points to the sexual and racial liberation of women.

The grandmother's gift of a life different from her own permits Janie to pursue dreams and visions beyond those that Nanny, "'a cracked plate'" (p. 37) damaged by slavery, could have projected. Janie creates her own future, the way to her individual happiness, at the same time that Hurston constructs a new legacy through the tale Janie tells. The story Janie tells Phoeby and the narrative the reader receives are vastly different from the shaping and socializing story Nanny tells Janie. In a sense, Nanny is the unreconstructed past, and Janie her fulfillment through a newly constructed present. Although the grandmother's narrative power has been repressed into further silence, Nanny still envisions the story she longed to tell: "'Ah wanted to preach a great sermon about colored women sittin' on high, but they wasn't no pulpit for me'" (pp. 31–32); but silence distorts this story to the point where the horizon of women's potential is constricted to the private sphere of domestic life. Through Janie, Hurston exposes the crack in the plate and preaches the liberating and defiant sermon that Nanny was never able to deliver and that black women, indeed all women, have been waiting to hear. Janie's story can be read as a new (hi)story constructed out of love and passed from one black woman to another.

The process of Janie's freedom from oppressive roles entails several steps and engenders predictable male opposition. Logan Killicks expresses his complaint about Janie's independence in racial terms: "'You think youse white folks by de way you act'" (p. 51). Joe Starks brings Janie closer to racial/cultural autonomy by escaping the control of white hegemony. His desire to be a "big voice" in a place beyond the authority of white men suggests change, chance, and the far horizon to Janie, although from the outset she realizes that Starks does not completely embody her vision: "He did not represent sun-up and pollen and blooming trees" (p. 50). From the day she rides off with him in a hired rig, sitting in a seat "like some high, ruling chair" (p. 54), Janie confronts the delimiting structures of language: "Her old thoughts were going to come in handy now, but new words would have to be made and said to fit them" (pp. 54–55). Hers is a new life beyond the limits of the imagined, demanding the creation of a new story for its expression.

Their Eyes Were Watching God is a novel about orality—of speakers and modes of speech: Joe's "big voice" wields power modeled on white culture; the grandmother speaks the language of slavery time; the story porch hosts "mule-talkers" and "big picture talkers"; and each town has its complement of gossips. Here, as everywhere, language produces power and knowledge as well as constraint; it is the ability to interpret and to transform experience. The townspeople perceive the equation of word and law, how Joe's big voice commands obedience; " 'You kin feel a switch in his hand when he's talkin' to yuh' " (p. 78); "He's de wind and we'se de grass. We bend which ever way he blows' " (p. 78). Commenting on this effect, Howard makes the clever observation that "It is no mistake that he [Joe] often prefaces his remarks with 'I, god.' "[18] Just as the town chorus is alienated by Joe's power of speech, they also note Janie's silence. In this world of lively speakers, Janie lives a speechless existence. At the town's dedication ceremony, Joe speaks when Janie is asked to say a few words. Although he robs her of this opportunity, she sees and reflects upon her loss: "She had never thought of making a speech, and didn't know if she cared to make one at all. It must have been the way Joe spoke out without giving her a chance to say anything one way or another that took the bloom off things" (pp. 69–70). Janie discovers the emptiness of class status, and especially of status by affiliation—the territory of women. In particular, she grows to understand the loneliness of silence, how orality is required for community. She loves the mule stories people tell on the store porch and creates her own tales in silence, but Joe restricts Janie's personal autonomy by prohibiting her participation in discourse. She can neither tell stories nor serve as a member of an audience—the folk community required for the telling.

Through the novel, Hurston also exposes phallocentrism and instructs her readers in the terms of discourse. By means of their oral skills, the porch speakers demonstrate the powerful effects of logocentrism: "They are the center of the world." As in white patriarchal culture, language serves as a locus for social control through its centrality within an order of meaning. Robert Hemenway and Roger Abrahams both comment on the importance of "negotiating respect" through verbal skill in the black community. In "Are You a Flying Lark or a Setting Dove?' Hemenway remarks that "negotiating for respect is not a static process dependent upon the institutions or instrumentalities offered to a woman by society—marriage, the home, the church—but a dynamic response to events growing out of a woman's capacity for self-expression."[19] Phallocentrism is so fundamentally pervasive that it is difficult to conceive of one's self, actions, and meaning outside of its system of control. To attempt to escape its constraints, Janie must use power in order to have power. By transforming her characteristic silence into speech, she stands a chance of establishing a different relationship with Joe, that is, a relationship based on acknowledging difference and accommodating change. Eventually she tires of his endless verbal disputes designed to bring about submission. Her silence in the external world reflects her internal repression until the hollow image of Joe Starks crashes from the shelf in her mind, and she discovers her emotional silence: "She had a host of thoughts she had never expressed to him, and numerous emotions she had

[18]Howard, *Zora Neale Hurston*, 100.

[19]Hemenway, "Are You a Flying Lark or a Setting Dove?," 145. See also Abrahams' "Negotiating Respect."

never let Jody know about. Things packed up and put away in parts of her heart where he could never find them. She was saving up feelings for some man she had never seen" (p. 112).

The three places in the text where Janie speaks publicly are marked in the novel. When Joe implements Janie's idea by freeing a persecuted mule—the analogue of black slaves, and especially of black women ("de mule uh de world")—Janie praises him. She gives a speech in which she compares Joe with Abraham Lincoln. The townspeople note her skill: "'Yo' wife is uh born orator, Starks. Us never knowed dat befo'. She put jus' de right words tuh our thoughts;" (p. 92). In the second instance, Hurston herself, through the omniscient narrative voice, underscores Janie's incursion into orality: "Janie did what she had never done before, that is, thrust herself into the conversation" (pp. 116–17). This time, instead of presenting an oblique defense of women through the suffering mule, Janie, like Freeman's Sarah Penn and Alice Walker's Celie, gets "too moufy" and preaches her sermon on women (the one Nanny never could deliver) to the men on the porch: "'Sometimes God gits surprised He was 'bout y'all turning out so smart after Him makin' yuh different; and how surprised y'all is goin' tuh be if you ever find out you don't know half as much 'bout us as you think you do. It's so easy to make yo'self out God Almighty when you ain't got nothin' tuh strain against but women and chickens'" (p. 117). The final instance of Janie's mastery that ultimately establishes her power occurs when, in retaliation for Joe's verbal abuse, she humiliates him in front of his male friends (pp. 122–23). She seizes his authority—language—and leaves him speechless.

No unquestioning user of language, Hurston creates her character as a critic of phallocentrism who speaks her defiance. As such, Janie positions herself in a different relation to discourse, moving beyond the exercise of language as a means of establishing power over others or of fixing absolute meaning, to "a practice of language" that Stephen Heath describes as "wild, on the body, unauthorised,"[20] Out of pity when Joe is on his death bed, Janie contemplates "what had happened in the making of a voice out of a man" (p. 134). Hélène Cixous's analysis of the politics of language clarifies what Hurston is doing through her character: "No political reflection can dispense with reflection on language, with work on language. For as soon as we exist, we are born into language and language speaks (to) us, dictates its law, a law of death: it lays down its familial model, lays down its conjugal model, and even at the moment of uttering a sentence, admitting a notion of 'being,' a question of desire, the desire that mobilizes philosophical discourse."[21] Constructing another course for black women, Hurston directs Janie's language toward the discovery of a discourse of emotion, a language she

[20]Heath, "Difference," 82.
[21]Cixous, "Castration or Decapitation?," 45.

learns through her relationship with Tea Cake who fulfills the bee and blossom imagery of the novel's opening. He demands a union of speech and feeling, and she asks that he speak "with no false pretense" (p. 165). He is the master linguist of "otherness"; as Janie tells Phoeby in the story within the story, "So in the beginnin' new thoughts had tuh be thought and new words said. After Ah got used tuh dat, we gets 'long jus' fine. He done taught me de maiden language all over'" (p. 173). This "maiden" language defies the social construction of difference and permits new perspectives to emerge from narrative action. For example, Janie rejects being "classes off" (p. 169), separated from other black people through her imprisonment in Joe's house and store as "his showpiece, his property."[22] To a degree, she frees herself from his story, another constriction of her horizon, and shares her perception with Phoeby: "An Ah'd sit dere wid de walls creepin' up on me and squeezin' all de life outa me'" (p. 169). Janie rejects the "race after property and titles" in favor of "uh love game" (p. 171). Recognizing that the exclusion of others is the repression of differences within one's self, she merges her life with the life of the black community, telling bog stories, listening to them, working along with the other women, and rejecting Mrs. Turner's politics of color—a pecking order that privileges white features over black.

By freeing herself from the oppressor's language and by learning a new integration of words and feeling, Janie develops her critique of color, class, and sex.[23] The narrator, Janie of the re-telling, speaks of the repression inherent in Nanny's "mis-love": "Nanny had taken the biggest thing God ever made, the horizon—for no matter how far a person can go the horizon is still way beyond you—and pinched it in to such a little bit of a thing that she could tie it about her granddaughter's neck tight enough to choke her. She hated the old woman who had twisted her so in the name of love" (p. 138). But this recognition becomes Janie's own and is modified by her interpretation of Nanny's circumstance—one can only dream the next dream, and until it is reached, its true value is unknown. Janie explains:

> "She was borned in slavery time when folks, dat is black folks, didn't sit down anytime dey felt lak it. So sittin' on porches lak de white madam looked lak uh mighty fine thing tuh her. Dat's whut she wanted for me—don't keer whut it cost. Git up on uh high chair and sit dere. She didn't have time tuh think whut tuh do after you got up on de stool uh do nothin'. De object wuz tuh git dere. So Ah got up on de high stool lak she told me, but Phoeby, Ah done nearly languished tuh death up dere. Ah felt like de world wuz cryin' extry and Ah ain't read de common news yet." (p. 172)

To a degree Hurston validates Nanny's dream for Janie through Phoeby who, less affluent than her friend, lends sympathy to the grandmother's way of thinking. At the same time, Hurston demonstrates how Nanny's values

---

[22]Christian, *Black Women Novelists*, 58.

[23]Lillie Howard presents a useful discussion of Hurston's treatment of race in *Zora Neale Hurston*, 108–10.

are the effects produced by the oppressed having internalized the oppressor's consciousness.

Robert Hemenway, commenting on Janie's effort to come to terms with Nanny's vision, maintains that "the vertical metaphor in this speech represents Hurston's entire system of thought, her social and racial philosophy. People erred because they wanted to be *above* others, an impulse which eventually led to denying the humanity of those below. Whites had institutionalized such thinking, and black people were vulnerable to the philosophy because being on high like white folks seemed to represent security and power."[24] In other words, if you haven't had it, power and status look good; so goes the hierarchical dream of the phallocentric economy. Reflecting her commitment to an essential relationship between experience and knowledge, Janie mitigates Tea Cake's regret over his decision not to stay when the hurricane was imminent: "'When yuh don't know, yuh just don't know'" (p. 240). She prefers not to trust the projections that, like Nanny's dream for Janie, reproduce the oppressor's logic. In a remarkable way, Hurston wages an early battle on behalf of oppressed people and anticipates black feminist writers such as Audre Lorde. Citing Paulo Freire's *The Pedagogy of the Oppressed*, Lorde proclaims: "The true focus of revolutionary change is never merely the oppressive situations which we seek to escape, but that piece of the oppressor which is planted deep within each of us, and which knows only the oppressor's tactics, the oppressors' relationships."[25] Hurston's effort to supplant the language and logic of this consciousness relates her to radical feminist writers today.

According to Hurston's defiant (deviant) narrative logic, only the Janie of the narrative frame, the one who returns to Eatonville, is capable of telling the story. The voiceless existence of the less experienced Janie prevented narration, except as the story might be presented through a third-person limited or omniscient narrator. This strategy, however, would have diminished the power of Janie's having come to speak, one of the highest forms of achievement and artistry in the folk community. Thus, Janie's story cannot be told and can only be re-told. Surely it is more than my illusion as a white feminist critic that Hurston presents us with a novel of the black woman's struggle to construct a language that destroys the conditions of her historic silence and creates the stories that articulate and make memorable a new (hi)story. Janie can return with an understanding she and Hurston share of the liberating force of language within the black community.

One of Janie's greatest lessons about language centers on its power to deconstruct and to construct, to kill or to give life. When she is on trial for Tea Cake's murder, she recognizes this potential in the black members of the audience: "They were there with their tongues cocked and loaded, the only real

[24]Hemenway, *Zora Neale Hurston*, 237.

[25]Lorde, *Sister Outsider*, 123.

weapon left to weak folks. The only killing tool they are allowed to use in the presence of white folks." (p. 275). This passage recalls the frame's opening segment in which Hurston describes the townspeople sitting on their porches at night: "They became lords of sounds and lesser things. They passed nations through their mouths. They sat in judgment" (p. 10). Adopting the traditional means of defense against gossip, Janie selects Phoeby, a trusted member of the community network, to whom she can provide an account of her behavior.[26] In addition to this pragmatic motive for narration, Janie uses language to give life and memory to feeling. Following the death of the mule, for example, it is memorialized in story by the porch talkers, just as the life of the black woman in slavery is fixed in Nanny's discourse when contrasted with Janie. Thus, according to the conventions of their discursive fields, Janie's story enters oral tradition while Hurston's novel passes into literary tradition. Through her character's discovery, the writer gives us a story of how language outwits time and exclusively patriarchal determinations of meaning, and the reader finds new significance in the frame's opening commentary comparing men, "whose dreams [are] mocked to death by Time," and women: "Now, women forget all those things they don't want to remember, and remember everything they don't want to forget. The dream is the truth. Then they act and do things accordingly" (p. 9).

Although the novel's work is conducted primarily through Janie's story, much of its significance rests in and in relationship to the narrative frame. The importance of the frame is that it permits Hurston to tell her story through a reconstituted subject. Hurston holds to this even at the expense of creating anomalies in Janie's story—the places where Phoeby is mentioned in the third person, dialogues between Phoeby and Janie in which Phoeby is presumably a participant in the telling, since Janie addresses her remarks to her friend. The story we receive is not constituted until Janie returns, changed. She arrives as the witness to a new epistemology: "you got tuh *know* there" (p. 285). Through Janie's story, Hurston presents an alternative conception of power as it operates in black female discourse. Rather than replicating verbal power as oppression, its form among whites and blacks imitating whites, Hurston espouses a form of narrative authority indigenous to black tribal tradition. As Ruth Borker notes of the Buhaya of Tanzania, "The key cultural concept for thinking about speech is that of 'knowing.'"[27] Janie operates according to a system whereby you don't know, and you can't know something until you experience it; or, as Jacques Derrida puts it, "the logocentrist or logocentric impulse is rocked by historical events, rocked by things that happen."[28] Having gone there, you are changed, and the story you have to tell is a

---

[26]Abrahams, "Negotiating Respect," 78–79.

[27]Borker, "Anthropology," 40.

[28]Derrida, et. al., "Deconstruction in America," 17.

different story. The interpretations of the phallocentric hegemony are called into question rather than assumed. This move wrests the control of meaning from a sexist, racist culture and locates the potential for change within the individual.

Besides the significance of how the story is changed by the fact that Janie has gone and returned, it is additionally important that Janie returns as a "speaking subject" to bring her story to the people. At this point, the changed Janie, Janie the storyteller, fuses with the author. Hurston designates the end of Janie's story with the novel's only authentic silence—one that is elected rather than imposed, and is as natural as the sounds that mark the ending: "There was a finished silence after that so that for the first time they could hear the wind picking at the pine trees" (p. 285). With the full resonance of the parallel, *Their Eyes Were Watching God* might well be understood as a "Portrait of the Artist as a Black Woman."

Through the overarching and elusive meaning of her title, Hurston confronts the dilemma of the phallocentric ground of determinate meaning. At the most critical moments in the novel, Janie and others scrutinize the heavens for a sign of God's intention. Like their African ancestors (and the Puritan interpreters), they are seeking a way through nature to unlock and interpret the meaning of events. They act out the reader's effort to interpret the text. In the novel's opening frame, we encounter the Watcher, an Everyman waiting for the ship of dreams to come in and trying to outwit Death who was "there before there was a where or a when or a then" (p. 129). Following Janie's sensual awakening, she desires validation for their dreams: "She was seeking confirmation of the voice and vision, and everywhere she found and acknowledged answers. A personal answer for all other creations except herself. She felt an answer seeking her, but where? When? How?" (p. 24). Only once does there seem to be a sign—the arrival of Tea Cake, which Janie invests with referential power taking us back to the blossoming pear tree and the bee: "He looked like the love thoughts of women. He could be a bee to a blossom—a pear tree blossom in the spring. He seemed to be crushing scent out of the world with his footsteps. Crushing aromatic herbs with every step he took. Spices hung about him. He was a glance from God" (p. 161).

While Janie accepts Tea Cake as a sign, his presence cannot resolve the problem of interpretation—the signification of events. When the hurricane is imminent, people consider God's purpose: "They sat in company with the others in other shanties, their eyes straining against crude walls and their souls asking if He meant to measure their puny might againt His. They seemed to be staring at the dark, but their eyes were watching God" (p. 236). The only answer given is the storm itself, suggesting that the people's question, as related by the narrator, contained its answer, that this was indeed a contest of force. The hurricane and Tea Cake's love for Janie ultimately contribute to his death, so that on a symbolic level, it would seem that what was once responsible for his presence is in the end responsible for his absence. Through the compelling imagery of the frame, Hurston refuses this simple dichotomy by rejecting the bipolar logic of absence: "Tea Cake, with the sun for a shawl. Of course he wasn't dead. He could never be dead until she herself had finished feeling and thinking. The kiss of his memory made pictures of love and light against the wall. Here was peace. She pulled in her horizon like a great fishnet. Pulled it from around the waist of the world and draped it over her shoulder. So much of life in its meshes! She called in her soul to come and see" (p. 286). The effect Derrida describes in approaching Sollers' *Numbers* expands our sense of Hurston's accomplishment here: "The text is out of sight when it compels the horizon itself to enter the frame of its own scene, so as to 'learn to embrace with increased grandeur the horizon of the present time.'"[29] Through Janie's exemplary insistence on a different (black and female) determination of meaning and value, and through her own narrative art as the teller within the tale, Hurston resists the binary opposition of phallocentrism as it inhabits Western metaphysics, just as she seeks to revise its attendant notion of interpretation. The present, as an unexperienced future, cannot unlock the meaning of what is to come. It has no predictive or determinative value.

In place of this practice, Hurston offers a particular concept of presence—the presence of a present—through Janie's re-telling. The only present is its illusion in narration, occasioned by and filling in for absence. Bringing the past into the present, Hurston gives both dimensions a particular reconstructed value, and propels the past, itself a former present, toward a future that exists only as an anticipated possibility for black women.[30] Thus, these elements of time remain fluid, each containing traces of the other. As storytellers, as speaking subjects, Janie and Hurston don't escape phallocentrism. Rather, they stage a critique from what Derrida calls "a certain inside of logocentrism. But it is an inside that is divided enough and tormented enough and obsessed enough by the other, by contradictions, by heterogeneity, for us to be able to say things about it without being simply 'outside of it.' And we say them within the grammar, within the language of logocentrism while allowing the alterity or the difference which obsesses this inside to show through."[31] By extricating herself from cultural control, Janie/Hurston creates culture. Through the re-telling of Janie's story, orality becomes textuality. Textuality is produced by Janie's learned orality, her participation in the oral tradition of the culture. She learns to be one of the people; thus, this is a story of her acculturation into black womanhood and her artistic entitlement to language. By chronicling Janie's development,

[29]Derrida, *Dissemination*, 334.

[30]Alice Walker achieves a similar effect through Nettie's letters in *The Color Purple*. While Walker's means are different, she accomplishes a similar goal by integrating the African presence (though some would argue that she subordinates it) into relationship with the lives of black American women today.

[31]Derrida et al., "Deconstruction in America," 17.

Hurston transforms the status of narrative from the temporality characteristic of oral tradition to the more enduring textuality required to outwit time's effect on memory. In doing so, she presents feminist readers with a map of a woman's personal resistance to patriarchy, and feminist writers—in particular Alice Walker—with the intertext for later feminist works.

Essays by Elizabeth Meese. "Orality and Textuality in Zora Neale Hurston's *Their Eyes Were Watching God*." Chapter 3 in *Crossing the Double-Cross: The Practice of Feminist Criticism*. Chapel Hill: University of North Carolina Press, 1986, pp. 39–53.

9

Marxism

"The most common and durable source of faction has been the various and un-equal distribution of property. . . . Those who hold, and those who are without property, have ever formed distinct interests in society."

JAMES MADISON, Federalist # 10

INTRODUCTION

With the collapse of communism and the Soviet empire in the late 1980s, many thought they heard the death knell of Marxism and its accompanying political and ideological structures. Down came the Berlin Wall, down came the Iron Curtain, and down came Marxism as an acceptable alternative to capitalism, as a form of government, and as an acceptable worldview. Capitalists rejoiced. Marxism had fallen. Seemingly, individual Marxists had only the glorious memories of the earlier decades of the twentieth century— a time when Stalin ruled Russia, when Marxist theory dominated both English and American writings, and when college campuses both in the East and the West were led and taught by intellectuals who pledged alliance to Marxist ideology. Now all that is gone!

But is it? Performing only a limited Internet search under the title *Marxism* results in a list of over 19,500 sites with titles such as "Marxism and Utopian Vision: El Salvador," "Marxism and the National Question," "Marxism and Problems of Linguistics," "Rethinking Marxism," "Marxism, Psychoanalysis, and Labor Competition," and "Baha's Future and Marxism," to name a few. In addition, announcements for newly published texts advocating sympathy for and support of Marxist ideology in all academic disciplines appear regularly. College courses in Marxist political theory, sociological concerns, literature, and literary theory abound. Perhaps the death knell for Marxism was struck prematurely.

What is it that fascinates intellectuals, politicians, and others about Marxism? Why did it not die out with the death of communism in the East?

Perhaps the answer lies in some of the core principles of Marxist thought: that reality itself can be defined and understood, society shapes our conscious-ness, social and economic conditions directly influence how and what we believe and value, and Marxism details a plan for changing the world from a place of bigotry, hatred, and conflict due to class struggle to a classless soci-ety where wealth, opportunity, and education are accessible for all people. By claiming to furnish us with a coherent, clear, and comprehensive worldview, Marxism asserts that it can provide answers to many of the complex ques-tions concerning life experiences and challenges other ideologies to provide answers for these same concerns. The same problems that gave rise to Marxism still exist today. Despite its glory decades of the 1900s and its present-day embattled position, Marxism declares that it provides a compre-hensive, positive view of human life and history and attempts to show humanity how it can save itself from a meaningless life of alienation and despair. Such a worldview that seemingly affords a bright promise for the future and a transformation of present-day society will not die quietly. Paraphrasing Mark Twain, "Announcements of Marxism's death have certainly been exaggerated."

HISTORICAL DEVELOPMENT

Karl Marx and Friedrich Engels

Unlike other schools of literary criticism, Marxism did not begin as an alternative theoretical approach to literary analysis. Before twentieth-century writers and critics embraced the principles of Marxism and used these ideas in their criticism, Marxism had already flourished in the nine-teenth century as a pragmatic view of history that offered the working classes of society an opportunity to change their world and therefore their lives. By providing both a philosophical system and a plan of action to cause change in society, Marxism offered to humanity a social, political, economic, and cultural understanding of the nature of reality, society, and the individ-ual. These and similar ideas have become the basis of what we know today as socialism and communism.

Without question, Marxist literary theory has its roots in the nineteenth-century writings of German social critic and philosopher Karl Heinrich Marx (1818–83). Marx himself, however, said little about the relationship of his ideas to literature. Marxist literary theory and criticism is a twentieth-century phenomenon. Using Marx's philosophical assumptions, twentieth-century critics have developed a variety of Marxist approaches of textual analysis that study the relationship between a text and the society that reads it. At the core of all these diverse approaches is Marx and his philosophical assumptions of the nature of reality itself.

Marx articulates his views on the nature of reality in two works: *The German Ideology* (1845) and *The Communist Manifesto* (1848), a work Marx coauthored with Friedrich Engels (1820–95). In *The German Ideology* Marx develops what has become known as **dialectical materialism,** the core beliefs of Marxism. In this work, Marx declares that "consciousness does not determine life: life determines consciousness." In other words, for Marx a person's consciousness is not shaped by some spiritual entity or means. Through daily living and interacting with each other, humans define themselves. According to Marx, our ideas and concepts about ourselves are fashioned in everyday discourse in the language of real life and are not derived from some Platonic essence or any other spiritual reality. In addition, Marx argues that the economic means of production within a society—what he calls the **base**—both engenders and controls all human institutions and ideologies—what Marx calls the **superstructure**, including all social and legal institutions, political and educational systems, religions, and art. The ideologies and institutions, then, develop as a direct result of the economic means of production, not the other way around.

Marx also declares that all societies are progressing toward communism. Believing progress is reactionary or revolutionary, Marx asserts that as a society progresses from a feudal system as its economic mode of production to a more market-based economy, the actual process for producing, distributing, and consuming goods becomes more complex. Accordingly, people's functions within the economic system become differentiated. And it is this differentiation that inevitably divides people into different social classes. Eventually, the desires and expectations of the various social classes will clash. Marx believes that such a clash or class conflict leads to a radical change in the economic base of society from a feudal system of power based on inherited wealth and status to a capitalist system based on the ownership of private property. This shift entails innumerable changes in the laws, customs, and religion of society. Overall, Marx cites four historical periods that were so developed by these forces: feudalism, capitalism, socialism, and communism. For Marx, socialism is not a true historical period but a transitional stage between capitalism and society's ultimate goal, communism. When society reaches this goal—what Marx called "the worker's paradise"—then benevolent self-rule will finally reign.

In their coauthored text *The Communist Manifesto*, Marx and Engels further develop Marxism's ideas. In this work, they declare that the capitalists, or the **bourgeoisie,** had successfully enslaved the working class, or the **proletariat**, through economic policies and production of goods. Now the proletariat must revolt and strip the bourgeoisie of their economic and political power and place the ownership of all property in the hands of the government, who will then fairly distribute the people's wealth.

In a later work, *Das Kapital* (1867), Marx enunciates his view of history that has become the basis for twentieth-century Marxism, socialism, and communism. According to Marx, history and therefore an understanding of people and their actions and beliefs is determined by economic conditions. Marx maintains that an intricate web of social relationships emerges when any group of people engage in the production of goods. For example, a few will be the employers, but many more will be the employees. It is the employers (the bourgeoisie) who have the economic power and who readily gain social and political control of their society. Eventually this upper class will articulate their beliefs, values, and even art. Consciously and unconsciously they will force these ideas, or what Marx calls their **ideology**, on the working class, otherwise known as the proletariat or the wage slaves. In effect, the bourgeoisie will develop and control the superstructure. In such a system, the rich become richer while the poor become poorer and more and more oppressed.

In such a system the bourgeoisie's ideology effectively perpetuates the system on which it was founded. Referred to as false consciousness, this ideology also describes the way in which the dominant social class shapes and controls an individual's self-definition or class consciousness.

In a capitalist society, Marx declares that such an ideology leads to fragmentation and alienation of individuals, particularly those of the proletariat. As a direct result of division of labor within the capitalist society, workers no longer have contact with the entire process of producing, distributing, and consuming material goods. Individuals are therefore cut off from the full value of their work as well as from each other, each performing discrete functional roles assigned to him or her by the bourgeoisie. To rid society of this situation, Marx believes that the government must own all industries and control the economic production of a country to protect the people from the oppression of the bourgeoisie.

Taken together, *The Communist Manifesto* and *Das Kapital* provide us with a theory of history, economics, politics, sociology, and even metaphysics. In these writings, little or no mention of literature, literary theory, or practical analysis of how to arrive at an interpretation of a text emerges. The link between the Marxism of its founding fathers and literary theory resides in Marx's concept of history and the sociological leanings of Marxism itself. Marx believed that the history of a people is directly based on the production of goods and the social relationships that develop from this situation. He also assumes that the totality of a people's experience—social interactions, employment, and other day-to-day activities—is directly responsible for shaping and developing an individual's personal consciousness. That our place in society and our social interaction determine our consciousness, or who we really are, is a theme Marx highlights throughout his writings.

Because the literary approach to a text that was common during Marx's time had similar sociological assumptions as did his own theories of society and the individual, Marx had no difficulty accepting his literary peers' methodology or hermeneutics for interpreting a text. Known today as the traditional historical approach, this critical position declares that a critic must place a work in its historical setting, paying attention to the author's life, the time period in which the work was written, and the cultural milieu of both the text and the author, all of these concerns being related to sociological issues. To these criteria, however, Marx and Engels add another: the economic means of production. This fourth factor addresses such concerns as who decides what texts should be published, when a text should be published, or how a text is to be distributed. Such questions necessitate an understanding of the social forces at work at the time a text is written or when it is being interpreted. In addition, this added criterion forces the critic to investigate the scheme of social relationships not only within the text itself but also outside the text and within the world of the author. By adding this sociological dimension, Marxism expands the traditional, historical approach to literary analysis by dealing with sociological issues that concern not only the characters in a work of fiction but also the authors and the readers. This added dimension, Marx believed, links literature and society and shows how literature reflects society and how it reveals truths concerning our social interactions.

Russia and Marxism

Thanks to G. K. Plehanov's Russian translation of *The Communist Manifesto*, Marx's theories soon gained wide exposure and prominence. Interestingly, Russia's fascination with Marxism's political ideas carried over into the aesthetic realm as well, for the Russian leadership at the beginning of the twentieth century insisted that the "man of letters" should also play a political role. Russia thus became the first country to promote Marxist principles as both aesthetic and literary guidelines.

Even before the Russian Revolution of 1919, party leaders insisted that literature promote the standards set forth by the party. For example, in 1905 Vladimir Ilyich Ulyanov (Lenin) wrote *The Organization and Party Literature*, in which he directly links good literature with the working-class movement. In this text he defends all kinds of literature, believing that something can be gleaned from any kind of writing. After the Bolshevik Revolution of 1917, however, Lenin amended his literary theory and argued that the Communist Party could not accept or support literary works that blatantly defied established party policies.

Soon after the Russian Revolution, revolutionary Leon Trotsky authored *Literature and Revolution* (1925) and in the process became the founding father of Marxist literary criticism. Advocating a tolerance for open, critical dialogue, Trotsky contends in this text that the content of a literary work need not be revolutionary. To force all poets to write about nothing but factory chimneys or revolts against capitalism, he believed, was simply absurd.

Unfortunately, Russia's next political leader, Joseph Stalin (1879–1953), was not as liberal as Lenin or Trotsky in his aesthetic judgments. Upon taking office, Stalin established the RAPP (the Russian Association of Proletarian

Writers), a group formed to guard against "liberal cultural" tendencies. But this group proved to be too tolerant for Stalin. In 1932 he established the Soviet Writer's Union, a group he himself headed. The union decreed that all literature must glorify party actions and decisions. In addition, such literature should exhibit revolutionary progress and teach about the spirit of socialism, revolving around Soviet heroes. Such aesthetic commandments quickly stifled many Russian writers, for the union allowed only politically correct works to be published. Not surprisingly, Stalin soon banished Trotsky, resulting in most Russian critics and writers succumbing to Stalin's guidelines rather than following Trotsky's public example. It was therefore left to critics outside Russia to explore and develop other Marxist approaches to literary criticism.

Georg Lukács

The first major branch of Marxism to appear outside Russia was that developed by Hungarian Georg Lukács. Lukács and his followers adapted and applied the techniques of formalism, believing that a detailed analysis of symbols, images, and other literary devices would ultimately reveal class conflict and would expose the direct relationship between the economic base and the superstructure. Known as **reflectionism**, this approach to literary analysis declares that texts directly reflect a society's consciousness. Reflection theorists such as Lukács are didactic, emphasizing the negative effects of capitalism such as alienation. Known today as **vulgar Marxism**, reflectionism insists on a one-way relationship between the base and the superstructure; that is, literature, as part of the superstructure, directly reflects the economic base. By giving a text a close reading, these critics believe they can reveal the "reality" of the text and the author's **Weltanschauung**, or worldview. It is the critic's job to show how the characters within the text are typical of their historical, socioeconomic setting and the author's worldview.

The Frankfurt School

Closely allied to Lukacs and reflection theory, another group of theorists emerged in Germany known as the Frankfurt school, a neo-Marxist group devoted to developing western Marxist principles. Included in this group are Theodor Adorno, Walter Benjamin, and Max Horkheimer. Agreeing with Lukács that literature reveals a culture's alienation and fragmentation, Frankfurt school critics such as Benjamin assert that a text is like any other commodity produced by capitalism. The market—that is, how well a commodity sells—ultimately determines what texts are published and when. Hence, there is no purely aesthetic activity that seeks to relate to human consciousness. That a text reveals a culture's fragmentation and not its wholeness is for Benjamin a useful notion for promoting socialist ideals.

Having stripped literature of what he calls its "quasi-religious aura," the enlightened reader can resist the bourgeoisie ideology embedded in the text and will not mindlessly acquiesce to the inane images, thinking, and desires depicted in some works.

Bertolt Brecht, a close friend of Benjamin, applies this new way of thinking directly to the theater. According to Brecht, dramatists believe they use the theater to express their ideas, but in fact the theater controls them. Instead of blindly accepting bourgeoisie conventionality as established through the various dramatic conventions, dramatists should revolt and seize the modes of production. Applying this principle to what became known as the **epic theater**, Brecht advocated an abandonment of the Aristotelian premise of unity of time, place, and action, including the assumption that the audience should be made to believe that what they are seeing is real. Accordingly, Brecht sought to create alienation effects such as frequently interrupting the drama by a direct appeal to the audience via a song or speech to keep the audience constantly aware of the moral and social issues to which they were being exposed in a drama. In the hands of Brecht, the epic theater became a tool for exposing the bourgeoisie ideology that had so pervasively permeated the arts.

Antonio Gramsci

Unlike Georg Lukács and his followers, who assert that the superstructure reflects the economic base, Italian critic Antonio Gramsci takes Marxism in another direction. Gramsci declares that there is a complex relationship between the base and the superstructure. How, Gramsci asks, are the bourgeoisie able to control and to maintain their dominance over the proletariat? According to Gramsci, the bourgeoisie establish and maintain what he calls **hegemony**. Because the bourgeoisie actually control the economic base and thereby establish all the elements that make up the superstructure—music, literature, art, and so forth—they gain the spontaneous accolades of the working class. It is the working people themselves who give their consent to the bourgeoisie and who adopt bourgeoisie values and beliefs. As sustainers of the economic base, the dominant class thus enjoys the prestige of the masses and controls the ideology (a term often used synonymously with hegemony) that shapes individual consciousness.

If literature, however, is only a part of the superstructure, then all literature actually concerns itself with the bourgeoisie. In effect, literature becomes a tool of the privileged class, and it cannot be used to further Marxist revolutions. Why write and study literature if it is only a reflection of the superstructure, which is, in itself, the reflection of bourgeoisie ideas established in the economic base? Although Gramsci concerned himself with this question, one of his followers provided the answer.

Louis Althusser

In seeking an answer to Gramsci's question, Louis Althusser rejects a basic assumption of reflection theory: that the superstructure directly reflects the base. His answer, known today as **production theory**, asserts that literature should not be strictly relegated to the superstructure. According to Althusser, the superstructure can and does influence the base. Art, then, can and does inspire revolution.

Althusser believes that the dominant hegemony, or prevailing ideology, forms the attitudes of people in society through a process he calls **interpellation,** or "hailing the subject." The people's worldview is thus craftily shaped by a complex network of messages sent to them through the elements contained in the superstructure, including the arts. Although the dominant class can use military and police force to repress the working class in order to maintain its dominant position and to achieve interpellation, it chooses to use the "Ideological State Apparatus," or the hegemony. In effect, it is the dominant class's hegemony that prevents the insurrection of the working class.

The dominant class's hegemony, however, is never complete. Such incompleteness suggests that alternative hegemonies exist and are competing with the dominant hegemony for supremacy. If the dominant class's interpellation or hailing the subject fails, then another hegemony can dominate and revolution can occur. Such a revolution can begin if working-class people create their own literature (dramas, poems, and novels), music, and paintings, thereby establishing an alternative hegemony to challenge the bourgeoisie's hegemony. Not through guns or battles or the shedding of blood, but through artistic expression of their own cultural activities can the working classes successfully revolt and usurp the hegemony of the dominant class.

Since Althusser, a number of post-Althusserian critics have continued to develop such Marxist thinking, including Pierre Macherey and Raymond Williams.

Marxist Theorists Today

Since the 1960s, Fredric Jameson in the United States and Terry Eagleton in Great Britain have dominated Marxist criticism. As a critic, Jameson merges psychoanalytic and Marxist theories. Borrowing Freud's idea of a repressed unconscious, Jameson discovers a **political unconscious**, or repressed conditions of exploitation and oppression. The function of literary analysis, Jameson believes, is to uncover the political unconscious present in a text.

Before his discovery of the political unconscious, Jameson developed **dialectical criticism**. In *Marxism and Form* (1971), a text which has become the Bible for American Marxist, Jameson asserts that all critics must be aware of their own ideology when analyzing a text and must therefore possess "dialectical self-awareness."

Perhaps the most influential Marxist critic today is British scholar Terry Eagleton, author of numerous works, including *Literary Theory*, a pivotal introductory text surveying literary criticism. Believing that literature is neither a product of pure inspiration nor the product of the author's feelings, Eagleton holds that literature in actuality is a product of an ideology, which is itself a product of history. This ideology is a result of the actual social interactions that occur between people in definite times and locations. One of the critic's tasks, then, is to reconstruct an author's ideology or the author's ideological milieu.

Throughout his long and prestigious career, Eagleton, like most critics, develops, changes, and redirects his own literary theory. At times he uses a variety of approaches to a text: the scientific approach of Louis Althusser, the psychoanalytic ideas of Lacan, and the poststructualism of Jacques Derrida. All his diverse approaches attack the bourgeoisie dominance of the hegemony and advocate revolution against such values.

From the mid-1970s to the present, Marxism has continued to challenge what it deems the bourgeoisie concerns of its literary counterparts through the voices of a variety of Marxist critics. Critical movements and theories such as structuralism, deconstruction, feminism, and New Historicism have all examined Marxism's basic tenets and share some of its social, political, and revolutionary nature. Like Marxism, these contemporary schools of criticism seek to change the way we think about literature and life. And from these various schools of thought present-day Marxism has borrowed many ideas and has evolved into an array of differing theories so that there no longer exists a single school of Marxist thought, but a variety of Marxist critical positions. Common to all these theoretical positions, however, is the assumption that Marx, no matter how he is interpreted by any of his followers, believed that change for the good in a society is possible if we will stop and examine our culture through the eyes of its methods of economic production.

ASSUMPTIONS

Marxism is not primarily a literary theory that can be used to interpret a text. Unlike other schools of criticism, it is first a set of social, economic, and political ideas that its followers believe will enable them to interpret and, more importantly, change their world. Although a variety of Marxist positions exist, most Marxists adhere to a similar understanding of the world.

Ultimate reality, declares Marxism, is material, not spiritual. What we know beyond any doubt is that human beings exist and live in social groups. All of our actions and responses to such activities as eating, working, and even playing are related in some way to our culture and society. In order to understand ourselves and our world, we must first acknowledge the interrelatedness of all our actions within society. For example, if we want to know who we are and how we should live, we must stop trying to find answers by looking solely to religion or philosophy and begin by examining all aspects of our daily activities within our own culture. Upon examining our daily routines, including our beliefs and values, we will discover that it is our cultural and our social circumstances that determine who we are. What we believe, what we value, and in many ways what we think are direct results of our culture and our society, not our religion or philosophy of life.

When we examine our society, declares Marxism, we will discover that its structure is built on a series of ongoing conflicts between social classes. The chief reason for these conflicts is the varying ways the members of society work and use their economic resources. According to Marx, the various methods of economic production and the social relationships they engender form the economic structure of society called the base. In America, for example, the capitalists exploit the working classes, determining their salaries and their working conditions, among many other elements of their lives. From this base, maintains Marx, arises the superstructure, or a multitude of social and legal institutions, political and educational systems, religious beliefs, values, and a body of art and literature that one dominant social class (the capitalists in America, for instance) uses to keep in check members of the working classes.

The exact relationship between the base and the superstructure is not easily defined. Some early Marxists posited what is known today as vulgar Marxism or reflection theory, believing that the base directly affects the superstructure and, in essence, determines its existence. Other Marxists assert that even Marx and Engels changed their opinions concerning this relationship and attest that the elements contained in the superstructure have a reality of their own, with each element affecting the other elements of the superstructure while simultaneously affecting the base. Whatever the position held by Marxists today, most agree that the relationship between the base and the superstructure is a complex one and will continue to remain a contentious point in Marxist theories.

The relationship between the base and the superstructure becomes clearer when we consider capitalistic America. Marxism declares that in America the capitalists hold the economic purse strings and therefore control the base, acting as the center of power in society. It is they who decree what beliefs are acceptable, what values are to be held, and what laws are to be formed. In other words, the capitalists, not the working classes, control society's ideology or hegemony (its social consciousness). It is they who, in effect, determine the acceptable standards of behavior and thoughts in their society.

Consciously and unconsciously, this social elite forces its ideas on the working classes. Almost without knowing it, the working classes have become trapped in an economic system that decrees how much money they will earn, when they will take vacations, how they will spend their leisure time, what entertainment they will enjoy, and even what they believe concerning the nature of humanity itself.

It is to the working classes that Marxism addresses its rallying cry. All working men and women can free themselves from the chains of social, economic, and political oppression if they will recognize that they are not free agents, but individuals controlled by an intricate social web dominated by a self-declared, self-empowered, and self-perpetuating social elite.

Because this social elite or the bourgeoisie shape a society's superstructure and its ideology, this social class necessarily controls its literature, for literature is one of many elements contained in the superstructure itself. From this perspective, literature, like any other element of the superstructure, becomes involved in a social process whereby the bourgeoisie indoctrinate the working classes with their elite ideology, as reflected in bourgeoisie literature. What becomes natural and acceptable behavior in that society is now pictured in its literature and, in essence, is controlled by the bourgeoisie who control the economic means of production.

Because literature is part of a society's superstructure, its relationship to other elements of the superstructure and to the base becomes the central focus in varying Marxist literary theories. For example, if a Marxist holds to the reflection theory concerning the relationship of the base to the superstructure, then this theorist posits that the economic base directly determines the literature. For such a critic, literature mirrors the economic base. On the other hand, if a Marxist theorist believes that elements of the superstructure have realities of their own and affect each other and also affect the base, a text may be responsible for altering not only other elements within the superstructure but also the base. And even the critics who pledge allegiance to this position hold differing opinions concerning a definition of a text and its relationship to other elements of the superstructure and to the base.

Although all Marxists assert that a text must be interpreted in light of its culture, how they define the text and its social relationships provides us with an array of Marxist literary theories and differing methods of analyses. Thus, there is not one Marxist theory of literature, but many, each hoping to change society.

METHODOLOGY

Because there is no absolute voice of authority who expounds "pure" Marxist principles, there can be no single Marxist approach to literary analysis. Like other methods of interpretation, Marxism includes an array of differing voices, with each articulating particular interests. These differing voices all agree, however, that Marxism, with its concerns for the working classes and the individual, provides the most workable and satisfying framework for understanding our world. Recognizing the interrelatedness of all human activities, Marxism, they believe, enables us to understand ourselves and how we as individuals relate to and are affected by our society. And these voices all assert that we must help direct and change our society, our culture, our nation, and our world by leading humanity toward an understanding and an acceptance of socialism.

As an approach to literary analysis, Marxism's methodology is a dynamic process declaring that a proper critique (*proper* being defined as one that agrees with socialistic or Marxist beliefs) of a text cannot be isolated from the cultural situation from which the text evolved. Necessarily, Marxists argue, the study of literature and the study of society are intricately bound. Such a relationship demands that a Marxist approach to a text deal with more than the conventional literary themes, matters of style, plot, or characterization, and the usual emphasis on figures of speech and other literary devices. Marxism must move beyond these literary elements to uncover the author's world and his or her worldview. By placing the text in its historical context and by analyzing the author's view of life, Marxist critics arrive at one of their chief concerns: ideology. It is the ideology expressed by the author, as evidenced through his or her fictional world, and how this ideology interacts with the reader's personal ideology that interests these critics.

Such an ideological and obviously political investigation, assert Marxist critics, will expose class conflict, with the dominant class and its accompanying ideology being imposed either consciously or unconsciously on the proletariat. The task of the critic, then, is to uncover and denounce such antiproletariat ideology and show how such a destructive ideology entraps the working classes and oppresses them in every area of their lives. Most importantly, through such an analysis the Marxist critic wishes to reveal to the working classes how they may end their oppression by the bourgeoisie through a commitment to socialism.

A Marxist critic may begin such an analysis by showing how an author's text reflects his or her ideology through an examination of the fictional world's characters, settings, society, or any other aspect of the text. From this starting point, the critic may then launch an investigation into that particular author's social class and its effects on the author's society. Or the critic may choose to begin textual analysis by examining the history and the culture of the times reflected in the text and then investigate how the author either correctly or incorrectly pictures this historical period.

Whatever method the critic chooses to use, a Marxist approach seeks to expose the dominant class, to demonstrate how the bourgeoisie's ideology controls and oppresses the working class, and to highlight the elements of society most affected by such oppression. Such an analysis, hopes the Marxist critic, will lead to action, social change, revolution, and the rise of socialism.

QUESTIONS FOR ANALYSIS

To gain a working understanding of a Marxist approach to literary analysis, Ira Shor, a Marxist critic and writer, suggests that we ask certain questions of any text, questions that will enable us to see the Marxist concerns that are evidenced or ignored in the text. The following questions, Shor believes, provide the framework for a close analysis of a text and demonstrate

Marxism's concern for the direct relationship between literature and society. These and other questions can be found in Shor's article "Questions Marxists Ask About Literature," found in *College English* 34 (2), 1974.

- Is there an outright rejection of socialism in the work?
- Does the text raise fundamental criticism about the emptiness of life in bourgeois society?
- In portraying society, what approximation of totality does the author achieve? What is emphasized? What is ignored?
- How well is the fate of the individual linked organically to the nature of societal forces? What are the work's conflicting forces?
- At what points are actions or solutions to problems forced or unreal?
- Are characters from all social levels equally well sketched?
- What are the values of each class in the work?
- What is valued most? Sacrifice? Assent? Resistance?
- How clearly do narratives of disillusionment and defeat indicate that bourgeoisie values (competition, acquisitiveness, chauvinism) are incompatible with human happiness?
- Does the protagonist defend or defect from the dominant values of society? Are those values in ascendancy or decay?

SAMPLE ESSAYS

In the student essay that follows, note how the critic applies Marxist principles in her interpretation of Tony Harrison's poem "Marked with a D." What is her main interest (class struggle, economics, social behavior, etc.)? Does she use any of Shor's questions in her analysis? If so, which ones? Does she successfully show the dynamic relationship between society and literature? And where in her analysis may she strengthen her interpretation?

In the professional essay that follows, note how the critic subtly applies Marxist theory to his analysis of *Huckleberry Finn*. When reading this essay, ask yourself what the critic sees as the novel's conflicting forces. In addition, note how the critic views the differing values portrayed in *Huckleberry Finn*. In particular, note how the critic pictures Huck's moral development as an ideological clash of values.

FURTHER READING

Adorno, Theodor W., Walter Benjamin, Ernst Block, Bertolt Brecht, and Georg Lukacs. *Aesthetics and Politics*. London: New Left Books, 1977.

Ahearn, Edward J. *Marx and Modern Fiction*. New Haven, CT: Yale University Press, 1989.

Eagleton, Terry. *Marxism and Literary Criticism*. Berkeley: University of California Press, 1976.

———. *Criticism and Ideology. A Study in Marxist Literary Theory.* New York: Schocken, 1978.
———. *Literary Theory: An Introduction.* Minneapolis: University of Minnesota Press, 1983.
Eagleton, Terry, and Drew Milne, eds. *Marxist Literary Theory.* Oxford, England: Blackwell, 1996.
Gottlieb, Roger S., ed. *An Anthology of Western Marxism: From Lukacs and Gramsci to Socialist-Feminism.* New York: Oxford University Press, 1989.
Hicks, Granville. *The Great Tradition.* New York: Macmillan, 1933, rev. 1935.
Jameson, Fredric. *Marxism and Form: Twentieth-Century Dialectical Theories of Literature.* Princeton, NJ: Princeton University Press, 1971.
———. *Postmodernism, or, the Cultural Logic of Late Capitalism.* Durham, NC: Duke University Press, 1991.
Jay, Martin. *Marxism and Totality.* Berkeley: University of California Press, 1990.
McMurtry, John. *The Structure of Marx's World-View.* Princeton, NJ: Princeton University Press, 1978.
Mulhern, Francis, ed. *Contemporary Marxist Literary Criticism.* New York: Longman, 1992.
Nelson, Cary, and Lawrence Grossberg, eds. *Marxism and the Interpretation of Culture.* London: Macmillan, 1988.

WEB SITES FOR EXPLORATION

http://www.shebeen.com/marx.htm
  Provides links to a variety of Marxist sites on the Web
www.trincoll.edu/~phil/philo/phils/marx.html
  Provides an overview of Karl Marx and provides links to many Marxist sites on the Web
www.edu.8080/~brians/hum_303/manifesto.html
  Provides a good overview and a study guide for *The Communist Manifesto*
www.idbsu.edu/surveyrc/Staff/jaynes/marxism/marxism.htm
  Provides access to the Marxism/Leninism Project
www.english-www.hss.cmu.edu/marx
  Provides access to the writings of Marx and Engels
www.shef.ac.uk/uni/academic/N-Q/psysc/staff/sihomer/mlg.html
  Provides a "Short History of the Marxist Literary Group"
www.colorado.edu/English/ENGL2012Klages/althusse.html
  Explains Louis Althusser's "Ideology and Ideological State Apparatuses"

∼ Student Essay ∼

Baking Bread for the Bourgeoisie

In Tony Harrison's poem "Marked with a D.," the persona records not only the thoughts and passions once voiced by a now deceased baker but also the persona's own evaluation of the baker's life. The speaker indicates that the baker had led a life of servanthood, always fulfilling the demands of others, while simultaneously contemplating his supposed serene and glorious reward awaiting him in Heaven, a place the persona is sure does not exist. After meditating on the baker's life, the persona concludes that revolution, not subservience to the will of others, is the goal toward which one should strive. A close reading of the poem quickly uncovers the speaker's references to such sentiments and to the oppression inherent in society that must necessarily lead to revolt.

The capitalist society portrayed in this poem is divided into "the haves," the bourgeoisie, and "the have-nots," the proletariat. "The haves" press "the have-nots" into serving them to increase the amount of capital and goods they possess. Through the enforcement of their values and interests, or their hegemony, the bourgeoisie deliberately oppress the proletariat.

Expressions of such oppression are present in the children's rhyming game "Pat-a-cake," alluded to by the title:

Pat-a-cake, Pat-a-cake, baker's man;
Bake me a cake as fast as you can;
Pat it and prick it, and *mark it with a "b,"*
Put it in the oven for baby and me.

The words to this popular game reflect the ideology of the bourgeoisie, for the bourgeoisie believe that anyone in the proletariat should necessarily serve "as fast as [they] can." In the case of the baker, the bourgeoisie believe that he should bake goods for them to eliminate the inconvenience of baking goods for themselves. And, unfortunately, the baker, a typical member of the "working class," faithfully serves the bourgeoisie all his life.

Daily the baker took "chilled dough" from his refrigerator and put it in the oven, dutifully performing his function in society. Like Marx himself, the baker believed that one's function in society comprises one's class—either proletariat or bourgeoisie—and subsequently one's identity. For him, as for Marx, "Life is not determined by consciousness, but consciousness by life." Life exists within the functions of eating, sleeping, obtaining shelter, and clothing one's self. And the "first historical act" is the manufacturing of these goods needed for survival. People like the baker must therefore produce these goods through the modes of production, or the base. As a member of the proletariat, the baker dutifully carried out his appointed mode of production, making baked goods. He thus existed within the base of baking dough, and his essence became equivalent to his existence. Just as the baker daily placed unbaked loaves into a stoked oven, so his body is now placed within "an oven/ Not unlike those he fueled all his life." In actuality, he is now not a dead man being cremated, but dough being baked.

The metaphor comparing the baker's chilled, stiff flesh to dough further enhances the relevance of the title, "Marked with a D." When the baker baked his dough, he kneaded it, formed it, and marked it with a "b," for baby or perhaps bourgeoisie. In the ideological bakery, the bourgeoisie treat the baker like a baked good. They mix all the ingredients together in their recipe to make ideal proletariat "dough," the baker himself. Then they "prick" him and "pat" him down, oppressing his true freedom by conforming and forming him to their mold. In the end, they mark him with a "D" for dead and place him in the crematory oven to bake his "doughy" flesh.

In contemplating the "baking process" of cremation, the persona imagines that the "diseased" eyes of the baker burn. Their burning, however, is not only the result of the literal fire within the crematory oven but also a result of a metaphorical fire—the desire to see the paradise of Heaven preached to him so often. His mouth opens, and "light [streams]" forth from his soul, yearning for a reunion with his wife "Florrie" on Heaven's celestial shore. Although in a formal bourgeoisie setting, "Florence and Flo" would have been the proper names used for addressing one's wife, the baker man called her Florrie. Being completely inappropriate for the seriousness of sophisticated bourgeoisie affairs, this pet name used by a member of the "lower class" further emphasizes the baker's place in society as an enslaved member of the proletariat.

As his mouth opens to alert Florrie to his coming, "his cold tongue [bursts] into flame." Unfortunately, the tongue is enflamed only "literally" in the cremation oven. As a member of the proletariat, he never spoke out concerning his oppression, nor did he ever vocalize a plan for revolution. One sadly wonders whether the baker man even realized that he was oppressed!

Once again bourgeoisie ideology has successfully prevented a member of the proletariat from realizing his oppression. Craftily, the ideology of the bourgeoisie promotes the idea of a literal Heaven to keep the proletariat like the baker in their service. By convincing them that Heaven exists, the proletariat will keep "pressing forward" in their earthly toil. Even if they believe they are oppressed, they will still labor on, trusting that someday they will reach the "pearly gates," behind which no one weeps, suffers, toils, or cries, and no one is oppressed. The idea of "Heaven" also implies a bourgeoisie ideology encompassing Christianity. Many philosophers view Christianity as a "slave religion." "Good" Christians submit themselves to God and to earthly "authority," and they even turn the other cheek if anyone abuses them in any way. What clever bourgeoisie would fail to utilize the full power of such an effective ideological state apparatus?

The persona, however, identifies the interpellation occurring in society, and he is "sorry for [the baker's] sake there's no Heaven to reach." He thus adopts a Marxist materialist philosophy. In this present moment, material possessions are all that exist. The persona's statement, "I get it all from earth, my daily bread," implies that a providential being and a transcendental signified do not reside in another "world." Meaning resides in the daily bread produced in the economic base of society itself.

The baker "hungered," however, for the ideological "bread of Heaven" that would "release [him] from mortal speech." The bourgeoisie utter their dictates and commands, and the proletariat obeys, whether in the production of goods or the adoption of values and beliefs in their personal lives. The word "mortal" not only signifies that the speech is human but also suggests its "deadliness" and "fatality." This fatal "speech" killed the baker's vision, his "sight" for "reality." Because of the bourgeoisie, he developed a metaphorical blindness as signified by his physical cataracts. Instead of seeing the physical state of society with his own eyes, he depended upon the "speech" of the bourgeoisie. Their "speech" dictated "reality" as viewed through their lenses, resulting eventually in his inability to see anything not "described" by the bourgeoisie. In addition, the "deadly" speech of the bourgeoisie also murdered his revolutionary spirit. "The tongue" pressing on him, "weighing like lead" upon his weary frame, "kept him down," working him to the grave.

The baker will not therefore "rise" from his grave to Heaven. Nor will he "rise" like the dough he baked, for he resembles a lump of dough without yeast. What he lacks is the "yeast" of revolution, an ingredient deliberately omitted from the recipe by the bourgeoisie ideology. He will never "rise"— dead or alive.

In the poem, Harrison uses the word "England" to symbolize the bourgeoisie culture whose ideology controlled the baker's life and being. "England" labeled the baker a "dull oaf," an "unintelligent, uninteresting, and clumsy person"; she never labeled him a threat, so he never thought of himself as one. As a "model member" of the proletariat, he embodied the bourgeoisie ideology. Yet the effects of his death and cremation could incite a revolution!

Reminiscent of the insignificance of his life, the smoke lingering from the burnt loaf of the baker's body could irritate someone's eyes. The baker died after a life of servility. He awaited the false hope of heaven instead of "uprising." He never took control of his life on earth to create the only option of paradise open for him and for all humanity. Only revolution can achieve paradise and can prevent such a tragic end to the "dough" of the entire proletariat body. The proletariat must therefore revolt and seize the modes of production in the bourgeoisie bakery. While so doing, they will form "one small loaf" with the "flour" of the baker man's ashes to symbolize a *former* life of servitude and oppression. This small loaf of revolution will never be marked with a "D" because it will not die under the oppression of the bourgeoisie.

JUANITA WOLFE

❧ Professional Essay ❧

Huckleberry Finn

In 1876 Mark Twain published *The Adventures of Tom Sawyer* and in the same year began what he called "another boys' book." He set little store by the new venture and said that he had undertaken it "more to be at work than anything else." His heart was not in it—"I like it only tolerably well as far as I have got," he said, "and may possibly pigeonhole or burn the MS when it is done." He pigeonholed it long before it was done and for as much as four years. In 1880 he took it out and carried it forward a little, only to abandon it again. He had a theory of unconscious composition and believed that a book must write itself; the book which he referred to as "Huck Finn's Autobiography" refused to do the job of its own creation and he would not coerce it.

But then in the summer of 1881 Mark Twain was possessed by a charge of literary energy which, as he wrote to Howells, was more intense than any he had experienced for many years. He worked all day and every day, and periodically he so fatigued himself that he had to recruit his strength by a day or two of smoking and reading in bed. It is impossible not to suppose that this great creative drive was connected with—was perhaps the direct result of—the visit to the Mississippi he had made earlier in the year, the trip which forms the matter of the second part of *Life on the Mississippi*. His boyhood and youth on the river he so profoundly loved had been at once the happiest and most significant part of Mark Twain's life; his return to it in middle age stirred memories which revived and refreshed the idea of *Huckleberry Finn*. Now at last the book was not only ready but eager to write itself. But it was not to receive much conscious help from its author. He was always full of second-rate literary schemes and now, in the early weeks of the summer, with *Huckleberry Finn* waiting to complete itself, he turned his hot energy upon several of these sorry projects, the completion of which gave him as much sense of satisfying productivity as did his eventual absorption in *Huckleberry Finn*.

When at last *Huckleberry Finn* was completed and published and widely loved, Mark Twain became somewhat aware of what he had accomplished with the book that had been begun as a journeywork and depreciated, postponed, threatened with destruction. It is his masterpiece, and perhaps he learned to know that. But he could scarcely have estimated it for what it is, one of the world's great books and one of the central documents of American culture.

Wherein does its greatness lie? Primarily in its power of telling the truth. An awareness of this quality as it exists in *Tom Sawyer* once led Mark Twain to say of the earlier work that "it is *not* a boys' book at all. It will be read only by adults. It is written only for adults." But this was only a manner of speaking, Mark Twain's way of asserting, with a discernible touch of irritation, the degree of truth he had achieved. It does not represent his usual view either of boys' books or of boys. No one, as he well knew, sets a higher value on truth than a boy. Truth is the whole of a boy's conscious demand upon the world of adults. He is likely to believe that the adult world is in a conspiracy to lie to him, and it is this belief, by no means unfounded, that arouses Tom and Huck and all boys to their moral sensitivity, their everlasting concern with justice, which they call fairness. At the same time it often makes them skillful and profound liars in their own defense, yet they do not tell the ultimate lie of adults: they do not lie to themselves. That is why Mark Twain felt that it was impossible to carry Tom Sawyer beyond boyhood—in maturity "he would lie just like all the other one-horse men of literature and the reader would conceive a hearty contempt for him."

Certainly one element in the greatness of *Huckleberry Finn*, as also in the lesser greatness of *Tom Sawyer*, is that it succeeds first as a boys' book. One can read it at ten and then annually ever after, and each year find that it is as fresh as the year before, that it has changed only in becoming somewhat larger. To read it young is like planting a tree young—each year adds a new growth ring of meaning, and the book is as little likely as the tree to become dull. So, we may imagine, an Athenian boy grew up together with the *Odyssey*. There are few other books which we can know so young and love so long.

The truth of *Huckleberry Finn* is of a different kind from that of *Tom Sawyer*. It is a more intense truth, fiercer and more complex. *Tom Sawyer* has the truth of honesty—what it says about things and feelings is never false and always both adequate and beautiful. *Huckleberry Finn* has this kind of truth, too, but it has also the truth of moral passion; it deals directly with the virtue and depravity of man's heart.

Perhaps the best clue to the greatness of *Huckleberry Finn* has been given to us by a writer who is as different from Mark Twain as it is possible for one Missourian to be from another. T. S. Eliot's poem, "The Dry Salvages," the third of his *Four Quartets*, begins with a meditation on the Mississippi, which Mr. Eliot knew in his St. Louis boyhood:

> I do not know much about gods; but I think that the river
> Is a strong brown god . . .

And the meditation goes on to speak of the god as

>   almost forgotten
> By the dwellers in cities—ever, however, implacable,
> Keeping his seasons and rages, destroyer, reminder of
> What men choose to forget. Unhonoured, unpropitiated
> By worshipers of the machine, but waiting, watching and waiting.[1]

Huckleberry Finn is a great book because it is about a god—about, that is, a power which seems to have a mind and will of its own, and which to men of moral imagination appears to embody a great moral idea.

Huck himself is the servant of the river-god, and he comes very close to being aware of the divine nature of the being he serves. The world he inhabits is perfectly equipped to accommodate a deity, for it is full of presences and meanings which it conveys by natural signs and also by preternatural omens and taboos: to look at the moon over the left shoulder, to shake the tablecloth after sundown, to handle a snakeskin, are ways of offending the obscure and prevalent spirits. Huck is at odds, on moral and aesthetic grounds, with the only form of established religion he knows, and his very intense moral life may be said to derive almost wholly from his love of the river. He lives in a perpetual adoration of the Mississippi's power and charm. Huck, of course, always expresses himself better than he can know, but nothing draws upon his gift of speech like his response to his deity. After every sally into the social life of the shore, he returns to the river with relief and thanksgiving; and at each return, regular and explicit as a chorus in a Greek tragedy, there is a hymn of praise to the god's beauty, mystery, and strength, and to his noble grandeur in contrast with the pettiness of men.

Generally the god is benign, a being of long sunny days and spacious nights. But, like any god, he is also dangerous and deceptive. He generates fogs which bewilder, and contrives echoes and false distances which confuse. His sand bars can ground and his hidden snags can mortally wound a great steamboat. He can cut away the solid earth from under a man's feet and take his house with it. The sense of the danger of the river is what saves the book from any touch of the sentimentality and moral ineptitude of most works which contrast the life of nature with the life of society.

The river itself is only divine; it is not ethical and good. But its nature seems to foster the goodness of those who love it and try to fit themselves to its ways. And we must observe that we cannot make—that Mark Twain does not make—an absolute opposition between the river and human society. To Huck much of the charm of the river life is human: it is the raft and the wigwam and Jim. He has not run away from Miss Watson and the Widow Douglas and his brutal father to a completely individualistic liberty, for in Jim he finds his true father, very much as Stephen Dedalus in James Joyce's *Ulysses* finds his true father in Leopold Bloom.[2] The boy and the Negro slave form a family, a primitive community—and it is a community of saints.

Huck's intense and even complex moral quality may possibly not appear on a first reading, for one may be caught and convinced by his own estimate of himself, by his brags about his lazy hedonism, his avowed preference for being alone, his dislike of civilization. The fact is, of course, that he is involved in civilization up to his ears. His escape from society is but his way of reaching what society ideally dreams of for itself. Responsibility is the very essence of his character, and it is perhaps to the point that the original of Huck, a boyhood companion of Mark Twain's named Tom Blenkenship, did, like Huck, "light out for the Territory," only to become a justice of the peace in Montana, "a good citizen and greatly respected."

Huck does indeed have all the capacities for simple happiness he says he has, but circumstances and his own moral nature make him the least carefree of boys—he is always "in a sweat" over the predicament of someone else. He has a great sense of the sadness of human life, and although he likes to be

[2] In Joyce's *Finnegans Wake* both Mark Twain and Huckleberry Finn appear frequently. The theme of rivers is, of course, dominant in the book; and Huck's name suits Joyce's purpose, for Finn is one of the many names of his hero. Mark Twain's love of and gift for the spoken language make another reason for Joyce's interest in him.

alone, the words "lonely" and "loneliness" are frequent with him. The note of his special sensibility is struck early in the story: "Well, when Tom and me got to the edge of the hilltop we looked away down into the village and could see three or four lights twinkling where there were sick folks, maybe; and the stars over us was sparkling ever so fine; and down by the village was the river, a whole mile broad, and awful still and grand." The identification of the lights as the lamps of sick-watches defines Huck's character.

His sympathy is quick and immediate. When the circus audience laughs at the supposedly drunken man who tries to ride the horse, Huck is only miserable: "It wasn't funny to me . . . ; I was all of a tremble to see his danger." When he imprisons the intending murderers on the wrecked steamboat, his first thought is of how to get someone to rescue them, for he considers "how dreadful it was, even for murderers, but I might come to be a murderer myself yet, and then how would I like it." But his sympathy is never sentimental. When at last he knows that the murderers are beyond help, he has no inclination to false pathos. "I felt a little bit heavy-hearted about the gang, but not much, for I reckoned that if they could stand it I could." His will is genuinely good and he has no need to torture himself with guilty second thoughts.

Not the least remarkable thing about Huck's feeling for people is that his tenderness goes along with the assumption that his fellow men are likely to be dangerous and wicked. He travels incognito, never telling the truth about himself and never twice telling the same lie, for he trusts no one and the lie comforts him even when it is not necessary. He instinctively knows that the best way to keep a party of men away from Jim on the raft is to beg them to come aboard to help his family stricken with smallpox. And if he had not already had the knowledge of human weakness and stupidity and cowardice, he would soon have acquired it, for all his encounters forcibly teach it to him—the insensate feud of the Grangerfords and the Shepherdsons, the invasion of the raft by the Duke and the King, the murder of Boggs, the lynching party, and the speech of Colonel Sherburn. Yet his profound and bitter knowledge of human depravity never prevents him from being a friend to man.

No personal pride interferes with his well-doing. He knows what status is and on the whole he respects it—he is really a very *respectable* person and inclines to like "quality folks"—but he himself is unaffected by it. He himself has never had status, he has always been the lowest of the low, and the considerable fortune he had acquired in *The Adventures of Tom Sawyer* is never real to him. When the Duke suggests that Huck and Jim render him the personal service that accords with his rank, Huck's only comment is, "Well, that was easy so we done it." He is injured in every possible way by the Duke and the King, used and exploited and manipulated, yet when he hears that they are in danger from a mob, his natural impulse is to warn them. And when he fails of his purpose and the two men are tarred and feathered and ridden on a rail, his only thought is, "Well, it made me sick to see it; and I was sorry for them poor pitiful rascals, it seemed like I couldn't ever feel any hardness against them any more in the world."

And if Huck and Jim on the raft do indeed make a community of saints, it is because they do not have an ounce of pride between them. Yet this is not perfectly true, for the one disagreement they ever have is over a matter of pride. It is on the occasion when Jim and Huck have been separated by the fog. Jim has mourned Huck as dead, and he, exhausted, has fallen asleep. When he awakes and finds that Huck has returned, he is overjoyed; but Huck convinces him that he has only dreamed the incident, that there has been no fog, no separation, no chase, no reunion, and then allows him to make an elaborate "interpretation" of the dream he now believes he has had. Then the joke is sprung, and in the growing light of the dawn Huck points to the debris of leaves on the raft and the broken oar.

> Jim looked at the trash, and then looked at me, and back at the trash again. He had got the dream fixed so strong in his head that he couldn't seem to shake it loose and get the facts back into its place again right away. But when he did get the thing straightened around he looked at me steady without ever smiling, and says:
>
> "What do dy stan' for? I'se gwyne to tell you. When I got all wore out wid work, en wid de callin' for you, en went to sleep, my heart wuz mos' broke bekase you wuz los', en I didn' k'yer no mo' what became er me en de raf'. En when I wake up en fine you back agin, all safe en soun', de tears come, en I could a got down on my knees en kiss yo' foot, I's so thankful. En all you wuz thinkin' 'bout wuz how you could make a fool uv old Jim wid a lie. Dat truck dah is *trash*; en trash is what people is dat puts dirt on de head er dey fren's en makes 'em ashamed."
>
> Then he got up slow and walked to the wigwam, and went in there without saying anything but that.

The pride of human affection has been touched, one of the few prides that has any true dignity. And at its utterance, Huck's one last dim vestige of pride of status, his sense of his position as a white man, wholly vanishes: "It was fifteen minutes before I could work myself up to go and humble myself to a nigger; but I done it, and I warn't sorry for it afterwards either."

This incident is the beginning of the moral testing and development which a character so morally sensitive as Huck's must inevitably undergo. And it becomes an heroic character when, on the urging of affection, Huck discards the moral code he has always taken for granted and resolves to help Jim in his escape from slavery. The intensity of his struggle over the act suggests how deeply he is involved in the society which he rejects. The satiric brilliance of the episode lies, of course, in Huck's solving his problem not by doing "right" but by doing "wrong." He has only to consult his conscience, the conscience of a Southern boy in the middle of the last century, to know that he ought to return Jim to slavery. And as soon as he makes the decision according to conscience and decides to inform on Jim, he has all the warmly gratifying emotions of conscious virtue. "Why, it was astonishing, the way I felt as light as a feather right straight off, and my troubles all gone. . . . I felt good and all washed clean of sin for the first time I had ever felt so in my life, and I knowed I could pray now." And when at last he finds that he cannot endure his decision but must sacrifice the comforts of the pure heart and help Jim in his escape, it is not because he has acquired any new ideas about slavery—he believes that he detests Abolitionists; he himself answers when he is asked if the explosion of a steamboat boiler had hurt anyone, "No'm, killed a nigger," and of course finds nothing wrong in the responsive comment, "Well, it's lucky because sometimes people do get hurt." Ideas and ideals can be of no help to him in his moral crisis. He no more condemns slavery than Tristram and Lancelot condemn marriage; he is as consciously *wicked* as any illicit lover of romance and he consents to be damned for a personal devotion, never questioning the justice of the punishment he has incurred.

Huckleberry Finn was once barred from certain libraries and schools for its alleged subversion of morality. The authorities had in mind the book's endemic lying, the petty thefts, the denigrations of respectability and religion, the bad language, and the bad grammar. We smiled at that excessive care, yet in point of fact *Huckleberry Finn* is indeed a subversive book—no one who reads thoughtfully the dialect of Huck's great moral crisis will ever again be wholly able to accept without some question and some irony the assumptions of the respectable morality by which he lives, nor will ever again be certain that what he considers the clear dictates of moral reason are not merely the engrained customary beliefs of his time and place.

We are not likely to miss in *Huckleberry Finn* the subtle, implicit moral meaning of the great river. But we are likely to understand these moral implications as having to do only with personal and individual conduct. And since the sum of individual pettiness is on the whole pretty constant, we are likely to think of the book as applicable to mankind in general and at all times and in all places, and we praise it by calling it "universal." And so it is; but like many books to which that large adjective applies, it is also local and particular. It has a particular moral reference to the United States in the period after the Civil War. It was then when, in Mr. Eliot's phrase, the river was forgotten, and precisely by the "dwellers in cities," by the "worshippers of the machine."

The Civil War and the development of the railroads ended the great days when the river was the central artery of the nation. No contrast could be more moving than that between the hot, turbulent energy of the river life of the first part of *Life on the Mississippi* and the melancholy reminiscence of the second part. And the war that brought the end of the rich Mississippi days also marked a change in the quality of life in America which, to many men, consisted of a deterioration of American moral values. It is of course a

human habit to look back on the past and to find it a better and more innocent time than the present. Yet in this instance there seems to be an objective
basis for the judgment. We cannot disregard the testimony of men so diverse
as Henry Adams, Walt Whitman, William Dean Howells, and Mark Twain
himself, to mention but a few of the many who were in agreement on this
point. All spoke of something that had gone out of American life after the
war, some simplicity, some innocence, some peace. None of them was under
any illusion about the amount of ordinary human wickedness that existed in
the old days, and Mark Twain certainly was not. The difference was in the
public attitude, in the things that were now accepted and made respectable
in the national idea. It was, they all felt, connected with new emotions about
money. As Mark Twain said, where formerly "the people had desired
money," now they "fall down and worship it." The new gospel was, "Get
money. Get it quickly. Get it in abundance. Get it in prodigious abundance.
Get it dishonestly if you can, honestly if you must."[3]

With the end of the Civil War capitalism had established itself. The relax-
ing influence of the frontier was coming to an end. Americans increasingly
became "dwellers in cities" and "worshippers of the machine." Mark Twain
himself became a notable part of this new dispensation. No one worshipped
the machine more than he did, or thought he did—he ruined himself by his
devotion to the Paige typesetting machine, by which he hoped to make a
fortune even greater than he had made by his writing, and he sang the praises
of the machine age in *A Connecticut Yankee in King Arthur's Court*. He associated intimately with the dominant figures of American business enterprise.
Yet at the same time he hated the new way of life and kept bitter memoranda
of his scorn, commenting on the low morality or the bad taste of the men who
were shaping the ideal and directing the destiny of the nation.

Mark Twain said of *Tom Sawyer* that it "is simply a hymn, put into prose
form to give it a worldly air." He might have said the same, and with even
more reason, of *Huckleberry Finn*, which is a hymn to an older America
forever gone, an America which had its great national faults, which was full
of violence and even of cruelty, but which still maintained its sense of reality, for it was not yet enthralled by money, the father of ultimate illusion and
lies. Against the money-god stands the river-god, whose comments are
silent—sunlight, space, uncrowded time, stillness, and danger. It was
quickly forgotten once its practical usefulness had passed, but, as Mr. Eliot's
poem says, "The river is within us."

In form and style *Huckleberry Finn* is an almost perfect work. Only one
mistake has ever been charged against it, that it concludes with Tom
Sawyer's elaborate, too elaborate, game of Jim's escape. Certainly this
episode is too long—in the original draft it was much longer—and certainly
it is a falling off, as almost anything would have to be, from the incidents of

---

[3] *Mark Twain in Eruption*, edited by Bernard DeVoto, p. 77.

the river. Yet it has a certain formal aptness—like, say, that of the Turkish initiation which brings Molière's *Le Bourgeois Gentilhomme* to its close. It is a rather mechanical development of an idea, and yet some device is needed to permit Huck to return to his anonymity, to give up the role of hero, to fall into the background which he prefers, for he is modest in all things and could not well endure the attention and glamour which attend a hero at a book's end. For this purpose nothing could serve better than the mind of Tom Sawyer with its literary furnishings, its conscious romantic desire for experience and the hero's part, and its ingenious schematization of life to achieve that aim.

The form of the book is based on the simplest of all novel-forms, the so-called picaresque novel, or novel of the road, which strings its incidents on the line of the hero's travels. But, as Pascal says, "rivers are roads that move," and the movement of the road in its own mysterious life transmutes the primitive simplicity of the form: the road itself is the greatest character in this novel of the road, and the hero's departures from the river and his returns to it compose a subtle and significant pattern. The linear simplicity of the picaresque novel is further modified by the story's having a clear dramatic organization: it has a beginning, a middle, and an end, and a mounting suspense of interest.

As for the style of the book, it is not less than definitive in American literature. The prose of *Huckleberry Finn* established for written prose the virtues of American colloquial speech. This has nothing to do with pronunciation or grammar. It has something to do with ease and freedom in the use of language. Most of all it has to do with the structure of the sentence, which is simple, direct, and fluent, maintaining the rhythm of the wordgroups of speech and the intonations of the speaking voice.

In the matter of language, American literature had a special problem. The young nation was inclined to think that the mark of the truly literary product was a grandiosity and elegance not to be found in the common speech. It therefore encouraged a greater breach between its vernacular and its literary language than, say, English literature of the same period ever allowed. This accounts for the hollow ring one now and then hears even in the work of our best writers in the first half of the last century. English writers of equal stature would never have made the lapses into rhetorical excess that are common in Cooper and Poe and that are to be found even in Melville and Hawthorne.

Yet at the same time that the language of ambitious literature was high and thus always in danger of falseness, the American reader was keenly interested in the actualities of daily speech. No literature, indeed, was ever so taken up with matters of speech as ours was. "Dialect," which attracted even our serious writers, was the accepted common ground of our popular humorous writing. Nothing in social life seemed so remarkable as the different forms which speech could take—the brogue of the immigrant Irish or the mispronunciation of the German, the "affectation" of the English, the reputed precision of the Bostonian, the legendary twang of the Yankee farmer, and the drawl of the Pike County man. Mark Twain, of course, was in the tradition of humor that exploited this interest, and no one could play with it nearly so well. Although today the carefully spelled-out dialects of nineteenth-century American humor are likely to seem dull enough, the subtle variations of speech in *Huckleberry Finn*, of which Mark Twain was justly proud, are still part of the liveliness and flavor of the book.

Out of his knowledge of the actual speech of America Mark Twain forged a classic prose. The adjective may seem a strange one, yet it is apt. Forget the misspellings and the faults of grammar, and the prose will be seen to move with the greatest simplicity, directness, lucidity, and grace. These qualities are by no means accidental. Mark Twain, who read widely, was passionately interested in the problems of style; the mark of the strictest literary sensibility is everywhere to be found in the prose of *Huckleberry Finn*.

It is this prose that Ernest Hemingway had chiefly in mind when he said that "all modern American literature comes from one book by Mark Twain called *Huckleberry Finn*." Hemingway's own prose stems from it directly and consciously; so does the prose of the two modern writers who most influenced Hemingway's early style, Gertrude Stein and Sherwood Anderson (although neither of them could maintain the robust purity of their model); so, too, does the best of William Faulkner's prose, which, like Mark Twain's own, reinforces the colloquial tradition with the literary tradition. Indeed, it may be said that almost every contemporary American writer who deals conscientiously with the problems and possibilities of prose must feel, directly or indirectly, the influence of Mark Twain. He is the master of the style that escapes the fixity of the printed page, that sounds in our ears with the immediacy of the heard voice, the very voice of unpretentious truth.

Essay by Lionel Trilling. "Huckleberry Finn" in *The Liberal Imagination: Essays on Literature and Society*. New York: Doubleday, 1957, pp. 100–13.

10

Cultural Poetics

or New Historicism

"I had dreamed of speaking with the dead, and even now I do not abandon this dream. But the mistake was to imagine that I would hear a single voice, the voice of the other. If I wanted to hear one, I had to hear the many voices of the dead. And if I wanted to hear the voice of the other, I had to hear my own voice. The speech of the dead, like my own speech, is not private property."

STEPHEN GREENBLATT, *Shakespearean Negotiations*, p. 20

INTRODUCTION

During the 1940s, 1950s, and 1960s, New Criticism, or formalism, was the dominant approach to literary analysis. At this time René Wellek and Austin Warren's text *Theory of Literature* became the Bible of hermeneutics, focusing the interpretive process on the text itself rather than historical, authorial, or reader concerns.

During this high tide of formalism, it would have been common to hear a college lecture like the following in a literature classroom.

A NEW CRITICAL LECTURE

"Today, class, we will quickly review what we learned about Elizabethan beliefs from our last lecture so that we can apply this knowledge to our understanding of Act I of Shakespeare's *King Lear*. As you remember, the Elizabethans believed in the interconnectedness of all life. Having created everything, God imposed on creation a cosmic order. At all costs, this cosmic order was not to be upset. Any element of the created universe that portended change in this order, such as a violent storm, eclipses of the sun or moon, or even disobedient children within the family structure suggested chaos that could lead to anarchy and the destruction of the entire earth. Nothing, believed the Elizabethans, should break any link in this Great

Chain of Being, the name given to this created cosmic order. With God and the angels in their place, with the King governing his obedient people in their places, and the animals being subdued and used by humankind in theirs, all would be right in the world and operate as ordained by God.

"Having gained an understanding of the Elizabethan worldview, let's turn to Act I, Scene ii, lines 101–12 of *King Lear*. You will recall that in this scene Edmund, the illegitimate son of the Duke of Gloucester, has persuaded the Duke that Edgar, the Duke's legitimate son and heir to the dukedom, wants his father dead so that he may inherit the Duke's title, lands, and wealth. Believing his natural son has betrayed both him and Edmund, the Duke says, 'These late eclipses in the sun and moon portend no good to us. Though the wisdom of nature can reason it thus and thus, yet nature finds itself scourged by the sequent effects. Love cools, friendship falls off, brothers divide.'

"What we see in these lines, class, is the Elizabethan worldview in operation. The Duke obviously believes in the interrelatedness of the created cosmic order and the concept of the Great Chain of Being. The significance of the eclipses of the sun and moon therefore rests in their representing change and chaos. Because the Duke believes that the macrocosm (the universe) directly affects the microcosm (the world of humanity on earth), he blames these natural occurrences (the eclipses) for interfering in familial relationships and destroying love between brothers, between father and daughters (King Lear having already banished his most beloved daughter, Cordelia), and between King and servant (Kent, King Lear's loyal courtier also having being expelled from the kingdom)."

OLD HISTORICISM

In this typical formalist lecture, the professor's method of literary analysis represents a good example of both New Criticism and what is known today as the old historicism. In this methodology, history serves as a background to literature. Of primary importance is the text, the art object itself. The historical background of the text is only secondarily important, for it is the aesthetic object—the text—that mirrors the history of its times. The historical context serves only to shed light on the object of primary concern, the text.

Underlying such a methodology is a view of history that declares that history, as written, is an accurate view of what really occurred. Such a view assumes that historians are able to write objectively about any given historical time period and are able to state definitively the truth about that era. Through various means of historical analysis, historians are seemingly capable of discovering the mindset, the worldview, or the beliefs of any group of people. For example, when the professor in our hypothetical lecture states the beliefs of the Elizabethans at the beginning of the lecture, he or she is articulating the Elizabethan worldview—the unified set of presuppositions or assumptions that all Elizabethans supposedly held concerning their world. By applying these assertions to the Elizabethan text *King Lear*, the professor believes he or she can formulate a more accurate interpretation of the play than if the teacher did not know the play's historical context.

THE NEW HISTORICISM

That historians can articulate a unified and internally consistent worldview of any given people, country, or time period and can reconstruct an accurate and objective picture of any historical event is a key assumption that **cultural poetics,** one of the most recent approaches to literary analysis, challenges. Appearing as an alternative approach to textual interpretation in the 1970s and early 1980s, cultural poetics—often called New Historicism in America and cultural materialism in Great Britain—declares that all history is subjective, written by people whose personal biases affect their interpretation of the past. History, asserts cultural poetics, can never provide us with the truth or give us a totally accurate picture of past events or the worldview of a group of people. Disavowing the old historicism's autonomous view of history, cultural poetics declares that history is one of many **discourses** or ways of seeing and thinking about the world. By highlighting and viewing history as one of many equally important discourses such as sociology and politics and by closely examining how all discourses (including that of textual analysis itself) affect a text's interpretation, cultural poetics or New Historicism claims to provide its adherents with a practice of literary analysis that highlights the interrelatedness of all human activities, admits its own prejudices, and gives a more complete understanding of a text than does the old historicism and other interpretive approaches.

HISTORICAL DEVELOPMENT

Although the assumptions of cultural poetics and its accompanying practices have been used by critics for several decades, the beginning of New Historicism dates to 1979–80 with the publication of several essays and texts such as "Improvisation and Power" and *Renaissance Self-Fashioning*, by Renaissance scholar Stephen Greenblatt, and a variety of works by Louis Montrose, Jonathan Dollimore, and others. Wishing to remain open to differing politics, theories, and ideologies, these critics share a similar set of concerns, not a codified theory or school of criticism. Of chief interest is their shared view that from the mid-1800s to the middle of the twentieth century historical methods of literary analysis were erroneous. During this time many scholars believed that history served as background information for textual analysis and that historians were able to objectively reproduce a given historical period and state "how it really was." In disclaiming these assumptions of old historicism and formulating its own theories of history and interpretive analysis, cultural poetics was first and aptly named New Historicism by one of its chief proponents, Stephen Greenblatt, in the introduction to a collection of Renaissance essays in a 1982 volume of the journal *Genre*. Because of its broader concerns with culture, history, literature, and a host of other factors that help determine a text's meaning, Greenblatt and his followers now believe that the term cultural poetics more aptly describes their approach to textual analysis than does New Historicism.

According to Stephen Greenblatt, cultural poetics was in large part shaped by the institutional character of American literary criticism during the 1960s and 1970s. During this time, one of the dominating influences in literary criticism was formalism, or New Criticism, with its accompanying theoretical assumptions and practical methodology. For example, during Greenblatt's graduate studies at Yale—a place he has since called the cathedral of High Church New Criticism—Greenblatt himself mastered New Critical principles. New Critical scholars, writers, and critics such as T. S. Eliot, Allen Tate, John Crowe Ranson, Cleanth Brooks, and Robert Penn Warren were revered and their methodology widely practiced throughout the country.

Aided early in its development by the publication and wide use of Cleanth Brooks and Robert Penn Warren's textbook *Understanding Poetry* (1939), New Criticism presented scholars and teachers a workable and teachable methodology for interpreting texts. From a theoretical perspective, New Criticism regards a literary text as an artifact or object with an existence of its own, independent of and not necessarily related to its author, its readers, the historical time it depicts, or the historical period in which it was written. From this viewpoint, a text's meaning emerges when readers scrutinize it and it alone. Such a close scrutiny results, the New Critics maintain, in perceiving a text as an organic whole wherein all parts fit together and support one overarching theme. A poem, a play, or a story, then, is highly structured and contains its meaning in itself and reveals that meaning to a critic-reader who examines it on its own terms by applying a rigorous and systematic methodology. Such an analysis is particularly rewarding, say the New Critics, for literature offers a unique kind of knowledge that presents us with the deepest truths related to humanity, truths that science is unable to disclose.

What New Criticism did not provide for Greenblatt and other critics was an attempt to understand literature from a historical perspective. From a New Critical perspective, the text was what mattered, not its historical context. Consideration of any given text as the result any historical phenomenon was devalued or silenced. In addition, Greenblatt felt that questions about the nature and definition of literature were not encouraged. He and other critics wished to discuss how literature was formed, whose interest it served, and what the term *literature* really meant. Do contemporary issues and the cultural milieu of the times operate together to create literature, they wondered, or is literature simply an art form that will always be with us?

Cultural poetics, then, began to develop as a direct result of New Criticism's dominance of literary criticism and its response or lack thereof to questions about the nature, definition, and function of literature itself. While Greenblatt was asking a different set of literary questions, a variety of new critical theories and theorists appeared on the literary scene. Deconstruction, Marxism, feminism, and Lacanian psychoanalysis also began to challenge the assumptions of New Criticism. Rejecting New Criticism's claim that the meaning of a text can be found, for the most part, in the text alone, these poststructural theories had been developing a variety of theoretical positions concerning the nature of the reading process, the part the reader plays in that process, and the definition of a text or the actual work of art. It is among this cacophony of voices that cultural poetics arose.

Upon reading sociological and cultural studies by Michel Foucault, Greenblatt and other critics admired and emulated Foucault's tireless questioning of the nature of literature, history, culture, and society; like Foucault, they refused to accept the traditional, well-worn answers. From the Marxist scholars (Georg Lukács, Walter Benjamin, Raymond Williams, and others) they learned that history is shaped by the people who live it, and they accepted the Marxist idea of the interconnectedness of all life. What we do with our hands and how we make our money does indeed affect how and what we think, they believed.

But unlike many of the poststructualist theories, especially deconstruction, cultural poetics struggled to find a way out of undecidability, or **aporia**, about the nature of reality and the interpretation of a text. Without denying that many factors affect the writing, production, and publication of texts, New Historicists sought to move beyond undecidability rather than simply assert that a text has many possible meanings. In so doing, they challenged the assumptions of the old historicism that presupposed that historians could actually write an objective history of any situation, they redefined the meaning of a text, and they asserted that all critics must acknowledge and openly declare their own biases.

Throughout the 1980s and 1990s, critics such as Catherine Gallagher, Jonathan Dollimore, Jerome McGann, Stephen Greenblatt, and many others voiced their concerns that the study of literature and its relationship to history has been too narrow. Viewing a text as culture in action, these critics blur the distinction between an artistic production and any other kind of social production or event. These cultural poetics critics want us to see that the publication of Swift's "A Modest Proposal" is a political act, for example, while noting that the ceremony surrounding the inauguration of a United States president is an aesthetic event with all the trappings of symbolism and structure found in any poem. Many similar examples of their critical practices can be found in their chief public voice, the journal *Representations*.

However, no consensus can be found among those who espouse the theory and practice of cultural poetics about theories of art, terminology, and practical methods of interpretation. Cultural poetics, like all other approaches to literary analysis, is best considered a practice of literary interpretation that is still in process, one that is continually redefining and fine tuning its purposes, philosophy, and practices while gaining new followers. Currently, its followers can be divided into two main branches: cultural materialists and New Historicists. Members of both groups continue to call for a reawakening of our historical consciousness, to declare that history and literature must be analyzed together, to place all texts in their appropriate contexts, and to understand that while we are learning about different societies that provide the historical context for various texts, we are simultaneously learning about ourselves, our own habits, and our own beliefs.

Cultural Materialism

Cultural materialism, the British branch of cultural poetics, is openly Marxist in its theories and overtly political and cultural in its aims. It finds its ideological roots in the writings of Marxist critics Louis Althusser and Raymond Williams. Believing that literature can serve as an agent of change in today's world, cultural materialists declare that any culture's hegemony is basically unstable. For literature to produce change, a critic must therefore read the works of the established canon "against the grain." By so doing, the critic will expose the political unconscious of the text and help debunk the social and political myths created by the bourgeoisie.

New Historicism

The American branch of cultural poetics is often called New Historicism. Its founding father, Stephen Greenblatt, along with a host of other scholars, holds that one's culture permeates both texts and critics. Just as all of society is intricately interwoven, so are critics and texts, both with each other and with the culture in which the critics live and the texts are produced. Because all critics are influenced by the culture in which they live, New Historicists believe that they cannot escape public and private cultural influences. Each critic therefore arrives at a unique interpretation of a text. Less overtly political than its British counterpart, New Historicism continues to be refined and redefined by its many practitioners.

ASSUMPTIONS

Like other poststructuralist practices, cultural poetics begins by challenging the long-held belief that a text is an autonomous work of art that contains all elements necessary to arrive at a supposedly correct interpretation.

Disavowing the old historical assumption that a text simply reflects its historical context—the mimetic view of art and history—and that such historical information provides an interesting and sometimes useful backdrop for literary analysis, cultural poetics redirects our attention to a series of philosophical and practical concerns that it believes will highlight the complex interconnectedness of all human activities. For example, it redefines the definition of a text and of history while simultaneously redefining the relationship between a text and history. Unlike the old historicism, New Historicism asserts that there is an intricate connection between an aesthetic object (a text or any work of art) and society while denying that a text can be evaluated in isolation from its cultural context. It declares that we must know the societal concerns of the author, the historical times evidenced in the work, and other cultural elements exhibited in the text before we can devise a valid interpretation. This new approach to textual analysis questions the very act of how we can arrive at meaning for any human activity such as a text, social event, long-held tradition, or political act.

Michel Foucault

Cultural poetics finds the basis for such concerns and a coherent body of assumptions in the writings of the twentieth-century French archaeologist, historian, and philosopher Michel Foucault. Foucault begins his rather complex and sometimes paradoxical theoretical structure by redefining the concept of history. Unlike many past historians, Foucault declares that history is not **linear**, for it does not have a definite beginning, middle, and end, nor is it necessarily **teleological**, purposefully going forward toward some known end. Nor can it be explained as a series of causes and effects that are controlled by some mysterious destiny or an all-powerful deity. For Foucault, history is the complex interrelationship of a variety of discourses or the various ways—artistic, social, political—that people think and talk about their world. How these discourses interact in any given historical period is not random, but dependent on a unifying principle or pattern Foucault calls the **episteme**: Through language and thought, each period in history develops its own perceptions of the nature of reality (or what it defines as truth) and sets up its own acceptable and unacceptable standards of behavior, in addition to its criteria for judging what it deems good or bad, and what people articulate, protect, and defend the yardstick whereby all established truths, values, or actions are deemed acceptable.

To unearth the episteme of any given historical period, Foucault borrows techniques and terminology from archaeology. Just as an archaeologist must slowly and meticulously dig through various layers of earth to uncover the symbolic treasures of the past, historians must expose each layer of discourse that comes together to shape a people's episteme. And just as an archaeologist must date each finding and then piece together the artifacts that define and help explain that culture, so must the historian piece together the various discourses and the interconnections among them and with nondiscursive practices (any cultural institution, such as a form of government) that will assist in articulating the episteme.

Seen from this point of view, history is a form of power. Because each era or people develops its own episteme, in actuality the episteme controls how that era or group of people views reality. History, then, becomes the study and unearthing of a vast, complex web of interconnecting forces that ultimately determines what takes place in each culture or society.

Why or how epistemes change from one historical period to another is unclear. That they change seemingly without warning is certain. Such a change occurred at the beginning of the nineteenth century—the change from the Age of Reason to romanticism, for example—and initiated a new episteme. In this new historical era a variety of different relationships developed among discourses that had not evolved or did exist and were deemed unacceptable in the previous historical period. Foucault asserts that such radical and abrupt changes that cause breaks from one episteme to another are neither good nor bad, valid nor invalid. Like the discourses that help produce them, different epistemes exist in their own right; they are neither moral nor immoral, but amoral.

According to Foucault, historians must realize that they are influenced and prejudiced by the epistemes in which they live. Because their thoughts, customs, habits, and other actions are colored by their own epistemes, historians must realize that they can never be totally objective about their own or any other historical period. To be a historian means one must be able to confront and articulate one's own set of biases before examining the various discourses or material evidence of past events that make up an episteme of any given period. Such an archaeological uncovering of the various discourses, Foucault believes, will not unearth a monological view of an episteme that presupposes a single, overarching political vision or design, but a set of inconsistent, irregular, and often contradictory discourses that will explain the development of that episteme, including what elements were accepted, changed, or rejected to form the "truth" and set the acceptable standards for that era.

Clifford Geertz

In addition to borrowing many of its ideas from Foucault, cultural poetics also uses theories and methodologies from cultural anthropologists such as Clifford Geertz. Geertz believes that there is "no human nature independent of culture," culture being defined by Geertz as "a set of control mechanisms—plans, recipes, rules, instructions," for the governing of behavior. Each person, then, must be viewed as a "cultural artifact." How each person views society is always unique, for there exists what Geertz calls an "information gap between what our body tells us and what we have to know in order to function in society." Such a gap also exists in society, for society cannot know everything that happens among all its people. Like individual people, society simply fills in the gaps with what it assumes to have taken place. And it is this information gap, within both people and society, that results in the subjectivity of history.

Cultural poetics also borrows and adapts Geertz's anthropological methodology for describing culture as "thick description." Geertz coined this term to describe the seemingly insignificant details present in any cultural practice. By focusing on these details, one can reveal the inherent contradictory forces at work within a culture. Borrowing this idea from Geertz, cultural poetics theorists declare that each separate discourse of a culture must be uncovered and analyzed in order to show how all discourses interact with each other and with institutions, peoples, and other elements of culture. This interaction among the many various discourses shapes a culture and thus interconnects all human activities, including the writing, reading, and interpretation of a text that the cultural poetics critic wishes to emphasize.

Texts, History, and Interpretation

Because texts are simply one of many elements that help shape a culture, cultural poetics critics believe that all texts are really social documents that not only reflect but also, and more importantly, respond to their historical situation. And because any historical situation is an intricate web of often competing discourses, cultural poetics scholars necessarily center on history and declare that any interpretation of a text is incomplete if we do not consider the text's relationship to the various discourses that helped fashion it and to which the text is a response. From this point of view, a text becomes a battleground of competing ideas among the author, society, customs, institutions, and social practices that are all eventually negotiated by the author and the reader and influenced by each contributor's episteme. By allowing history a prominent place in the interpretive process and by examining the convoluted webbings of the various discourses found within a text and its historical setting, cultural poetics declares, we can negotiate a text's meaning.

Overall, cultural poetics posits the interconnectedness of all our actions. For a cultural poetics critic, everything we do is interrelated to a network of practices embedded in our culture. No act is insignificant; everything is important. In our search to attach meaning to our actions, cultural poetics critics believe that we can never be fully objective, for we are all biased by cultural forces. Only by examining the complex web of these interlocking forces or discourses that empower and shape culture and by realizing that no one discourse reveals the path to absolute truth can we begin to interpret our world or a text.

For cultural poetics, the goal of interpretive analysis is really the formation and an understanding of a "poetics of culture," a process that sees life and its sundry activities as being more like art than we think, a more metaphorical interpretation of reality than an analytic one. Through the practice of their analysis, cultural poetics critics maintain that we will discover not only the social world of the text but also the present-day social forces working on us as we negotiate meaning with printed material. Like history itself, however, our interaction with any text is a dynamic, ongoing process that will always be somewhat incomplete.

METHODOLOGY

Like other approaches to literary analysis, cultural poetics includes an array of techniques and strategies in its interpretive inquiries, with no one method being dubbed the correct form of investigation. No matter what the technique, however, cultural poetics scholars begin by assuming that language shapes and is shaped by the culture that uses it. By language, cultural poetics critics mean much more than spoken words. For them, language includes discourse, writing, literature, social actions, and any social relationship whereby a person or a group imposes ideas or actions on another.

Included in this definition of language is history. Like literature, writing, or other relationships that involve a transfer or a relationship of power, history becomes a narrative discourse. As in literature or any other narrative discourse, history must be viewed as a language that can never be fully articulated or completely explained. From this perspective, history and literature are nearly synonymous, both being narrative discourses that interact with their historical situations, authors, readers, and present-day cultures. Neither can claim a complete or objective understanding of its content or historical situation, for both are ongoing conversations with their creators, readers, and cultures.

Because cultural poetics critics view history, literature, and other social activities as forms of discourse, they strongly reject the old historicism that sees history as necessary background material for the study of literature. For cultural poetics critics, a work of art—a text—is like any other social discourse that interacts with its culture to produce meaning. No longer is one discourse superior to another, but all are necessary components that shape and are shaped by society. And no longer do clear lines of distinction exist among literature, history, literary criticism, anthropology, art, the sciences, and other disciplines. Blurring the boundaries between the disciplines, cultural poetics scholars investigate all discourses that affect any social production. Because they believe that meaning evolves from the interaction of interwoven social discourses, no hierarchy of discourses can exist, for all are necessary and must be investigated in the process of textual analysis. Included in this interpretive process must also be a questioning of the methodological assumptions for discerning meaning for each discourse and for every practitioner, for no one discourse or method or critic can reveal the truth about any social production in isolation from other discourses.

Because cultural poetics critics view an aesthetic work as a social production, a text's meaning resides for them in the cultural system composed of the interlocking discourses of the author, text, and reader. To unlock textual meaning, a cultural poetics critic investigates three areas of concern: the life of the author, the social rules and dictates found within a text, and a reflection of a work's historical situation as evidenced in the text. Because an actual person authors a text, his or her actions and beliefs reflect both individual concerns and those of the author's society and are therefore essential elements of the text itself. In addition, the standard of behavior as reflected in a society's rules of decorum must also be investigated because these behavioral codes simultaneously helped shape and were shaped by the text. And the text must also be viewed as an artistic work that reflects on these behavioral social codes. To begin to understand a text's significance and to realize the complex social structure of which it is a part, cultural poetics critics declare that all three areas of concern must be investigated. If one area is ignored, the risk of returning to the old historicism, with its lack of understanding of a text as a social production, is great. And during this process of textual analysis critics must not forget to question their own assumptions and methods, for they too are products of and influences on their culture.

To avoid the old historicism's "error" of thinking that each historical period evidences a single political worldview, cultural poetics avoids sweeping generalizations and seeks out the seemingly insignificant details and manifestations of culture usually ignored by most historians and literary critics. Because cultural poetics critics view history and literature as social discourses and therefore battlegrounds for conflicting beliefs, actions, and customs, a text becomes culture in action. By highlighting seemingly insignificant happenings such as a note written by Thomas Jefferson to one of his slaves or a sentence etched on a window pane by Hawthorne, these critics hope to reveal the competing social codes and forces that mold a given society. Emphasizing a particular moment or incident rather than an overarching vision of society, a cultural poetics critic will often point out nonconventional connections such as that between Sophia Hawthorne's having a headache after reading *The Scarlet Letter* and the ending of Nathaniel Hawthorne's next romance, *The House of the Seven Gables*, or between the climate and environs of Elmira, New York, and some locations, descriptions, and actions in Mark Twain's *Huckleberry Finn*. Cultural poetics scholars believe that an investigation into these and similar happenings will demonstrate the complex relationship that exists among all discourses and show how narrative discourses such as history, literature, and other social productions interact, define, and are in turn shaped by their culture. By applying these principles and methodologies, say the cultural poetics critics, we will learn that there is not one voice but many to be heard interpreting texts and culture: our own voices, those of others, and those of the past, the present, and the future.

QUESTIONS FOR ANALYSIS

- Read Tony Harrison's poem "Marked with a D." and ask yourself what voices you hear in the poem. What is the text saying about its culture? About its readers? About itself?
- After reading Hawthorne's "Young Goodman Brown," see whether you can discover any propaganda in the story. What was Hawthorne's position on the nature of sin? Of Puritan theology? Of the devil?
- Does cultural poetics ask us to make any connections between the 1840s and the 1640s? If so, what are these connections?
- How does Hawthorne's "Young Goodman Brown" question dominant cultural values of his day? Of the 1640s?
- What is a working definition of the word *sin* as used in our present culture? In Hawthorne's day? In the 1640s? Why would cultural poetics be interested in this definition?
- How is our reading of "Marked with a D." and "Young Goodman Brown" shaped by our history? Our understanding of our history?
- Identify four discourses operating in "Young Goodman Brown" and "Marked with a D." Show how these discourses interconnect to enable the reader to arrive at an interpretation of each of the works.
- Examine the student essay written at the end of Chapter 9. Describe the student's hegemony on the basis of this essay. Provide evidence to support your answer.

SAMPLE ESSAYS

For the student essay, "Hawthorne's Understanding of History in 'The Maypole of Merry Mount,'" show how or whether the critic investigates the three major areas of concern for cultural poetics. Is one area emphasized more than another? Does the author highlight a historical moment or a culture's single vision of reality? Does the critic admit her own prejudices and methodology? Is history used as background or brought to the center of the literary analysis? And what would be different about this essay if it were written from old historicism's point of view?

In the professional essay, "Is Literary History Still Possible?" what is Arthur Kinney's definition of a text? According to Kinney what makes a text literary? Explain Kinney's four working premises or axioms for examining texts. How do these axioms support cultural poetics' principles?

FURTHER READING

Brooks, Cleanth, and Robert Penn Warren. *Understanding Poetry*. New York: H. Holt and Company, 1939.

Collier, Peter, and Helga Geyer-Ryan, eds. *Literary Theory Today*. Ithaca, NY: Cornell University Press, 1990.

Dollimore, Jonathan. *Radical Tragedy: Religion, Ideology and Power in the Drama of Shakespeare and His Contemporaries*, 2nd ed. Durham, NC: Duke University Press, 1993.

During, Simon. "New Historicism." *Text and Performance Quarterly* 11 (July 1991): 171–89.

Foucault, Michel. *The Foucault Reader*, Paul Rabinow, ed. New York: Pantheon, 1984.

Greenblatt, Stephen. *Renaissance Self-Fashioning: From More to Shakespeare*. Chicago: University of Chicago Press, 1980.

———. Introduction. "The Forms of Power and the Power of Forms in Renaissance." *Genre* 15 (Summer 1982): 3–6.

———. *Shakespearean Negotiations: The Circulation of Social Energy in Renaissance England*. Berkeley: University of California Press, 1988.

Howard, Jean E. "The New Historicism in Renaissance Studies." *English Literary Renaissance* 16 (Winter 1986): 13–43.

Montrose, Louis. "Renaissance Literary Studies and the Subject of History." *English Literary Renaissance* 16 (Winter 1986): 5–12.

Murfin, Ross C., ed. *Heart of Darkness: A Case Study in Contemporary Criticism*. New York: St. Martin's, 1989.

Robertson, D. W. Jr. "Historical Criticism" in *English Institute Essays: 1950*, Alan S. Downer, ed. New York: Columbia University Press, 1951, pp. 3–31.

Thomas, Brook. "The Historical Necessity for—and Difficulties with—New Historical Analysis in Introductory Literature Courses." *College English* 49 (September 1987): 509–22.

Vesser, H. Aram, ed. *The New Historicism*. New York: Routledge, 1989.

Wellek, René, and Austin Warren. *Theory of Literature*, 3rd ed. New York: Harcourt, Brace & Co., 1964.

Williams, Raymond. *Marxism and Literature*. Oxford, England: Oxford University Press, 1977.

WEB SITES FOR EXPLORATION

http://www.sou.edu/English/IDTC/Issues/History/Intros/nhintro2.htm
    Provides an overview of New Historicism, including people and terms, and provides links to other New Historicist sources

www.sun3.lib.uci.edu/~scctr/hri/historicisms/greenblatt.html
    Provides a detailed bibliography on the writings of Stephen Greenblatt

www.english.tamu.edu/ighs/
    Provides access to the Interdisciplinary Group of Humanities Studies

www.stg.brown.edu/projects/h...ext/lando/SSPCluster/Foucault.html
    Provides links and information concerning Michel Foucault

www.trincoo.edu/~phil/philo/phils/foucault.html
    Provides a variety of links concerning the works of Michel Foucault
www.csun.edu/~hfspc002/foucault.home.html
    Provides access to "The World of Michel Foucault"

~ Student Essay ~

Hawthorne's Understanding of History in "The Maypole of Merry Mount"

Synonymous with the flowering of America literature during the 1840s and 50s is the name Nathaniel Hawthorne. Known particularly for his four romances—*The Scarlet Letter, The House of the Seven Gables, The Blithedale Romance,* and *The Marble Faun*—Hawthorne also penned over sixty short stories, including "The Maypole of Merry Mount" (c. 1829). Based upon an actual event occurring at Mount Wollaston or Merry Mount between the fun-loving, anti-Puritan Thomas Morton and the Puritan leader William Bradford, this tale presents a mirthful scene suddenly brought to a close by the arrival of the staunch Puritans.

    More frequently than not, scholars such as Richard Harter Fogle, Randall Stewart, John T. Frederick, and many others note that Hawthorne paints the revelers of Merry Mount as "immitigable zealot[s]" whereas the Puritans are "most dismal wretches." Put another way, Hawthorne embodies in the conflict between Merry Mount and Plymouth two distinct personality types: the jolly colonists versus the gloomy Puritans. That his sympathies reside with the Lord and Lady of the May are undoubtable, but if he were forced to choose between the rivaling parties, Hawthorne would have sided with Endicott, for life, after all, is not a party but a rather serious affair. And his story, assert Hawthorian scholars, demonstrates that the Puritan worldview with its accompanying assumptions about the nature of reality triumphs over the colonists because the Puritans, not the fun-loving revelers, are in tune with the nature of reality itself.

    Such an interpretation rests upon the standards set by the old historicism. Yes, Hawthorne was a historian, and he did understand Puritan theology and history. But the history Hawthorne understood was itself a narrative written by historians who can at best only present their own personal and biased understanding of the past. From a New Historicist's point of view, there exists no definitive view of the Puritans, no definitive view of Hawthorne, and no definitive understanding of "The Maypole of Merry Mount." What we can gain from rereading this tale from a New Historicist viewpoint is a glimpse of how Hawthorne saw life in early America and how he himself was shaped by his own historical era. Such an understanding will reveal how seemingly insignificant events in Hawthorne's life and what appears as arbitrary information within the text of the short story reveal insights into our understanding and enjoyment of this tale.

Hawthorne sets "The Maypole of Merry Mount" in Salem, Massachusetts. Once a thriving seaport during the Puritan era, the Salem of Hawthorne's time is now relatively quiet and in decay. Gone are the boisterous sailors, the many schooners unloading their goods at Derby's Wharf, and the crowded streets. In their place Hawthorne saw gabled housetops, decaying docks, and old maids scurrying from the crumbling mansions of Chestnut Street and Federal Street to buy books at the once-profitable bookstores of downtown Salem. From Hawthorne's point of view, Salem must have resembled the ancient cities of mediaeval Europe that were, like Salem, displaced by modern towns and trades. And like these all but forgotten cities, the spirit of the Gothic hung over Salem.

In Hawthorne's Salem there was no need to invent tales of horror, of witchcraft, or any other kind of legend, for wherever Hawthorne went—on Charter Street near the town's cemetery, nearby Crystal Hills once populated by the Indians, or on the fringes of Salem society known for their superstitious ways—Hawthorne heard tales of sea adventures, wizards, witches, and of the "Maypole's" Endicott and a time when the Puritan punishment for even small sins or mistakes was harsh and swift.

Hawthorne's Salem, a center of legends and Gothic tales, was a city where reality and symbols blended into each other. Where the supernatural began and physical reality ended was often confused, ignored, or avoided. And Hawthorne himself was not immune to his town's Gothic tales and horrors. Van Wyck Brooks notes in *The Flowering of New England* that Hawthorne saw apparitions in his family yard located on Herbert Street. At least in Hawthorne's mind a ghost or apparition haunted the yard, peering into the windows, passing through the house's gate, or simply staring at family members as they entered the house. And Hawthorne knew the identity of this ghost and why it haunted his family: Hawthorne's first American ancestor, William Hathorne, settled in Puritan Salem and quickly became known for his persecution of Quakers. William's son, John Hathorne, followed in his father's footsteps and became one of the judges and interrogators during the Salem witch trials of the 1690s. According to Nathaniel Hawthorne, his family's land was cursed because of the enormous sins committed by his Puritan ancestors upon many undeserving people who were accused, tried, and convicted of witchcraft. It is his personal shame of such unspeakable deeds that causes Hawthorne to question Puritanism, to ask why such supposedly God-fearing people could be filled with so much hate, so much destruction. How could their God be so harsh, Hawthorne wondered. How could they not see the joy in life: a dance, a party, bright and colorful clothing? How could they be so spiritually minded and of so little earthly good?

It was thus the Gothic nature of his Salem, the ubiquitous telling of old wives' tales of ghosts and wizards, and the reappearing apparition in the yard outside his family's home that helped shaped Hawthorne's opinion of his Puritan ancestors. Although he had studied Puritan history, it was his town's milieu, his personal experience with ghosts, and his personal identification with the horrors of the Salem witch trials that ultimately formed his understanding of Puritan theology, the supernatural, and his own guilt of the past. And it is these factors that directly contribute to his writing of "The Maypole of Merry Mount."

Like all historians, Hawthorne's view of his Puritan ancestors is tainted by his own historical era and its existing cultural milieu. Hawthorne knew, of course, that his Puritan ancestors came to America to escape the oppression that faced them in England. Seeking religious freedom, Hawthorne's ancestors immigrated to the New World and established their own culture. As a result, the social boundaries and restrictions of their past changed. Now they were in the dominant social position. Now they were the ruling class rather than the oppressed. And such a change is affirmed by Hawthorne in "The Maypole of Merry Mount." Knowing his history, Hawthorne knew the mistakes of his ancestors and their prejudices. But the Puritans he knew were not the actual Puritans, but concoctions created by his own mind and the stories and tales of his contemporary Salem.

Puritans, said Hawthorne and his contemporary historians, hated gaiety, parties, beautiful clothes, and alcoholic beverages. Although present-day historians have proved all these assumptions to be in error— the Puritans loved to throw parties, drink brandy, engage in wrestling matches, and wear brightly-colored clothing—Hawthorne writes that the revelers of Merry Mount were "gaily decked." Indeed, he notes that "Bright were the days at Merry Mount, when the Maypole was the banner staff of that gay colony!" And the leaders of the colony, the Lord and Lady of the May, were a "youth in glistening apparel" and "a fair maiden," each holding the other's hand while dancing together. Waiting to marry this fair couple was the English priest, who, Hawthorne notes, waited "decked with flowers, in heathen fashion." Although this priest is actually of English descent, he is apparently shaking off his loyalty and giving in to his wild nature.

When the Puritans arrive, John Endicott, the Puritan leader, cuts down the Maypole and contemplates the penalties the worshipers are to receive. After some time, Endicott decides that part of the punishment of the Lord and Lady of the Maypole is that their hair must be cut. "Crop it forthwith, and in the true pumpkin-shell fashion." Such a punishment may appear slight or even trifling, but in actuality it is not. According to Hawthorne's understanding of Puritan theology with its accompanying rules and punishments, all youths must have shortly cropped hair, a symbol of acceptance by and of Puritan customs, laws, and theology. In addition to having their hair cut, the revelers must also don "garments of a more decent fashion." Once again, we observe the Puritans oppressing those who disagree with them and wielding their newfound power over the New Englanders. And last of all, Endicott commands his lieutenant to "bestow on them a small matter of stripes apiece," a punishment that was common during the late 1690s for those who went against Puritan standards.

When writing his romances and short stories like "The Maypole of Merry Mount," Hawthorne was unable to escape his own history. In his stories we catch small glimpses of his life as it was shaped by his culture and his own readings and how his Puritan ancestors and his contemporary Salem contribute to the ideas and questions he had concerning the theology and beliefs of his Puritan forefathers. Throughout his writings, he continually questions the Puritans' so-called perfection while emphasizing their sinfulness. Although his historical facts are sometimes inaccurate, he reveals in "The Maypole of Merry Mount" the power struggle existing in the Puritan society of the late 1690s while examining Puritan religion and its newly-developing culture. In writing this tale, Hawthorne really gives us two contrasting views of American society, the first being his personal understanding of Puritan theology and the second our glimpse of American society in the mid-1840s through the eyes of Hawthorne.

KRISTA ADLHOCK

❧ Professional Essay ❧

Is Literary History Still Possible?*

III

But is literary history still possible? My title is taken from a recent study, published in 1992, by David Perkins. He is writing against a simplified "old" history in which events are linked to causes, and works to sources—as *The Winter's Tale* by Shakespeare is discovered in Robert Green's *Pandosto*. The shortcomings of this kind of literary history have been set forth succinctly by Jean E. Howard:

> How a literary text relates to a context, whether verbal or social, is one of the many issues rethought in the last several decades of literary study. In the past, contextualizing a literary work often meant turning it into an illustration of something assumed to be prior to the text, whether that something were an idea, a political event, or a phenomenon such as social mobility. This reading strategy had several problematic consequences. First, it seemed to suggest that

*Parts I and II of this essay are not reproduced here; footnotes appear as in original text.

texts had one primary determining context and that textual meaning could be stabilized by aligning a text with its "proper" context. Second, it seemed to suggest that literary texts were always responses to, reflections of, something prior to and more privileged than themselves by which they could be explained. This denied literature an initiatory role in cultural transformations or social struggles, and it seemed to foreclose the possibility that literature could have an effect on other aspects of the social formation, as well as being altered by them. Third, using literature as illustration of a context invited a flattening of that text, a denial of its plurality and contradictions in favour of a univocal reading of its relations to a particular contextual ground.[13]

A new literary history would free itself of such charges by seeing literary texts as the convergence of a number of ideas and forces at the given moment of writing the text, not all of them conscious. Moreover, the ruptures and discontinuities that we now know characterize a series (but not necessarily a sequence) of past events in turn disrupts any attempt at forging an overriding thesis or organicism. Literary history, then, begins as the late E. H. Carr, Wilson Professor of International Politics at the University College of Wales at Aberystwyth, says history itself does—"when men begin to think of the passage of time in terms not of natural processes—the cycle of the seasons, the human life-span—but of a series of specific events in which men are consciously involved and which they can consciously influence."[14] Such a history is dynamic and discontinuous. Yet both the old and the new history— more or less recording, more or less creating—are interventions into the flow of time governed by conceptualization and reflection of events from which the historian, as the literary historian, stands apart. Such reflection for Fredric Jameson leads in short order to *historicism*, however, if the historian himself is not passively witnessing but actively engaged in the project of history; for Jameson, historicism is "our relationship to the past, and of our possibility of understanding the latter's monuments, artifacts, and traces."[15] This is a postmodernist sense of history that is not only disjunctive but, by being fruitfully partial, attempts to be all-encompassing. This is a postmodernist sense of history that, for John Kronik, can mean a cobbler's stew.

In the past few years, Gertrude Himmelfarb has been the most trenchant critic of such postmodern historicism. She locates the beginnings of such a postmodernist history—and by extension postmodernist literary history—in a man like Theodore Zeldin:

> Traditional, or narrative, history, he argued, is dependent upon such "tyrannical" concepts as causality, chronology, and collectivity (the latter including such categories as nationality and class). To liberate it from these constraints, he proposed a history on the model of a *pointilliste* painting, composed entirely of unconnected dots. This would have the double advan-

[13]Jean E. Howard, *The Stage and Social Struggle in Early Modern England* (London and New York: Routledge, 1994), 47.

[14]E. H. Carr, *What Is History?* 2d ed. (London: Macmillan, 1986), 134.

[15]Fredric Jameson, "Marxism and Historicism," *New Literary History* 11 (1979): 43.

tage of emancipating the historian from the tyrannies of the discipline, and emancipating the reader from the tyranny of the historian, since the reader would be free to make "what lines he thinks fit for himself."[16]

Himmelfarb's Zeldin thus comes close to the practice that Stephen Greenblatt and his followers have made a trademark of New Historicist readings and criticism. Their storytelling, both in a recovered incident and its filiations to other recovered incidents, to which they draw lines, however disjunctive or remote, is often composed by or into a narration or implied narration: this is a postmodernist possibility for literary history that is at once historical and (through its close readings of texts especially) literary.

For Himmelfarb, one historian who practices a similar connection between data and narrative is Hayden White:

> For White, as for post-modernism generally, there is no distinction between history and philosophy or between history and literature. All of history, in this view, is aesthetic and philosophic, and its only meaning or "reality" [in the created narrative] is that which the historian chooses to give it in accord with his own sensibility and disposition. What the traditional historian sees as an event that actually occurred in the past, the post-modernist sees as a "text" that exists only in the present—a text to be parsed, glossed, construed, interpreted by the historian, such as a poem or novel is by the critic. And, like any literary text, the historical text is indeterminate and contradictory, paradoxical and ironic, so that it can be "textualized," "contextualized," "recontextualized" and "intertextualized" at will—the "text" being little more than a "pretext" for the creative historian (pp. 12–13). At the greatest reaches, then, there would be as many histories as historians—something Himmelfarb finds both absurd and intolerable.
>
> From this perspective of history, Brook Thomas identifies two fundamental "strains of the new historicism" that follow naturally. "One tries to offer new narrative structures to present the past. The other retains traditional narrative structures but offers new voices from which to tell the past,"[17] voices often marginalized or silenced until now. In Louis A. Montrose's famous chiasmus of "the textuality of history and the historicity of texts,"[18] Greenblatt elides and erases any boundary between them "in order to reopen texts to a dynamic field of discursive play," according to Thomas (40). Indeed, according to Howard Felperin, a distinguishing characteristic of the practice of New Historicists writing literary history is "the extent that traditional opposition between the 'literary' and the 'historical' has been shown . . . to be deconstructible, as *constructed intertextuality*."[19]

[16]Gertrude Himmelfarb, "Telling It As You Like It: Postmodernist History and the Flight from Fact," *Times Literary Supplement* 4672 (October 16, 1992), 16.

[17]Brook Thomas, *The New Historicism and Other Old-Fashioned Topics* (Princeton: Princeton Univ. Press, 1991), 24–25.

[18]Louis A. Montrose, "Renaissance Literary Studies and the Subject of History," *English Literary Renaissance* 16, no. 1 (1986): 8.

[19]Howard Felperin, "'Cultural Poetics' versus 'Cultural Materialism': The Two New Historicisms in Renaissance Studies," in *Uses of History: Marxism, Postmodernism and the Renaissance*, "The Essex Symposia," ed. Francis Barker, Peter Hulme, and Margaret Iversen (Manchester: Manchester Univ. Press, 1991), 77.

Such an understanding, says Felperin, permits us to separate the older literary history from the new, "for their 'conventionist' understanding of culture as an intertextual construction supersedes an older 'empiricist' or 'realist' identification of the meaning of an historical text with the biographical author's intention or his contemporary audience's understanding of it, as if such things were once monolithically present or linguistically transparent—even for the historical culture concerned—and retain an integrity untouched by the terms and methods of our enquiry into them" (78). He goes on:

> The very term "representation" at once recuperates and sublates this older historicist and naively realist objective of "making present again" a past culture conceived not only as chronologically but *ontologically* prior to any construction of it. In so doing, it partly rehabilitates a residually referential aspiration, if not to "commune," at least to correspond with the past. . . . [Indeed], such problems have already been confronted and effectively transcended by the post-structuralist move by which the "traces" of history and constructs of culture have been re-framed on the linguistic model of "texts" and "discourses" requiring an ever fresh and renewable "construction" rather than the pseudo-empiricist model of "documents" and "facts" to be "read off" in the effort of definitive reconstruction. (80, 82)

Like Pierre Bourdieu, who influenced him, Greenblatt finds formal and historical concerns inseparable while, unlike Bourdieu, de- emphasizing or dismissing the importance of extra-textual social and historical concerns, a material culture, in his acts of mediating recovery. But if Greenblatt's particular view ignores the material artifacts of a culture, Felperin writes, he seems at odds metaphorically when, disjoining himself from the cultural materialists in Great Britain, he returns with a Marxist lexicon. As Felperin puts it, "Does Greenblatt's latest terminology of 'circulation,' 'negotiation,' 'social energy' and 'exchange' —basically mercantile, even strangely monetarist, as it is—not effectively render Elizabethan England in terms of a generative grammar of economic exchange common to all societies? On this account, we might be excused for wondering whether we have blundered into a kind of universal bazaar teeming with rug dealers" (84). But if old history is too narrow in its focus on principal events chronologically or causally arranged, and if new history is flawed by incompleteness and dispersal, how can we write a literary history in our age that is foreshadowed in the seventeenth-century work of Ralegh, for example? And if we could write such a history—seemingly organic; actually juxtapositional—what makes it "literary"?

IV

These issues are as interrelated as they may seem to be separate. J. R. DeJ. Jackson provides a means for addressing the first of them in *Historical Criticism and the Meaning of Texts* when he defines historical criticism as "criticism that tries to read past works of literature in the way in which they were read when they were new."[20] Jackson also sketches a methodology for this:

[20]J. R. deJ. Jackson, *Historical Criticism and the Meaning of Texts* (London: Routledge, 1989), 77.

> If the aim of the recovery is to know a past literary environment as it was known in its own time so that reference to it in particular works will be comprehensible, three aspects will need to be considered: the range of works that existed; the portion of that range that was well enough known for authors to be able to take it for granted; and the way in which that portion was understood, in so far as it differs from the way in which a modern reader might be expected to understand it. (109)

It is, I think, in just such a semiotic practice as this—of reading texts, customs, and actions as similar and related cultural documents, all constitutive signs of a cultural moment that will impinge on a literary text—that our best and brightest hope for a literary history now rests. One method toward this end is described in the work of Marc Bloch, who argues that history must extend beyond conventional archival resources to include all kinds of evidence—verbal, nonverbal, extraverbal. "Everything that man says or writes, everything that he makes, everything he touches can and ought to teach us about him," Bloch writes in *The Historian's Craft* (posthumously translated and published in 1954). "It would be sheer fantasy," he continues,

> to imagine that for each historical problem there is a unique type of document with a specific sort of use. On the contrary, the deeper the research, the more the light of the evidence must converge from sources of many different kinds. What religious historian would be satisfied by examining a few theological tracts or hymnals? He knows full well that the painting and sculpture of sanctuary walls and the arrangement and furnishing of tombs have at least as much to tell him about dead beliefs and feelings as a thousand contemporary manuscripts.[21]

Bloch's own studies of feudalism or of the royal touch, like his disciple Fernand Braudel's massive study of the Mediterranean, while not themselves poststructuralist, invite the use of other and all disciplines for the self-correcting synchronic presentation of culture that can also provide a fuller, if disjunctive and so postmodernist, foundation for writing (or rewriting) literary history.

The other question is equally important, if apparently in the different and perhaps somewhat distant field of aesthetics. The distance is more apparent than real. Leah Marcus puts her finger on the issue of literary history in early modern England when in *Puzzling Shakespeare* she asks about "the place of art" in the Renaissance: "[a]uthors were caught between the need for currency, the need to attract an immediate public" by topicality as well as by popular convention "and a newly emerging desire for permanence and monumentality."[22] As one of my students in a seminar at New York University put it a few weeks ago, "When does a performance become a poem?"; when does a performative text become a literary one? When does *Volpone* become a candidate for

---

[21]Marc Bloch, *The Historian's Craft*, trans. Peter Putnam (Manchester: Manchester Univ. Press, 1954), 66–67.

[22]Leah Marcus, *Puzzling Shakespeare: Local Reading and Its Discontents* (Berkeley: Univ. of California Press, 1988), 37.

a folio *Works of Benjamin Jonson,* and is it thereby transformed by the very
fixing of it in print? For Marcus the answer must be both diachronic and
synchronic. For her the useful "localization of Shakespeare is based on the
assumption that a similar cross-fertilization between the mapping of 'cross-
cultural' analysis favored by anthropologists and the longitudinal sequential
analysis characteristically practiced by historians will create a range of new
vantage points from which to consider how the plays create meaning" (37).
The literary linkage, then, is the representational image, or to paraphrase
Jonson, what is for all time in the ways it captures and thus represents the
moment. A text is literary in, through, and by its metaphoric functioning.

Such a concept is also found in Gandamer's *Truth and Method,* in which
he argues that in making an image, verbal or nonverbal, the literary artist
makes that image both immediately present and more lastingly representative. Consciously or not, Hans Robert Jauss elaborates on this in his very
helpful concern with what he calls the "horizon of expectations":

> The reconstruction of the horizon of expectations, in the face of which a
> work was created and received in the past, enables one . . . to pose questions
> that the text [initially] gave answer to, and thereby [permits us] to discover
> how [our] contemporary reader [who reads the work "as if it were new"]
> could have viewed and understood the work. This approach corrects the
> most unrecognized norms of a classicist and modernizing understanding of
> art, and avoids a circular recourse to a general "spirit of the age." It raises to
> view the hermeneutic difference between the former and the current under-
> standing of a work [the "cultural moment" instead of "for all time"]; it
> raises to consciousness the history of its reception, which mediates both
> positions; and it thereby calls into question as a platonizing dogma of philo-
> logical metaphysics the apparently self-evident claims that in the literary
> text, literature is eternally present, and that its objective meaning, deter-
> mined once and for all, is at all times immediately accessible.[23]

Such an attempt to forge a postmodernist literary history appears in *Puzzling
Shakespeare* when Marcus speaks for a "new topicality," which, as Richard
Wilson elsewhere defines it, "will restore history to the plays through metic-
ulous 'local reading' of their discursive contexts, allied to an 'awareness that
our activity has local coordinates of its own.'"[24] For as Marcus claims, "topicality cuts across static explanatory systems and closed cultural forms, opening them to the vagaries of historical process" (37). Felperin also helps us to
this larger vision that can contain both the wider society and its wider and
more varied linguistic constructions by introducing something of the semiotics we have already associated with Saussure. "Unless Elizabethan literature and society are viewed, not simply as a textual *system* operating on its
own terms—arbitrary, autonomous, as it were, autochthonic," he proposes,

[23]Hans Robert Jauss, "Literary History as a Challenge to Literary Theory" in *Critical Theory Since 1965,* ed.
Hazard Adams and Leroy Searle (Tallahassee: Florida State Univ. Press, 1986), 171.

[24]Richard Wilson, *Will Power: Essays on Shakespearean Authority* (Exeter: Wayne State Univ. Press, 1993), 16.

"but as a cultural *moment*, laden with the traces of earlier and latencies of subsequent moments, there can be any number of anthropological descriptions, 'thick' and 'thin,' but no historical interpretation" (86). It is just such a semiotic practice of reading texts, customs, and actions as similar cultural documents, all constitutive signs of a cultural moment, that can be the basis for a significant (and significantly different) postmodernist literary history. Such moments are, granted, composed of change and continuity—of factors demarcating development and the relatively stable conditions and ideas that sequential moments share. Both are part of a representational, metaphor-oriented text that attempts to mediate or negotiate them. Shakespeare's *Macbeth*, for instance, openly mediates the continuing theory of monarchial rule with the more particularized example of an absolutist Scottish ruler that negotiates tenth-century Scotland with its own Jacobean England.

<h2 style="text-align:center">V</h2>

In practice, then, we should acknowledge that signifying texts—verbal and nonverbal texts—both register and interrogate the ideas and values of a culture at the same time presentational imaging and metaphorizing of such ideas and values are a literary means of intervening in that culture and so helping to constitute—and to reconstitute—it. We call "literary" those texts that have great imagining and metaphoric power, and we choose cultural moments that surround or are embedded in those specially striking texts. In this sense, the signs that matter are the signs that inform and illuminate the literary text, being the cultural signs that help constitute it. Some complexly representative texts, operating with metaphoric power within their cultural moments, will show what I have in mind.

When Sir Philip Sidney's Euarchus, at the close of the comprehensive fiction of *Arcadia*, finds himself unable to accommodate the guilt of his son because the laws of justice do not admit exceptions, the author makes a forceful comment favoring the newer courts of equity and an equally forceful questioning of the courts of common law, dependent wholly on precedent, under Elizabeth I. The fiction does not stop being a fiction, nor the romance a romance, but at the same time the imaging text interrogates the Tudor legal system and interrupts the smugness with which other writers were praising it in London and in the provinces. When Iago in *Othello* is able to challenge the self-confident judgment of his general by showing in the person of the drunken Cassio that Othello chose an inferior man as his lieutenant, that Othello's autocratic wisdom can be called to account and found wanting, Shakespeare not only draws directly for literary representation on military manuals of his day, he also demonstrates the inherent limitations of a military conditioning and mind-set given to absolute commands and irrevocable decisions that can be fallible and opposed to each other—and in his Jacobean reception toward the clear and present danger of James I, who also displays a stubborn self-confidence in writing and publishing his political doctrine of enlightened absolutism. When, in "The Collar," the poet George Herbert, self-exiled to the small village parish of Bemerton in distant Wales, writes: "I struck the board, and cry'd, No more. /I will abroad," he is not merely announcing a frustration with the Christian faith or exemplifying the Christian state of near despair. He is also demonstrating through his textual register of meditative poetry a representational image of how the Christian in this cultural moment who is neither Genevan nor papist can yearn for more than the Erastian provisos of the Church of England. He is talking about the plight of the religious in a nation that charts contradictory and unsettled religious paths. In *Will Power*, Richard Wilson has recently shown how James's presence interrupts the text of *Measure for Measure*; how Brian Annesley's will, recognizing Kentish *gavelkind*, divides his property at his death equally among his children, including the youngest, Cordelia, some four or five years before *King Lear*; how actual riots inform *2 Henry VI, Julius Caesar*, and *Coriolanus*; and how Tudor enclosures inform and are informed by *As You Like It*. Elsewhere I have argued how Thomas Deloney's *Jack of Newburie* is a fictional rewriting of a petition he wrote with William Muggins and one Willington in support of the London weavers of his own day, "To the Minister and Elders of the French Church in London," which sent him to prison,[25] and how certain anachronistic words—such as "imperial theme," "twofold balls and treble sceptres," and "equivocation" transfer Shakespeare's account of Macbeth from that of his source, the eleventh-century history of Francis Thynne for Holinshed's *Chronicles*, to seventeenth-century Jacobean England,[26] much as Bacon rewrites biblical history making it too contemporary and charged with political freight. Such matters as these are surely the concern of any literary history (if appropriate and natural for a postmodern literary history), because they lead us, by showing us something about what that work meant when it was new, to the greater representative and metaphorical range inherent in—and at times dynamic to—the literary text. They are constitutive of both literature *and* history.

VI

Signs may also come in much more subtle ways, first introduced into contemporary critical study by Derrida in his essay on Jusserl as "le trace." According to Derrida, "The trace is not a presence but is rather the simulacrum of a presence that dislocates, displaces, and refers beyond itself"[27]; according to his follower Emmanuel Levinas,

> The trace is not a typical sign, but it may play the role of a sign. It may be taken for a sign. The detective examines everything that marks the scene of the crime as a revealing sign, the intentional or unintentional work of the criminal; the hunter follows the trace of the game, which reflects the activity and the tread of the animal he seeks; the historian discovers ancient civi-

---

[25]Arthur F. Kinney, "Situational Poetics," *Prose Studies* 11, no. 2 (1988): 13–17.

[26]Arthur F. Kinney, "Imagination and Ideology in Macbeth," in *The Witness of Times: Manifestations of the Ideology in Seventeenth-Century England*, ed. Gerald J. Schiffhorst and Katherine Z. Keller (Pittsburgh: Duquesne Univ. Press, 1993), 148–73.

[27]Jacques Derrida, *Speech and Phenomena and Other Essays on Jusserl's Theory of Signs*, trans. David B. Allison (Evanston: Northwestern Univ. Press, 1973), 156.

lizations, beginning with the vestiges left by their existence, as horizons to our world.[28]

Sheldon P. Zitner, for instance, has seen the intense controversy over the Elizabethan Court of Wards in traces in *All's Well That Ends Well*, a play written and first performed when the controversy was at its height. The practice then established, which enabled the crown to profit from the persons and inherited property of minors by selling—or, for a fee, allowing its nobility to sell—the guardianship of orphans, informs the situation of both Helena and Bertram. Helena is clearly such a ward, in effect surrendered by the Countess of Rossillion to the king as a chattel whose perquisite it is to assign control of her for profit; Bertram, on the other hand, is equally without control of property because his father had the bad fortune to die before his son came of age.[29] *All's Well*, then starts with two recently orphaned youth of different genders whose actions display a hierarchical and relatively closed society. The play is about what they *do*. It is also, from this perspective, about what they *can do*; court and military service for him; nursing and the convent for her. From another perspective, the play conducts a rigorous examination of rank and gender in late Tudor England (as well as France, where the action putatively takes place).

In a different way, *The Merry Wives of Windsor* intervenes in its cultural moment. I think it is no accident that this play is set uniquely in Shakespeare's contemporary England; it means to question the economic conditions of that time and place. Windsor, the play's sole location, was then a royal borough, but it was also a village devastated (as were other parts of the country) by four years of bad harvests between 1593 and 1597, by unusual dearth, poverty, starvation, and death. In this context the gluttonous Falstaff serves as the perfect ironic sign. As in the history plays, he is "out at heeles" (fol. 1, sig. D3), while the merchants of the play, the Pages and the Fords, stuff themselves at feast after feast. *The Merry Wives* is a play about the haves and the have-nots, about the deepening economic divide in the late "golden years" of Elizabeth I. This play, too, functions as commentary, entering into the culture for its material, returning that material to the culture as farce. But why farce? Perhaps in analogy to the invention of screwball comedies in Hollywood, musical comedies on Broadway, and the game of Monopoly based on Atlantic City during our Great Depression—to relieve economic distress by making light of it.[30] That, too, is part of its constituent, representational, metaphoric meaning.

Such simultaneity alerts us to redolent dimensions of a cultural moment. Karen Newman's examination of Shakespeare's *Taming of the Shrew* func-

[28]Emmanuel Levinas, "Le trace," *Humanisme de l'autre Homme*, trans. Peter Sokolowski (Montpellier: Fata Morgana, 1972), 66.

[29]Sheldon P. Zitner, ed. *All's Well That Ends Well*, Twayne's New Critical Introductions to Shakespeare (Boston: Twayne Publishers, 1989), 42–46.

[30]I develop this argument in greater detail in "Textual Signs in *The Merry Wives of Windsor*," *Yearbook of English Studies* 23 (1993): 206–34.

tions somewhat differently. Newman likens the play, which we customarily date around 1593–94, to an event in Wetherden, Suffolk:

> A drunken tanner, Nicholas Rosyer, staggers home from the alehouse. On arriving at his door, he is greeted by his wife with "dronken dogg, pisspott and other unseemly names." When Rosyer tried to come to bed to her, she "still raged against him and badd him out dronken dog dronken pisspot." She struck him several times, clawed his face and arms, spit at him, and beat him out of bed. Rosyer retreated, returned to the alehouse, and drank until he could hardly stand up. Shortly thereafter, Thomas Quarry and others met and "agreed amongest themselfs that the said Thomas Quarry who dwelt at the next howse . . . should . . . ryde abowt the towne upon a cowlstaff whereby not onely the woman which had offended might be shunned for her misdemeanors towards her husband but other women also by her shame might be admonished to offence in like sort."[31]

Newman dates this event "Plough Monday, 1604," well beyond our accepted date of Shakespeare's play, but before the first instance of the play being entered in the Stationer's Register (to one J. Smethwick on 19 November 1607). Perhaps the revival of public punishing of shrews—or the continuation of such punishment—prompted a revival of Shakespeare's play or suggested to the commercially minded Smethsick a new financial possibility. I was myself puzzled by the number of distinct verbal echoes in *Macbeth* of Marlowe's *Tamberline*, first published in 1590, a full fifteen years before Shakespeare's play, until I learned by consulting the Short Title Catalog that *Tamberline* was reprinted (and restaged?) in 1604. The cultural moment thus includes the possibilities of renewing past events and anticipating future ones; the literary cultural moment has no fixed period or lines of demarcation.

VII

Such instances, which help to constitute a literary history in terms of cultural moments, have led me to formulate four working premises or axioms—starting places for examining texts and signs that may be subject to change, addition, or suspension but which nevertheless function as heuristic points of departure:

1. No text is ever entirely unmarked by its time and place—and its fullest range of meaning depends to a greater or lesser degree on such knowledge.

2. Every text always has some intention; even when the intention is misconceived, unrealized, or misunderstood, no text is innocent of purpose or reception.

3. Every text potentially contains multiple readings through multiple interpreters and multiple occasions on which it is interpreted or conveyed.

[31]Karen Newman, *Fashioning Femininity and English Renaissance Drama* (Chicago: Univ. of Chicago Press, 1991), 35.

4. No text is completely unequivocal or conclusive; all texts are contingent on further understanding of their cultural moment, when they are new.

The limitation when working with a past period such as the early modern period is that the only cultural signs that are preserved are those in written or pictorial records or in material remains: even our knowledge of Essex's rebellion relies on extant verbal documents that relate or interpret it. Such documents may be as formal as court proceedings or statutes or as informal as gossip recorded in letters or diaries, but they survive as potential objects of our knowledge because they are in written or printed form. In the absence of other means of knowledge, they have privileged writing, and this in turn has often historically privileged literature. But the uniqueness of written transmission does not make literature autonomous nor the only evidence to which it can be made to relate. The *Annales* school forcefully reminds us that other matters—such as Brian Annesley's will or Nicholas Rosyer's punishment—are part of a literary text's meaning at its original moment or time and may be some of the meaning of that text even now. Shakespeare's *Tempest*, written and presented in 1611, for instance, may recall contemporary voyage pamphlets, but it may also recall a much earlier one, in 1606, which tells of five American Indians—potential originals for Caliban in the mind of Shakespeare and in the minds of his audience, for they were still on display in London in 1611, and could be viewed on the way to the theater. Similarly, Henry Smith's 1591 sermon on Jonah finds its echoes in the play and potentially in its significant relationship to Prospero and to Alonso; likely it was still being preached, as it was still being printed, in 1611, in later editions of Smith's works.

Finally, crucial cultural signs at a later moment of a literary text's origination may not be evident signs at a later moment of reading. But that likelihood should not prevent us from searching out the signs in force at the cultural moment when the literary text under examination was first conceived and produced, and both are part of a literary history we can now write, or rewrite. The traces and latencies of subsequent moments in such texts have always made reading them richer and more difficult, but we shall never register the fullest possible readings, based on such traces and latencies as well as on the texts, until we first attend closely to all we can recover of the originary moment itself. Just such acts, however, will continue to make literary history—even postmodernist literary history—possible.

Essay by Arthur F. Kinney. *Ben Jonson Journal* 2: 199–221.

11

Cultural Studies

INTRODUCTION

The 1960s saw a revolution in literary theory. Until this decade, New Criticism dominated literary theory and practice with its insistence that one ultimately correct interpretation of a text could be discovered if the critical reader followed the methodology prescribed by the New Critics. Believing that a text contained its meaning within itself, New Critics paid little attention to a text's historical context or to the feelings, beliefs, and ideas of a text's reader. For the New Critics, a text's meaning was inextricably bound to ambiguity, irony, and paradox found within the structure of the text. By analyzing the text alone, New Critics believed that an astute critic would be able to identity a text's central paradox and be able to explain how the text ultimately resolved that paradox while at the same time supporting the text's overarching theme.

Into this seemingly self-assured system of hermeneutics marched Jacques Derrida and his friends in the 1960s. Unlike the New Critics, Derrida, the founding father of deconstruction, denied the objective existence of a text. Disavowing this basic assumption of New Criticism, Derrida and other poststructural critics also challenged the definitions and assumptions of both reading and writing and from a philosophical perspective asked what it actually means to read and to write. Joined by reader-response critics, these postmodern thinkers insisted on questioning what part not only the text but also the reader and the author play in the interpretive process.

Joined by a host of authors and scholars—Stanley Fish, J. Hillis Miller, Michel Foucault, and many others—these philosopher–critics also questioned the language of texts and of literary analysis. Unlike the New Critics, who believed that the language of literature was somehow different from the language of science and everyday conversation, these postmodernists insisted that the language of texts is not distinct from the language used to analyze such writings. For these critics, all language is discourse. In other words, the discourse or language used in literary analysis helps shape and form the text being analyzed. We cannot separate the text and the language used to critique it. Language, then, helps create what we call objective reality.

Believing that objective reality can be created by language, many postmodernists posit that all reality is a social construct. From this point of view, there is no objective reality, but many subjective understandings of that reality—as many realities as there are people. How, then, do we come to agree on public and social concerns such as values, ethics, and the common good? According to many postmodern thinkers, each society or culture contains within itself a dominant cultural group who determines that culture's ideology or its hegemony—its dominant values, its sense of right and wrong, and its sense of personal self-worth. All people in a given culture are consciously and unconsciously asked to conform to the prescribed hegemony.

What happens when one's ideas, one's thinking, and one's personal background do not conform? For example, what happens when the dominant culture consists of white, Anglo-Saxon males and you are a black female? Or how does one respond to a culture dominated by these same white males when you are a Native American? For people of color living in Africa or the Americas, for Native Americans, for females, and for a host of others, the traditional answer has been silence. Live quietly, work quietly, think quietly. The message sent to them by the dominant culture has been clear: Conform and be quiet; deny yourself and all will be well.

But many have not been quiet. Writers and thinkers such as Toni Morrison, Alice Walker, Gabriel García Márquez, Carlos Fuentes, Gayatri Spivak, Edward Said, and Frantz Fanon have dared and continue to challenge the dominant cultures and the dictates such cultures decree. They have not been silenced. Defying the dominant culture, they believe that an individual's view of life, values, and ethics does matter. Not one culture, but many; not one cultural perspective, but a host; not one interpretation of life, but countless numbers is their cry.

Joined by postmodern literary theorists and philosophers, Africans, Australians, Native Americans, women, and many other writers are finding their voices among the cacophony of dominant and overpowering cultural voices. Believing that they can effect cultural change, these new voices refuse to conform and be shaped by their culture's hegemony. These newly heard but long-existent voices can now be overheard at the discussions taking place at the literary table, where they present their understanding of reality, society, and personal self-worth.

Known as **cultural studies**, an analysis and an understanding of these voices can be grouped into three approaches to literary theory and practice: postcolonialism, African-American criticism, and gender studies. Although each group has its personal concerns, all seek after the same thing: to be heard and understood as valuable and contributing members of society. Their individual and public histories, they assert, do matter. They believe that their past and their present are intricately interwoven. By denying and suppressing their past, they declare that they will be denying themselves. Their desire is to be able to articulate their feelings, concerns, and assumptions about the nature of reality in their particular cultures without becoming marginalized. Often called **subaltern writers**—a term used by Marxist critic Antonio Gramsci to refer to the classes who are not in control of a culture's ideology or its hegemony—these writers provide new ways to see and understand cultural forces at work in literature and in ourselves. Although each approach's literary theory and accompanying methodology are still developing, a brief overview of the central tenets of each of the three approaches will enable us to catch a glimpse of their diverse visions of literature's purposes and functions in today's world. Although no sample student essay is provided, following the synopsis of each of the three approaches is a professional essay that demonstrates the concerns and theoretical interests of postcolonialism.

POSTCOLONIALISM: THE EMPIRE WRITES BACK

Postcolonialism or **post-colonialism** (either spelling is acceptable, but each represents slightly different theoretical assumptions) can be defined as an approach to literary analysis that concerns itself particularly with literature written in English in formerly colonized countries. It usually excludes literature that represents either British or American viewpoints, and concentrates on writings from colonized cultures in Australia, New Zealand, Africa, South America, and other places and societies that were once dominated by but outside of the white, male European cultural, political, and philosophical tradition. Often called third-world literature by Marxist critics—a term many other critics think pejorative—postcolonial literature and theory investigate what happens when two cultures clash and when one of them with its accompanying ideology empowers and deems itself superior to the other.

The beginnings of such literature and theoretical concerns date back to the 1950s. During this decade, France ended its long involvement in Indochina, Jean-Paul Sartre and Albert Camus parted ways on their differing views about Algeria, Fidel Castro delivered his now-famous speech "History Shall Absolve Me," and Alfred Sauvy coined the term *Third World* to represent countries that philosophically, politically, and culturally were not defined by Western metaphysics. During the 1960s, Frantz Fanon, Albert Memmi, George Lamming, and other authors, philosophers, and critics began publishing texts that would become the cornerstone of postcolonial writings.

The terms *post-colonial* and *postcolonialism* first appear in the late 1980s in many scholarly journal articles and as a subtitle in Bill Ashcroft, Gareth Griffiths, and Helen Tiffin's text *The Empire Writes Back: Theory and Practice in Post-Colonial Literatures* (1989) and again in 1990 in Ian Adam and Helen Tiffin's *Past the Last Post: Theorizing Post-Colonialism and Post-Modernism*. By the mid-1990s, the terms had become firmly established in scholarly writing, and now postcolonialism usually refers to literature of cultures colonized by the British Empire.

Like deconstruction and other postmodern approaches to textual analysis, postcolonialism is a heterogenous field of study where even its spelling provides several alternatives. Some argue that it should be spelled postcolonialism with no hyphen between *post* and *colonialism*, whereas others insist on using the hyphen as in *post-colonialism*. Many of its adherents suggest there are two branches: those who view postcolonialism as a set of diverse methodologies that possess no unitary quality, as suggested by Homi Bhabha and Arun P. Murkerjee, and those who see postcolonialism as a set of cultural strategies centered in history. Even this latter group however, can be subdivided into two branches: those who believe postcolonialism refers to the period after the colonized societies or countries have become independent and those who regard postcolonialism as referring to all the characteristics of a society or culture from the time of colonization to the present.

However postcolonialism is defined, that it concerns itself with diverse and numerous issues becomes evident when we examine the various topics discussed in one of its most prominent texts, Ashcroft, Griffiths, and Tiffin's *The Post-Colonial Studies Reader* (1995). Such subjects include universality, difference, nationalism, postmodernism, representation and resistance, ethnicity, feminism, language, education, history, place, and production. As diverse as these topics appear, all of them draw attention to one of postcolonialism's major concerns: highlighting the struggle that occurs when one culture is dominated by another. As postcolonial critics are ever ready to point out, to be colonized is to be removed from history. In its interaction with the conquering culture, the colonized or indigenous culture is forced to go underground or to be obliterated.

Only after colonization occurs and the colonized people have had time to think and then to write about their oppression and loss of cultural identity does postcolonial theory come into existence. Born out of the colonized peoples' frustrations, their direct and personal cultural clashes with the conquering culture, and their fears, hopes, and dreams about the future and their own identities, postcolonial theory slowly emerges. How the colonized respond to changes in language, curricular matters in education, race differences, and a host of other discourses, including the act of writing, become the context and the theories of postcolonialism.

Because different cultures that have been subverted, conquered, and often removed from history will necessarily respond to the conquering culture in a variety of ways, no one approach to postcolonial theory, practice, or concerns is possible or even preferable. What all postcolonialist critics emphatically state, however, is that European colonialism did occur, that the British Empire was at the center of this colonialism, that the conquerors not only dominated the physical land but also the hegemony or ideology of the colonized people, and that the effects of these colonizations are many and are still being felt today.

An inherent tension exists at the center of post-colonial theory, for those who practice this theory and provide and develop its discourse are themselves a heterogeneous group of critics. On one hand, critics such as Fredric Jameson and Georg Gugelberger come from a European and American cultural, literary, and scholarly background. Another group that includes Gayatri Spivak, Edward Said, Homi K. Bhabha, and many others were raised in Third World cultures but now reside, study, and write in the West. And still another group that includes writers such as Aijaz Ahmad live and work in the Third World. A theoretical and a practical gap occurs between the theory and practice of those trained and living in the West and the Third World, subaltern writers living and writing in non-Western cultures. Out of such tension postcolonial theorists have and will continue to discover problematic topics for exploration and debate.

Although a number of postcolonial theorists and critics such as Frantz Fanon, Homi K. Bhabha, and Gayatri Chakravorty Spivak have contributed to postcolonialism's ever-growing body of theory and its practical methodology, the key text in the establishment of postcolonial theory is Edward W. Said's *Orientalism* (1978). In this text, Said chastises the literary world for not investigating and taking seriously the study of colonization or imperialism. According to Said, nineteenth-century Europeans tried to justify their territorial conquests by propagating a manufactured belief called Orientalism— the creation of non-European stereotypes that suggested "Orientals" were indolent, thoughtless, sexually immoral, unreliable, and demented. The European conquerors, Said notes, believed that they were accurately describing the inhabitants of their newly conquered land. What they failed to realize, maintains Said, is that all human knowledge can be viewed only through one's political, cultural, and ideological framework. No theory, either political or literary, can be totally objective.

That no political, social, or literary theory can be objective also holds true for a person living and writing in a colonized culture. Such an author must ask of himself or herself three questions: Who am I? How did I develop into the person that I am? To what country or countries or to what cultures am I forever linked? In asking the first question, the colonized author is connecting himself or herself to historical roots. By asking the second question, the author is admitting a tension between these historical roots and the new culture or hegemony imposed on the writer by the conquerors. And by asking the third question, the writer confronts the fact that he or she is both an individual and a social construct created and shaped by the dominant culture. And the writing penned by these authors will necessarily be personal and always political and ideological. Furthermore, its creation and its reading may also be painful, disturbing, and enlightening. Whatever the result, the story will certainly be a message sent back to the Empire, telling the Imperialists what they did wrong and how their Western hegemony damaged and suppressed the ideologies of those who were conquered.

Postcolonialism and African-American Criticism

The growing interest in postcolonialism in American literary theory during the late 1970s to the present provided a renewed interest in African-American writers and their works. To say that postcolonialism or other postmodern theories initiated African-American criticism and theory, however, would be incorrect. For the first seven decades of the twentieth century, African-American criticism was alive and well, its chief concern being the relationship between the arts (writing, music, theater, poetry, etc.) and a developing understanding of the nature of African-American culture. During this time, writers such as Langston Hughes (*Not Without Laughter, The Weary Blues*), Richard Wright (*Black Boy, Native Son*), Zora Neale Hurston (*Their Eyes Were Watching God, Dust Tracks on a Road*), James Baldwin (*Go Tell It on the Mountain, The First Next Time*), and Ralph Ellison (*The Invisible Man*), wrote texts depicting African-Americans interacting with their culture. In this body of literature, these subaltern writers concerned themselves mainly with issues of nationalism and helped to expose the treatment of African Americans—a suppressed, repressed, and colonized subculture—at the hands of their white conquerors. Presenting a variety of themes in their fiction, essays, and autobiographical writings, such as the African American's search for personal identity; the bitterness of the struggle of black men and women in America to achieve political, economic, and social success; and both mild and militant pictures of racial protest and hatred, these authors gave to America personal portraits of what it meant to be a black writer struggling with personal, cultural, and national identity.

Although literature authored by black writers was gaining in popularity, more often than not it was interpreted through the lens of the dominant culture, a lens that, for the most part, could see only one color: white. A black aesthetic had not yet been established, and critics and theorists alike applied the principles of Western metaphysics and Western hermeneutics to this ever-evolving and steadily increasing body of literature. Although theoretical and critical essays by W. E. B. DuBois, Langston Hughes, Richard Wright, and Ralph Ellison had begun to announce to America and the literary world that black literature was a distinctive literary practice with its own aesthetics and should not be dubbed a subcategory or a footnote of American literature, it was not until the late 1970s and 1980s that black theorists began to articulate the distinctiveness of African-American literature.

In this ever-increasing group of literary critics, two stand out: Abdul R. JanMohamed and Henry Louis Gates, Jr. The founding editor of *Cultural*

Critique, JanMohamed is one of the most influential postcolonial theorists. A professor of English at the University of California at Berkeley, JanMohamed has authored a variety of scholarly articles and texts that stress the interdisciplinary nature of literary criticism. Raised in Kenya (and therefore not considered by some to be an African American), JanMohamed witnessed first hand the British Imperialists' attempt to dominate and eliminate the colonized culture. He has thus spent his life studying the effects of colonization with its accompanying economic and social dynamics, concerning both the conqueror and the conquered. Of particular importance is his text *Manichean Aesthetics: The Politics of Literature in Colonial Africa* (1983). In this work, JanMohamed argues that literature authored by the colonized (Africans in Kenya and African-Americans in America, for example) is more interesting for its **noematic** value—the complexities of the world it reveals— than its **noetic** or subjective approach to what it perceives. Consequently, JanMohamed delineates the antagonistic relationship that develops between a hegemonic and a nonhegemonic literature. In African-American literature, for example, he notes that black writers such as Richard Wright and Frederick Douglass were shaped by their personal socioeconomic conditions. At some point in their development as writers and as people who were on the archetypal journal of self-realization, these writers became "agents of resistance" and were no longer willing to "consent" to the hegemonic culture. According to JanMohamed, subaltern writers, at some time, resist being shaped by their oppressors and become literary agents of change. It is this process of change from passive observers to resistors that forms the basis of JanMohamed's aesthetics.

Perhaps the most important and leading African-American theorist, however, is Henry Louis Gates, Jr. Unlike many African-American writers and critics, Gates directs much of his attention to other African-American critics, declaring that they and he "must redefine 'theory' itself from within [their] own black cultures, refusing to grant the premise that theory is something that white people do. . . .We are all heirs to critical theory, but we black critics are heir to the black vernacular as well" ("Authority, [White] Power, and the [Black] Critic," 344). Accordingly, Gates attempts to provide a theoretical framework for developing a specifically African-American literary canon. In this new framework, he insists that African-American literature be viewed as a form of language, not a representation of social practices or culture. For black literary criticism to develop, he contends that its principles must be derived from the black tradition itself and must include what he calls "the language of blackness, the signifying difference which makes the black tradition our very own." In his texts *The Signifying Monkey* (1988) and *Figures in Black: Words, Signs, and the "Racial" Self* (1987), Gates develops these ideas and announces the "double-voicedness" of African-American literature— that is, African-American literature draws on two voices and cultures, the white and the black. It is the joining of these two discourses, Gates declares, that produces the uniqueness of African-American literature.

Along with other theorists such as Houston Baker and a host of African-American feminist critics, present-day African-American critics believe that they must develop a culturally specific theory of African-American literature. Theirs, they believe, is a significant discourse that has for too long been neglected. The study of this body of literature, they insist, must be reformed. The beginnings of this reformation have brought to the foreground another body of literature that has also been ignored or at least relegated to second-class citizenship: the writings of females with its accompanying literary theory, gender studies.

GENDER STUDIES: NEW DIRECTIONS IN FEMINISM

What do Toni Morrison, Alice Walker, and Gloria Naylor have in common? All are African-American women writers who have successfully bridged the gap between subaltern authors and the dominant culture. Each has achieved a place of prominence in American culture, with Toni Morrison winning the Nobel Prize for Literature in 1993. Thanks, at least in part, to an increasing interest in postcolonial literature, these female authors have bridged not only the cultural but also the gender gap. As models for other women, these writers have found their voice in a society dominated by males and Western metaphysics, and their works have become seminal texts in feminist and gender studies.

Concerned primarily with feminist theories of literature and criticism and sometimes used synonymously with feminism or feminist theories (see Chapter 8 for an explanation of feminist theories and practice), gender studies broadens traditional feminist criticism to include an investigation not only of femaleness but also maleness. What does it mean, it asks, to be a woman or a man? Like traditional feminist theory, gender studies continues to investigate how women and men view such terms as *ethics*, definitions of truth, personal identity, and society. Is it possible, gender specialists question, that women view each of these differently than men?

Into the multivoiced feminist theories, gender studies adds the ever-growing and ever-diverse voices of black feminists, the ongoing concerns of French feminism, and the impact of poststructural theories on customary feminist issues. Its authors include the almost canonical status of writers such as Adrienne Rich, Bonnie Zimmerman, and Barbara Smith, along with those of Elaine Showalter, Sandra Gilbert, Susan Gubar, Gayatri Chakravorty Spivak, and Toril Moi. But new authors and critics such as Yvvonne Vera, Anne McClintlock, Sara Suleri, Dorothea Drummond Mbalia, and Sara Mills also appear, asking and adding their own unique questions to feminist theory.

Striving to develop a philosophical basis of feminist literary theory, gender studies re-examines the canon and questions traditional definitions of the family, sexuality, and female reproduction. In addition, it continues to articulate and investigate the nature of feminine writing itself. And it joins feminist scholarship with postcolonial discourses, noting that postcolonial literature and feminist writings share many characteristics, the chief being that both are examples of oppressed peoples.

As with feminist theory, the goal of gender studies is to analyze and challenge the established literary canon. Women themselves, gender specialists assert, must challenge the hegemony and free themselves from the false assumptions and the long-held prejudices that have prevented them from defining themselves. By involving themselves in literary theory and its accompanying practices, gender specialists believe women and men alike can redefine who they are, what they want to be, and where they want to go.

SAMPLE ESSAY

In the professional essay that follows, note how Peter Hulme uses the principles and theories of postcolonialism to arrive at his conclusions. After carefully reading this article, be able to cite the postcolonial terms, interests, and theories that Hulme uses. Do you agree or disagree with Hulme's analysis? Be able to defend your position.

FURTHER READING

Adam, Ian, and Helen Tiffin, eds. *Past the Long Post: Theorizing Post-Colonialism and Post-Modernism*. Hemel Hempstead, London: Harvester Wheatsheaf, 1991.

Ashcroft, Bill, Gareth Griffiths, and Helen Tiffin. *The Empire Writes Back: Theory and Practice in Post-Colonial Literatures*. London: Routledge, 1989.

Ashcropt, Bill, Gareth Griffiths, and Helen Tiffin. *The Post-Colonial Studies Reader*. New York: Routledge, 1995.

Bhabha, Homi K., ed. *Nation and Narration*. New York: Routledge & Kegan Paul, 1990.

Fanon, Frantz. *The Wretched of the Earth*. Trans. Constance Farrington. New York: Grove, 1968.

Gates, Henry Louis Jr. *Figures in Black: Words, Signs, and the "Racial" Self*. Oxford: Oxford University Press, 1990.

———. *The Signifying Monkey: A Theory of African-American Literary Criticism*. New York: Oxford UP, 1988.

———. *Loose Canons: Notes on the Culture Wars*. New York: Oxford UP, 1992.

JanMohamed, Abdul R. *Manichean Aesthetics: The Politics of Literature in Colonial Africa*. Amherst: University of Massachusetts Press, 1983.

Niranjana, Tejaswine. *Sitting Translation: History, Post-Structuralism, and the Colonial Context*. Berkeley: University of California Press, 1990.

Rushdie, Salman. *Imaginary Homelands: Essays and Criticism, 1981–91*. London: Penguin, 1991.

Said, Edward. "Figures, Configurations, Transfigurations." *Race & Class* 1 (1990).
———. *Orientalism*. New York: Vintage, 1979.
Spivak, Gayatri Chakavorty. "The Making of Americans, the Teaching of English, and the Future of Culture Studies." *New Literary History* 21 (1990): 781–798.
Suleri, Sara. "Woman Skin Deep: Feminism and the Postcolonial Condition." *Critical Inquiry*, 18 (4) (Summer), 1992.
———. *The Rhetoric of English India*. Chicago: University of Chicago Press 1992.

WEB SITES FOR EXPLORATION

HTTP://www.stg.brown.edu/projects/hypertext/landow/post/poldiscourse/theorists.html
Includes discussions of eighteen postcolonial theorists
www.stg.brown.edu/projects/hypertext/landow/post/misc/postov.html
Includes links to postcolonial authors, history, politics, religion, theory, bibliographies, and gender matters.
www.ualberta.ca/~amatavi/gender.htm
Includes links to feminism and women's resources, men's issues, women's studies, gender studies, sexuality, and a host of other sites
www.stg.brown.edu/projects/hypertext/landow/post/gender/genderov.html
Provides an overview of gender theory and other critical concerns
www.tile.net/tile/listserv/amfalit.html
Provides a list serve originating from Kent State University with links to news groups and a variety of other souces concerning African-American literature
www.asu.edu/~meltro/aflit/christian/bib.html
Provides a detailed bibliography of African-American women authors, Black studies, and women's studies

∼ Professional Essay ∼

Columbus and the Cannibals

The primary *OED* definition of "cannibal" reads: "A man (*esp.* a savage) that eats human flesh; a man-eater, an anthropophagite. Originally proper name of the man-eating Caribs of the Antilles." The morphology or, to use the *OED*'s word, form-history of "cannibal" is rather more circumspect. The main part of its entry reads:

> (In 16th c. pl. *Canibales*, a. Sp. *Canibales*, originally one of the forms of the ethnic name *Carib* or *Caribes*, a fierce nation of the West Indies, who are recorded to have been anthropophagi, and from whom the name was subsequently extended as a descriptive term . . .)

This is a "true" account of the morphology of the word "cannibal" in English, yet it is also an ideological account that functions to repress important historical questions about the use of the term—its discursive morphology, perhaps, rather than its linguistic morphology. The trace of that repression is the phrase "who are recorded to have been," which hides beneath its blandness—the passive tense, the absence (in a book of authorities) of any ultimate authority, the assumption of impartial and accurate observation—a different history altogether.

The tone of "who are recorded to have been" suggests a nineteenth-century ethnographer sitting in the shade with notebook and pencil, calmly recording the savage rituals being performed in front of him. However unacceptable that might now seem as "objective reporting," it still appears a model of simplicity compared with the complexities of the passages that constitute the record in this instance.

On 23 November 1492 Christopher Columbus approached an island "which those Indians whom he had with him called 'Bohio.'" According to Columbus's *Journal* these Indians, usually referred to as Arawaks:

> said that this land was very extensive and that in it were people who had one eye in the forehead, and others whom they called "canibals." Of these last, they showed great fear, and when they saw that this course was being taken, they were speechless, he says, because these people ate them and because they are very warlike. (Columbus [1825] 1960 68-9)

This is the first appearance of the word "canibales" in a European text, and it is linked immediately with the practice of eating human flesh. The *Journal* is, therefore, in some sense at least, a "beginning text."

But in just what sense is that name and that ascription a "record" of anything? For a start the actual text on which we presume Columbus to have inscribed that name disappeared, along with its only known copy, in the middle of the sixteenth century. The only version we have, and from which the above quotation is taken, is a handwritten abstract made by Bartolome de Las Casas, probably in 1552, and probably from the copy of Columbus's original then held in the monastery of San Pablo in Seville. There have subsequently been various transcriptions of Las Casas's manuscript. So the apparent transparency of "who are recorded to have been" is quickly made opaque by the thickening layers of language: a transcription of abstract of a copy of a lost original. This is chastening, but to some extent contingent. More telling is what might be called the internal opacity of the statement. Columbus's "record," far from being an observation that those people called "canibales" ate other people, is a report of other people's words; moreover, words spoken in a language of which he had no prior knowledge and, at best, six weeks' practice in trying to understand.

Around this passage cluster a whole host of ethnographic and linguistic questions. . . . But the general argument here will be that, though important, these questions take second place to the textual and discursive questions. What first needs examination, in other words, are not isolated passages taken as evidence for this or that, but rather the larger units of text and discourse, without which no meaning would be possible at all.

To write about the text we call "el diario de Colón" (Columbus's journal) is to take a leap of faith, to presume that the transcription of the manuscript of the abstract of the copy of the original stands in some kind of meaningful relationship to the historical reality of Columbus's voyage across the Atlantic and down through the Caribbean islands during the winter months of 1492–3.

It would be perverse and unhelpful to presume that no such relationship exists, but credulous and unthinking to speak—as some have done—of the *Journal's* "frank words, genuine and unadorned." Circumspection would certainly seem called for. Yet if the *Journal* is taken not as a privileged eyewitness document of the discovery, nor as an accurate ethnographic record, but rather as the first fable of European beginnings in America, then its complex textual history and slightly dubious status become less important than the incredible narrative it unfolds.

This is not an argument in favour of somehow lifting Columbus and his *Journal* out of history. . . . But it is an argument in favour of bracketing particular questions of historical accuracy and reliability in order to see the text whole, to gauge the structure of its narrative, and to chart the interplay of its linguistic registers and rhetorical modalities. To read the *Journal* in this way is also to defer the biographical questions: the Columbus of whom we speak is for the moment a textual function, the "I" of the *Journal* who is occasionally, and scandalously, transformed into the third person by the intervention of the transcriber's "I."

The *Journal* is generically peculiar. It is in part a log-book, and throughout records the navigational details of Columbus's voyage. Commentators have usually accepted that it was written up almost every evening of the six-and-a-half-month journey, not revised or rewritten, and not constructed with a view to publication. It certainly gives that impression, which is all that matters here: Columbus is presented by the *Journal* as responding day by day to the stimulus of new challenges and problems. Yet if its generic shape is nautical the *Journal* is also by turns a personal memoir, an ethnographic notebook, and a compendium of European fantasies about the Orient: a veritable palimpsest.

"From whom the name was subsequently extended as a descriptive term." Linguistic morphology is concerned only with the connection made between the term "cannibal" and the practice of eating human flesh. We have seen how the very first mention of that term in a European text is glossed with reference to that practice, and for the linguist it is satisfactory, but not of intrinsic interest, to note how that reference is always present, either implicitly or explicitly, in any recorded use of the word "cannibal" from Columbus's on 23 November 1492 onwards. It was adopted into the bosom of the European family of languages with a speed and readiness which suggests that there had always been an empty place kept warm for it. Poor "anthropophagy," if not exactly orphaned, was sent out into the cold until finding belated lodging in the nineteenth century within new disciplines seeking authority from the deployment of classical terminology.

All of which makes it even stranger that the context of that beginning passage immediately puts the association between the word "cannibal" and the eating of human flesh into doubt. Las Casas continues:

> The admiral says that he well believes that there is something in this, but that since they were well armed, they must be an intelligent people [gente de razon], and he believed that they may have captured some men and that, because they did not return to their own land, they would say that they were eaten. (Columbus 1960: 69)

This passage is of no interest to linguistic morphology since Columbus's scepticism failed to impinge upon the history of the word. Ethnographically it would probably be of scant interest, showing merely Columbus's initial scepticism, and therefore making him a more reliable witness in the end. Even from the point of view of a revisionist ethnography that wanted to discount suggestions of native anthropophagy the passage could only be seen as evidence of the momentary voice of European reason soon to be deafened by the persistence of Arawak defamations of their traditional enemy. Attention to the discursive complexities of the text will suggest a different reading. The great paradox of Columbus's *Journal* is that although the voyage of 1492–3 was to have such a devastating and long-lasting effect on both Europe and America, and is still celebrated as one of the outstanding achievements of humanity, the record itself tells of misunderstandings, failures and disappointments. The greatest of these—that he had not reached Asia—was too overwhelming for Columbus ever to accept. The minor ones are in some ways even more telling. . . .

In brief, what a symptomatic reading of the *Journal* reveals is the presence of two distinct discursive networks. In bold outline each discourse can be identified by the presence of key words: in one case "gold," "Cathay," "Grand Khan," "intelligent soldiers," "large buildings," "merchant ships"; in the other "gold," "savagery," "monstrosity," "anthropophagy." Even more boldly, each discourse can be traced to a single textual origin, Marco Polo and Herodotus respectively. More circumspectly, there is what might be called a discourse of Oriental civilization and a discourse of savagery, both archives of topics and motifs that can be traced back to the classical period. It is tempting to say that the first was based on empirical knowledge and the second on psychic projection, but that would be a false dichotomy. There was no doubt a material reality—the trade that had taken place between Europe and the Far East over many centuries, if intermittently. In pursuit of, or as an outcome of, this trade there were Europeans who travelled to the Far

East, but their words are in no way a simple reflection of "what they saw." For that reason it is better to speak of identifiable discourses. There was a panoply of words and phrases used to speak about the Orient: most concerned its wealth and power, as well they might since Europe had for many years been sending east large amounts of gold and silver. Marco Polo's account was the best known deployment of these topoi. The discourse savagery had in fact changed little since Herodotus's "investigation" of Greece's "barbarian" neighbors. The locations moved but the descriptions of Amazons, Anthropophagi and Cynocephali remained constant throughout Ctesias, Pliny, Solinus and many others. This discourse was hegemonic in the sense that it provided a popular vocabulary for constituting "otherness" and was not dependent on *texual* reproduction. Textual authority was however available to Columbus in Pierre d'Ailly and Aeneas Sylvius, and indeed in the text that we know as "Marco Polo," but which is properly *Divisament dou Monde*, authored by a writer of romances in French, and itself already an unravellable discursive network.

In the early weeks of the Columbian voyage it is possible to see a certain jockeying for position between these two discourses, but no overt conflict. The relationship between them is expressed as that between present and future: this is a world of savagery, over there we will find Cathay. But there are two potential sites of conflict, one conscious—in the sense of being present in the text; the other unconscious—in the sense that it is present only in its absence and must be reconstructed from the traces it leaves. The conscious conflict is that two elements, "the soldiers of the Grand Khan" from the discourse of Marco Polo and "the maneating savages" from the discourse of Herodotus, are competing for a single signifier—the word "canibales." Columbus's wavering on 23 November belongs to a larger pattern of references in which "canibal" is consistently glossed by his native hosts as "maneater" while it ineluctably calls to his mind "el Gran Can." In various entries the phonemes echo each other from several lines' distance until on 11 December 1492 they finally coincide:

> it appears likely that they are harassed by an intelligent race, all these islands living in great fear of those of Caniba. "And so I repeat what I have said on other-occasions," he says, "the Caniba are nothing else than the people of the Grand Khan [*que Caniba no es otra cosa sino la gente del Gran Can*], who must be very near here and possess ships, and they must come to take them captive, and as the prisoners do not return, they believe that they have been eaten." (Columbus 1960: 92-3)

The two "Can" are identified as one, the crucial identification is backdated, and "canibal" as man-eater must simply disappear having no reference to attach itself to.

Except of course that it does not disappear at all. That would be too easy. In fact the assertion of the identity of "Caniba" with "gente del Can," so far from marking the victory of the Oriental discourse, signals its very defeat; as if the crucial phonetic evidence could only be brought to texual presence once its power to control action had faded.

Essay by Peter Hume. *Colonial Encounters: Europe and the Native Carribean 1492–1797*. London. Methuen, 1986.

An Overview of the Schools of Literary Criticism

School of Criticism	No. of Correct Interpretations Per Text	Place Where Meaning Ultimately Resides	Truth and Values	Goal	Evaluation of Critic
New Criticism	one	text alone	text reveals truth	organic unity	elitist
Reader-Response	many	reader + text	reader and text create truth	reader's reaction	not elitist
Structuralism	many	mainly text	no referential truth in text	structural relationships	not elitist
Deconstruction	many	intertextuality	truth is relative	incongruity	not elitist
Psychoanalytic	many	text, author, and reader	texts reveal the author's truth and truth about the author	motivation of author and response of reader	not elitist
Feminism	many	text, author, and reader	text reveals author's views on women	discovery of woman in text and text in the woman; response of female reader	not elitist
Marxism	many	text, history, and ideology	text reveals oppression and class conflict and promotes socialism	the exposure of ideology and calls for revolution	not elitist
New Historicism	many	intertextuality	truth is relative	blurring the boundaries between literature and history	not elitist
Postcolonialism	many	intertextuality	truth is relative	shows oppression of colonized peoples	not elitist

References

CHAPTER 1

Beardsley, Monroe C., Robert W. Daniel, and Glenn H. Leggett. *Theme and Form: An Introduction to Literature.* Englewood Cliffs, NJ: Prentice-Hall, 1969.

Daiches, David. *Critical Approaches to Literature.* New York: Longman, 1981.

Danziger, Marlies, and W. Stacy Johnson. *An Introduction to Literary Criticism.* Boston: D.C. Heath, 1961.

Eagleton, Terry. *Literary Theory: An Introduction.* Minneapolis: U of Minnesota P, 1983.

Grebanier, Bernard. *The Enjoyment of Literature.* New York: Crown, 1975.

Holman, C. Hugh, and William Harmon. *A Handbook to Literature.* 6th ed. New York: Macmillan, 1992.

Lentricchia, Frank, and Thomas McLaughlin, eds. *Critical Terms for Literary Study.* Chicago: U of Chicago P, 1990.

Rosenblatt, Louise M. The *Reader, the Text, the Poem: The Transactional Theory of the Literary Work.* Carbondale: Southern Illinois UP, 1978.

Sire, James W. *The Joy of Reading: A Guide to Becoming a Better Reader.* Portland, OR: Multnomah, 1978.

———. *The Universe Next Door.* 2nd ed. Downers Grove, IL: InterVarsity, 1988.

Staton, Shirley F., ed. *Literary Theories in Praxis.* Philadelphia: U of Pennsylvania P, 1987.

Stevens, Bonnie, and Larry Stewart. *A Guide to Literary Criticism and Research.* Fort Worth: Holt, 1992.

Twain, Mark. *The Adventures of Huckleberry Finn.* New York: Harcourt, 1961.

CHAPTER 2

Alighieri, Dante. *Eleven Letters.* Trans. Charles Sterret Latham. Boston: Houghton, 1892.

———. *The Divine Comedy.* Trans. Charles S. Singleton. Princeton, NJ: Princeton UP, 1975.

Aristotle. *Poetics.* Trans. Ingram Bywater. *On the Art of Poetry.* Oxford, UK: Clarendon, 1920.

———. *Poetics.* Trans. Leon Golden. Englewood Cliffs, NJ: Prentice-Hall, 1968.

Arnold, Matthew. *Essays in Criticism: First Series.* New York: Macmillan, 1895.

Auerbach, Erich. *Dante: Poet of the Secular World.* Trans. R. Manheim. Chicago: Chicago UP, 1961.

Bate, Walter J. *From Classic to Romantic*. Cambridge, MA: Harvard UP, 1946.

Bradley, A. C. *Oxford Lectures on Poetry*. London: Macmillan, 1909.

Brody, Jules. *Boileau and Longinus*. Geneva: Droz, 1953.

Butcher, S. H. *Aristotle's Theory of Poetry and Fine Art*. 3rd ed. London: Macmillan, 1902.

Casey, John. *The Language of Criticism*. London: Methuen, 1960.

Clubbe, John, and Ernest J. Lovell. *English Romanticism: The Grounds of Belief*. London: Macmillan, 1983.

Cooper, Lane. *The Poetics of Aristotle: Its Meaning and Influence*. New York: Cooper Square, 1963.

D'Alton, J. F. *Horace and His Age*. London: Longman Green, 1917.

Daugerty, Sandi B. *The Literary Criticism of Henry James*. Athens: Ohio UP, 1981.

Devereux, James A. "The Meaning of Delight in Sidney's Defense of Poesy." *Studies in the Literary Imagination* 15 (1982): 85–97.

Eliot, T. S. *John Dryden: The Poet, the Dramatist, the Critic. Three Essays*. New York: Haskell House, 1966.

Ells, John Shepard. *The Touchstones of Matthew Arnold*. New York: Bookman Associates, 1955.

Else, Gerald F. *Aristotle's Poetics: The Argument*. Cambridge, MA: Harvard UP, 1957.

———. *Plato and Aristotle on Poetry*. Chapel Hill: U of North Carolina P, 1986.

Fenner, Arthur, Jr. "The Unity of Pope's Essay on Criticism." *Philological Quarterly* 39 (1960): 435–56.

Fergusson, Francis. "On the Poetics." *Tulane Drama Review* 4 (1960): 23–32.

Garrod, Deathcote William. *Poetry and the Criticism of Life*. New York: Russell, 1963.

Goad, Caroline. *Horace in the English Literature of the Eighteenth Century*. New Haven: Yale UP, 1918.

Griffin, Dustin. *Alexander Pope: The Poet in the Poems*. Princeton, NJ: Princeton UP, 1978.

Grube, G. M. *Plato's Thought*. London: Methuen, 1935.

Hamilton, Paul. *Coleridge's Poetics*. Oxford, UK: Blackwell, 1983.

Henn, T. R. *Longinus and English Criticism*. Cambridge, MA: Cambridge UP, 1934.

Herrick, Marvin T. *The Fusion of Horatian and Aristotelian Literary Criticism*. Urbana: U of Illinois P, 1946.

Hill, John Spencer, ed. *The Romantic Imagination: A Casebook*. London: Macmillan, 1977.

Hirsch, E. D. *Wordsworth and Schelling*. New Haven, CT: Yale UP, 1950.

Hollander, R. *Allegory in Dante's Commedia*. Princeton, NJ: Princeton UP, 1969.

Hughes, Herbert Leland. *Theory and Practice in Henry James*. Ann Arbor, MI: Edwards, 1926.

Hume, Robert D. *Dryden's Criticism*. Ithaca, NY: Cornell UP, 1970.

James, Henry. *The Art of the Novel: Critical Prefaces*. Introduction by R. P. Blackmur. New York: Scribner, 1932.

Jones, Henry John. *The Egotistical Sublime: A History of Wordsworth's Imagination*. London: Chatto & Windus, 1970.

Lanser, Susan S. *The Narrative Act: Point of View in Prose Fiction*. Princeton, NJ: Princeton UP, 1981.

Lodge, Rupert C. *Plato's Theory of Art*. New York: Humanities Press, 1953.

Mason, H. A. "An Introduction to Literary Criticism by Way of Sidney's Apology for Poetrie." *Cambridge Quarterly* 12. 2–3 (1984): 79–173.

Mishra, J. B. *John Dryden: His Theory and Practice of Drama*. New Delhi: Bahir, 1978.

Modrak, Deborah. *Aristotle: The Power of Perception*. Chicago: U of Chicago P, 1987.

Monk, S. *The Sublime: A Study of Critical Theories in XVIII-Century England*. Ann Arbor: U of Michigan P, 1960.

Olson, Elder. *Aristotle's Poetics and English Literature*. Chicago: U of Chicago P, 1965.

———. "The Argument of Longinus's On the Sublime." *On Value Judgments in the Arts and Other Essays*. Chicago: U of Chicago P, 1976.

Owen, W. J. B. *Wordsworth as Critic*. Toronto: Toronto UP, 1971.

Pechter, E. *Dryden's Classical Theory of Literature*. London: Cambridge UP, 1975.

Perkins, David. "Arnold and the Function of Literature." *ELH* 18 (1951): 287–309.

Plato. *The Republic*. Trans. B. Jowett. 3rd ed. Oxford, UK: Clarendon, 1888.

Roberts, Morris. *Henry James's Criticism*. Cambridge, MA: Harvard UP, 1929.

Robinson, Forrest Glen. *The Shape of Things Known: Sidney's Apology in Its Philosophical Tradition*. Cambridge, MA: Harvard UP, 1972.

Rollinson, Philip. *Classical Theories of Allegory and Christian Culture*. Pittsburgh: Duquesne UP, 1981.

Russell, D. A., ed. *"Longinus" on the Sublime*. Oxford, UK: Clarendon, 1964.

Sharma, L. S. *Coleridge: His Contribution to English Criticism*. New Delhi: Arnold-Heinemann, 1981.

Shorey, Paul. *What Plato Said*. Chicago: U of Chicago P, 1933.

Singleton, Charles S. *Dante Studies*. 2 vols. Cambridge, MA: Harvard UP, 1958.

Smith, Nowell C., ed. *Wordsworth's Literary Criticism*. Bristol, England: Bristol Classical P, 1980.

Stack, Frank. *Pope and Horace: Studies in Imitation*. New York: Cambridge UP, 1985.

Taine, Hippolyte A. *The History of English Literature*. 4 vols. Trans. H. Van Laun. Philadelphia: David McKay, 1908.

Taylor, A. E. *Plato*. Ann Arbor: U of Michigan P, 1960.

Thorpe, C. D. "Coleridge as Aesthetician and Critic." *Journal of the History of Ideas* 1 (1944): 387–414.

Trilling, Lionel. *Matthew Arnold*. New York: Norton, 1939.

Warren, Austin. *English Poetic Thenjo 1825–1865*. Princeton, NJ: Princeton UP, 1950. *Pope as Critic and Humanist*. Princeton, NJ: Princeton UP, 1929.

———. *Alexander Pope as Critic and Humanist*. Princeton, NJ: Princeton UP, 1963.

Watson, George. *John Dryden: Of Dramatic Poesy and Other Critical Essays*. 2 vols. London: J. Dent, 1962.

Wood, Allen G. *Literary Satire and Theory: A Study of Horace, Boileau, and Pope*. New York: Garland, 1985.

CHAPTER 3

Bagwell, J. Timothy. *American Formalism and the Problem of Interpretation*. Houston: Rice UP, 1986.

Brooks, Cleanth. *Modern Poetry and the Tradition*. Chapel Hill: U of North Carolina P, 1939.

———. *The Well-Thought Urn: Studies in the Structure of Poetry*. New York: Harcourt, 1947.

———. "My Credo: Formalist Critics." *Kenyon Review* 13 (1951): 72–81.

———. "In Search of the New Criticism." *American Scholar* 53 (Winter 1983/84): 41–53.

Brooks, Cleanth, and Robert B. Heilman. *Understanding Drama: Twelve Plays*. New York: Holt, 1948.

Brooks, Cleanth, and Robert Penn Warren. *Understanding Poetry: An Anthology for College Students*. New York: Holt, 1939.

Cain, William E. *The Crisis in Criticism: Theory, Literature, and Reform in English Studies.* Baltimore: Johns Hopkins UP, 1984.

Eliot, T. S. "Tradition and the Individual Talent." *The Sacred Wood.* London: Methuen, 1928.

———. "The Function of Criticism." *Selected Essays.* New York: Harcourt, 1950.

———. *Notes Towards the Definition of Culture.* London: Faber, 1965.

Elton, William. *Seven Types of Ambiguity.* New York: Noonday Press, 1958.

Empson, William. *A Glossary of the New Criticism.* Chicago: Modern Poetry Association, 1949.

Handy, William J. *Kant and the Southern New Critics.* Austin: U of Texas P, 1963.

Jancovich, Mark. *The Cultural Politics of the New Criticism.* Cambridge, MA: Cambridge UP, 1993.

Krieger, Murray. *The New Apologists for Poetry.* Minneapolis: U of Minnesota P, 1956.

Lentricchia, Frank. *After the New Criticism.* Chicago: U of Chicago P, 1980.

Patnaik, J. N. *The Aesthetics of the New Criticism.* New Delhi: Intellectual Publishing House, 1982.

Ransom, John Crowe. *The New Criticism.* New York: New Directions, 1941.

———. *The World's Body. 1938.* Baton Rouge: Louisiana State UP, 1968.

———. *Beating the Bushes: Selected Essays: 1941–1970.* New York: New Directions, 1972.

Richards, I. A. Principles of Literary Criticism. New York: Harcourt, 1924.

———. *Practical Criticism.* New York: Harcourt, 1929.

Schiller, Jerome P. *I. A. Richards' Theory of Literature.* New Haven, CT: Yale UP, 1969.

Schorer, Mark. "Technique as Discovery." *Hudson Review* 1 (Spring 1948): 67–87.

Simpson, Lewis P., ed. *The Possibilities of Order: Cleanth Brooks and His Work.* Baton Rouge: Louisiana State UP, 1976.

Tate, Allen. *Reason in Madness.* New York: Putnam, 1941.

———. "What I Owe to Cleanth Brooks" in *The Possibilities of Order: Cleanth Brooks and His Work,* Lewis P. Simpson, ed. Baton Rouge: Louisiana State UP, 1976.

Warren, Robert Penn. "Pure and Impure Poetry," *Kenyon Review* 5 (Spring 1943): 229–54.

Wellek, René. "The New Criticism: Pro and Contra." *Critical Inquiry* 4 (Summer 1978): 611–24.

Wellek, René, and Austin Warren. *Theory of Literature. 1942.* San Diego: Harcourt Brace Jovanovich, 1977.

Wimsatt, W. K. *The Verbal Icon.* Lexington: U of Kentucky P, 1954.

Wimsatt, W. K. Jr., and Monroe Beardsley. "The Affective Fallacy" in *The Verbal Icon: Studies in the Meaning of Poetry,* W. K. Wimsatt Jr., ed. Lexington: U of Kentucky P, 1954, pp. 21–39.

Wimsatt, W. K. Jr., and Cleanth Brooks. *Literary Criticism: A Short History.* New York: Knopf, 1957.

Winters, Yvor. *In Defense of Reason.* Denver: Swallow, 1947.

CHAPTER 4

Barthes, Roland. "From Work to Text." *The Rustle of Language.* Berkeley: U of California P, 1989.

Bleich, David. *Readings and Feelings: An Introduction to Subjective Criticism.* New York: Harper, 1977.

————. *Subjective Criticism*. Baltimore: Johns Hopkins UP, 1978.

Booth, Stephen. "On the Value of *Hamlet*," in *Reinterpretations of Elizabethan Drama*, Norman Rabkin, ed. New York: Columbia UP, 1969, pp. 77–99.

Booth, Wayne C. *The Rhetoric of Fiction*. Chicago: U of Chicago P, 1978.

Eco, Umberto. *The Role of the Reader: Explorations in the Semiotics of Texts*. Bloomington: Indiana UP, 1979.

Fish, Stanley E. "Literature in the Reader: Affective Stylistics." *New Literary History* 2 (1970): 123–61.

————. *Self-Consuming Artifacts: The Experience of Seventeenth-Century Literature*. Berkeley: U of California P, 1972.

————. *Is There a Text in This Class? The Authority of Interpretive Communities*. Cambridge, MA: Harvard UP, 1980.

Freund, Elizabeth. The *Return of the Reader: Reader-Response Criticism*. New York: Methuen, 1987.

Holland, Norman N. *The Dynamics of Literary Response*. New York: Oxford UP, 1968.

————. *Poems in Persons: An Introduction to the Psychoanalysis of Literature*. New York: Norton, 1973.

————. "Unity, Identity, Text, Self." *PMLA* 90 (1975): 813–22.

————. *Holland's Guide to Psychoanalytic Psychology and Literature-and-Psychology*. Oxford, UK: Oxford UP, 1990.

————. "A *Portrait* as Rebellion: A Reader-Response Perspective." In *"A Portrait of the Artist as a Young Man": Complete, Authoritative Text with Biographical and Historical Contexts, Critical History, and Essays from Five Contemporary Critical Perspectives*, R. B. Kershner, ed. Boston: Bedford Books-St. Martin's, 1993, pp. 279–94.

Holub, Robert C. *Reception Theory: A Critical Introduction*. New York: Methuen, 1984.

Iser, Wolfgang. *The Implied Reader: Patterns of Communication in Prose Fiction from Bunyan to Beckett*. Baltimore: Johns Hopkins UP, 1974.

————. *The Act of Reading. A Theory of Aesthetic Response*. Baltimore: Johns Hopkins UP, 1978.

————. *Prospecting: From Reader Response to Literary Anthropology*. Baltimore: Johns Hopkins UP, 1989.

Jauss, Hans Robert. *Aesthetic Experience and Literary Hermeneutics*. Minneapolis: U of Minnesota P, 1982.

Mailloux, Steven. "Reader-Response Criticism?" *Genre* 10 (1977): 413–31.

————. "Learning to Read: Interpretation and Reader-Response Criticism." *Studies in the Literary Imagination* 12 (1979): 93–108.

————. *Interpretive Conventions: The Reader in the Study of American Fiction*. Ithaca, NY: Cornell UP, 1982.

Ong, Walter S. J. *Orality and Literacy*. New York: Methuen, 1982.

Prince, Gerald. "Introduction to the Study of the Naratee," in *Reader-Response Criticism: From Formalism to Post-Structuralism*, Jane O. Tompkins, ed. Baltimore: Johns Hopkins UP, 1980, pp. 177–96.

"Reading Interpretation, Response." Special section of *Genre* 10 (1977): 363–453.

Rosenblatt, Louise M. "Towards a Transactional Theory of Reading." *Journal of Reading Behavior* 1 (1969): 31–47.

Suleiman, Susan R., and Inge Crosman, eds. *The Reader in the Text: Essays on Audience and Interpretation*. Princeton, NJ: Princeton UP, 1980.

CHAPTER 5

Bannet, Eve Tavor. *Structuralism and the Logic of Dissent.* Chicago: U of Illinois P, 1989.

Barthes, Roland. *Elements of Semiology.* Trans. A. Lavers and C. Smith. London: Cape, 1967.

———. *S/Z.* Trans. R. Miller. New York: Hill & Wang, 1971.

———. *Critical Essays.* Trans. R. Howard. Evanston, IL: Northwestern UP, 1972.

———. *Selected Writings.* Intro by Susan Sontag. London: Fontana, 1983.

Blonsky, Marshall, ed. *On Signs.* Baltimore: Johns Hopkins UP, 1985.

Connor, Steven. "Structuralism and Post-structuralism: From the Centre to the Margin" in *Encyclopedia of Literature and Criticism,* Martin Coyle, Peter Garside, Malcolm Kelsall, and John Peck, eds. London: Routledge, 1990.

Crystal, David. *A Dictionary of Linguistics and Phonetics.* 2nd ed. Cambridge, MA: Basil Blackwell, 1985.

Culler, Jonathan. *Structuralist Poetics: Structuralism, Linguistics and the Study of Literature.* London: Routledge, 1975.

———. *Ferdinand de Saussure.* Baltimore: Penguin, 1976.

———. *The Pursuit of Signs: Semiotics, Literature, Deconstruction.* Ithaca, NY: Cornell UP, 1981.

De George, Richard T., and M. Fernande, eds. *The Structuralists from Marx to Lévi-Strauss.* Garden City, NY: Doubleday, 1972.

Detweiler, Robert. *Story, Sign, and Self: Phenomenology and Structuralism as Literary Critical Methods.* Philadelphia: Fortress, 1978.

Ehrmann, Jacques, ed. *Structuralism.* Garden City, NY: Doubleday, 1970.

Genette, Gerard. *Narrative Discourse.* Oxford, UK: Blackwell, 1980.

Hawkes, Terence. *Structuralism and Semiotics.* London: Methuen, 1977.

Innes, Robert E., ed. *Semiotics: An Introductory Reader.* London: Hutchinson, 1986.

Jakobson, Roman. *Fundamentals of Language.* Paris: Mouton, 1975.

Jameson, Fredric. *The Prison-House of Language: A Critical Account of Structuralism and Russian Formalism.* Princeton, NJ: Princeton UP, 1972.

Krieger, Murray, and L. S. Dembo, eds. *Directions for Criticism: Structuralism and Its Alternatives.* Madison: U of Wisconsin P, 1977.

Lane, Michael, ed. *Introduction to Structuralism.* New York: Harper, 1972.

Lévi-Strauss, Claude. *Structural Anthropology.* Trans. C. Jacobson and B. G. Schoepf. London: Allen Lanne, 1968.

Lodge, David. *Working with Structuralism: Essays and Reviews on Nineteenth-and Twentieth-Century Literature.* Boston: Routledge & Kegan Paul, 1981.

———. *Working with Structuralism.* London: Routledge, 1986.

Macksey, Richard, and Eugenio Donato, eds. *The Structuralist Controversy.* Baltimore: Johns Hopkins UP, 1970.

Prince, Gerald. *Narratology: The Form and Functioning of Narrative.* New York: Mouton, 1982.

Propp, Vladimir. *The Morphology of the Folktale.* Austin: Texas UP, 1968.

Robey, David, ed. *Structuralism: An Introduction.* Oxford, UK: Clarendon, 1973.

Saussure, Ferdinand de. *Course in General Linguistics.* Trans. W. Baskin. London: Collino, 1974.

Scholes, Robert. *Structuralism in Literature: An Introduction.* New Haven: Yale UP, 1974.

———. *Semiotics and Interpretation.* New Haven, CT: Yale UP, 1982.

Sturrock, John. *Structuralism and Since*. New York: Oxford UP, 1979.

Selz, Dorothy B. "Structuralism for the Non-Specialist: A Glossary and a Bibliography." *College English* 37 (1975): 160–66.

Tatham, Campbell. "Beyond Structuralism." *Genre* 10. no. 1 (1977):131–55.

Todorov, Tzvetan. *The Fantastic: A Structural Approach to a Literary Genre*. Ithaca, NY: Cornell UP, 1973.

———. *The Poetics of Prose*. Trans. Richard Howard. Ithaca, NY: Cornell UP, 1977. Includes "The Typology of Detective Fiction."

CHAPTER 6

Abrams, M. H. "The Deconstructive Angel." *Critical Inquiry* 3 (1977): 425–38.

Anderson, Danny J. "Deconstruction: Critical Strategy/Strategic Criticism" in *Contemporary Literary Theory*, G. Douglas Atkins and Laura Morrow, ed. Amherst: U of Massachusetts P, 1989, pp. 137–57.

Arac, Jonathan, Wlad Godzich, and Wallace Martin, eds. *The Yale Critics: Deconstruction in America. Theory and History of Literature*, vol. 6. Minneapolis: U of Minnesota Press, 1983.

Atkins G. Douglas. *Reading Deconstruction: Deconstructive Reading*. Lexington: UP of Kentucky, 1983.

Barthes, Roland. *S/Z*. Trans. Richard Miller. New York: Hill, 1974.

———. *The Pleasure of the Text*. Trans. Richard Miller. New York: Noonday, 1976.

———. "The Death of the Author" in *Image-Music-Text*. Trans. S. Heath. New York: Hill & Wang, 1977.

Bloom, Harold. *A Map of Misreading*. New York: Oxford UP, 1975.

Bloom, Harold, et al., eds. *Deconstruction and Criticism*. New York: Seabury P, 1979.

Bruns, Gerald L. "Structuralism, Enconstruction, and Hermeneutics." *Diacritics* 14 (1984): 12–23.

Cain, William E. "Deconstruction in America: The Recent Literary Criticism of J. Hillis Miller." *College English* 41 (1979): 367–82.

Caputo, John D. "The Good News About Alterity: Derrida and Theology." *Faith and Philosophy* 10.4 (Oct. 1993): 453–70.

Cascardi, A. J. "Skepticism and Deconstruction." *Philosophy and Literature* 8 (1984): 1–14.

Con Davis, Robert, and Ronald Schleifer, eds. *Rhetoric and Form: Deconstruction at Yale*. Norman: U of Oklahoma P, 1985.

Crowley, Sharon. *A Teacher's Introduction to Deconstruction*. Urbana, IL: National Council of Teachers of English, 1989.

Culler, Jonathan. *Structuralist Poetics: Structuralism, Linguistics and the Study of Literature*. Ithaca, NY: Cornell UP, 1975.

———. *The Pursuit of Signs: Semiotics, Literature, Deconstruction*. Ithaca, NY: Cornell UP, 1981.

———. *On Deconstruction: Theory and Criticism After Structuralism*. Ithaca, NY: Cornell UP, 1982.

de Man, Paul. *Blindness and Insight: Essays in the Rhetoric of Contemporary Criticism*. New York: Oxford UP, 1971.

———. *Allegories of Reading*. New Haven: Yale UP, 1979.

———. *The Rhetoric of Romanticism*. New York: Columbia UP, 1984.

Derrida, Jacques. *Of Grammatology*. Trans. Gayatri Spivak. Baltimore: Johns Hopkins UP, 1974. Trans. of *De la grammatologie*, 1967.

——. "Structure, Sign, and Play in the Discourse of the Human Sciences" in *The Structuralist Controversy: The Languages of Criticism and the Sciences of Man*, Richard Macksey and Eugenio Donato, eds. Baltimore: Johns Hopkins UP, 1970, pp. 247–65.

——. *Speech and Phenomena, and Other Essays on Husserl's Theory of Signs*. 1973. Trans. David B. Allison. Evanston, IL: Northwestern UP, 1978.

——. *Writing and Difference*. 1967. Trans. Alan Bass. Chicago: U of Chicago P, 1978.

——. "Living On: Border Lines" in *Deconstruction and Criticism*, by Harold Bloom et al. New York: Seabury, 1979, pp. 75–175.

——. *Acts of Literature*. 2nd ed. Minneapolis: U of Minnesota P, 1983.

——. *A Derrida Reader: Between the Blinds*, Peggy Kamuf, ed. New York: Columbia UP, 1991.

——. *Dissemination*, Derek Attridge, ed. New York: Routledge, 1992.

Ellis, John M. *Against Deconstruction*. Princeton: Princeton UP, 1989.

Fisher, Michael. *Does Deconstruction Make Any Difference?* Bloomington: Indiana UP, 1987.

Flores, Ralph. *The Rhetoric of Doubtful Authority: Deconstructive Readings of Self-Questioning Narratives, St. Augustine to Faulkner*. Ithaca, NY: Cornell UP, 1984.

Foucault, Michel. *The Foucault Reader*. Paul Rabinov, ed. New York: Pantheon, 1984.

Gasche, Rodolphe. "Deconstruction as Criticism." *Glyph Textual Studies* 6 (1979): 177–215.

——. *The Tain of the Mirror*. Cambridge, MA: Harvard University Press, 1986.

Hartman, Geoffrey. *Criticism in the Wilderness: The Study of Literature Today*. New Haven, CN: Yale University Press, 1980.

Hartman, Geoffrey. *Saving the Text: Literature/Derrida/Philosophy*. Baltimore: Johns Hopkins UP, 1981.

Hartman, Geoffrey H., et al. *Deconstruction and Criticism*. New York: Continuum, 1979.

Jefferson, Ann. "Structuralism and Post Structuralism." *Modern Literary Therory: A Comparative Introduction*. Totowa, NJ: Barnes, 1982, pp. 84–112.

Johnson, Barbara. *The Critical Difference: Essays in the Contemporary Rhetoric of Reading*. Baltimore: Johns Hopkins UP, 1980.

Leitch, Vincent B. "The Laterial Dance: The Deconstructive Criticism of J. Hillis Miller." *Critical Inquiry* 6 (1980): 593–607.

——. *Deconstructive Criticism: An Advanced Introduction*. New York: Columbia UP, 1983.

Megill, Allan. *Prophets of Extremity: Nietzsche, Heidegger, Foucault, Derrida*. Berkeley: U of California P, 1985.

Miller, J. Hillis. Introduction. *Bleak House*. By Charles Dickens. Ed. Norman Page. Harmondsworth, UK: Penguin, 1971, pp. 11–13.

——. "Tradition and Differance." *Diacritics* 2. 4 (1972): 6–13.

——. "Narrative and History." *EHL* 41 (1974): 455–73.

——. *Tropes, Parables, and Performatives: Essays in the Contemporary Rhetoric of Reading*. Baltimore: Johns Hopkins UP, 1980.

——. *Fiction and Repetition: Seven English Novels*. Cambridge, MA: Harvard UP, 1982.

Norris, Christopher. *Deconstruction: Theory and Practice*. New York: Methuen, 1982.

——. *The Deconstructive Turn: Essays in the Rhetoric of Philosophy*. New York: Methuen, 1983.

——. *Deconstruction and the Interests of Theory*. Oklahoma Project for Discourse and Theory 4. Norman: U of Oklahoma P, 1989.

Rajnath, ed. *Deconstruction: A Critique.* New York: Macmillan, 1989.

Rorty, Richard. *Consequences of Pragmatism.* Minneapolis: U of Minnesota P, 1982.

———. "Deconstruction and Circumvention," *Critical Inquiry* 11 (1984): 1–23.

Ryan, Michael. *Marxism and Deconstruction.* Baltimore: Johns Hopkins UP, 1982.

Said, Edward W. *The World, The Text, and the Critic.* Cambridge: Harvard UP, 1983.

Saussure, Ferdinand de. *Course in General Linguistics.* Charles Baly and Albert Reidlinger, eds. Trans. Wade Baskin. New York: Philosophical Library, 1959.

———. *Course in General Linguistics.* New York: McGraw-Hill, 1966.

Scholes, Robert. "Deconstruction and Criticism." *Critical Inquiry* 14, (1988): 278–95.

Spivak, Gayatri. "Reading the World: Literary Studies in the 1980s." *College English* 43 (1981): 671–79.

Taylor, Mark C., ed. *Deconstruction in Context: Literature and Philosophy.* Chicago: U of Chicago P, 1986.

Todorov, Tzvetan. *The Fantastic: A Structural Approach to a Literary Genre.* Trans. Richard Howard. Ithaca, NY: Cornell UP, 1975.

Young, Robert, ed. *Untying the Text: A Post-Structuralist Reader.* London: Routledge & Kegan Paul, 1981.

White, Hayden. *Tropics of Discourse.* Baltimore: Johns Hopkins University Press, 1978.

CHAPTER 7

Barrett, William. "Writers and Madness" in *Literature and Psychoanalysis.* Edith Kurzweil and William Phillips, eds. New York: Columbia UP, 1983.

Basler, Roy P. *Sex, Symbolism, and Psychology in Literature.* New York: Octagon, 1975.

Benvenuto, Bice, and Roger Kennedy. *The Works of Jacques Lacan: An Introduction.* New York: St. Martin's, 1986.

Bodkin, Maud. *Archetypal Patterns in Poetry.* New York: Vintage, 1958.

Bonaparte, Marie. *The Life and Works of Edgar Allen Poe.* Trans. John Rodker. London: Imago, 1949.

Campbell, Joseph. *The Hero with a Thousand Faces.* New York: Pantheon, 1949.

———. *The Hero with a Thousand Faces.* 2nd ed. Princeton: Princeton UP, 1968.

———. *The Power of Myth.* With Bill Moyers. Betty Sue Flowers, ed. New York: Doubleday, 1988.

Caroll, David. "Freud and the Myth of Origins." *New Literary History* 6 (1975): 511–28.

Crews, Frederick C., ed. *Psychoanalysis and Literary Process.* Cambridge UK: Winthrop, 1970.

———. *Out of My System.* New York: Oxford UP, 1975.

Davis, Robert Con, ed. *The Fictional Father: Lacanian Readings of the Text.* Amherst: U of Massachusetts P, 1981.

———, ed. *Lacan and Narration: The Psychoanalytic Difference in Narrative Theory.* Baltimore: Johns Hopkins UP, 1983.

———, ed. Special issue on "Psychoanalysis and Pedagogy." *College English* 49 6/7 (1987).

Erikson, Erik. *Childhood and Society.* New York: Norton, 1963.

Feder, Lillian. *Madness in Literature.* Princeton, N.J.: Princeton UP, 1980.

Felman, Shoshana, ed. *Literature and Psychoanalysis: The Question of Reading: Otherwise.* Baltimore, Md.: Johns Hopkins UP, 1982.

————. *Writing and Madness (Literature/Philosophy/Psychoanalysis)*. Trans. Martha Noel Evans and Shoshana Felman. Ithaca, NY: Cornell UP, 1985.

————. *Jacques Lacan and the Adventure of Insight: Psychoanalysis in Contemporary Culture*. Cambridge, MA: Harvard UP, 1987.

Freud, Sigmund. *Totem and Taboo*. Trans. A. A. Brill. New York: Moffat, 1918.

————. *Introductory Lectures on Psycho-Analysis*. Trans. Joan Riviere. London: Allen, 1922.

————. *The Basic Writings of Sigmund Freud*. Trans. and ed. A. A. Brill. New York: Modern Library, 1938. (Includes *Psychopathology of Everyday Life, The Interpretation of Dreams, Three Contributions to the Theory of Sex, Wit and Its Relation to the Unconscious, Totem and Taboo*)

————. *The Interpretation of Dreams*. Trans. A. A. Brill. New York: Random House, 1950.

————. *Group Psychology and the Analysis of the Ego*. Trans. James Strachey. New York: Norton, 1990.

Frye, Northrop. *Anatomy of Criticism*. Princeton, NJ: Princeton UP, 1957.

Gallop, Jane. *Reading Lacan*. Ithaca, NY: Cornell UP, 1985.

Gilbert, Sandra, and Susan Gubar. *Madwoman in the Attic: The Woman Writer and the Nineteenth Century Literary Imagination*. New Haven, CT: Yale University Press, 1979.

Gilman, Sandor, ed. *Introducing Psychoanalytic Theory*. New York: Brunner-Mazel, 1982.

————. *Reading Freud's Reading*. New York: New York UP, 1994.

Girard, René. *Violence and the Sacred*. Trans. Patrick Gregory. Baltimore: Johns Hopkins UP, 1977.

————. "The Bible Is Not a Myth." *Literature and Belief* 4 (1984): 7–15.

Gutheil, Emil. *The Handbook of Dream Analysis*. New York: Liveright, 1951.

Hartman, Geoffrey. *Psychoanalysis and the Question of the Text*. Baltimore: Johns Hopkins UP, 1979.

Hoffman, Frederick J. *Freudianism and the Literary Mind*. 2nd ed. Baton Rouge: Louisiana State UP, 1957.

Holland, Norman N. *The Dynamics of Literary Response*. New York: Oxford UP, 1968.

————. "The 'Unconscious' of Literature" in *Contemporary Criticism*, Norman Bradbury and David Palmer, eds. Stratford-upon-Avon Series, vol. 12. New York: St. Martin's, 1970.

————. "Literary Interpretation and the Three Phases of Psychoanalysis," *Critical Inquiry* 3 (1976): 221–33.

————. *The I*. New Haven: Yale UP, 1985.

Jung, Carl G. *Symbols of Transformation*, 2nd ed. Translated by R.F.C Hull. Princeton University Press, 1967. (Bollingen Series XX, The Collected Works of C. G. Jung, vol. 5.)

Jung, C. G. *The Collected Works of C. J. Jung*, Sir Herbert Read, Michael Fordhan, and Gerhard Adler, eds. 20 vols., plus supplements. New York: Bollingen Foundation, 1953–83.

Kazin, Alfred. "Freud and His Consequences." *Contemporaries*. Boston: Little, Brown, 1962.

Klein, George. *Psychoanalytic Theory: An Exploration of Essentials*. New York: International Universities P, 1976.

Knapp, Bettina Liebowitz. *A Jungian Approach to Literature*. Carbondale: Southern Illinois UP, 1984.

Kramer, Samuel Noah, ed. *Mythologies of the Ancient World*. New York: Anchor-Doubleday, 1961.

Kurzweil, Edith, and William Phillips, eds. *Literature and Psychoanalysis*. New York: Columbia UP, 1983.

Lesser, Simon O. *Fiction and the Unconscious*. Boston: Beacon, 1957.

Lévi-Strauss, Claude. "The Structural Study of Myth" in *Structural Anthropology*. Trans. Claire Jacobson and Brooke Grundfest Schoepf. New York: Basic, 1963, 206–31.

Lewis, C.S. "Myth." *An Experiment in Criticism*. Cambridge, UK: Cambridge UP, 1961, 40–49.

———. "The Anthropological Approach" and "Psycho-analysis and Literary Criticism" in *Selected Literary Essays*, Walter Hooper, ed. Cambridge: Cambridge UP, 1969. 301–11, 286–300.

Meisel, Perry, ed. *Freud: A Collection of Critical Essays*. Englewood Cliffs, NJ: Prentice-Hall, 1981.

———. ed. *Freud: Twentieth Century Views*. Englewood Cliffs, NJ: Prentice-Hall, 1981.

Mitchell, Juliet. "Introduction: I." in *Feminine Sexuality: Jacques Lacan and the École Freudienne*, Juliet Mitchell and Jacqueline Rose, eds. Trans. Jacqueline Rose. New York: Norton, 1982, pp. 1–26.

Muller, John P., and William J. Richardson. *The Purloined Poe: Lacan, Derrida, and Psychoanalytic Reading*. Baltimore: Johns Hopkins UP, 1988.

Nagele, Rainer. *Reading After Freud*. New York: Columbia UP, 1987.

Natoli, Joseph, and Frederik L. Rusch, comps. *Psychocriticism: An Annotated Bibliography*. Westport, CT: Greenwood, 1984.

Paris, Bernard J. *A Psychological Approach to Fiction: Studies in Thackeray, Stendhal, George Eliot, Dostoevsky, and Conrad*. Bloomington: Indiana UP, 1974.

Porter, Laurence M. *The Interpretation of Dreams: Freud's Theories Revisited*. Twayne's Masterwork Studies Series. Boston: Hall, 1986.

Reppen, Joseph, and Maurice Charney. *The Psychoanalytic Study of Literature*. Hillsdale, NJ: Analytic, 1985.

Schafer, Ray. *The Analytic Attitude*. New York: Basic Books, 1982.

Scott, Wilbur. *Five Approaches to Literary Criticism*. London: Collier-Macmillan, 1962.

Skura, Meredith Anne. *The Literary Use of Psychoanalytic Process*. New Haven: Yale UP, 1981.

Strelka, Joseph P., ed. *Literary Criticism and Psychology*. University Park, PA: Pennsylvania State UP, 1976.

Tennenhouse, Leonard, ed. *The Practice of Psychoanalytic Criticism*. Detroit: Wayne State UP, 1976

Trilling, Lionel. *Freud and the Crisis of Our Culture*. Boston: Beacon, 1955.

Wright, Elizabeth. *Psychoanalytic Criticism: Theory in Practice*. New York: Methuen, 1984.

Wyatt, Jean. *Reconstructing Desire: The Role of the Unconscious in Women's Reading and Writing*. Chapel Hill: U of North Carolina P, 1990.

CHAPTER 8

Abel, Elizabeth, ed. *Writing and Sexual Difference*. Chicago: U of Chicago P, 1982.

Abel, Elizabeth, and Emily K. Abel. *The Signs Reader: Women, Gender & Scholarship*. Introduction. Chicago: U of Chicago P, 1983.

Anzaldúa, Gloria, ed. *Making Face, Making Soul: Haciendo Caras: Creative and Critical Perspectives of Women of Color*. San Francisco: Aunte Lute Foundation Books, 1990.

Auerbach, Nina. *Communities of Women: An Idea in Fiction*. Cambridge, MA: Harvard UP, 1978.

Bauer, Dale M. *Feminist Dialogics: A Theory of Failed Community*. Albany: State U of New York P, 1988.

Baym, Nina. *Women's Fiction: A Guide to Novels by and About Women in America, 1820–1870*. Ithaca, NY: Cornell UP, 1978.

Beauvoir, Simone de. *The Second Sex*. 1949. Ed. and Trans. H. M. Parshley. New York: Modern Library, 1952.

Belsey, Catherine, and Jane Moore, eds. *The Feminist Reader. Essays in Gender and the Politics of Literary Criticism*. London: Macmillan, 1989.

Carby, Hazel V. *Reconstructing Womanhood: The Emergence of the Afro-American Woman Novelist*. New York: Oxford UP, 1987.

Cixous, Hélène. "The Character of 'Character.'" *New Literary History* 5 (1974): 383–402.

———. "The Laugh of the Medusa." Trans. Keith Cohen and Paula Cohen. *Signs* 1 (1976): 875–94.

———. "Castration or Decapitation?" Trans. Annette Kuhn. *Signs* 7 (1981): 41–55.

———. *Readings: The Poetics of Blanchot, Joyce, Kafka, Kleist, Lispector and Tsvetayeva*. Trans. and ed. Verena Andermatt Conley. Hemel Hempstead, UK: Harvester Wheatsheaf, 1992.

Cixous, Hélène, and Catherine Clement. *The Newly Born Woman*. Paris: Union Générale d'Editions, 1975.

Cohen, Ralph, ed. "Feminist Directions." *New Literary History: A Journal of Theory and Interpretation* 19.1 (Autumn 1987).

Conley, Verena Andermatt. *Hélène Cixous*. Hemel Hempstead, UK: Harvester Wheatsheaf, 1992.

Diamond, A., and L. Edwards, eds. *The Authority of Experience: Essays in Feminist Criticism*. Amherst: U of Massachusetts P, 1977.

Donovan, Josephine, ed. *Feminist Literary Criticism: Explorations in Theory*. Lexington: Kentucky UP, 1975.

Eagleton, Mary, ed. *Feminist Literary Theory: A Reader*. Oxford, UK: Basil Blackwell, 1986.

———, ed. *Feminist Literary Criticism*. New York: Longman, 1991.

Edwards, Lee, and Arlyn Diamond, eds. *The Authority of Experience: Essays in Feminist Criticism*. Amherst: U of Massachusetts P, 1977.

Eisenstein, Hester. *Contemporary Feminist Thought*. London: Unwin, 1984.

Eisenstein, Hester, and Alice Jardine, eds. *The Future of Difference*. Boston: G.K. Hall, 1980.

Ellmann, Mary. *Thinking About Women*. New York: Harcourt, 1968.

Felman, Shoshana. "Rereading Femininity." *Yale French Studies* 62 (1981): 19–44.

Fetterley, Judith. *The Resisting Reader: A Feminist Approach to American Fiction*. Bloomington: Indiana UP, 1978.

Flynn, Elizabeth A., and Patrocinio Schweickart, eds. *Gender and Reading: Essays on Readers, Texts, and Contexts*. Baltimore: Johns Hopkins UP, 1986.

Fowler, Rowena. "Feminist Criticism: The Common Pursuit." *New Literary History* 19.1 (Autumn 1987): 51–62.

French Feminist Theory. Special issue, *Signs* 7 (1981).

Gallop, Jane. *The Daughter's Seduction: Feminism and Psychoanalysis*. Ithaca, NY: Cornell UP, 1982.

Gilbert, Sandra M., and Susan Gubar. *The Madwoman in the Attic: The Woman Writer and the Nineteenth-Century Literary Imagination*. New Haven: Yale UP, 1979.

———. *A Classroom Guide to Accompany the Norton Anthology of Literature by Women*. New York: Norton, 1985.

————. *No Man's Land: The Place of the Woman Writer in the Twentieth Century*. Vol. 1, *The War of the Words*. New Haven, CT: Yale UP, 1988.

————. *No Man's Land: The Place of the Woman Writer in the Twentieth Century*. Vol. 2, *Sexchanges*. New Haven, CT: Yale UP, 1988.

Greene, Gayle, and Coppelia Kahn, eds. *Making a Difference. Feminist Literary Criticism*. New York: Methuen, 1985.

Humm, Maggie, ed. *Feminisms: A Reader*. Hemel Hempstead, UK: Harvester Wheatsheaf, 1992.

Irigaray, Luce. "When Our Lips Speak Together." Trans. Carolyn Burke. *Signs* 6 (1980): 69–79.

————. *This Sex Which Is Not One*. Trans. Catherine Porter. Ithaca, NY: Cornell UP, 1985.

Jacobus, Mary. *Reading Woman: Essays in Feminist Criticism*. New York: Columbia UP, 1986.

————, ed. *Women Writing and Writing About Women*. London: Croom Helm, 1979.

Jardine, Alice, and Paul Smith, eds. *Men in Feminism*. New York: Methuen, 1987.

Jay, K., and J. Glasgow, eds. *Lesbian Texts and Contexts: Radical Revisions*. New York: New York UP, 1986.

Jones, Ann Rosalind. "Writing the Body: Toward an Understanding of *l'Écriture Féminine*" in *The New Feminist Criticism: Essays on Women, Literature, and Theory*, Elaine Showalter, ed. New York: Pantheon, 1985, pp. 361–77.

Kaplan, Cora. "Radical Feminism and Literature: Rethinking Millett's *Sexual Politics*" *Feminist Literary Criticism*, Mary Eagleton, ed. New York: Longman, 1991.

Kauffman, Linda, ed. *Gender and Theory: Dialogues on Feminist Criticism*. New York: Basil Blackwell, 1989.

Kolodny, Annette. *The Lay of the Land. Metaphor as Experience in American Life and Letters*. Chapel Hill: U of North Carolina P, 1975.

————. "Some Notes on Defining a 'Feminist Literary Criticism.'" *Critical Inquiry* 2 (1975): 75–92.

————. "Dancing Through the Minefield: Some Observations on the Theory, Practice, and Politics of a Feminist Literary Criticism." *Feminist Studies* 6.1 (1980): 1–25.

Kristeva, Julia. *Desire in Language: A Semiotic Approach to Literature and Art*. Trans. Thomas Gora, Alice Jardine, and Leon S. Roudiez. Ed. Leon S. Roudiez. New York: Columbia UP, 1980.

Marks, Elaine, and Isabelle de Courtivron, eds. *New French Feminisms*. New York: Schocken, 1981.

Meese, Elizabeth. *Crossing the Double-Cross: The Practice of Feminist Criticism*. Chapel Hill: U of North Carolina P, 1986.

————. *(EX)Tensions: Re-Figuring Feminist Criticism*. Urbana: U of Illinois P, 1990.

Millett, Kate. *Sexual Politics*. New York: Doubleday, 1970.

Minnich, Elizabeth, Jean O'Barr, and Rachel Rosenfeld, eds. *Reconstructing the Academy: Women's Education and Women's Studies*. Chicago: U of Chicago P, 1988.

Moers, Ellen. *Literary Women: The Great Writers*. New York: Doubleday, 1976.

Moi, Toril. *Sexual/Textual Politics: Feminist Literary Theory*. New York: Methuen, 1985.

Mulvey, Laura. *Visual and Other Pleasures*. Bloomington: Indiana UP, 1989.

Munt, Sally, ed. *New Lesbian Criticism: Literary and Cultural Readings*. Brighton, UK: Harvester Press, 1987.

Newton, Judith, and Deborah Rosenfelt, eds. *Feminist Criticism and Social Change. Set Class and Race in Literature and Culture*. New York: Methuen, 1985.

Nicholson, Linda J. *Feminism/Postmodernism*. New York: Routledge, 1990.

Pacteau, Francette. "The Impossible Referent: Representations of the Androgyne" in *Formations of Fantasy*, Victor Burgin, James Donald, and Cora Kaplan, eds. London: Methuen, 1986, pp. 62–84.

Rich, Adrienne. *On Lies, Secrets, and Silence: Selected Prose* 1966–1978. London: Virago, 1980.

Ruthven, K. K. *Feminist Literary Studies: An Introduction.* New York: Cambridge UP, 1984.

Schriber, Mary Suzanne. *Gender and the Writer's Imagination: From Cooper to Wharton.* Lexington: UP of Kentucky, 1987.

Schuster, Marilyn R., and Susan R. Van Dyne, eds. *Women's Place in the Academy: Transforming the Liberal Arts Curriculum.* Totowa, NJ: Rowman & Allanheld, 1985.

Showalter, Elaine. *A Literature of Their Own: British Women Novelists from Brontë to Lessing.* Princeton, NJ: Princeton UP, 1977.

———, ed. *The New Feminist Criticism: Essays on Women, Literature, Theory.* New York: Pantheon, 1985.

———. *Sexual Anarchy: Gender and Culture at the Fin de Siècle.* New York: Viking-Penguin, 1990.

Spivak, Gayatri Chakravorty. *In Other Worlds: Essays in Cultural Politics.* New York: Methuen, 1987.

Suleiman, Susan Rubin. "(Re)writing the Body: The Politics and Poetics of Female Erotocism" in *The Female Body in Western Culture*, Susan Rubin Suleiman, ed. Cambridge, MA: Harvard UP, 1986, pp. 7–29.

Todd, Janet. *Feminist Literary History.* New York: Routledge, 1988.

———. *Feminist Literary Theory: A Defence.* Oxford: Polity, 1988.

Tong, Rosemarie. *Feminist Thought: A Comprehensive Introduction.* Boulder, CO: Westview, 1989.

Walker, Alice. *Living by the Word: Selected Writings, 1973–1987.* New York: Harcourt Brace Jovanovich, 1988.

Warhol, Robyn R., and Diane Price Herndl, eds. *Feminisms: An Anthology of Literary Theory and Criticism.* Basingstoke: Macmillan, 1992.

Waugh, Patricia. *Feminine Fictions: Revisiting the Postmodern.* New York: Routledge, 1989.

Weedon, Chris. *Feminist Practice and Poststructuralist Theory.* Oxford: Basil Blackwell, 1987.

Whitford, Margaret. *Luce Irigaray: Philosophy in the Feminine.* London: Routledge, 1991.

Wittig, Monique. *Les Guerilleres.* Trans. David Le Vay. New York: Avon, 1973.

Wollstonecraft, Mary. *A Vindication of the Rights of Women.* Harmondsworth, England: Penguin Books, 1975.

Woolf, Virginia. *A Room of One's Own.* London: Hogarth, 1929; London: Grafton, 1987.

———. *Collected Essays.* London: Hogarth, 1966.

———. *Women and Writing.* London: Women's Press, 1979.

Wyatt, Jean. *Reconstructing Desire: The Role of the Unconscious in Women's Reading and Writing.* Chapel Hill: U of North Carolina P, 1990.

CHAPTER 9

Adorno, Theodor W. *Prisms.* London: Neville Spearman, 1967.

———. *Aesthetic Theory.* Trans. C. Lenhardt. ed. Gretel Adorno and Rolf Tiedemann. London: Routledge and Kegan Paul, 1984.

Adorno, Theodor W., Walter Benjamin, Ernst Block, Bertolt Brecht, and Georg Lukács. *Aesthetics and Politics.* London: New Left Books, 1977.

Adorno, Theodor W., and Max Horkheimer. *Dialectic of Enlightenment.* London: Allen Lane, 1972.

Ahearn, Edward J. *Marx and Modern Fiction.* New Haven, CT: Yale UP, 1989.

Althusser, Louis. *For Marx.* New York: Pantheon, 1969.

Arvon, Henri. *Marxist Aesthetics.* Trans. H. Lane. Ithaca, NY: Cornell UP, 1973.

Baxandall, Lee, and Stefan Morowski, eds. *Marx and Engels on Literature and Art.* New York: International General, 1973.

Benjamin, Walter. *Illuminations.* New York: Schocken, 1970

———. *The Origins of German Tragic Drama.* Trans. John Osborne. London: New Left Books, 1977.

———. *Reflections: Essays, Aphorisms, Autobiographical Writings.* Trans. Edmund Jephcott. Ed. Peter Dementz. New York: Harcourt Brace Jovanovich, 1978.

Bennett, Tony. *Formalism and Marxism.* London: Methuen, 1979.

Craig, David, ed. *Marxists on Literature.* Harmondsworth, UK: Penguin, 1975.

Demetz, Peter. *Marx, Engels and the Arts: Origins of Marxist Literary Criticism.* Chicago: U of Chicago P, 1967.

Dowling, William C. *Jameson, Althusser, Marx: An Introduction to the Political Unconscious.* Ithaca, NY: Cornell UP, 1984.

Eagleton, Terry. *Criticism and Ideology: A Study in Marxist Literary Theory.* London: New Left Books, 1976.

———. *Marxism and Literary Criticism.* Berkeley: U of California P, 1976.

———. *Literary Theory: An Introduction.* Minneapolis: U of Minnesota P, 1983.

———. *The Function of Criticism: From the Spectator to Post-Structuralism.* London: Thetford, 1984.

Eagleton, Terry. "Capitalism, Modernism, and Postmodernism." *New Left Review* 152 (1985): 60–72.

Eagleton, Terry, and Drew Milne, eds. *Marxist Literary Theory.* Oxford, England: Blackwell, 1996.

Fekete, John. *The Critical Twilight.* Boston: Routledge & Kegan Paul, 1976.

Frow, John. *Marxism and Literary History.* Ithaca, NY: Cornell UP, 1986.

Goldmann, Lucien. *The Hidden God.* London: Routledge & Kegan Paul, 1964.

———. "Marxist Criticism" in *The Philosophy of the Enlightenment.* Cambridge, MA: MIT, 1973, pp. 86–97.

Gottlieb, Roger S., ed. *An Anthology of Western Marxism: From Lukács and Gramsci to Socialist-Feminism.* New York: Oxford UP, 1989.

Gramsci, Antonio. *Selections from the Prison Notebooks.* Quintin Hoare and Geoffrey Nowell Smith, eds. New York: International Publishers, 1971.

Hicks, Granville. *The Great Tradition.* New York: Macmillan, 1931, rev. 1935.

Horkheimer, Max, and Theodor W. Adorno. *The Dialectic of Enlightenment.* Trans. John Cumming. New York: Seabury, 1972.

James, C. Vaughan. *Soviet Socialist Realism: Origins and Theory.* New York: Macmillan, 1973.

Jameson, Fredric. *Marxism and Form: Twentieth-Century Dialectical Theories of Literature.* Princeton, NJ: Princeton UP, 1971.

———. *The Prison-House of Language. A Critical Account of Structuralism and Russian Formalism.* Princeton, NJ: Princeton UP, 1972.

————. *The Political Unconscious: Narrative as a Socially Symbolic Art*. Ithaca, NY: Cornell UP, 1981.

————. *Postmodernism, or, the Cultural Logic of Late Capitalism*. Durham, NC: Duke UP, 1991.

Jay, Martin. *The Dialectical Imagination: A History of the Frankfurt School*. London: Heinemann, 1973.

Jay, Martin. *Marxism and Totality*. Berkeley: U of California P, 1990.

Lentricchia, Frank. *Criticism and Social Change*. Chicago: U of Chicago P, 1983.

Lukács, Georg. *The Historical Novel*. London: Merlin, 1962.

————. *The Meaning of Contemporary Realism*. London: Merlin, 1963.

————. *Writer and Critic and Other Essays*. London: Merlin, 1970.

————. *Essays on Realism*. Trans. David Fernbach. Ed. Rodney Livingstone. Cambridge, MA: MIT P, 1981.

Macherey, Pieffe. *A Theory of Literary Production*. Trans. G. Wall. London: Routledge & Kegan Paul, 1978.

Marcuse, Herbert. *The Aesthetic Dimension: Toward a Critique of Marxist Aesthetics*. Boston: Beacon, 1978.

McMurtry, John. *The Structure of Marx's World-View*. Princeton, NJ: Princeton UP, 1978.

Mulhern, Francis, ed. *Contemporary Marxist Literary Criticism*. New York: Longman, 1992.

Nelson, Cary, and Lawrence Grossberg, eds. *Marxism and the Interpretation of Culture*. London: Macmillan, 1980.

Prawer, S. S. *Karl Marx and World Literature*. Oxford: Oxford UP, 1978.

Sartre, Jean-Paul. *What Is Literature?* New York: Philosophical Library, 1949.

Trotsky, Leon. *Literature and Revolution*. Ann Arbor: U of Michigan P, 1971.

Wellmer, Albrecht. "Reason, Utopia, and the *Dialectic of Enlightenment*" in *Habermas and Modernity*, Richard J. Bernstein, ed. Cambridge, MA: MIT P, 1985, pp. 35–66.

Willett, John, ed. *Brecht on Theatre*. London: Methuen, 1964.

Williams, Raymond. *Culture and Society, 1780–1950*. London: Chatto and Windus, 1958.

————. *Marxism and Literature*. Oxford, UK: Oxford UP, 1977.

Wilson, Edmund. *Axel's Castle*. New York: Scribner, 1961.

Wright, Elizabeth. *Postmodern Brecht: A Re-Presentation*. London: Routledge, 1988.

CHAPTER 10

Brooks, Cleanth, and Robert Penn Warren. *Understanding Poetry*. New York: H. Holt and Company, 1939.

Collier, Peter, and Helga Geyer-Ryan, eds. *Literary Theory Today*. Ithaca, NY: Cornell UP, 1990.

Cooper, Barry. *Michel Foucault: An Introduction to the Study of His Thought*. New York: Edwin Mellen, 1982.

Cousins, Mark, and Athar Hussain. *Michel Foucault*. New York: St. Martin's, 1984.

Cox, Jeffrey N., and Larry J. Reynolds, eds. *New Historical Literary Study: Essays on Reproducing Texts, Representing History*. Princeton, NJ: Princeton UP, 1993.

Dollimore, Jonathan. *Radical Tragedy; Religion, Ideology, and Power in the Drama of Shakespeare and His Contemporaries*. Chicago: U of Chicago P, 1984.

Dollimore, Jonathan, and Alan Sinfield, eds. *Political Shakespeare: New Essays in Cultural Materialism*. Manchester, UK: Manchester UP, 1985.

During, Simon. "New Historicism." *Text and Performance Quarterly* 11 (July 1991): 171–89.

Foucault, Michel. *Madness and Civilization.* Trans. Richard Howard. New York: Pantheon, 1965.

———. *The Order of Things.* New York: Pantheon, 1972.

———. *Discipline and Punishment: The Birth of the Prison.* Trans. Alan Sheridan. New York: Vintage, 1979.

———. *The Foucault Reader,* Paul Rabinow, ed. New York: Pantheon, 1984.

Fox-Genovese, Elizabeth. "Literary Criticism and the Politics of the New Historicism" in *The New Historicism,* H. Aram Veeser, ed. New York: Routledge, 1989, pp. 213–24.

Gane, Mike, ed. *Towards a Critique of Foucault.* London: Routledge & Kegan Paul, 1987.

Geertz, Clifford. *The Interpretaion of Cultures: Selected Essays.* New York: Basic Books, 1973.

———. *Negara: The Theatre State of Nineteenth-Century Bali.* Princeton, NJ: Princeton UP, 1980.

Goldberg, Jonathan. *James I and the Politics of Literature: Jonson, Shakespeare, Donne, and Their Contemporaries.* Baltimore: Johns Hopkins UP, 1983.

Graff, Gerald, and Reginald Gibbons, eds. *Criticism in the University.* Evanston, IL: Northwestern UP, 1985.

Greenblatt, Stephen. *Renaissance Self-Fashioning: From More to Shakespeare.* Chicago: U of Chicago P, 1980.

———. Introduction. "The Forms of Power and the Power of Forms in the Renaissance." *Genre* 15 (Summer 1982): 3–6.

———. *Shakespearean Negotiations: The Circulation of Social Energy in Renaissance England.* Berkeley: U of California P, 1988.

———. "Towards a Poetics of Culture" in *The New Historicism,* H. Aram Veeser, ed. New York: Routledge, 1989, pp. 1–14.

———. *Learning to Curse: Essays in Early Modern Culture.* New York: Routledge, 1991.

Howard, Jean E. "The New Historicism in Renaissance Studies." *English Literary Renaissance* 16 (Winter 1986): 13–43.

Hunt, Lynn, ed. *The New Cultural History.* Berkeley: U of California P, 1989.

Lindenberger, Herbert. "Toward a New History in Literary Study" in *Profession: Selected Articles from the Bulletins of the Association of Departments of English and the Association of Departments of Foreign Languages.* New York: MLA, 1984, pp. 16–23.

MaGann, Jerome. *The Beauty of Inflections: Literary Investigations in Historical Method and Theory.* Oxford: Oxford UP, 1985.

———. *Historical Studies and Literary Criticism.* Madison: U of Wisconsin P, 1985.

———. *Social Values and Poetic Act: The Historical Judgment of Literary Work.* Cambridge, MA: Harvard UP, 1988.

Michaels, Walter Benn. *The Gold Standard and the Logic of Naturalism: American Literature at the Turn of the Century.* Berkeley: U of California P, 1987.

Montrose, Louis. "Renaissance Literary Studies and the Subject of History." *English Literary Renaissance* 16 (Winter 1986): 5–12.

———. "Professing the Renaissance: The Poetics and Politics of Culture" in *The New Historicism,* H. Aram Veeser, ed. New York: Routledge, 1989, pp. 15–36.

———. "New Historicisms" in *Redrawing the Boundaries: The Transformation of English and American Literary Studies,* Stephen Greenblatt and Giles Gunn, eds. New York: Modern Language Association, 1992, pp. 392–418.

Morris, Wesley. *Toward a New Historicism.* Princeton, NJ: Princeton UP, 1972.

New Historicisms, New Histories, and Others. Special issue of *NLH* 21 (1990).

Murfin, Ross C., ed. *Heart of Darkness: A Case Study in Contemporary Criticism*. New York: St. Martin's, 1989.

Orgel, Stephen. *The Illusion of Power, Political Theater in the English Renaissance*. Berkeley: U of California P, 1975.

Rabinow, Paul, ed. *The Foucault Reader*. New York: Pantheon, 1984.

Robertson, D. W., Jr. "Historical Criticism" in *English Institute Essays: 1950*, Alan S. Downer, ed. New York: Columbia UP, 1951, pp. 3–31.

Sheridan, Alan. *Michel Foucault*. New York: Horwood and Tavistock, 1985.

Thomas, Brook. "The Historical Necessity for—and Difficulties with—New Historical Analysis in Introductory Literature Courses." *College English* 49 (September 1987): 509–22.

Turner, Victor. *Celebration: Studies in Festivity and Ritual*. Washington, DC: Smithsonian Institution, 1982.

Vesser, H. Aram, ed. *The New Historicism*, New York: Routledge, 1989.

Wellek, René, and Austin Warren. *Theory of Literature*. 3rd ed. New York: Harcourt, Brace, & Co., 1964.

Wicke, Jennifer A. *Advertising Fictions: Literature, Advertisement, and Social Reading*. New York: Columbia UP, 1988.

Williams, Raymond. *Marxism and Literature*. Oxford, England: Oxford UP, 1977.

CHAPTER 11

Achebe, Chinua. "An Image of Africa: Racism in Conrad's *Heart of Darkness*." *Massachusettes Review* 18 (1977): 782–94.

Adam, Ian, and Helen Tiffin. *Past the Long Post: Theorizing Post-Colonialism and Post-Modernism*. Hemel Hempstead, London: Harvester Wheatsheaf, 1991.

Appiah, Kwame Anthony. *In My Father's House: Africa in the Philosophy of Culture*. New York: Oxford UP, 1992.

Ashcroft, Bill, Gareth Griffiths, and Helen Tiffin. *The Empire Writes Back: Theory and Practice in Post-Colonial Literatures*. London: Routledge, 1989.

Benjamin, Walter. *The Origin of German Tragic Drama*. Trans. John Osborne. London: New Left Books, 1997.

Bhabha, Homi K., ed. *Nation and Narration*. New York: Routledge & Kegan Paul, 1990.

———. "Postcolonial Critiscism" in *Redrawing the Boundaries: The Transformation of English and American Literary Studies*, Stephen Greenblatt and Giles Gunn, eds. New York: Modern Language Association, 1992, pp. 437–65.

———. *The Location of Culture*. London: Routledge, 1994.

Brantlinger, Patrick. "History and Empire." *Journal of Victorian Literature and Culture*, 1992 (19): 317–27.

Carby, Hazel V. *Reconstruction Womanhood: The Emergence of the Afro-American Woman Novelist*. New York: Oxford UP, 1987.

Chatterjee, Partha. "More on Modes of Power and the Peasantry" in *Selected Subaltern Studies*, Ranajit Guha and Gayatri Chakravorty Spivak, eds. New York: Oxford UP, 1988, pp. 351–90.

Chinweizu, Onwuchekwa Jemie, and Ihechukwu Madubuike. *Toward the Decolonization of African Literature*. Vol. 1, *African Fiction and Poetry and Their Critics*. Washington, DC: Howard UP, 1983.

Cronin, Richard. *Imagining India*. London: Macmillan, 1990.

Davis, Angela Y. *Women, Race, and Class*. New York: Vintage, 1983.

Dirlik, Arif. *The Postcolonial Aura: Third World Criticism in the Age of Global Capitalism*. Boulder, CO: Westview, 1997.

During, Simon. "Postmodernism or Post-Colonialism Today." *Textual Practice* 1.1 (1987): 32–47.

Evans, Malcolm. *Signifying Nothing: Truth's True Contents in Shakespeare's Text*. Athens: U of Georgia P, 1986.

Fanon, Frantz. *A Dying Colonialism*. Trans. Haakon Chevalier. New York: Grove, 1965.

———. *Black Skin, White Masks*. Trans. Charles Lam Markmann. New York: Grove, 1967.

———. *Toward the African Revolution: Political Essays*. Trans. Haakon Chevalier. New York: Grove, 1967.

———. *The Wretched of the Earth*. Trans. Constance Farrington. New York: Grove, 1968.

Gates, Henry Louis Jr., ed. *Black Literature and Literary Theory*. New York: Methuen, 1984.

———, ed. *"Race," Writing, and Difference*. Chicago: U of Chicago P, 1986.

———. *Figures in Black: Words, Signs, and the "Racial" Self*. New York: Oxford UP, 1987.

———. *The Signifying Monkey: A Theory of African-American Literary Criticism*. New York: Oxford UP, 1988.

———. "Authority, (White) Power, and the (Black) Critic; or, It's All Greek to Me" in *The Future of Literary Theory*, Ralph Cohen, ed. New York: Routledge, 1989, pp. 324–46.

———. "Critical Fanonism." *Critical Inquiry* 17.3 (1991): 457–70.

———. *Loose Canons: Notes on the Culture Wars*. New York: Oxford UP, 1992.

Guha, Ranajit, and Gayatri Chakravorty Spivak, eds. *Selected Subaltern Studies*. New York: Oxford UP 1988.

Hutcheon, Linda. "Introduction: Complexities Abounding" in *Colonialism and the Postcolonial Condition*. Special issue of *PMLA* 110.1 (1995): 7–16.

Jameson, Fredric. "Third-World Literature in the Era of Multinational Capitalism." *Social Text* 15 (1986): 65–88.

JanMohamed, Abdul R. *Manichean Aesthetics: The Politics of Literature in Colonial Africa*. Amherst: U of Massachusetts P, 1983.

Lamming, George. *The Pleasure of Exile*. London: Michael Joseph, 1960.

Lazarus, Neil. *Resistance in Postcolonial African Fiction*. New Haven: Yale UP, 1990.

Llosa, Mario Vargas. *The Storyteller*. Trans. Helen Lane. New York: Penguin, 1989.

McClintock, Anne. *Imperial Leather: Race, Gender, and Sexuality in the Colonial Context*. London: Routledge, 1995.

Mitchell, W. J. T. "Postcolonial Culture, Postimperial Criticism." *Transition* 56 (1992): 11–19.

Ngugi wa Thiong'o. *Decolonising the Mind: The Politics of Language in African Literature*. London: James Currey, 1986.

Niranjana, Tejaswine. *Sitting Translation: History, Post-Structuralism, and the Colonial Context*. Berkeley: U of California Press, 1990.

Owomoyela, Oyekan, ed. *A History of Twentieth-Century African Literatures*. Lincoln: U of Nebraska P, 1993.

Richards, Thomas. *The Imperial Archive: Knowledge and the Fantasy of Empire*. London: Verso, 1993.

Rodney, Walter. *How Europe Underdeveloped Africa*. Dar es Salaam: Tanzania Publishing House, 1972.

Rushdie, Salman. *Imaginary Homelands: Essays and Criticism, 1981–91*. London: Penguin, 1991.

Said, Edward. *Orientalism*. New York: Vintage, 1979.

———. *The World, the Text, and the Critic*. Cambridge, MA: Harvard UP, 1983.

———. "Figures, Configurations, Transfigurations." *Race & Class* 1 (1990).

———. *Culture and Imperalism*. New York: Knopf, 1993.

Spivak, Gayatri Chakravorty. "Subaltern Studies: Desconstructing Historiography" in *Subaltern Studies: Writings on South Asian History and Society*, Vol. 4, Ranajit Guha, ed. Delhi: Oxford UP, 1985, pp. 330–63.

———. "Can the Subaltern Speak?" in *Marxism and the Interpretation of Culture*, Cary Nelson and Lawrence Grossberg, eds. Urbana: U of Illinois P, 1988, pp. 271–313.

———. *In Other Worlds: Essays in Cultural Politics*. New York: Routledge, 1988.

———. *The Post-Colonial Critic: Interviews, Strategies, Dialogues*, Sarah Harasym, ed. New York: Routledge, 1990.

———. "The Making of Americans, the Teaching of English, and the Future of Culture Studies." *New Literary History* 21 (1990): 781–98.

Suleri, Sarah. *The Rhetoric of English India*. Chicago: U of Chicago P, 1992.

———. "Woman Skin Deep: Feminism and the Postcolonial Condition." *Critical Inquiry* 18.4 (Summer 1992).

Trimmer, Joseph, and Tilly Warnock, eds. *Understanding Others*. Urbana: National Council of Teachers of English, 1992.

Viswanathan, Gauri. *Masks of Conquest: Literary Study and British Rule in India*. New York: Columbia UP, 1989.

Williams, Raymond. *Keywords: A Vocabulary of Culture and Society*. Rev. ed. Oxford, UK: Oxford UP, 1983.

Wolf, Eric R. *Europe and the People Without History*. Berkeley: U of California P, 1982.

Zahar, Renate. *Frantz Fanon: Colonialism and Alienation*. New York: Monthly Review, 1974.

Bibliography

INTRODUCTORY AND GENERAL SURVEYS OF LITERARY CRITICISM

Atkins, G. Douglas, and Laura Morrow, eds. *Contemporary Literary Theory*. Amherst: U of Massachusetts P, 1989.

Berman, Art. *From the New Criticism to Deconstruction: The Reception of Structuralism and Post-Structuralism*. Chicago: U of Illinois P, 1988.

Booker, M. Keith. *A Practical Introduction to Literary Theory and Criticism*. White Plains, NY: Longman, 1996.

Cowles, David. *The Critical Experience: Literary Reading, Writing, and Criticism*. 2nd ed. Dubuque, IA: Kendall/Hunt, 1994.

Coyle, Martin, et al., eds. *Encyclopaedia of Literature and Criticism*. London: Routledge, 1990.

Daiches, David. *Critical Approaches to Literature*. 2nd ed. New York: Longman, 1981.

Davis, Robert Con, and Laurie Finke, eds. *Literary Criticism and Theory: The Greeks to the Present*. New York: Longman, 1989.

Davis, Robert Con, and Ronald Schleifer. *Contemporary Literary Criticism: Literary and Cultural Studies*. 2nd ed. New York: Longman, 1989.

Eagleton, Terry. *Literary Theory: An Introduction*. Minneapolis: U of Minnesota P, 1983.

Groden, Michael, and Martin Kreiswirth. *The Johns Hopkins Guide to Literary Theory & Criticism*. Baltimore: Johns Hopkins UP, 1994.

Jefferson, Ann, and David Robey, eds. *Modern Literary Theory: A Comparative Introduction*. 2nd ed. London: Batsford, 1986.

Keesey, Donald. *Contexts for Criticism*. 3rd ed. Mountain View, CA: Mayfield, 1998.

Lodge, David. *20th Century Literary Criticism*. New York: Longman, 1972.

———. *Modern Criticism and Theory: A Reader*. New York: Longman, 1988.

Murfin, Ross, ed. *The Scarlet Letter: Case Studies in Contemporary Criticism*. Boston: St. Martin's, 1991.

Natoli, Joseph, ed. *Tracing Literary Theory*. Chicago: U of Illinois P, 1987.

Newton, K. M. ed. *Twentieth-Century Literary Theory*. London: Macmillan, 1988.

Richter, David, ed. *The Critical Tradition: Classic Texts and Contemporary Trends*. New York: St. Martin's, 1989.

Selden, Raman, and Peter Widdowson. *A Reader's Guide to Contemporary Literary Theory*. 4th ed. Upper Saddle River NJ: Prentice-Hall, 1998.

Staton Shirley, ed. *Literary Theories in Praxis*. Philadelphia: U of Pennsylvania P, 1987.

Wellek, René. *A History of Modern Criticism: 1750–1950*. New Haven, Yale UP, 1986.

Credits

Krista Adlhock. "Hawthorne's Understanding of History in 'The Maypole of Merry Mount.' "

Julie Claypool. "A Structuralist Look at Glaspell's *Trifles*."

Cleanth Brooks. "Keats's Sylvan Historian: History Without Footnotes" from *The Well Wrought Urn: Studies in the Structure of Poetry, Second Edition*. Copyright © 1947 and renewed © 1975 by Cleanth Brooks. Reprinted with the permission of Harcourt Brace and Company.

Tony Harrison. "Marked with a D" from *Selected Poems*. Copyright © 1981 by Tony Harrison. Reprinted with the permission of Gordon Dickerson for the author.

David Johnson. "A Psychoanalytic Approach to Poe's 'The City in the Sea.' "

Norman Holland. "*Hamlet*—My Greatest Creation" from *Journal of the American Academy of Psychoanalysis* 3 (1975): 419–27. Copyright © 1975 by the American Academy of Psychoanalysts. Reprinted with the permission of The Guilford Press.

Peter Hulme. "Columbus and the Cannibals" from *Colonial Encounters: Europe and the Native Caribbean 1492–1797*. Copyright © 1986 by Peter Hulme. Reprinted with the permission of Methuen.

Arthur Kinney. "Is Literary History Still Possible?" from *The Ben Jonson Journal* vol. 2 (1995). Copyright © 1995 by the University of Nevada Press. Reprinted with the permission of the publishers.

John Leax. "Sacramental Vision" from *The Task of Adam*. Copyright © 1985 by John Leax. Reprinted with the permission of Zondervan Publishing House.

Elizabeth A. Meese. "Orality and Textuality in Zora Neale Hurston's *Their Eyes Were Watching God*" from *Crossing the Double-Cross: The Practice of Feminist Criticism*. Copyright © 1986 by The University of North Carolina Press. Reprinted with the permission of the publishers.

J. Hills Miller. "On Edge: The Crossways of Contemporary Criticism" from *Bulletin of the American Academy of Arts and Sciences* 32 (January 1979). Copyright © 1979. Reprinted with the permission of the author.

"The Parable of the Wedding Banquet," Matthew, Ch. 23, from the *Holy Bible: New International Edition*. Copyright © 1973, 1978, 1984 by Zondervan Publishing House. All rights reserved.

Index

Absolutist critic, 5
Adam, Ian, 265
Adlhock, Krista, 249–52
Adorno, Theodor, 215
Aesthetic criticism. *See* New Criticism
Aesthetic experience, 41
Aesthetic reading, 67
Aesthetics, 10–11
Aesthetic theory, 148
Affective Fallacy, 42
African-American criticism, 9, 268–70
Ahmad, Aijaz, 267
Allophones, 90, 97
Althusser, Louis, 217, 218, 241
Altizer, Thomas, 118
Ambiguity, 43, 44, 45
American feminism, 185–86
Anal stage, 151
Analytical psychology, 148, 155
Anthropology, cultural, 243–44
Aporia, 240
Applied criticism (practical criticism), 5, 10
Aquinas, St. Thomas, 181, 189
Archetypal criticism, 155, 162
Archetypes, 154–55
Arche-writing (archi-écriture), 126–27
Aristotle, 5, 10, 12, 18–21, 23, 30, 64, 180, 189
Arnold, Matthew, 4, 30–31, 33, 66
Artifacts, 11
Ashcroft, Bill, 265, 266
Aspirated, 122
Atwood, Margaret, 191, 193
Augustine, St., 181

Bachelard, Gaston, 71
Bacon, Francis, 116
Bad critics, 46
Baker, Houston, 270
Baldwin, James, 268
Barthes, Roland, 70, 96–97, 114
Base, 212, 215, 216

relationship between superstructure and, 219–20
Beauvoir, Simone de, 182, 183
Behavioral social codes, 246
Benjamin, Walter, 215–16, 240
Bhabha, Homi, 266, 267
Binary oppositions, 125
Blackmur, R.P., 39
Blake, William, 161
Bleich, David, 73, 74
Bourgeoisie, 212, 220
    hegemony of, 216–17
Brecht, Bertolt, 216
British feminism, 186
Brontë, Charlotte, 184
Brooks, Cleanth, 39, 47, 52–61, 239

Camus, Albert, 265
Capitalism, 213, 219
Carus, C.G., 149
Castration complex, 152
Castro, Fidel, 265
Catalyst, 42
Catharsis, 20
Chopin, Kate, 184
Chora, 187–88
Cixious, Helene, 187, 188
Claypool, Julie, 101–4
Close readers, 38
Close reading, 46
Coleridge, Samuel Taylor, 26, 43, 181
Collective unconscious, 154–55
Communism, 212
Competence, literary, 99
Concretized text, 72–73
Condensation, 153
Connotation, 44
Conscious, 149, 150
    personal, 154
Criticism. *See* Literary criticism
Culler, Jonathan, 70, 98–99, 114
Cultural anthropology, 243–44
Cultural materialism, 241